Rebordering the Mediterranean

General Editor: **Jacqueline Waldren**, *Institute of Social Anthropology,*
University of Oxford

REBORDERING THE MEDITERRANEAN

*Boundaries and Citizenship
in Southern Europe*

Liliana Suárez-Navaz

Berghahn Books
NEW YORK · OXFORD

Published in 2004 by
Berghahn Books

www.berghahnbooks.com

© 2004 Liliana Suárez-Navaz
First paperback edition printed in 2006

Library of Congress Cataloging-in-Publication Data

Suárez-Navaz, Liliana.
   Rebordering : boundaries and citizenship in southern Europe /
Liliana Suárez-Navaz.
    p. cm. — (New directions in anthropology ; v. 17)
   Includes bibliographical references and index.
   ISBN 1-57181-472-8 (alk. paper)
    1. Granada (Spain : Province)—Social conditions. 2. Group identity—
Spain—Granada (Province). 3. Africans—Spain—Granada (Province)—
Social conditions. 4. Immigrants—Spain—Granada (Province)—Social condi-
tions. 5. Citizenship—Spain. 6. Immigr I. Title. II. Series.

HN590.G7S83 2003
306'.09—dc21

                          2002043660

British Library Cataloguing in Publication Data

A catalogue record for this book is available from
the British Library.

Printed in the United States on acid-free paper

To the memory of those who died crossing national borders.

For Granada and its peoples.

For Andrea Yara and Iker with love.

Contents

ACKNOWLEDGMENTS

*M*y personal circumstances forced me to move and adapt to different places and peoples, and I am happy to say that everything I learned is marked by my migratory and intercultural experiences. I encourage anybody in similar circumstances to move forward, no matter the efforts she has to make, to be able to make the most of our world. It certainly is a challenge, however, to acknowledge all of the people scattered in three continents who helped in so many ways to carry this project through.

The financial support of several institutions was essential for completion of this project. A joint Fulbright/Spanish Ministry of Education scholarship supported me during my Ph.D. training. My fieldwork and the writing of my dissertation were financed by generous grants from the National Science Foundation (SBR-94/11667), the Institute for International Studies at Stanford, the Mellon Foundation, and Stanford's Department of Anthropology. I also thank the American Anthropological Association, the Law and Society Association, and the Minda de Gunzburg Center for European Studies at Harvard University for support to attend conferences where I received important feedback for this work.

My primary thanks go to George A. and Jane F. Collier, both of whom have helped and guided me since I began graduate studies at Stanford. I am deeply indebted to them for their consistent commitment to furthering my work, for their personal and professional support, and for their endless generosity. Jane F. Collier introduced me to anthropology of law and she has been the single most important influence in my interest in the "culture" of modernity. As my advisor, George A. Collier taught me much about methods and ethnohistorical analysis; but above all, I thank the legacy of American anthropology he transmitted to me. As a classical master, he taught me how to be a good anthropologist in the field as well as in the academic environment—and most especially, how to be a good advisor in the future with my own students.

In my graduate years at Stanford I was immersed in one of the most complete and demanding training programs an anthropologist could desire. Renato Rosaldo was an inspiring help, always teaching me to find new ways to listen to words and silences, and to bring the invisible to the forefront. I also thank Professors Paulla Ebron, Jim Gibbs, Akhil Gupta, Terry Karl, Cheleen Mahar, Mary Prat, Philippe Schmitter, Silvia Yanagisako, and others. Rodolfo Stavenhaven has been a continuous support throughout these years, and much of what I know about ethnicity and nationalism I learned from him. In American academia, I also want to mention Davydd Greenwood, who helped me understand much about ethnogenesis in Spain, and Michael Kearney, who inspired my work on transnational migration.

My Stanford colleagues gave me too much to record here: moral support, intellectual inspiration, generosity, and crucial feedback during my graduate years. I thank most especially, for their intellectual input and for their friendship, Federico Besserer, Paco Ferrándiz, Hellen Gremillon, Stefan Helmreich, Saba Mahmood, Bill Maurer, Sara Miller, Víctor Ortíz, Heather Paxson, Sandra Razieli, Apen Ruíz, Teresa Sierra, Nikolai Ssorin-Chikov, and Mukund Subramanian. Most especially I want to thank the sisterhood of the group of "las brujas"—Francisca James-Hernández and R. Aida Hernández—with whom I shared the most happy times and my most deep concerns.

Without the generosity and support of people in Granada and Senegal who shared so much of themselves with me, this work would not exist. I engaged in several fieldwork periods from 1992 to 1995, and in each of them many people made my work possible, helping me not just by answering my questions, but also by allowing me to enter their lives as if I were one of them. Here, to preserve their anonymity I will only use their first names. I want to thank most especially: Isa and Nando, and Eduardo, Rosalía, and Mati, for generously hosting me when I first arrived in Granada; the people of Granada Acoge, the Human Rights Association; Acción Alternativa; and Comisiones Obreras, most particularly Antonio, Mari Carmen, Miguel, Encarna, Jesús, and others with whom I shared my concern about the increasing racism in Andalusia. At the university, I thank Javier García Castaño and Rafael Pulido for their help when I initiated my fieldwork, and for allowing me to use the results of a study done with Granada Acoge about Senegalese, and José Cazorla for offering me his library on emigration and encouraging me to pursue my interest in highlighting how previous Andalusian emigration can help us understand today's immigration.

Essential in this work was the support of many immigrants in Granada and Alfaya for my research, allowing me to share daily life with them so I could understand Africans' life in Andalusia, and inviting me to their formal and informal gatherings so I could also understand the way their life extended beyond Andalusia. Among them, I want to thank deeply four people for their generosity, support, friendship, and for teaching me about Islam: Cheick, Assane, Omar, and Tarik. In Alfaya, my work would have been impossible without the help of Juan Miguel, who taught me from his privileged perspective much more than I could assimilate about peasants, their economy, and their culture. His family and Puri, who generously hosted me, provided me with a friendly and sympathetic environment, without which I could hardly have survived the difficult periods of my fieldwork. Most people in Alfaya helped me answering my questions and some went far beyond that, providing me with key clues for understanding the complexities of their lives; I express my deepest gratitude to Eduardo, Emiliano, Nati, Teresa, Dori, Isabel, Rafa, Reme, Rafael, Carmen, Domingo, Mari, Pepe Luis, Antonio P., Pepe C., Luis, Salvador, Nono, Javi, Salva, Jose Antonio, Manolo, Miguelón, Imma, Santiago, Teresa, Trini, Chola, Paco, Ramón, Antonio, Dolores, Victoria, María, Jose, Miguel, Carlos, Josefa, Yolanda, Mari Luz, and Pitillo.

In Senegal, my deepest gratitude goes to the family Diouf, Niang, Dieng, Dieye, and Sene, and most especially to Cheick and Rama Niang, who are now part of my family, to Salla, to Khadi and the Center for Disabled People of Mbour, to the people of the Cultural and Sport Association of Darou-Salam in Sébikotane, to Miguel in the Spanish Consulate, to Abdoulaye Diof in IFAM-CAD, and to Silvie Bredeuloup in ORSTON. Angela was a friend and a colleague during fieldwork, always struggling to defy the gender and race borders marked by conventions and to open new paths for dialog and understanding.

In Spain, where I now live and work, there are many people I would like to mention here for their support and friendship. I thank first my colleagues in the Anthropology Department at the Universidad Autónoma of Madrid, and most especially Carlos Giménez and members of the program on Migration and Multiculturalism, with whom I have shared dreams and efforts to construct an intercultural university and society, and most particularly to Pilar, Paloma, Chus, and the Master and Ph.D. students who have worked with me, Raquel, Luzmar, Arantxa, Meme, Paloma, Lydia, Patricia, etc. With my return to Spain, colleagues from Madrid, Barcelona, Tarragona, and Sevilla have helped me to understand the Spanish academy and start a professional life here, an objective that is not an easy task for an "outsider" like me and impossible without the support of these colleagues and friends. Spanish anthropologists abroad, such as J. Llobera, have also helped with their support to make this transition an easier task.

Last, but not least, I am also indebted to the support of family and friends who believed this book was an important achievement. I thank Alvaro for his love, help, and support during the last years, and the del Val family; my aunt Cari for her generosity and for offering my children and myself a sanctuary close to the beach to finish this book; my father and my brother Juan and his family, Mada and Alejandra; and the sisters I have chosen—Ana, Graciela, Angela, and Aida—as well as other close friends who helped me in my efforts to be a mother, a woman, and a professional all at the same time. The smiles and warmth of my children, Andrea Yara and Iker, have inspired me much while writing; this book is dedicated to both of them.

Motril, February 2004

Rebordering the Mediterranean

INTRODUCTION

We are living times of fear and anxiety about terrorists who, in the name of Islam, want to destroy icons of modernity and secular development. Arguments for a future of civilizational opposition maintained by several intellectuals around the world will surely conjure up the terrible images of the destruction that occurred on the 11th of September, 2001, in New York. Rhetorics of revenge grow at a global level, reconfigured as a new scenario of competing sacred and universal destinies. The complex dynamics of interethnic relations around the world, the new spaces of rich hybridization, and the historical experiences of peaceful interreligious *convivencia*[1]—a relevant historical experience for Andalusia and a key concept in this book—all dissolve in the new powerfully created antagonism between secularized Western Christianity and Islam.

There is an urgent need to put forward case studies where this oppositional dynamic is clearly shown as historically constructed, and thus surmountable. This book offers an alternative vision of these processes through a situated cultural analysis of how global, national, and local discourses and practices crystallized in the construction of social borders between Spanish citizens and Muslim immigrants in Granada (Andalusia, Spain) and the way these boundaries are challenged in the moral and cultural repertoires used in daily interactions.

What I call the rebordering of the Mediterranean refers to the extension of European frontiers to include southern European countries in the mid 1980s, and to the construction of new social boundaries in the innerland. The Spanish economic boom of the 1960s, fostered by tourism, industrialization, and a new capitalist rationality, together with the establishment of a stable democratic system, paved the way for the country's full membership in the European Community (EC) in 1986. In 1985, the Spanish government enacted the Alien Law, or *Ley Orgánica de Extranjería* 7/1985 (LOE),[2] designed to close up the southern European border in view of Spain's petition to become a full member of what was then called the European Economic Community (EEC). As a result of these shifts, we witness a final redrawing of the frontiers between north and south. The Pyrenees, once the legal and symbolic border between Spain and a "Europe" that lay to the north, disappeared in the process of the construction of a free market and a European citizenship. Or rather, the Pyrenees moved south, as the situation has often been depicted in the mass media. This political and economic conjuncture defines African immigrants' presence in Spain today. The situation is determined primarily by the openness of internal borders in the European Union (EU). The need to protect the new imagined community—a European ethos based on a common citizenship—promotes racist and xenophobic discourses about the African workers. This process is not taking place without resistance. Associations representing new immigrants and Spaniards protest daily against discrimination and repression. In the new multicultural and democratic Spain, national and regional identities have yet to be defined. To explore these complex processes is one of the main objectives of this book.

The gradual tendency toward segmentation and reduction of interethnic relational spaces in Andalusia is thus framed in the broader processes shaping structures of exclusion and inclusion in contemporary Western societies. But the case study of Muslim African immigration in southern Europe brings into the center of analysis a non-core European perspective that has been underexplored in the literature on postwar European immigration. I trace the historical process by which Andalusians have experienced the shift from being poor southern emigrants to northern Europe, to being privileged citizens of the southernmost borderland of the EU, where thousands of African immigrants came in search of a better life. This ethnographic perspective also brings a corrective to the assumption of fixed national, cultural, and socioeconomic boundaries vis-à-vis outside migration in core countries.

My intended contribution to the debate about the limits of citizenship in areas such as the European Union thus lies in ethnographic investigation of the social processes that underlie the construction of modern citizenship, its limitations, and its alternatives. Drawing from anthropology and sociology of law, the concept of citizenship is considered here not just as a clearly bounded legal concept but as a dominant model of representation of belonging, both at the level of rights as well as through identity. I analyze citizenship as a cultural product created in a particular geohistorical conjunction, scrutinizing the sociospatial relations drawn through the daily practices and discourses where the category is actually constructed. The rebordering of the Mediterranean thus refers not just to the construction of legal and political boundaries with the south but to the exploration of the social effects of the new symbolic spaces of belonging and exclusion in the innerland. From this perspective, the blurry and marginal area where membership is denied to some people becomes a privileged site from which to grasp the complex web of ethnic, religious, regional, national, and transnational identities in play in the construction of contemporary societies. This is intended to counteract the powerful hegemonic construction of the so-called war between civilizations.

Identities and Citizenship in the Andalusian Borderland

How did the rebordering of the Mediterranean take place during the last fifteen years in southern Europe? How have Andalusians and Africans made sense of it? The social agents involved in this process do not fit into clear-cut social categories, and the cultural repertoires informing their actions are far from neatly bounded. Those involved in the process drew boundaries in a fluid landscape, redefining the meaning of community and bringing the criteria for membership and exclusion into contention.

Granada, the Andalusian province where I conducted most of my fieldwork during the first half of the 1990s, combines various characteristics that make it an especially fascinating case for studying the refiguring of social differences and cultural identities. First, its experience with migration during past thirty years is marked by a profound paradox. In the 1960s and 1970s the Andalusian poor migrated to northern Europe as part of the Mediterranean reserve army of labor that experienced deprivation of political rights, economic exploitation, and ethnic discrimination in host countries. Yet today Andalusians have become European citizens who hold political, legal, and economic privileges denied to Mediterranean immigrants coming from Africa to work for them in Andalusia.

Second, and in contrast to core European countries, Spain has experienced a major shift from an authoritarian political system based on an imposed homogeneous "principle of nationality" to a democratic system based on a multicultural idea of a decentralized Spanish state, in the context of a revival of nationalist regional identities. Third, after fifty years of international ostracism, Spain's incorporation into the EC in 1986 has produced strong rhetoric about a "European ethos" based on a common citizenship, occurring simultaneously with the definition of Africans as different from, and antagonistic to, the Spanish/European population.

Finally, Andalusians, especially those from the province of Granada, largely define their cultural uniqueness in terms of their Muslim past, which makes analysis of interethnic relations between Africans and Granadans even more compelling in the present historical context. The ethnographic account is rich in detail about the way religious imageries anchored in historical experiences are incorporated by both Andalusian citizens (both Catholics and Muslim converts) and Muslim Africans in their daily sociocultural interactions. The official discourse about a romanticized harmonious coexistence during Al-andalus, the medieval Muslim Spain, coexists with one of opposition between Muslim societies—where immigrants come from—and Western societies. Today, Muslims have finally come to be considered a threat to the recently adopted democratic regime in Spain, thus relegating to an old and nationalized time the level of tolerance and mutual interethnic respect achieved in the medieval Al-Andalus.

* * *

To explore how people living today in Granada make sense of the rebordering of the Mediterranean, I use an ethnohistorical perspective and much participant observation as essential methodological devices.[3] Through the compilation of oral histories and other ethnohistorical techniques, I trace the way social difference and cultural identities have been structured and challenged in Andalusia during last fifty years, focusing on the way new and old notions of personhood and of belonging to an imagined community are used in daily discourses and practices. The use of multisited ethnography also proved to be a good instrument to capture both the nomadic lifestyle of migrants and the way global interconnection shapes the creation of difference in a contested public space.

This perspective derives from a consideration of the social agents as not determined by a priori and unitary subject positions. People engage in conflict and negotiation over the minimum norms of behavior and the common feeling of belonging to a political community that is not necessarily nationally bounded. The case of the Granadan Valley of Alfaya[4] were I conducted most of my ethnographic work, is a good example of this. In spite of historically entrenched ethnic and religious boundaries differentiating Spaniards from the so-called Moors (broadly used to refer to Muslim North African peoples), most people from the Alfayan valley saw African immigrants in the early 1990s as equal peasant workers. These newly arrived workers, irrespective of their legal status and nationality, were perceived as being entitled to cross borders to earn a living for themselves and their families, as Andalusian peasants themselves had done before. Most Andalusians welcomed them, remembering their own experiences of the poverty, hunger, marginalization, humiliation, and exploitation that they suffered in northern Europe as emigrants up to the mid 1970s. They thought of the Africans as belonging to a similar economic class and as sharing an ingrained cultural identity as people from the south, proudly different from Europeans and yet holding a nagging internalized feeling of inferiority and backwardness vis-à-vis the northern "civilized" nations.

During the course of my fieldwork in Granada from 1992 to 1995, the boundaries between Andalusians and African immigrants were dramatically redrawn along new legal and ethnic lines, dividing citizens from foreigners, Europeans from Africans, and Christians from Muslims. Class solidarity among those who, in local terms, "honestly work the land with their own hands" and local peasants' utopia of equality and autonomy from outside forces were progressively displaced by a new ideological universe of impartiality and equality of citizens newly constituted before the law, under the aegis of a purportedly rational and neutral state. Left at the margins of this process were African immigrants, now categorized as foreign, disposable workers, racially and religiously marked; they had become "dangerous" men, with no rights to settle down. Being categorized as "illegals,"[5] their access to a shrinking welfare state was now seen as an illegitimate threat.

It is difficult to overemphasize how fiercely both immigrants and villagers experienced this process of redrawing sociospatial boundaries between them. The relational process through which identities were defined and membership criteria were forged involved conflict, pain, violence, and negotiation on both sides, as did the imagining of alternative spaces for interaction, dialog, and mutual respect. Yet one might ask the question, Why so much noise, if in fact the number of immigrants in Andalusia and Spain was extremely low compared with the rest of European countries (and still is), and if newcomers were actually incorporating themselves smoothly into local relations of production and social networks? This indeed challenges the typical explanations of ethnic conflict as being a consequence of a purportedly clear-cut threshold of tolerance and of imagined primordial cultural incompatibilities.

An important factor shaping this anxiety was, of course, the broader public concern about an uncontrolled wave of "desperate" immigrants competing for jobs and scarce resources. This concern was framed in a climate of moral panic created through the alarmist tone of the national mass media and politicians, who revived entrenched fears of a silent southern "invasion" of the national territory. But this factor in itself does not explain local perceptions of the situation. National concerns are not automatically assumed by peasants as their own, due to peasants' historically marginal class and spatial location within the Spanish social structure, as well as to their ingrained reticence and suspicion of the state's demagoguery and forms of domination.

In contrast, some crucial local experiences played a major role in creating anxiety and feelings of frustration. The poverty, segregation, and exploitation that resurfaced with the advent of African immigration stirred up painful memories that Andalusians had tried to cover up. But the moral concerns of the mainly leftist and Catholic peasants did not prevail over anxiety about defending the villagers' hard-won new social position in a context of local economic development and new national and supranational alignments. Class segmentation and the defense of nationals' newly acquired privileges vis-à-vis the state played a major role in the rebordering of local space, but this in itself is still a limited explanation.

As I will show in this book, a key factor in the creation of such disproportionate concern lay in the fact that the presence of immigrant workers was used by the state as a powerful symbolic and concrete mechanism through which Andalusians themselves were transformed into something beyond their control. Andalusians painfully learned the price of modernization and of the duties entailed in their new status as citizens-namely, having to submit to the machinery of the state- initially deployed to regulate the situation of immigrants. Immigration functions as a major force of modernization, creating a modern bounded citizenship. However much the state was accountable to nationals' interests, and however powerful the imagery of future secure well-being within the European symbolic space, this process of normalization and of legitimization of legality also brought unexpected consequences for natives.

At the same time, both immigrants and citizens learned that in the new global space, boundaries are not set in stone. This learning of citizenship—of its forms of domination and its spaces of resistance—does not stop where the border is marked. And as the imagery of incompatible differences and the formulation of differential legal statutes crystallize, people left behind and beyond the space where entitlements are acknowledged daily engage in the practical challenge of making their voices heard and attaining the respect they deserve.

Modernity in the Making: The Reinscription of Difference in a Legally Bounded Space

In this book I discuss the social process of boundary making between those who are considered members of a political community and those who are categorized as outsiders and newcomers. Most research done in Spain about immigration in Spain focuses primarily on the newcomers, leaving unexplored the cultural transformations associated with the new status of Spaniards as citizens of a modern democratic state and full members of the European Union and the Western developed world. Cultural identities of Spaniards and Africans are assumed to be primordially different, and considered an a priori element shaping the construction of social boundaries. In these accounts, racism is described as an autonomous force, an additional factor shaping late capitalist forces toward class segmentation. The general impression is that new workers are excluded, exploited, and marginalized as a consequence of two quite independent forms of domination: class, narrowly conceived on the basis of economic interests; and ethnicity or "race," analyzed as either "emanating" from specific relations of production (and thus reduced to class) or as based on primordial traits and collective identities, adding a new system of stratification to that of class.

In making explicit the theoretical perspective from which I undertake the cultural analysis of the new social borders being constructed in the Andalusian borderland, it is convenient to start with the most basic point, one that is already well established in anthropology. Ethnic, and by extension, cultural identity is not, of course, a primordial trait but rather a sociocultural product. What is primordial is the construction of social boundaries; it is, in fact a basic cultural expression of social relations.[6] Identity is a relational process that shifts through time. This implies two things: (1) classification is a necessary exercise of human perception, and (2) identity is a mode of consciousness relative to the historical forces that are simultaneously cultural and structural. The word "cultural" here refers to the semantic and pragmatic properties of the daily practices of human beings—the system of lived meanings that are available to inform action. Structural here refers to a set of patterns of distribution of power, exerted by institutions and social agents in both agentive and non-agentive form, that is, by control, coercion, and the manipulation of the limits of representation.[7]

This work assumes, therefore, that humans engage in processes of self-identification in opposition to those categorized and perceived as "others," a process that changes through time along with cultural and structural processes. My analysis of cultural transformations includes both Spaniards and Africans, and considers how the construction of social boundaries effects new notions of identity and belonging among all social agents engaged in daily interactions. I do not assume that the constructed opposition between "us/them" is necessary, nor that the contrast is set in ethnic terms. Indeed, there are processes of boundary construction that do not imply an oppositional dynamic, although of course legitimating exclusion or domination is a latent function of boundaries. The contrast between us/them is not necessarily ethnic or cultural; indeed, it is only one form of marking collective differences. Other boundaries operating in social processes include, for example, wealth, prestige, religion, "race," sex, and age. Common to all of these forms of identification and differentiation is the fact that they are shaped by inequality, by a differential distribution of power. Also common to all of these structures of inequality is the fact that they are legitimized on the basis of a purportedly natural endowment, beyond the control of human beings, couched in the terms of a divine or natural Law, or a modern secular legality. In a relational process shaped by inequality, identity comes to the forefront as a cultural expression of forms of domination and of regulation, and also as a form of resistance.

I am concerned with the naturalization of difference as a mechanism for legitimating inequality (in the form of exclusion or domination), as well as with the naturalization of identity as a form of regulation of homogenizing standards of behavior. I consider each as a part of the same relational process, because I understand them as interdependent processes. Moreover, I believe that this concrete coupling is a central feature of modern hegemony, or rather, the hegemony of modernity. I underscore two aspects of modernity: (1) the concern with legitimating inequality (because a universal equality is assumed), and (2) the concern with producing homogeneous standards of behavior (because difference is seen as a threat). These issues have been analyzed in the literature about nationalism, racism, and sexism. Although I draw from these perspectives, which underline the structural relationship between the three forms of naturalization, I do not enter in the polemic over what comes first in a causal relationship and when each form is produced historically. Instead, I am interested in how naturalization of identity and difference are still present in current forms of legitimization of inequality and exclusion, shaping modern social forms of segmentation and stratification.

Let me return to the specific case explored in this book. From the perspective of Andalusians, the southern border has acquired a relevance that was lacking only thirty years ago. In the historical experience of the Andalusians on whom this research focuses, the border marking the "others" was twofold: one border separated those who could not live on their own from those who held economic, political, and cultural power in the Francoist regime; the second border, to the north, separated "backward" Spaniards from the "civilized" world—namely, Europe. For a historically informed ethnography such as this one, this point is crucial. Following F. Barth's seminal work on ethnic identities, I will not explore the notion of belonging to a community through the analysis of the Barth dixit "cultural stuff" that separates members from nonmembers; rather, I will privilege the role of space and place in boundary creation and its effects on the redefinition of "difference." I have chosen to privilege analytically the open semantic range of naturalization mechanisms intended to legitimize inequality and differentiation in order to better grasp the mutually informing dynamic between class and the construction of "others." I trace sociospatial mechanisms of power that traditionally have shaped the production of difference of local disadvantaged groups inhabiting physical and material locations within a particular locality or territory. Instead of analyzing the current location of immigrants within a space treated as "dead nature" where social relations take place, I incorporate the efforts of critical geography to understand spatiality as simultaneously being a social product (or outcome) and a shaping force (or medium) in social life.[8]

As I show through ethnographic analysis in the following chapters, the cultural repertoires informing new social boundaries between Andalusian and African workers are nourished by the broader task of transforming a corporatist and authoritarian regime into a new, modern democratic political community ordained by the rule of law. With the 1986 incorporation of Spain into the EC and the promulgation of the Alien Law in 1985, Spain consolidated as a modern nation-state, where membership is regulated by the legal category of citizenship, anchored to territorialized notions of cultural belonging to an "imagined community," the nation (Anderson 1991). However, this consolidation took place at a moment in both Spain and the rest of Europe when the national model of membership was challenged by several crucial transformations. Major political transformations were underway within and beyond the nation-state (formation of the European Union, the Europe of the regions). Millions of non-nationals entitled to many membership rights were incorporated into polities and a pervasive international normative frame of rights as entitled to all human beings was coming into play, weakening the ability of states to link membership rights to a bounded territory (Soysal 1994).

In view of these transformations, current theory and research has refocused attention to issues of citizenship. T. H. Marshall's seminal work (1950) on class and citizenship in modern England showed that the historical expansion of the rights (civil, political, and social) granted to full members of a political community served as an equalizing mechanism for the social classes displaced by capitalist relations of production. Marshall argued that the history of citizenship produced not only formal rights but social entitlements: "the whole range from the right to a modicum of economic welfare and security to the right to share to the full in the social heritage and to live the life of a civilized being according to the standards prevailing in society" (1950, 11; Somers 1993). This definition of citizenship is increasingly considered unsatisfactory by recent social theory and research, due both to major transformations in national- and world-level institutional frameworks and processes and to the problematization of long-held assumptions about the nation, the state, and social identities as unified and bounded entities.

The most obvious criticism of Marshall's work lies in the fact that in defining citizenship as a status bestowed on full members of a national community he "assumes a given collectivity … [not] as an ideological and material construction, whose boundaries, structures and norms are a result of constant processes of struggles and negotiations, or more general social developments. Any dynamic notion of citizenship must start from the processes which construct the collectivity" (Yuval-Davis 1990, 3). Marshall's assumptions about the political community as a given and of citizenship as a status that one either has or does not have are also apparent in the literature on postwar European migration. The case of southern Europe enables me to question the essentialist notions of social and cultural identity held implicitly in these studies. I shall consider the national political community whose borders are marked as a sociocultural construct, an outcome of cultural and moral hegemonic processes through which the state reproduces itself as the "natural embodiment of history, territory and society."[9]

Spanish hegemonic representation of the nation, imagined as a community of shared blood, heritage, and destiny, contrasts with Anderson's overly sharp distinction between the secular and the religious. In the case of Spanish nationalism, in contrast to the French case, religion was never considered incompatible with the creation of a modern secular project. Religious differences strongly informed the nationalist projects, both in the case of the centuries of opposition between

Spanish Catholics and the Islamic "Moors" as well as opposition between Catholics and other European Christians. This religious component becomes strengthened in the new European Union's symbolic space couched in the new terms of incompatibilities and cultural antagonism between secularized Western Christianity and Islam. European postcolonial imagery further nourished this new community with redefined racial connotations. The traditional use of the "Hispanic race" and the "Gypsy race" transforms into a continuum between the white and black "races," influenced by the pervasive Anglo-Saxon racial categorization present in the hegemonic North American cultural framework.

Whether the nation was based on territoriality as in France, or on common descent and ethnicity as in Germany, the "principle of nationality" (Hobsbawm 1990) endowed the notion of citizenship with ethnic content whose peculiarity was that it is made invisible in relation to other purportedly less universal, more locally focused cultural identities designated as "ethnic groups" or "cultural minorities."[10] The cultural inscription of the liberal model of citizenship is furthermore made invisible in multinational states such as Spain, where it appears as a neutral legal framework with a merely "integrative" function of "differentiated citizenship" (Kymklicka 1996). A central concern of this book will be to show how this invisibility informs the daily practices constructing social boundaries in the civil sphere. Even if membership in the national political community is increasingly detached from a homogeneous national cultural heritage, as in the case of Spain, the model of modern citizenship relies on the mythical character of the universalist project imbued in nationalism "to actualize in political terms the universal urge for liberty and progress" (Chatterjee 1986, 2). As Peter Fitzpatrick has argued "[a]s for that supra-national or universal dimension of nationalism, law in Weberian terms is the very figure of the 'legal-rational' authority characteristic of modernity. And 'law' is now increasingly invoked with indicative facility as a universal measure of appropriate behavior, as a new *jus gentium*" (1992, 117). Universalism blends together with a new form of power that characterizes modernity, a non-agentive and decentered form of domination whose aim is the creation of a new subjectivity, whose techniques operate not so much by negative prohibition as by control and surveillance, and whose object is the body, the creation of the individual subject (Foucault 1977, 1980).

Citizenship is a dominant model of regulation of belonging and entitlement essentially associated with the project of modern state reproduction in the context of global capitalist relations. It is, as I will show, embedded with redefined forms of imagining an objectified community, and in a dialectic relation with these, with new forms of naturalizing differences that legitimate social inequalities. As my colleagues and I have argued elsewhere, modern legal power and its application through mundane modern techniques of administration and decentered power create a new subjectivity that inscribes both identity and difference as "natural":

Bourgeois law, by requiring equal treatment for all subjects, appears to ignore differences that exist before or outside of law. Yet we suggest bourgeois legality plays a major role in producing such differences. It does so, however, in two contradictory ways. First, by declaring everyone equal before the law, it constructs a realm outside of law where inequalities flourish.... Second, bourgeois law demands difference even as it disclaims it, both soliciting expressions of difference and enforcing the right of people to express their differences even as law requires people to stress their similarities in order to enjoy equality. (Collier et al. 1995, 2)

Foucault's notion of power and governamentality guided me through the analysis of processes of normalization, regulation, and discipline by which general standards are internalized by the subject, shaping social agents' behavior and, most important, constituting them as social personas in their belonging to society. The making of citizenship needs a strong state that combines regulative and coercive forms and agencies, because it

defines, in great detail, acceptable forms and images of social activity and individual and collective identity.... Fundamental social classifications, like age and gender [as well as ethnicity and "race," sedentarism and nomadism], are enshrined in law, embedded in institutions, routinized in administrative procedures and symbolized in rituals of state. Certain forms of activity are given the official seal of approval, others are situated beyond the pale. This has cumulative, and enormous, cultural consequences; consequences for how the people identify ... themselves and their "place" in the world. (Corrigan and Sayer 1985, 4)

Through the study of the normalization of immigration and its impact on both immigrants and Spaniards, I aim to show how this new legal culture embedded in the model of citizenship is slowly becoming a "common sense" or "doxa" in the Bourdieuan sense, and how, even when contested and negotiated from particular regional, ethnic, gender, and class interests that characterize internal differentiation in hegemonic formations, it is effectively shaping the limits of social action and the specific forms of discursive possibility.[11]

However, this new hegemony is "not, except analytically, a system or a structure. It is a realized complex of experiences, relationships, and activities, with specific and changing pressures and limits.... It has continually to be renewed, recreated, defended, and modified. It is also continually resisted, limited, altered, challenged by pressures not at its own" (Williams 1977, 112). Citizenship has to be understood as a moral and cultural project rather than as an achievement; it is highly dependent on the creation of a manageable polity, self-disciplined subjects, and effective state apparatuses (Roseberry 1994, 364). But, as will be demonstrated here, this is always a complex and incomplete task, continuously jeopardized by pervasive contradictions and clashes of interests between the different levels of state administration, and by the uneven ability of regulatory powers to homogenize regional, local, and class sectors of the social formation. Following these insights, I explore the impact of the cultural assumptions of modern citizenship in a historically constituted, socially situated field of power and resistance, constituted through "the articulation between universal rules and institutions on one hand, and the political cultures and identities of different [local, regional, and transnational] communities" (Somers 1993, 608).

My perspective on the creation of citizenship also brings the creation of deterritorialized transnational communities into the analysis, incorporating the challenge of recent theory and research to take seriously the criticism of "a ruptured landscape of independent nations and autonomous cultures ... [by] understanding social change and cultural transformation as situated within interconnected spaces ... [and by] rethinking difference *through* connection" (Gupta and Ferguson 1992, 8). By studying Senegalese transnationalism as a facet of Andalusian immigration, I point out the continuities between the colonial system of administration and the current focus of migratory policies on control and integration. I explore the legacy of the racialized colonial civil sphere in contemporary Senegal, and the role of relatively autonomous, culturally encapsulated, indigenous authorities in continuously reproducing the Senegalese state. I bring to light the crucial role of socioreligious intermediary structures in the migratory space and the way their power as the legitimate authorities of "authentic" black Muslim traditions is reinscribed in the diaspora, through the appropriation of legal space opened in Western political communities to state-enforced cultural others. Through this multisited ethnographic perspective, I explore some crucial theoretical points addressed in the literature on transnationalism and deterritorialized nation-states.[12]

Culture and Gender in Ethnographic Work

When I first went to Granada as an anthropologist, I was returning to a city I had loved and visited for many years, though I did not have a concrete personal or familial connection to it. I was just one more person attracted by its *embrujo,* or bewitchment. The city has inspired hundreds of artists to sing to it, to research its past, and to write about its peoples and streets in a highly romanticized tone that exalts the Muslim past (see, for example, the works by the American author Washington Irving). Far from this orientalizing perspective, my own interest was to understand how people living in Granada were relocating themselves as Europeans, and how this process was serving to legitimize the new xenophobic and racist sentiments toward Muslims arriving to the city as immigrants.

In the past, when I had visited the city and the province, I had noted a widespread feeling of backwardness, and even inferiority, in relation to "other" Europeans, and as in the rest of Spain, a strong desire to become accepted as full members of the European Community. Contrary to the approach taken by most anthropologists, I was rather suspicious of bounded notions of cultural identity, and the way people in Granada experienced the rebordering of the Mediterranean seemed a strategic vantage point from which to understand further how the bounding was taking place in a territory historically situated at the margins of clear-cut identities.

Part of my perspective grew out of my own nonconformity with so-called normal patterns of cultural identification. As for many other transnational and highly nomadic people, my own cultural identity was far from clear. Or at least so I thought before living in California, where my contact with people from all over the world, and most especially with Chicanas/os, rendered rather problematic a fixed territorial and cultural notion of culture and origin. My apparent conflict became evident each time people asked me the hated question "Where are you from?"—a question that, at least in Spain, is almost invariably asked when your origin is not really clear to the person with whom you are interacting.

The problem was not my accent, since when I returned from Colombia, where I was born, I promptly adapted to both the accent and manners considered normal to social interaction in the north of Spain, where I spent most of the second decade of my life. Rather, the problem was a deep, though confusing, attachment to several places at the same time, a notion of belonging that was not territorially or biologically defined. To answer the dreaded question, I invariably used a sentence that started with Latin America and followed with Navarra and Madrid.

A theoretical pretext exists for this description of my origins, relevant to my positioning during fieldwork and as a writer. I do not want to simply reproduce the confessional postmodern mood that has invaded anthropological literature in recent years. Rather, in talking about a deterritorialized and nonunivocal sense of belonging, I want to raise the question of considering culture as detached from a territorially bounded location (Gupta and Ferguson 1992) and as not being synonymous with difference (Rosaldo 1989). The frustrating experience of my own fractured sense of belonging was incorporated into my research and analysis as a symptom of a broader space of signifying practices shaping normality and constituting me as lacking something-namely, a clear sense of belonging marked by biological and territorial links to a bounded place. My interest as an anthropologist has been to understand what kind of social processes shaped this normality, and how people situated at the margins of the hegemonic "either-or" (Kearney 1995) notion of belonging resisted their displacement.

There is another sense in which my own experience informs my theoretical view of cultural analysis: time changes people and cultures. As obvious as this may seem, the very notion of culture as something that one either has or does not have historically has been built on an essentialized understanding of the way people make sense of the world and represent themselves and others. There are several tempos from which this dynamic can be incorporated into a cultural analysis, for the tempo of daily social practices runs much quicker than the tempo of collective social transformations. The experiences of displacement and movement across borders, and the new interactions and conflicts derived from those relocations, force people to act in these new contexts through "necessary improvisation" (Bourdieu 1977, 8). Cultural analysis has to incorporate uncertainty and improvisation as a central feature of social practices in order to escape from an objectifying view of the cultural matrix as determining the way social agents engage in practice. Taking into account the tempo of collective transformations requires considering the limits of improvisation, as set up by objective structures conditioning the embodied range of possibilities opened by social actors in their practical actions. Both tempos together, considered as feeding back on each other, in a dialectical relation, allow us to avoid a teleological view of history while also scrutinizing why and how reproduction of power takes place.

As an anthropologist, my situation in Granada did not fit the normal relationship between the observer and those observed. For many in Granada, I was a "Castilian" woman living in the United States who came to study "Moors and blacks." This was well understood by locals, since it was obvious that the "weird" people, the ones scholars should "study," were the immigrants. This was all well and good until I started to approach Granadans and villagers themselves. This produced a strange feeling among many of them, the typical discomfort felt by anyone (or at least by me) who has been scrutinized as an interesting object of study. The inverted gaze of my study did not resemble "studying up," since I was accorded a more or less similar status to that of villager, especially among youth. Yet I often had to take pains to dispel suspicions about my hidden interests in showing the racism of the villagers. Villagers frequently evinced surprise, a mixed feeling of distrust and complacency toward my interests. As one of my neighbors asked me, "Are we so strange that you want to study us?" [¿Tan raros somos que quieres estudiarnos?]. As my interest in learning more about Andalusians' experiences became accepted, people happily provided me with what they viewed as the most authentic accounts of the valley's traditions and legends—what they considered their own culture. Inexorably, the habitus of a highly romanticized and anthropologized people reemerged among Andalusians, molded also by the current context of ethnogenesis induced by Spain's system of "Autonomous Communities" in search of "authentic" cultural traditions (Greenwood 1992). Only occasionally did people understand that what I was interested in was precisely the cultural shape of their purportedly noncultural normality.

In addition to the complex way cultural positioning shaped fieldwork, gender dynamics proved to be a main structuring force for both my personal experience as a fieldworker and for interethnic relations between immigrants and natives. I will briefly refer to this before explaining the organization of this book.

My situation as a woman was a highly uncomfortable one, as it was for other women working as volunteers in NGOs and associations or as social workers. Being a woman in the field among "blacks and Moors," with whom I spent hours chatting, and to whom I gave rides in my car, produced rumors among villagers questioning my "real" status and my "honor" as an "upstanding" woman. I knew this and could not avoid the tension it produced for me. Similarly, I frequently found myself uncomfortable with immigrants, especially Moroccans, who did not understand how my husband could let me be alone in the field and not be present to defend his "property." The precautions I took to avoid any kind of harassment included long and loose clothing and a prudent attitude combined with a fierce defense of my independence. My awareness about the impact of the sex and gender implications of fieldwork was strong and permanent, and I learned to live with it.

I did experience a case of real harassment, however, which serves to illustrate both the way racism is internalized and the interaction between sexism and racism. It happened when I was doing archival research in the municipal council, precisely when I assumed I was "safe" and reduced my precautions. Amazed and furious as I was, I discovered the way prominent progressist villagers knew about and tolerated the common harassment of female employees by the council secretary. Those women decided to remain silent to avoid losing their jobs or being shamed by jokes about their "oversensitivity." Unfortunately, sexual harassment and violence is as common in Alfaya as it is in the rest of the country, and there was little I could do about it at the moment.

I mention this incident here not only to take a humble revenge in the name of women who have to silently endure this kind of harassment in a context where everybody advises us to just "forget about it," but also to underscore the way gender violence is invisibilized or visibilized in contexts of interethnic relations. Had this incident happened involving the "blacks and Moors" with whom I was working, villagers would have reacted in a completely different way. Sex and gender are one of the most prominent arenas of ethnic stereotyping, especially when "Moors" are involved. This had happened a couple of times before this incident, and invariably served to reinforce the characterization of Africans as "dangerous men"—sexually aggressive and sexist. These are the typical charges used to categorically scorn other cultures and legitimize the urge for assimilation—the least radical of possible racist complaints and claims. When sexual harassment is part of "our" culture, then the reading is much more indulgent toward the harassers.

In Alfaya this was further fuelled by the fact that most immigrants were men and most Spaniards who established close relationships with them beyond the workplace (in associations as in leisure time) were women. The gendered features of this restructuring of work sectors and of the new Spanish civil spheres are related to increasing privatization of state responsibility for those who are excluded and/or marginalized by contemporary Western societies. This has further consequences for depoliticizing claims for equality, for strengthening the links between racism and sexism, and for perpetuating the gender division of labor in capitalist relations of production.

* * *

This book is divided into seven chapters, which I will very briefly describe to guide the reader to concrete interests. In the first chapter I describe the overall transformation and relocation of Alfaya's peasants during the last forty years, drawing from collected oral histories, ethnographic material of the 1960s and 1970s in Andalusia, and social theory related to the transformation of sociopolitical rural structures in southern Europe. The detailed analysis of peasants' customary notions of rights, justice, and the community; their experiences as guest workers in northern Europe; and their struggle during the transition period to transform the segmented and stratified social space will help shed light on the way immigrants are received in the 1990s and how interethnic relations are shaped at the local level. After describing what villagers call the "price of modernization" (dependence on outside economic actors and capitalist markets and the depoliticizing of rural Spain), in the final section I present the dominant and alternative narratives of the origins of the valley, showing how inclusive and exclusive criteria of belonging are related to the way Arabs' historical presence in Andalusia and Alfaya is represented.

The second chapter introduces the reader to the political economy and the legal factors shaping the rebordering of the Mediterranean. After describing in a broad outline the relatively recent arrival of African immigrants to Spain and the 1985 Alien Law, I offer a detailed description of the contradictions arising from the enforcement of the law in a the context of a deeply entrenched informal economy. These contradictions intensify when considering the particular complexity of the construction of the new European imagery in Andalusia, and the way the purportedly fixed borders are strongly contested by immigrants, both by materially crossing them, and by appropriating Andalusia's Muslim past to claim rights and belonging. The chapter concludes by introducing Assane D., one of the first Senegalese to arrive in Alfaya, whose experiences are described through extensive quotations from his oral history. Through his testimonies I describe the first popular movement of resistance to the new European borders imposed in the Andalusian borderland, and the lack of credibility and legitimization of the law in a region where it has served the powerful for decades. This ethnographic account will also set the stage for understanding the political struggles surrounding immigration, which are described in the next chapter.

The third chapter focuses on the process of reproduction of a segmented social space in the Andalusian rural landscape, looking at the continuities and changes between Francoist times and today. I trace the sociospatial mechanisms of power that have traditionally shaped the difference of disadvantaged groups inhabiting physical and material locations within the valley and beyond as nomads, showing how new and old meanings of social displacement intertwine or contradict each other in daily social relations shaping immigrants' location in social space. The so-called immigration problem ushered in a local political debate about who belongs where and why, who has the right to move across and to settle in a specific space, what the requirements are to dwell in a particular site, and how these requirements are maintained in practice. Finally, the analysis moves from local politics to the broader cultural politics, underlining the move toward putting immigrants in their (social) place, looking at the tacit customary rules for everyday use and occupancy of the public space according to an individual's class, age, gender, and ethnicity.

In the fourth chapter, the symbolic and political manufacturing of the legitimization of legality is analyzed, as well as its effects on the daily construction of social boundaries between Andalusian citizens and African foreigners. I explore how disciplinary techniques and relations of power extend beyond the limits of the state, looking at how social groups of civil society, which act as intermediaries between the state and immigrants, embrace legality as an inclusive framework that can incorporate immigrants as legal subjects with rights. I will show how these groups of civil society become complicit in the disciplining of immigrants, and how they themselves are transformed in the process. Describing the disciplinary methods involved in what I call the "fetishism of papers," the chapter shows the cultural effects of these sociolegal processes. I will explain in detail immigrants' critiques of legality as in fact reproducing structural inequalities, and of citizenship as in fact guided by a mercantilized notion of rights and belonging.

The fifth chapter analyzes the discourses and implementation of immigration policies during a specific segment of time, the summer of 1994, and in a geographically bounded social space, the Valley of Alfaya. The goal is to highlight the contradictions arising from the imagining of integration and multiculturalism in a context of forces of exclusion shaped by the application of the Alien Law. The summer of 1994 saw a shift in immigration policies from control and coercion of foreigners to a more inclusive focus on both Spaniards and immigrants as subjects of a modern rationality requiring compliance with the law. When modern rationality applied the law inclusively to shape social action and discursive possibility in Andalusia, it conjured up an image of consensus building and *convivencia* between Spaniards and immigrants. In practice, however, the legitimization of legality among villagers accelerated the process of normalization of the Alfayan social space and worldview. However limited and ambiguous, complicit acceptance of the rule of law subtly coerced villagers to transform customary rules of their own behavior and productive relations. Villagers in Alfaya found themselves constituted through these processes as citizens with rights but also with duties to comply with the law. This painful process of learning about citizenship was not without consequences for both nationals and immigrants. Nationals saw Africans as a threat to the maintenance of their privileges, especially because the racial visibility of immigrants made peasants' informal economic practices much easier for the state to control. Immigrants were further pushed toward invisibility and vulnerability, independent of their legal status, as racially marked scapegoats of peasants' reluctance to be accountable to the state.

In the sixth and seventh chapters, I illuminate the link between the politics producing a culturally differentiated immigrant worker in Spain and those producing a culturally abiding emigrant worker in Senegal. Linked together, such politics serve as a powerful mechanism through which nation-states perpetuate their clienteles in late capitalism. In chapter 6, I focus on the contested social space where Senegalese migrant workers negotiate, resist, or adopt a transnational postcolonial framework. In earlier chapters I analyzed how Andalusians bring cultural and historical particularities of their background into their experience of the new legal and ethnic inner boundaries shaping social space. Here I provide an analogous case study of the Senegalese diaspora and how it builds on the legacy of the racialized colonial civil sphere and the state's reproduction of relatively autonomous, culturally encapsulated, indigenous authorities. I will show how idiosyncratic Senegalese modes of social organization successfully extend to a migratory transnational space to incorporate youth from the lowest ranks of the global labor market and at the margins of a transstate civil sphere where legal subjects are acknowledged, and how these new transnational practices reinvent a relatively autonomous space from which to challenge global inequalities. Finally, we will see the extent to which Senegalese organization in diaspora facilitates or hinders the questioning of the national status quo.

Having spelled out the particularities of the Senegalese transnational social space, I return to Alfaya and Granada in chapter 7 to examine how different understandings of integration and *convivencia* work out in daily social processes. *Convivencia* requires a theoretical approach to ethnic relations that looks beyond conflict to processes of exchange, mutual respect, and understanding. I argue that in order to transcend categories and structures of difference, the analyst should take full account of these complexities as they shape day-to-day interactions, where rivalry and suspicion go hand in hand with mutual interaction and creative influence. To appreciate the complexities of the social dynamics of cultural interaction, the analyst has to attempt to transcend difference by relativizing it, in addition to historicizing it.

Immigrants in Andalusia and Spain engage in the active construction of *convivencia*, forging both common rules of social behavior (ultimately a shared notion of justice) and notions of common belonging to a shared civil sphere that makes room for a nonhomogeneous and transnational cultural identification and belonging (ultimately a shared multicultural citizenship). I draw on several ethnographic examples to explore moments and instances of *convivencia* where immigrants struggle to achieve respect, resolutely drawing on local customary notions of rights due to those who work honestly with their own hands, maintaining the pride and dignity to which every person is entitled. In the last section, I examine collective processes of *convivencia,* drawing mainly on the case study of Senegalese in Granada, a highly symbolic place for Muslims, and contrast their strategies of entitlement and belonging with the formal recognition of their rights as different "others." From the perspective of most immigrants, *convivencia* implies a daily negotiation and resistance to the prejudices toward different "others" that are imposed on them and that shape their marginal location in the civil sphere. I will show how, notwithstanding this situation, the revaluation of cultural identity and of human rights as privileged channels of participation in the civil sphere opens up spaces of struggle for civil participation and representation in the Spanish social sphere and beyond.

Notes

1. Literally "living together," *convivencia* was the concept coined by historians to refer to the coexistence and cultural interbreeding of Muslims, Jews, and Christians in the medieval times, just before the Spanish nation-state was founded as a territorial unit in the Iberian peninsula (the sense in which it is used above). Today it is a somewhat loose term that applies to (1) a formal/informal meeting with a spiritual, congregational, or ecumenical approach (the sense in which it is used above), (2) the daily interaction among people, and (3) a particular model governing collective rules of a political community, as in the expression democratic *convivencia.* For my theoretical approach to this term, see the end of chapter 6 and chapter 7, where I provide an empirical analysis of processes of *convivencia* in Granada.

2. The Organic Law 7/1985 (July 1), on "Rights and Liberties of Foreigners in Spain," known as the *Ley de Extranjería* will be cited in this book as the Alien Law, or LOE (*Ley Orgánica de Extranjería*). The law was further elaborated upon in the associated Regulations [*Reglamento*], Royal Decree 1119/1986 (May 26). Additional legislation includes the European Council and other international agreements (see *Boletín Oficial del Estado* [*BOE*] 1991, "Ley y Reglamento de Extranjería"). The associated Regulations were reformed in 1996, and in 2000, a new reform of the law took place (Organic Law 4/2000, with the highly polemic reforms of 8/2000). During the editing of this book in 2003, a new final reform is being drafted; we are receiving new critiques and comments from important unions, political parties, and NGOs, but this is all still unofficial. See De Lucas and Torres 2002 for a recent review of the new normative, policies, and political debate about migration in Spain.

3. I base my analysis on fieldwork conducted for my dissertation from 1992 to 1995 in Granada and Madrid (Spain) and in Dakar, Sébikotane, and Louga (Senegal). I did participant observation in Alfaya (see note 4 below), Granada, and Senegal, collected oral histories, taped more

than fifty hours of interviews, reviewed the local and national press and archives, and surveyed two samples of thirty families each—one in Alfaya and the other in Sébikotane—on their social, economic, and political strategies in recent years. I also collected a variety of materials of cultural production by Alfayan peasants in the valley and abroad, by African immigrants, and by NGOs, associations, and other groups working on issues relating to migratory movements. Since 1998, once established professionally in Madrid, I have continued doing research about immigration issues in Spain, following closely the processes analyzed here.

4. Alfaya is a pseudonym. Throughout this book I use pseudonyms and acronyms for places and names of informants to guarantee the confidentiality of information and people who collaborated in this research. I included some data that could help to locate the informant only when he or she agreed to appear in the book without pseudonyms.

5. Throughout this book I retain the commonly used term "illegal" instead of other more descriptive concepts such as "undocumented" or "irregular" (immigrants) in order to retain the connotations and impact of the term as it is used in the local context.

6. See Barth 1969; Comaroff 1987.

7. See Comaroff and Comaroff 1991; Gramsci 1971; Williams 1979.

8. See Harvey 1989; Soja 1989, 7.

9. See Anderson 1991; Cohn and Dirks 1989, 2; Hobsbawm 1990; Hobsbawm and Ranger 1983.

10. See Balibar and Wallerstein 1991; Fitzpatrick 1992; Rosaldo 1993, 1994a; Williams 1989.

11. See Bourdieu 1977; Gramsci 1971; Hunt 1993; Williams 1977.

12. See Blash et al. 1994; Kearney 1995, 1996.

1. PEOPLES OF ALFAYA
The Relocation of Peasants
in Southern Europe

*T*he overall theme of this chapter is the analysis of the transformations of Andalusian peasants' identity and class position over the last fifty years in the Valley of Alfaya. First I review the abject situation of *jornaleros,* or day laborers, in post–Civil War Spain (from the 1940s thorough the 1950s); their experience of stigmatization during their forced emigration, and the changes emigration brought upon autochthonous notions of rights (from the 1960s through the early 1970s); and their newly won economic autonomy through innovative family-based intensive agriculture (in the 1970s). By the early 1980s, class positions had equalized. Civil, political, and socioeconomic rights definitively replaced the previous politics of fear, and a progressive social majority representing many of the dispossessed of earlier years began to assume power at the local level (and soon in the central government as well). By the late 1980s the "social vision of the village" appeared to be possible, though it would soon be followed by disappointment. As a solidary class consciousness and a vibrant public sphere have been lost in an increasingly capitalistic Alfaya, peasants have begun to assess what they refer to as the price of modernization. They find themselves in a new relationship with the state, dependent on subsidies and informal economic practices to maintain their new standard of living. Today they see themselves as vulnerable people with rights. Peasants see those rights as strongly fought-for consequences of their own actions and work. Very soon they will be forced to reconceptualize and negotiate them anew according to new criteria of belonging, criteria such as nationality, culture, and citizenship.

Analysis of the emigration period shows that one cannot assume that autochthonous notions of rights and the legitimacy of law correspond to political philosophy manuals. Nor can one assume as a given the social criteria of belonging

Notes for this chapter begin on page 45.

to an imagined community (in particular whether these are conceptualized as culture or ethnic difference). Rather, one must study how these criteria are created and changed. For this purpose, in the last section I examine the village's narratives of origin, where much of villagers' self-conception as a community is embedded. I show that many of these narratives expose an inclusive criterion of belonging based on "being a person," implying respect for certain core values in the relationship with others and in work; this self-conception sets the stage for the initial reception of African immigrants in the valley as described in chapter 2. At the same time, one can find the seeds of certain exclusionary criteria that will prove crucial for later developments in the relationship between villagers and African immigrants.

Although Spanish peasants did not yet realize it, immigrants coming from Africa beginning in the mid 1980s were to become a force in relocating them as peasants of southern Europe: as citizens with rights more extensive than those of foreigners; as reluctant enforcers of the European Union's southern frontier and its closest point to Africa; as newly privileged nationals. Class, for peasants, ceased to be the defining factor of their social position; at the same time, peasants came to see and actively contribute to the marginalization of a new "wretched class" (Carr and Fussi 1979, 8), now defined along the lines of ethnicity and legal status.

Peasants in Francoist Times

I will begin with a brief description of the social panorama in which most adults in Alfaya were raised. It is worth remembering that this period began after a traumatic civil war: two generations matured in times of famine, ruralization, and class polarization maintained through an authoritarian ideology based on national Catholicism.[1]

Peasants became a political force in Spain, and especially in Andalusia, a region dominated by a few *latifundistas* (quasi-feudal owners of large landed states) from the second half of the nineteenth century. Anarchists, communists, and socialists struggled for years to achieve agrarian reform, involving redistribution of the land and reforms in the relations of employment. Some of their claims found political channels during the Second Republic.[2] The establishment of the Francoist dictatorship, which existed from 1939 to 1975, meant the destruction of organized labor, the repression of those who had sided with the Republic, and an economic nationalism of autarky.

The governments of western Europe ostracized Spain as a fascist state, while the Franco government legitimated its isolation with a nationalist demagoguery that emphasized the need to "save" the unity of Spain as united by its imperial past and cultural uniqueness, one that was symbolically opposed to that of the

Europeans.[3] Meanwhile, the regime conjured up the category of "peasant" as the essence of the "Spanish race" [*sic*], as "noble and rightful," and as the "moral reserve of the nation." This idealization of the peasantry (or *soberanía del campesinado*, in the words of Sevilla Guzmán 1979) coexisted with an otherwise "agrarian fascism" that reinforced the class-based rural social structure. Famine and rationing lasted for over a decade. Regional disparities increased, and while Catalonia and the Basque Country slowly became industrialized, the laborers of Andalusia continued being "the most wretched class in Europe" (Carr and Fussi 1979, 8).

Well after the Spanish Civil War, by the end of the 1950s, the social structure of the Valley of Alfaya consisted of three main groups: (1) a small and traditionally powerful group of *caciques* (political bosses) who effectively controlled economic, political, and legal institutions;[4] (2) a preponderance of small-propertied peasant families whose domestic economy had to be complemented with salaried work on the lands of elites, either as day laborers, land renters, or sharecroppers;[5] and (3) a heterogeneous group of day laborers without land, or *jornaleros*, in the strict sense, also known in the valley as *choceños*, or *cortijeros*.[6] Elites used discretionary power to keep smallholders tied to the land yet dependent on their power to contract them.[7] The lack of *autonomía*, as powerfully demonstrated by G. Collier in his work in Huelva, united *jornaleros* with or without land in their subordination to *caciques*: "*autonomía* epitomized the proprietor's prerogative of protecting his family honor and developing his family interests as he wished, free from others' control" (1987, 5; see also the concept *vivir de lo suyo*, or "live on their own," used by García Muñoz 1995).

Law and order was locally controlled through representatives of authoritarian power, the *caciques*, the administrative civil servants, and the Civil Guard. *Caciques* and civil servants traditionally used their power to engage in clientelism, patronage, and paternalistic relationships with their subordinates, exchanging "favors" (influences, documents, promises of help, access to social benefits such as health care, education, and subsidies for the most needy people) for submission and exploitation in labor relations.[8] *Caciques* used political power to obtain the "circulation permits" required to transport wheat, selling this surplus production in the black market. They controlled and restrained alternative strategies of survival for those who lacked *autonomía* (see first section of chapter 3; see also Fraser 1979; Martínez Alier 1971).

Little could be done to undermine this agrarian system at the time. After the dramatic repression of anarchists, communists, and socialists who struggled in the Second Republic for agrarian reform, an imposed "apoliticism" prevailed among the offspring of the vanquished in the postwar years (Collier 1987). The poor were forced to maintain a submissive attitude, humble and obedient to the wishes of employers, political bosses, and state security forces. In general, it was the employer who gave references attesting to a worker's "ideological purity" or whether or not he was "trustworthy," thus condemning those who did not submit to employers' rules to permanent hiding, emigration, or nomadism (Sevilla Guzmán 1979, 176). As one of my neighbors in Alfaya put it, such social positions were maintained through the forces of fear: "There are still rich and poor people, but now things are different because we have leveled off [*nos hemos igualao*]. Before, there was that tremendous fear; one could not say a word to the *cacique*—we had to talk to them with the head bent downward. We coped with everything because we were afraid of their power, of the possibility of reprisals" (R.G., summer 1995).

I wish to highlight three basic features of the agrarian system that, although redefined, still play an enduring role in the rural landscape of the 1990s. First, we find deeply embedded practices supporting an underground economy and conscious fraud against the state that conform to a historical habitus shared across classes. Second, class differences are maintained and reproduced through a politics of fear based on an authoritarian political system that used security forces against poor and ideologically suspicious people. Third, the system effectively linked forced nomadism and hiding with chronic poverty to create a reserve army of agrarian labor to keep wages down. As I will show in detail in the third chapter, reproduction of these features in today's rural Andalusia also maintains a symbolic form of domination based on the naturalization of these latter groups as different from or marginal to the imagined community.

Rights and the Experience of Emigration

In this section, I examine preexisting notions of rights and cultural difference among Alfayan peasants in relation to their experiences of migration, as a necessary preliminary task to understanding the way African immigration was received in the late 1980s. The ethnohistorical material collected among Granadan peasants of various generations prevents us from projecting upon them a liberal and individualistic notion of justice produced in democratic systems governed by the rule of law. Rather, debates about rights among Andalusian peasants in the context of today's immigration should be understood as being shaped by the peasants' historical experience of migration and their position in the social structure. Their understanding of cultural difference is not mainly related to "exotic" cultures; rather, it is constructed from a bitter experience of recent emigration to Europe. The assimilationist[9] idea that prevails among peasants is not informed by a strong and historically rooted notion of what makes a citizen, as in France, for instance, but rather by a painful experience of having being excluded from rights warranted to nationals in the European countries where Andalusians lived as emigrants in the 1960s and 1970s.

Most people I knew in Alfaya's valley withstood humiliating treatment during the Francoist regime because of a lack of food or lack of *autonomía*. As we have seen, agrarian fascism managed to keep both small landowners and *jornaleros* without land linked to Alfaya, dependent on a labor market fully controlled by *caciques*. Those who were forced to emigrate outside Alfaya before the 1960s did so only temporarily because they were not welcome to stay longer than needed in the Andalusian agrarian sites where they were hired. These emigrants, many of whom I interviewed in the 1990s in Alfaya, lacked basic human rights and experienced only an authoritarian regime, if not the horrors of the Civil War that brought it. As late as the 1960s, nobody paid taxes or believed in institutionalized justice as being neutral and fair; nor did they consider the state as a guarantor of general collective interests.

The early 1960s marked a shift in Francoist policies away from autarky and toward new economic policies to foster industrialization and create a market economy in Spain. This shift, Franco told the nation in his 1964 New Year's message, was the beginning of a "new era" (Carr and Fussi 1979, 54). Rapid, uncontrolled growth produced economic polarization and the impoverishment of rural regions such as Andalusia. Poor peasants began the rural exodus to more developed areas, participating in the broader "Mediterranean reserve army of labor" for northwestern European countries. Andalusians' experiences with Catalan or European racism against them have been extensively reported by novelists and social scientists.[10] In this context, Alfayans began a forced emigration, which once again spread the community across the bounds of the local territory, this time across Spain and Europe. Some of the people who left definitively settled abroad, changing their permanent residence, though most still come to the valley during vacation periods. But most Alfayans returned to the valley in the 1970s and 1980s, coinciding with a general national trend of return of former emigrants and exiles.

In the Valley of Alfaya, and more generally in Andalusia, the battle for rights is a long-standing affair. As peasants and as Andalusians, many of them have been discriminated against, exploited, and alienated. They have been characterized as the most folkloric, Catholic, and rabid nationalists (Burgos 1972), as well as quintessential the perfect examples of the backwardness and ignorance of southern Europe and of the cultural difference of Catholics and Mediterraneans (Castles and Kosack 1985).[11] Peasants' notions of "basic rights" are closely related to the notion of *autonomía* referred to previously: autonomy for feeding one's family and for refusing orders that endanger the pride and dignity that every person is entitled to defend. As a neighbor in his thirties told me: "This valley has witnessed the most essential Andalusian struggle, that of the *jornalero*, not even for land but for bread. For us, emigration was a blessing because those in power here wanted us tied. My family would go to beg to [a friend's grandfather's] house, and sometimes they would not even look at us. As if we were animals, I say! That is what is not fair." Listening to such a young villager, one can imagine the situation during Franco's dictatorship, when the majority of the village, small landowners or day laborers who could not live on their own, were faced with the attitudes of those in powerful classes, as masterfully articulated by Arguedas: "God made man with a destiny that men would have to split into two groups of individuals, one superior to the other. The superiors have the duty and the right to command, to write laws, to dictate orders to which inferiors must submit so as to keep social peace" (1968, 204f.).

Because of the labor exploitation, political submission, and all-too-frequent personal humiliation they have experienced, peasants have historically developed a profound egalitarianism based on the notion of being a person. The struggle for recognition as "persons" is thus the most basic fight for human and civil rights, as they are conceptualized in the autochthonous tradition of Andalusian peasants. This is not an abstract or individualistic notion, in contrast with the current notion of citizenship and human rights. On the contrary, being a person refers to a set of communal rules and values that affect all members of a given collective and their duties and rights. The definition of being a person is related to someone's behavior with respect to his or her peers and job. These minimum rules of behavior are viewed as a requirement of pacific coexistence. According to the most traditional local narratives, nobody deserves or has a right to anything unless he or she behaves as a "person," adhering to certain moral values such as being "a good worker," "noble," "respecting commitments," being "grateful," not provoking or betraying others, and respecting a certain notion of "fairness."[12] Systematically, peasants give priority to these autochthonous rules of behavior when judging who has a right to what in the valley, so that "rights" can be either deserved or not: "He was very honest, kept his commitments, was very formal, that's why he never lacked a day-salary and nobody attacked him.… I mean, he deserved it" (P.M., spring 1995).

But this notion of justice most often did not match reality, a reality in which the rich and powerful would not acknowledge the status of peasants as "persons," disrespecting their basic right to have bread to feed their families and to live free from humiliation. This position of dependence, submission, and lack of autonomy is described as only appropriate to animals. Within the borders of Andalusia, "We would leave the village because we didn't have anything to eat here, we went, all the family together, with the four things we need, and thus we lived, as animals in the field" (A.M., spring 1995). And among those who left, "We left the village, herded like cattle or sheep, in a train wagon … wearing something like an arrow on our bodies, to indicate we were emigrants,… it was like an emblem, a pin attached to our jackets" (C.G., summer 1994).

The poor, and those who had to emigrate, generally believe that current welfare state rights are something that should be acquired by paying and do not necessarily match the rights that one "deserves" as a person. Having access to today's welfare rights is equated with upward social mobility and with the privileges of class, gender, or nationality. In a conversation about rights, three peasants discussed who has a right to what and how these rights have changed. Referring to village life in the past, one said, "In the past we never paid any rights [*no pagábamos derechos*], because nobody had anything, and so it was, that nothing [no rights] were accorded to us." A former emigrant commented, "I paid all my rights, to work as others there [abroad], I paid my rights, I was in the same situation as them [native workers in Europe]" (P.M. and A.M., spring 1995). A woman who emigrated to Germany and who had to work illegally (as did many others) resented that she hadn't had minimal rights either abroad or after her return: "I don't get the unemployment subsidy here, I didn't have rights there to be able to work, nor do I have rights here to get subsidies, or for having suffered a war, nor any kind of right at all.… Uff, I'm now in my sixties and I have no right to anything, not even a holiday. [I'm] a slave, a slave" (M.C., summer 1994).

Interestingly, it was in emigration that emigrants encountered the notion of "right" as understood in liberal democracies. Migrants' narratives contrasted the experience abroad with earlier experiences in Andalusia. Most felt that as emigrants they were treated as "persons," even though without full rights. One woman contrasted her experiences as an emigrant in Andalusia and abroad as follows: "I admire the way people behaved toward me in Switzerland; here some would look at you askance just because you were an emigrant … but there you are looked upon as a 'normal' person.[13] And there they value your work, one gets credit for work done. Here it was never like that. Here they always wanted more from you, you never did enough, you were never equal to them" (A.R., spring 1995). Credit for work done echoes again the idea of deserving to be treated as "normal." Many were surprised to find that being "equal before the law" effectively translated into fair application of the law. An emigrant to Switzerland remembers how a Swiss policeman was fined for incorrectly filling out his migratory documents: "Uff, I said [with a sigh of relief at having avoided the expected worst], if this had happened in Spain, I'm the one who would have had to pay the fine! And the interpreter told me, here it's not that way; in Switzerland, the one responsible for the infraction is the one who pays" (C.G., summer 1994).

But it is also in emigration that many current inhabitants of the Valley of Alfaya learned the value of nationality as the basis for certain privileges from which they were excluded for being foreigners. Migrants not only learned to link unequal relations with foreignness, but they also saw how the legal status of foreigner became filled with content through the notion of "cultural difference," seeing themselves categorized as people from the Mediterranean, Catholics, Spaniards, southern Europeans, or even just as immigrants. The testimony of A.P., a day laborer who emigrated to France to work as a unionized construction worker, is quite revealing: "I went first to Catalonia; they spoke Catalan and thought of themselves as superior to us Andalusians, something which I have never tolerated, nobody is more than an Andalusian." In France it was different because there he was treated as a "person," even though A.P. had to adapt to French customs: "They would criticize our way of being [*nuestra forma de ser*] even when we [Spaniards] grouped together, building a 'piece' of Spain with our customs…. Once we went to watch a play by García Lorca, and just because one of us said *Olé* a policeman came to complain. I felt bothered, and told him that that's what we say in our village—could we not even express ourselves?" A.P. emphasized that, as workers and residents, Spaniards had certain rights that were respected, even though their status as foreigners and Spaniards made it impossible for them to feel they were equal members of French society: "At work and at home we had the same rights as the French, and nobody could bother us, but we could not vote or open a shop or small business" (A.P., summer 1994).

Irrigation, Intensive Labor, and the Autonomous Entrepreneur

The process of modernization is perceived at the local level as being a result of peasants' own efforts to overcome traditional class stratification and segmentation through both agricultural innovation and grassroots political struggle.[14] In the 1960s, with the rural exodus and the implementation of the new "modernizing" political economic policies, peasants with modest land holdings tried to survive by combining several domestic strategies, such as finding part-time work for their family members both in agriculture and in other economic sectors, inside and outside the valley.[15] The key to such transformation was the opening up of a free market of labor within and beyond Spain. This involved the proletarization of the peasantry, but also their access to cash from salaried work and to class-based political struggle within clandestine unions and political parties in Spain and abroad—key factors in the relocation of peasants in the new "modernized" rural landscape.

At the same time, during the 1960s, some villagers started innovating with techniques of intensive horticulture, taking what advantage they could of Alfaya's distinctive microclimate to enter into the otherwise very competitive business of agricultural production. Families used remittances of members working abroad to invest in land and irrigation in the village. Other cash earners invested in transportation, one of the more successful ways of rapidly accumulating capital, which could, in turn, be invested in land and irrigation infrastructure. Through irrigation horticulture, many of those whom the economy had traditionally condemned to dependence attained the wished-for *autonomía* previously restricted to *caciques*. As one pioneer horticulturist explained to me:

The "General" [a prominent *cacique* of the village] had always lent me money when there was no work. He was a usurer, and poor people accumulated debts to him that were so large they were forced to turn over their land to him. I hated him. He would always come over to my land to tell me how to work my farm. But in that first year of irrigation I discovered that I could earn more in three months than in the whole year. Then when the "General" came by to sneak around, as he always had done, I told him: "Can't you see the borders of this land? Well, from here to there is mine, and only mine, so here I do what I want." This was a terrible insult to a *cacique*, mind you, and he did not talk to me for more than twenty years, but in fact I never ever needed him again. (E.O., spring 1995)

The traditional landed class was slow to adopt such new techniques as tapping underground water for irrigation and using intensive domestic labor. The old elite expected to keep the privileges of the system based on land capital (Sevilla Guzmán 1979, 227). While others innovated, the old elite chose instead to increase the old-fashioned rain-fed cultivation of cereals such as wheat. At the beginning of the 1960s, thirty to forty of the valley's wealthiest residents bought a tractor and other new machinery for cereal cultivation. The ten richest land-owners formed a "cereal association," popularly known as the "Ten Command-ments," to take advantage of subsidies given to cereal producers (A.V., spring 1995). They soon realized, however, that both increased wages and the new tech-niques for irrigation had permanently changed agricultural production in the val-ley. Some landowners sold part of their land to cash earners such as emigrants or truckers to begin investing in the new irrigation agriculture. Although most of their descendants today work the lands with their own hands along with every-one else, the rich initially resisted acknowledging the new value of labor and the concomitant importance of strategies of domestic self-exploitation as the basis for successful intensive horticulture: "The thing with the 'Ten Commandments' didn't work out, because once we hired 'outsiders' [that is, nonfamily members] it didn't pay. Either you gave them 'social security' or you had to pay them more, because they knew you needed the work done" (D.M., spring 1995). A common strategy to retain ownership of land has been to invest in irrigation infrastructure in order to rent it out or to put it in *medianería* with families of small peasants or day laborers without land (see note 5). As one peasant told me, important dif-ferences persisted between rich and poor in terms of land capital and relations of production. But the general perception was that the displacement of land as the basis for social prestige by work and money had somewhat leveled the social dif-ferences in the valley: "Everybody here speaks to one another as equals now" (M.A., summer 1995).

The transformation of traditional agriculture into capitalist enterprises has been very rapid in Alfaya, as it has been in other newly developed areas in south-ern Europe. To adjust to the new agrarian capitalism, peasants were forced to make heavy, and sometimes risky, capital investments, whose returns increasingly depended on off-farm inputs (seeds, fertilizers, pesticides, and irrigation technologies), outside labor, and unpredictable market variations.[16] Most family enterprises in Alfaya traditionally used links between families and neighbors to lower production costs, effectively combining formal and informal economic strategies with both legal and sometimes fraudulent uses of state public resources. Despite their new outside dependence from off-farm inputs, immigrant labor, and market variations, peasants who entered agribusiness during the early irrigation period saw themselves as having won well-deserved *autonomía* as well as a strong measure of popular sovereignty, as will be shown in the next section.

Politics of Change: The Social Vision of the Village

After less than a decade of developing and pursuing irrigation horticulture, the economic autonomy peasants had won allowed them to question authoritarian political practices in the context of the "revolutionary" times of the 1970s. During Spain's transition to democracy, a strong local political leadership emerged in Alfaya in the form of a collective of people who had been persecuted as "suspects" in the last years of the Franco dictatorship and who had become resolute organizers of endless evening political meetings and tireless activists in all areas of social mobilization. Influenced by Marxist and Catholic left-wing militants of the burgeoning clandestine resistance to the Franco regime in the mid 1970s, the leaders of this collective had been arrested repeatedly and fined for their public challenges to the local established power holders. But such repression only fueled resistance in the church following the sermons of the *cura obrero* (worker-priests),[17] in the streets as seen in demonstrations, hunger strikes, and graffiti, and in the organization of cultural events that publicized the work of forbidden "reds" (leftist) authors such as García Lorca.

When democracy finally allowed for the establishment of political organizations, these militants formed new political parties and unions. They carried their activism into the arena of production by founding a cooperative for horticulture and by fighting for higher wages for dayworkers and for unemployment benefits and social rights. They thus promoted a new social vision of the valley based on an imagined collective community, the *pueblo* (both in the sense of "village" and "people").[18] This new social vision of the *pueblo* was based on an autochthonous notion that the people deserved autonomy from local agents of the state (*caciques*, professionals, and civil servants) and from the external agents of capitalist production who were appropriating the benefits of the new agrarian production, such as *corredores* and *representantes*.[19] The slogans they used in their political struggle clearly illustrate this vision: "The valley, united, will never be defeated"; "Our protest is peaceful, our situation violent"; "Justice for the lettuces. Let us weed out intermediaries"; "We are fed up with the imposition of a price for our work" "[Intermediaries] lie to the peasants and cheat consumers,"; "Dear Three Kings: We want a nice, hard-working, and elected judge, and we ask you to bring charcoal to those who support the one we have now from Granada." In addition, the movement worked to link itself to a revival of an autochthonous traditional culture of "conscious peasants":[20] mottoes such as *pueblo, ha nacido la esperanza* (*pueblo,* hope is born), and *construyendo pueblo* (building *pueblo*) appeared in posters and pamphlets. Artistic exhibitions heralded traditional agrarian tools, autochthonous customs, occupations, and cultural associations. There was the revival of an almost forgotten local dance, the *fandango,* and public events featured invited speakers from an array of political and cultural personalities, groups, and parties.

The utopia of imagined primordial equality, social harmony, and autonomy seemed to have been achieved in the 1980s. The poverty and inability to feed one's own family, the lack of *autonomía,* the forced nomadism, and social and political submission to authorities that had been imposed by the authoritarian regime were all thought to have been overcome by the peasants' active participation in broader forces of modernization and democracy. In the newly democratic regime, peasants used the press as a tool to denounce the situation in the village, directly appealing to the central government for support in their struggles to abolish the local privileges of and abuses by, among others, teachers, doctors, judges, and pharmacists (J. Moreno 1987). Prior to this time, a notion of restricted access to the public sphere had prevailed in Alfaya. Now activists in the municipal council, initially from the Communist Party and later (after 1991) the Socialist Party, worked to open public spaces to all villagers, most of whom had been formerly marginalized from decision-making institutions as "ignorant peasants," or as emigrants.

Two main ideological currents, Marxism and social Catholicism, deeply shaped the dominant "imagined community," its main symbols, categories, and normative principles. The poem below illustrates the optimistic mood of the mid 1980s, just before Spain's entry into the European Union and the enactment of the new Alien Law were felt at the local level. The poem expresses the principles guiding popular mobilization: solidarity between those who "work the land with their hands" and those who emigrated, and the work ethic that ennobles the *pueblo* by availing it of the fertile resources of mother nature. Yet the poem is ironically also a swan song of the revolutionary need to keep up the struggle "until utopia comes."

Alfaya,
a line in the sand,
broke the gates,
will not stop
so that its people won't go.
Look at your land,

your wells,
join your efforts
with joy,
will your mountains be
warm breasts
for your desires.
Your plain
makes brothers
of all who work them
from dawn to dusk
with their hands.
Noble
lean men
who make the land
engender solidary fruits.
Alfaya,
do not stop,
keep up the fight
until utopia comes.[21]

The Price of Modernization: Loss of *Autonomía* in a Global Space

The years in which peasants became agro-entrepreneurs as well as citizens with full rights are generally remembered as golden: "Those were really exciting times ... the whole valley struggled for common goals. It was part of that era, we were more romantic and we would go for anything ... it was unbelievable! Now the village is much better off economically, but we have given up our culture; we need more solidarity, more awareness of the need to get organized. Market, money, benefits ... maybe it's just inevitable" (J.M.O., peasant and councilor, summer 1993). It is not unusual to find such a high level of reflection and such strong historical consciousness in villages. The new circumstances contrasted sharply with the traditional practices and values that dominated in the preceding era. Yet in this testimony one of the leaders of the collective identifies an unexpected paradox: even though people live much better now, "culture" has been left behind. Surprisingly, what this leader means by culture is the habitus of collectively creating options for everybody in the valley, of thinking about one's own interests as mediated by the publicly discussed interests of others. He longs for the popular participation in social affairs that fueled the initial struggle for the formal democratic system. Against this background, his assessment of the present of the village appears to be negative, if not fatalist. He feels that control of the local situation now lies elsewhere, beyond the valley, embodied in impersonal forces such as the market, money, and benefits. In an unconscious expression of

Weberian pessimism and Marxist humanism, this leader regrets the unintended effects of his own struggles: rationalization of objectives guided by a reductionist search for profit; abdication of utopian views, generating a crisis of peasants' "identity"; and retreat from passion, improvisation, and enthusiasm. The village is portrayed as unable to control its destiny. At the same time, such verdicts on the present may help frame alternative visions of the future.

Other testimonies similarly underscore the high cost of modernization in cultural terms:

> We are paying a high price to become modern. Before, one would never see a street door closed, for there was no fear, no distrust. Now, just take a walk around town and tell me: Who do you see in the streets? What houses are still open, inviting you to enter? (E.A., teacher, summer 1992)

> When I arrived here to work as a secretary it was fun. The municipal council's assemblies were crowded, everybody used to attend, not just the councilors. People debated every single issue for hours, meetings used to wind down at two or three in the morning. And mind you, everyone gathered in groups afterwards, and many went off later to informal meetings in their own houses! (M.C.A., secretary of the local council, summer 1994)

> Things have really changed here. I really think we communicated with each other better before. Now people stay at home in front of the TV; before, nothing could keep us at home. Even when you were exhausted after a hard day, even if we didn't have a penny in our pocket, we knew how to appreciate the simple pleasures of life. You see, we used to polish up our old shoes and go for a walk with our friends. We would walk out to the end of town, where we would eat berries and wild asparagus—we found them delicious! Now everyone is much more influenced by what people do on TV, and their behavior progressively mirrors what they see there. (J.A., housemaid, summer 1994)

> The good thing about the time of transition was that the whole village participated, at all levels. People attended the locally produced theater and the popular ferias, they took an interest in exhibitions about the village's past, they drew again and again on their own experiences and abilities to enrich the collective. (E.O., peasant, spring 1995)

The good aspects of the past are remembered in contrast with the perception of current individualism, passivity, and consumerism. Houses were open, assemblies were crowded, and people took advantage of a vibrant public sphere. People shared in a collective identity and the moral sense that those who could not live on their own could nonetheless build class solidarity from the shared struggle to make a living, through honest work rather than inherited patrimony, and to achieve personal *autonomía* through democratic participation. These three basic moral values—solidarity, the need to work in order to live with dignity, and *autonomía*—seem to break down in modern times. Today, it is said, each person "minds his or her own business," and people rest at ease in comfortable houses equipped with all kinds of modern appliances.

In a village such as Alfaya, the outcomes of the socioeconomic revolution are hard to swallow. For a time, peasants had forged a proud identity for themselves as conscious and combatant citizens who were able to work with their own hands to create a new destiny for themselves (see section on narratives of the past later in this chapter). Yet now, people are described as obsessed with production, money, and market, holed up in their houses with their families, indifferent to what happens beyond the limits of their own interests. Local leaders complain that no one cares about sociocultural issues unless they deal with improvements in production, taxes and bureaucratic processes, or subsidies. Political hostilities between the village's leaders and their emphasis on ideological issues are perceived to be the cause of the economic problems that have kept Alfayan cooperatives from becoming modern, productive enterprises. By the end of each summer, during which most agricultural production occurs, familial production units and cooperatives alike struggle to garner profits sufficient enough to pay off debts and to provide for their annual living expenses. The new dependence of most peasants on loans and markets has dramatically affected their place in the social structure as well as their collective identities. Astonishingly, no union currently exists that deals with workers' rights. In 1994 I was not even able to find the current *convenio del campo* (the rural collective bargaining agreement on labor relations) anywhere in the village, not even in the houses of former union activists.

A New Relationship with the State

Alfaya has been caught up in the new, capital-intensive agricultural production, dependent on off-farm inputs, outside labor, and market fluctuations. Alfaya shares with the rest of rural Andalusia in a depoliticization of peasants' struggles, a phenomenon that several Andalusian scholars have interpreted as symptomatic of a profound "identity crisis."[22] A major factor explaining this is the new relationship between peasants and the state, which was forged primarily during the 1980s. Despite the economic transformations of Alfaya, and the equalization in economic relations that they brought about, the seasonality of agricultural production and the risks associated with profit-oriented agriculture still leaves many unable to earn enough to support themselves for the entire year. Meanwhile, the state has attempted to make up the difference; thus, dependence on *caciques* has been replaced by a new dependence of peasants on the state.

The politics of rural subsidies instituted by the Socialist Party in 1984 were in fact a redefined continuation of the late Francoist rural employment plans. The two key changes in the new system were the shift from families to individuals as the basis for subsidies, and from control by local landowners and employers (based on vertical and corporatist syndicates) to administrative control that emphasizes the individual links between citizens and the state at the local, regional, and national levels. The Régimen Especial Agrario (REA) is a special labor program for rural Andalusia and Extremadura designed to address problems specific to agrarian production in less-developed areas in Spain, such as chronic unemployment (which, as of 1996, stood at 30 percent in rural Andalusia). In theory, each citizen who works in agriculture has to declare occupation and income, either as an autonomous or salaried worker. But people have resisted the coupling of their obligations as taxpayers to their rights as subsidized peasants. The new rural employment funds have been instrumental in the massive incorporation of peasants in the REA in order to obtain the employment benefits granted to rural citizens who proved having worked for at least sixty or ninety days (depending on age) as *jornaleros,* and whose patrons have paid the required social security costs. Each of the worked days are known as *peonadas.* Commonly referred to as *el paro* and *el PER,* which stand respectively for the Agrarian Unemployment Subsidy, or SDA (Subsidio de Desempleo Agrario), and the Rural Employment Plan, or PER (Plan de Empleo Rural), the new unemployment plans provide each subsidized person with a modest nine-month salary to cover structural rural temporary unemployment. Peasants have incorporated these subsidies into their economic domestic strategies: progressively more women and youth have registered in the REA as rural workers to become eligible for unemployment funds. Some formal limits, such as that requiring employers to "sign" *peonadas* for members of the family, are easy to circumvent through exchange of *peonadas* with other families so that both families' dependent members get unemployment funds. In the PER, where employment funds are used by the municipal council to hire people for public works, clientelist relationships have prevailed, according to scholars and to the only peasant union that continues working for agrarian reform (Rural Workers' Union, or SOC, Sindicato Obrero del Campo). Irregular practices do not restrict the receipt of subsidies, however, and should be understood within the context of a close coexistence of registered and underground economic exchanges.

Peasant acceptance of a subsidized status and a nonpolitical role in Spanish social structure conflicts with a central symbol in Andalusian history: the peasants' struggle against an overpowerful rural oligarchy, a struggle that peasants now appear to have abandoned. Paradoxically, Andalusian social researchers attribute peasants' depoliticization and the crisis in their identity to the access peasants have gained to social rights as rural citizens through public policies enacted to countervail the endemic regional rural unemployment. Peasants have shifted the focus of their collective mobilization away from class-based struggles (between peasants or *jornaleros* and *caciques*) centered on working conditions and landed property. Instead, they now focus on strategies to retain access to public subsidies (for unemployment or production), while profiting from the prosperous underground economy. As Moreno puts it, "[Confrontations and claim-making shifted from those] between *jornaleros* and *terratenientes* (large landowners) over employment, to those between workers and the state, to demand unemployment funds" (1991a, 28). Whereas the 1970s witnessed a strong, if ephemeral, increase in the visibility of the peasants' struggle, a central peasant concern in the 1990s was to "avoid being 'portrayed' (*retratados*)[23] by the state" (J.O., summer 1993), to become as invisible as peasants can be in relation to the state to continue combining formal and informal economic strategies with both legal and fraudulent use of public resources.

The analysis of social relations of production in Alfaya also underscores the effects of globalization in semiperipheral areas of southern Europe, here characterized by strong dependency on public subsidies and at the same time, by an underground economy linked to a nondeclared work force comprised of both local and foreign workers. One villager emphasized how this situation is perceived at the local level:

> We are peasants, even though nowadays we have to think more in terms of production and benefits and have to be like businessmen.... But we are actually scared of what is happening. Before, we had autonomy, an unfair autonomy, but autonomy at last.... Now, the state wants to control the little money we make, to take it away from us. We don't like to be "portrayed" [by the state];[24] we try to hide what is really going on because we still don't make it for the whole year.... Here, any given family has one or two members receiving unemployment benefits while working in the black market, you see? Who is going to throw the first stone? How can you pretend to control this situation when the whole valley is involved in it in one way or another? (A.N., summer 1993)

In addition to this ambiguous relationship between peasants and the state, there are obvious contradictions in the way a semiperipheral European state deals with marginal and vulnerable economic sectors and regions such as rural Andalusia. On the one hand, public intervention is necessary to deal with such structural distortions as the high unemployment rate and to develop foreign policy initiatives that would open markets for Spanish agrarian production in the European Union. On the other hand, European Union requirements for a common currency impose policies of austerity in public expenditures. Spain has tolerated the underground economy and illegal labor conditions, especially at harvest time, but increasingly the state is held accountable for guaranteeing the socioeconomic rights of Spaniards and of legal foreign workers, and for preventing exploitation in the workplace.[25]

In this politically delicate situation where people are co-opted by the state in exchange for the state's toleration of supposedly invisible socioeconomic exchanges that foster the reproduction of clientelist relations,[26] the state has skillfully chosen to intervene on the basis of a "need to control illegal African immigration," a theme that recurs often in this study. Suffice it to say that the mechanisms employed by the state against immigrants are greatly resented at the local level (see, in particular, the section "Politics of Invisibility: A Racial Geography of Labor Relations" in chapter 5), because they endanger, albeit indirectly, the underground hiring practices that peasants find necessary for economic survival. But even though locals resent intervention by the state at the local level (because it tends to strip them of their *autonomía*), they also fall prey to the way this indirect intervention conjures up a landscape in which Africans are characterized as a danger to the interests of European citizens. These processes foster an emergent identity for Andalusians that feeds upon the new legal ideology characteristic of bourgeois liberalism in which "formal equality and freedom mask and serve to legitimate exploitative economic relations. Each legal subject stands as an individual one-to-one relation with the state without the potentially disruptive mediation of class" (Fitzpatrick 1980, 33).

Alfaya in the Narratives of the Past: Inclusive versus Exclusive Criteria of Belonging

In this section I will analyze several narratives dealing with the elucidation of who are thought to be the primordial occupants of the valley and where the sociocultural boundaries and the normative principles guiding the social vision of the imagined community are situated. I will show how the dominant narrative embodies a symbolic imagery rooted in a peasant work ethic and class struggle while, at the same time, incorporating nationalist imagery based on a deeply embedded historical process of nation-building, which, in Spain, was characterized by an externalization of Islam and an oppositional dynamic between "Moors" and Spanish Catholicism.

The exploration of narratives of origin is useful for problematizing studies that privilege dominant categories of belonging, such as those supported and promoted by a government, be it national or regional. The labels "peasants," "citizens," and "foreigners" are only some of the identity categories people use to interact with others and resist processes of marginalization. Their narratives reveal much about how villagers see themselves and others. By looking at the way they refer to their imagined community, we can, as Rosaldo (1989, 217) has put it, discern the "borrowing and lending across porous national and cultural boundaries that are saturated with inequality, power, and domination," which is characteristic of the interdependent late twentieth century. The intention is to go beyond the "boundaries of officially recognized cultural units, but also less formal interactions, such as those of gender, age, status, and distinctive life experiences," as well as class, "race," and ethnicity in order to explore the borderlands (Rosaldo 1989, 29). In the individual narratives, we can explore the representational activities of a person, understood not as " the ego of a type of singular *cogito,* but as the individual trace of a whole collective history" (Bourdieu 1987, 129). We can locate the dispersed spatial nodes and past events that make up collective identities, and at the same time, trace the different uses and interpretation of hegemonic "common sense." Last but not least, by incorporating narratives into the analysis, I want to engage the anthropological approach that attends to "other people's narrative analysis … to take account of subordinate, nonhegemonic, forms of knowledge" (Rosaldo 1989, 147f.).

When I arrived in Granada in 1992, my research focused on racism and antiracist practices in the context of the rebordering of the Mediterranean. Soon after, I made contact with the main NGO in Granada working with immigrants and was invited to visit Alfaya to see what was happening there with immigrants working in the agricultural harvest. Before we went, a person in the NGO's network who lived in the village of Alfaya agreed to answer questions about the situation there. A civil servant in a rural adult education program, he recounted his own trajectory from the theological seminary, to the Legión,[27] into left-wing parties, and on to activism in new social movements and nongovernmental associations. At the time of the interview, he was involved in the struggle to provide lodging for some one hundred homeless African immigrants. Immediately after we met, he began to tell us a story as if we were among the students he normally taught. It was a well-informed narrative that tells us much more about the present than the past of the village, for, as Wallerstein puts it, "The past can only be told as it truly is, not was. For recounting the past is a social act of the present done by men [*sic*] of the present and affecting the social system of the present" (1974, 9).

Alfaya is a name that in Arab means "land of shepherds." Arabs started using this valley as a refuge for their cattle in the hot days of burnt pasture in the surrounding areas. As for many places here in Andalusia, the names are Arab, you see, because they discovered the multiple uses of land and lived from their work. This is the first period of the valley. The second starts when Alfaya is colonized by *malagueños,*[28] people from the surrounding villages who couldn't make a living across the mountains and who came here to farm the up-to-then virgin land. There were many struggles with the people paid by the *caciques* from the head of the county [*cabeza de comarca*], because they wanted to maintain their rights over the land for their cattle. Peasants won, and since then, Alfaya has been an agricultural valley. Yet the third stage comes with the discovery of the underground treasure that makes this valley what it is today: water. Irrigation, small properties, and huge benefits mark this last stage, the one we are living now.[29] (E.A., summer 1992)

In this narrative Arabs are portrayed as the primordial inhabitants of the valley; they are the ones who named the valley, an action that retains all of its symbolic weight in this account. The leader of the NGO invited us to embrace his perspective, an alleged revision of traditional historiography and popular history under a nonracist lens in that it reverses the silencing of the Arab and Jewish past in Spain and Andalusia. Although in recent years the state and civil society have made a manifest effort to render this past visible, much has yet to be done. In this case, emphasis on the Arab presence runs counter to the dominant narratives in the valley that, in contrast, emphasize the second stage as the foundation moment of the "mythico-history," as I show below (Malkki 1995). The author of this narrative has rhetorical reasons for naming Arabs as the valley's original inhabitants: as pioneers of the land, it is ironic that today Arabs are deprived of the most elemental right—the right to work to make an honest living. Yet, his use of an ethnic category (Arab) to refer to this supposedly aboriginal population, which was instead historically characterized in religious and multiethnic terms (Andalusian Muslims), implicitly incorporates the long-held biologist imagining of the Spanish "race," an essentialist trait opposed to that of "Arabs."[30] Thus, Arabs, or "Moors" in the most colloquial use, are incorporated into the valley's narratives, yet at the same time, they are marked as ethnically different from villagers. This perspective is not in itself wrong or right; it does not revolve around verifiable "facts," but does reveal symbols that are crucial in the exploration of villagers' cultural repertoires.

The narrative most Alfayans refer to when asked about the origin of the valley emphasizes the cultural and territorial attachment that primordial inhabitants had to the land—in contrast to the minority narratives of origin discussed above, which highlight Arabs' original presence in the valley. In the more common narrative, emphasis falls on the actual process of farming the land and constructing the settlement that was to become Alfaya. What the NGO leader described as a second stage of the valley's historical process is treated in the more common narrative as the first stage. Earlier influences in the valley are reduced to mere anecdotes about passersby *(gente de paso),* whose fleeting presence contrasts with the "permanence" of sedentary farmers. I have chosen to reconstruct the narrative of an old peasant who is well known as an important figure in the development of the valley, both as one of the visionaries to gamble on new irrigation methods and intensive labor and as a protagonist in the Communist politics that dominated the village beginning in the late 1980s. This man has astonishing knowledge of the people and recent history of the valley. In addition to the wealth of information provided by our first informant, the old peasant's accounts were full of localisms, poetry, and moral reflections about history, love, and power.[31] As a rhetorical tool, he shortens historical time to exclude people that "pass" through the valley but did not "actually live" there:

> We come from people from … [the] villages located at this side of the mountains, which belongs administratively to Málaga, not Granada. And however close we got with people of the county, we are very different: we are innovative, clever, because

from the beginning we have struggled with the land, the climate, and the ruinous political authorities that have governed this area. In the beginning we all struggled against the landowners, who misused this fertile land, paying indigent salaries to the shepherds they hired to look after their cattle. We come from poor peasant families without lands, who stepped forward to seize what was theirs in honest law [*en buena ley*], because it is not right to eat and not to work. We won because we fought with arms to expel the landowners from the valley, because we worked the land with our hands to make the most of it, and because, at the same time, we built our *chozas* [thatched cottages or huts][32] here, for that is the original name of the village, *Las chozas*. In 1815, we were finally recognized as an autonomous parish and council. Since then, there has been much suffering, because life for peasants is not easy, especially with little or no land in the *secano* [area of dry farming]. Not everyone had even bread for their families. There were difficult times of famine, except for the *caciques* of course, who had a good life, as they do everywhere else. They have always held the reins of power because the system benefited them: more land, more power— economic, political, cultural, and all. We paid them our debts, we worked for them, we obeyed them. But not anymore. (E.O., spring 1995)[33]

In this narrative, the foundational moment is symbolized by struggle for the property of the land and by the construction of the *chozas*, the characteristic dwellings of poor peasants. The emphasis on the rights of peasants over the land should be read as part of peasants' notions of utopia as being able to "live on their own." Work in the land is set as the main criterion establishing rights over it, an open category of belonging that excluded and was set in contrast to landed classes who did not work the land on their own, the classic *señorito* or *cacique*. As Moreno explains, the land acquires a symbolic content: "Transforming the property of the land means, in the Andalusian collective imaginary, to radically transform society; it means, whether it is true or not, to change the world" (1991a, 25).

There is thus a revolutionary component in the narrative of this peasant, a moral social vision entailing a strong element of class solidarity and a work ethic linked both to modern notions of people's sovereignty and to what historians and anthropologists have described as indigenous peasant ideologies.[34] As explored in detail later, the work ethic and class solidarity characteristics of peasants' autochthonous ideology figure prominently in today's debates about the "place" of African immigrants in the valley's social structure; it plays a part in an inclusive dynamic that joins the contemporary internationalization of human and workers' rights discourses that challenge the right claimed by the nation-state to exclude non-nationals from equality under the law.

This open notion of belonging is reinforced by former Andalusian emigrants' experiences as "foreigners" or "immigrant" workers deprived of the same rights accorded to natives, be these Catalans or Germans, among others. The collective imagery that links contemporary experience back to Andalusians' earlier experience of marginality and exclusion has to be incorporated into the contemporary picture. During the epoch of rural modernization and exodus, the local community stretched across national boundaries to include those members of the community abroad. In a related way, Andalusians' experience of earlier migration helps delegitimate the way migratory laws exclude emigrants from rights acquired as workers and residents: "Because we know about migration, we know the difference between legal and 'illegal' [migrants] is not a person's difference. There is nothing legal or illegal in working to feed your family. Everybody has the right to eat. We did anything we could to achieve this in the north and it is only normal that these people [African immigrants] should do the same here" (A.P., spring 1995).

This narrative exemplifies how both inclusion and exclusion simultaneously shape the boundaries of the community, in a way similar to how narratives construct the imagined community of the nation and of "race."[35] Here we find the inclusionary openness of entitlement to rights based on working the land with one's own hands, but we find it combined with a sedentary, territorialized, ethnically pure, and, hence, exclusionary vision of the foundation of the valley. The exclusion of Arab shepherds and other nomadic peoples from the historical picture is in itself meaningful. This narrative depicts an imaginary collective strongly attached to a bounded territory, thus setting apart as "marginal" the styles of life of deterritorialized groups such as migrant workers. Even Andalusian emigrants' narratives illustrate this feeling of exclusion from a strongly territorialized local culture: "We [emigrants] were seen as different from the rest of the people who stayed in the valley. We lived outside many years working hard to make a living, but when you arrive here there is no recognition of this work." As another emigrant put it, "I always felt marginalized in the village. Because we were always traveling, like other emigrant families, I couldn't attend school with the rest of the children of the village. I was always on the move" (M.C., summer 1994; A.R., spring 1995).

At the same time, pioneers are characterized in cultural terms as having passed on to today's inhabitants of the valley a certain characteristic style of life and an idiosyncratic personality. The dominant ideology links bounded territory, an inherited style of life, and rights of sovereignty and autonomy with one another. Together they construct an exclusionary criterion of belonging that ends up privileging the property of the land and/or inherited cultural membership. The nationalist overtones of this thinking mark a clear boundary distinguishing people born in the valley, and thus sharing a peasant Andalusian cultural logic, from the outsiders, or those who are excluded from the imagined community. The testimony of a recent emigrant to Germany illustrates how such nationalist ideology gets reproduced for Alfayans, even in a context of transnationalization:

I feel pity toward these blind "mahometans" [*sic*], leaving scraps of life around.... Migration is not a good deal, and if I could come back, I would rather stay here.... When I arrived in Germany to join my husband, illegal and illiterate, I almost went insane, as many did in migration, like my husband who is mentally ill now.... When you live abroad it is as if your homeland were bigger.... When we lived there [in Germany] they looked at us as foreigners, one of the many of the bottom, like the last monkey. They called us *ausländer* [foreigner], and to command us to leave, they told us *raus* [get out], and each day more and more, and that problem will remain because "foreigner" means work and pain. A migrant wants to find a job and save money to return. We were not interested in learning about other cultures or meeting other peoples, but rather to fulfill some needs we had. Once we return our rights should be acknowledged, because I did not have rights to work there, but now I am entitled to receive benefits here as any villager. (M.C., summer 1994)

In addition to the autochthonous notion of primordial equality between all people, established in terms of class struggle, Andalusian emigrants have also embraced the European notions of justice and equality of rights that they learned through their experiences abroad. However, this adoption of the dominant criteria of entitlements and rights is two-edged: on the one hand, emigrants learn to appreciate the rights entitled to them as workers and human beings, but on the other hand, they come to legitimize the privileges of nationals in relation to foreigners through their exclusion from full rights in the places to which they emigrated. Legal boundaries between nationals and foreigners are thus ultimately implemented in the valley as a consequence of the modernization process, despite the initial resistance to criminalization of incoming African immigrants. Cultural boundaries of the thus-imagined community, whether set up around nationalist, ethnic, religious, or racial differences, further strengthen the idea of rights as privileges of nationals from modern countries such as Spain today.

The final important element suggested in M.C.'s narrative is a notion of progress, represented through the heroic figures of peasants who struggled through centuries to obtain today's autonomy. It is precisely this evolutionary logic that immigrants' narratives question by substituting a somewhat transcendental law governing historical development, the *Mizan*. By contrast, the peasants' cultural logic claims responsibility for progress as a consequence of collective organizing around a social vision of the valley based on democratic and egalitarian policies. Among many of the villagers, who matured in a climate of secular politics, purportedly transcendental or religious laws are interpreted negatively within the legacy of the extreme anticlericalism characteristic of the locally dominant cultural Left. Even Catholics who participate in the revolutionary perspective of the church as the "parish of the poor" share the post-Enlightenment, secular notion of the public sphere and of history. They thus problematize the traditionally dominant national Catholicism, criticizing its role in having once maintained the status quo of powerful social corporations.

Along with the dominant ethnocentric notion of progress, Westerners see the maintenance of religious social principles as a hindrance to modernization, especially when the religion involved is Islam (Said 1978, 1981). Moreover, in the particular case of Andalusia and Spain, the historically dominant notion of Spanish and Andalusian identities systematically built upon religious categories that legitimated the exclusionary biological principle of "purity of blood" and of the civilizing project of Spanish colonization. In an indirect way, these Iberian narratives stir up old fears of invasion and a medieval imagery, which, as I will show later, feed the cultural resources that are used to deny current temporary workers from Africa the right to live and work in the valley. The overwhelming identification of Alfayan villagers with the European model of development thus strongly incorporates both old and new hegemonic meanings of "Moors" and Islam as a threat to what they regard as Christian, democratic, European civilization.

This, then, is the context in which peasants tap both historic cultural resources and modernity to draw the boundary between those who have a so-called European destiny and those who challenge it from an Islamic political-religious perspective. The transformation of the hierarchical and unequal rural Andalusian social structure is imagined accordingly in terms of the central recognition of Andalusians as holding the individual rights of European citizens—which are equal for landowners, day laborers, leftists and rightists, men and women, Gypsies and *Payos* (non-Gypsies)—in contrast to non-European Africans.

Summary and Preliminary Conclusions

An underground economy and a high level of fraud in the acceptance of unemployment subsidies are key features in the repositioning of peasants as entrepreneurs and citizens with social benefits, as well as in the shift from class to ethnicity and legal status as the "dominant medium through which the social order is interpreted and navigated" (Comaroff 1987, 311). This is not to suggest that class is an inadequate analytic category, but, as Kearney has argued in his book *Reconceptualizing the Peasantry*, class differentiation and segmentation within the broader objective position of peasant has deepened, "eroding any possible single, unitary subject position as a basis of a subjective class identity" (1996, 145).

Andalusia has recently been transformed into a borderland space, by forces well beyond the control of the "autonomous" peasants. Andalusian peasants have repositioned themselves in the new structures of power as the guardians and enforcers of European privileges against new African *jornaleros*. In other words, the class position of the nomadic *jornalero* still exists. Yet within this class position, one group—commonly referred to as the "Moors," the "illegals," the "immigrants," and, in political and legal terms, "foreign workers"—is being deprived of rights and persecuted in the name of law enforcement. While another group—Andalusian *jornaleros*—continue occupying a very similar class position to that of Africans, they are now entitled to a series of rights and liberties not just as workers, but as citizens and nationals.

Today, Andalusian peasants have a strong consciousness of themselves as vulnerable "people with rights." They perceive their rights as a consequence of their own actions in the political arena and in working the land. Many witnessed through their experiences as emigrants a model of citizenship that excluded them on legal grounds as foreigners, but they also saw a notion of equality before the law that was respected. Learning to be a citizen involves a transformation of customary principles ingrained in the underprivileged people of rural Andalusia. Economic autonomy in a modern democratic society requires from citizens their contribution as taxpayers to the common good; this is perceived as a loss of political autonomy, since it involves central management of citizens' resources. The fight for dignity was also won. As my neighbor in Alfaya said, "we have leveled off": status and class differences have diminished as a result of economic autonomy, democratic decision making, and state-provided services and subsidies.

As political actors, peasants recognize interlocutors beyond those of agrarian society, as within the political institutions of the European Union in Brussels and the state and regional administrations, who can help advocate for their rights. Although peasants acknowledge that the new systems of agricultural production make them dependent on finance capital, transnational agribusiness, and global markets, they value highly their new rights as "citizens," such as social benefits, the freedom to advocate for their own political rights through parties and associations, open tolerance of the underground economy and of unemployment fraud, freedom of movement, and the disappearance of the politics of fear that characterized the Francoist regime.

In this context, the reproduction of clientelist relationships among people is no longer based on submission. Instead, most access to public resources is locally interpreted as negotiated through the personal exchange of favors and privileges (state, political parties, and labor clientelism according to Cazorla's 1994 conceptualization). It is here that a key but underexplored feature of clientelism should be considered: prejudice toward others. When favors are negotiated in terms of the privileges of citizens to the detriment of noncitizen "others," clientelism serves to reinforce a new nationalist dialectic where membership and entitlement to rights may end up being defined in terms of legal status (as a possession) and cultural identity (as a primordial attachment). My situated knowledge of Andalusian rural society is one where its redefined position as the southern sociocultural European frontier is most salient: Spain has reconfigured the "national" Spanish state by replacing a traditionally homogeneous notion of Spanish national identity with the multicultural model of "Autonomous Communities" and the supranational model of European citizenship. For their part, peasants have been co-opted into this exclusionary imagery, as they themselves have become efficient agents and enforcers of the new north-south oppositional dynamic characteristic of the post–Cold War late capitalist world order.

Notes

1. It was not until the 1970s that scholars shifted emphasis from internal integration, patronage, and the cultural system of honor and shame (e.g., Pitt-Rivers 1954) to the politically oriented class struggle muted by the politics of fear used by the repressive dictatorship (Collier 1987; Fraser 1973; Gilmore 1980; Lisón Tolosana 1966; Martínez Alier 1971; Mintz 1982).

2. See Brenan 1980; Collier 1987; Díaz del Moral 1984; Fraser 1979; Gilmore 1980; Malefakis 1970; Martínez Alier 1971; Mintz 1982; Sevilla Guzmán 1979. See Ferrer 1982 for a historical and geographical perspective centered on Alhama.

3. Spanish textbooks stressed the national unity of Spain in terms of a common race, customs and religion, and the historical imperial spirit that distinguished Spain from foreign ideologies, that is, those of democratic capitalist countries (*Nueva Enciclopedia Escolar* 1954, [New Student Encyclopedia]). See the works of Carandell (1970) and Sopeña Monsalve (1994) for a humorous exploration of these textbooks and other popular culture materials of the Franco era.

4. The term *cacique* originally meant "the principal person in a village," but in the Nineteenth century it acquired negative connotations referring to anybody who is considered to hold power in an illegitimate, arbitrary, and corrupt way. Uses of the term are related to the ascendance of a local bourgeoisie in the creation of a capitalist agrarian society (Contreras 1991, 503; Joaquín Costa 1978).

5. *Arrendatarios* are land renters, and *aparceros* and *medianeros* are sharecroppers to whom the landowner supplies land, seed, capital investment, and other kinds of clientelistic favors, while the worker contributes the animal team and labor. Finally, *comuneros* are more strongly linked to a particular land plot, paying a minimum rent and acquiring some rights over the land through the years, and even across generations linking owner and worker families.

6. In the village, poor people used to live in *chozas*, described as thatched cottages or huts by Mintz (1982) in his wonderful piece of ethnohistorical research. *Choceños* are those people who lived in the *chozas*. Similarly, *cortijeros* are the people who live in the *cortijos*, which, in contrast to the typical Andalusian elite rural houses, in this part of Andalusia refer to small houses scattered in the valley (see also the section "Landscapes of Inequality" on the spatial distribution of the valley in chapter 3).

7. Maintenance of a combination of large and small landowners proved to be essential for keeping a large part of Alfaya's population linked to the land in spite of poverty and exploitation, as described for agrarian systems elsewhere in Andalusia and Spain (Contreras 1991; Martínez Veiga 1991; Sevilla Guzmán 1979).

8. Clientelism and patronage have received important attention from scholars working in the Mediterranean area; see Cazorla 1994; Contreras 1991; Corbin 1979; Costa, 1982; Frigolé 1981, 1991; Gilmore 1980; Gellner and Waterbury 1977; Littlewood 1979; Waterbury 1977.

9. In this work I argue that an assimilationist attitude prevails in Granada, but this should be read as grounded in historical experiences and relevant cultural imageries. This is also shown in the section "Naturalizing Difference" in chapter 3, where local and supranational variables are taken into account to investigate the senses that assimilation and other concepts acquire "in the hands" of social subjects.

10. See Candel 1967; Garamendía 1981; Gregory 1978; Solé 1982.

11. The depictions of Andalusians and other "backward" peoples in postwar ethnography and migration studies worked from a clearly ethnocentric perspective, imposing a derogatory image which nevertheless had a strong impact on the consciousness of the populations thus subjugated; see I. Moreno Navarro(1986) for an anthropological critique of such depictions of Andalusia in European and North American ethnographies.

12. Local expressions for these requirements are *comportarse como una persona, ser trabajador, noble, cumplidor, agradecido, no meterse con nadie, ser justo.* All these, with the local idiomatic variations one may find, can be found in classic ethnographies of the Iberian peninsula, and particularly Andalusia. Regarding the notion of "fairness," research of peasants' customary notions of "the dignity of a person" and consciously held "egalitarianism," has pointed out the irrelevance of "law" in itself as a guarantor of "rights," and so forth (Lisón Tolosana 1966, 207 passim; Arguedas 1968; Martínez Alier 1971; Fraser 1973).

13. "Normal" here does not mean that people were treated as equals; the statement should be seen as referring to the successful completion of a process of normalization in which Spanish migrants moved out of the system of hierarchical statuses of Spanish society of the 1960s.

14. See Harding (1984) for a similar perspective on the importance of local agency in the transformation of rural landscape and her wonderful analysis of the way the "iron fist" and the "invisible hand" of capitalism interacted to construct this perception.

15. For analyses of the effects of rural emigration and programs of modernization, among others see, Aceves 1971; Aceves and Douglass 1976; Berger and Mohr 1975; Brandes 1975; Buecher 1991; Cazorla Pérez 1965, 1989; Douglass 1975; Giner and Salcedo 1978; Greenwood 1976, 1977; Gregory 1978; Iszaevich 1991; Martin Díaz 1991; Martínez Veiga 1991; Rhoades 1978; and Solé 1982.

16. See Gavira 1991; Moreno Navarro 1991a, 1991b; Palenzuela 1991, 1992; Sevilla Guzmán and González de Molina 1992.

17. Inspired by liberation theology's critical view of orthodox clergy, worker-priests actively contributed to resistance to Franco's regime in the 1960s and 1970s. Similarly to what happened in Latin America, activism developed under the umbrella of the parishes was at least initially tolerated in view of the traditional moral authority conferred to priests in Francoist national-Catholicism.

18. See Velasco 1991 and Contreras 1991 for a good analysis and review of theoretical perspectives on the polysemic notion of *pueblo.*

19. *Corredores* (literally runners) are those who link individual producers with customers, obtaining a good commission for each business deal. In the eyes of peasants, this way of earning money was considered a "immoral," as they have told me, because no (physical) "work" was involved, no risk was assumed, and because *corredores* enrich themselves at the expense of both producers and consumers. *Representantes* (agents) of a particular firm are similarly considered immoral.

20. In the years being discussed, the traditional category of "men with ideas" or "conscious men" was broadly used. See, among others, Collier, 1987; Contreras 1991; García Muñoz 1995; Martínez Alier 1971; Mintz 1982; Moreno Navarro 1991b; Sevilla Guzmán 1979.

21. Poem written by Esteban Tabares (quoted in J. Moreno 1987): "Alfaya,/punto y raya,/rompió la valla/no se calla/para que su gente/no se vaya./Mira tu tierra/tus pozos/aúna los esfuerzos/ con gozo/que tus montañas/sean cálido seno/a tus anhelos./Tu llano/hace hermanos/a cuantos

lo trabajan/de sol a sol/con sus manos./Con hombres nobles/enjutos/que hacen parir/a la tierra/solidarios frutos./Alfaya/no te detengas/sostén la batalla/hasta que la utopía/venga." Unless otherwise noted, all translations are my own.

22. The most interesting research groups on this issue can be found in Seville, around the figure of Moreno; in Córdoba, around Sevilla Guzmán; and in Granada around Cazorla, Alcantud, and Briones.

23. "Being portrayed by the state" is a particular local idiom that refers to the state's acquisition of accurate records of a person's real economic and labor situation. More generally, it refers to peasants' desires to not be controlled by the state.

24. See note 23.

25. *Boletín Oficial del Estado (BOE),* April 9, 1990. This is a claim advanced by several social sectors at the same time, political parties, work unions, and the new NGOs dedicated to immigrants' issues. Modernization is assumed to go hand in hand with the disappearance of nonregistered, and usually exploitative, social relations of production. However, social scientists have long acknowledged the structural role of the informal sector in the development of capitalism both in peripheral countries (see the work of Benería, Carbonetto, Castells, Hardy, Jelin, Lomnitz, Matos Mar, Prebisch, Portes, Quijano de Soto, Touraine) and in core countries (Fernández-Kelly 1983; Portes, Castells and Benton, 1989; Sassen-Koob 1988).

26. Cazorla Pérez (1994) has used national and regional (Andalusian) examples to demonstrate the persistence of clientelist relationships in the structuring of social relations. He particularly emphasizes the clientelism in political parties, which ultimately control public resources of the welfare state, as fostering labor clientelism characteristic of the PER and unemployment subsidies in rural Andalusia.

27. The Legión was a pseudo-paramilitary force in Franco times linked to the Moroccan protectorate and to hypernationalist symbols, such as the flag, the destiny of the Spanish nation, and the national-Catholic regime. The Legión has recently been given a new role as part of the Peace Corps of NATO or the UN.

28. Situated within the southwest border of the province of Granada with Málaga, Alfaya has always maintained a stronger connection with the neighboring villages of the province of Málaga.

29. Caro Baroja provides historical confirmation of this: the name of the valley is found in the "General Description of Africa" by the Granadan author Luis Mármol de Carvajal in 1573. Caro Baroja links the Muslim shepherds to the *moriscos hortelanos* of the Alpujarra (a Muslim horticultural population that stayed in Granada after the conquest by the Catholic kings and that revolted against the kings' abrogation of the Capitulations of Santa Fe, which initially allowed non-Catholic groups to maintain their religion and social habits) (Caro Baroja [1957] 1977, chap. 3).

30. The polemic between Américo Castro and Sánchez Albornoz is basic for a good understanding of Spanish historiography. Sánchez Albornoz defended the centrality of Castilian heritage and Catholicism for Spanish history against challenges posed by Américo Castro emphasizing the foundational influence of *convivencia* (coexistence) of the peninsula's "three castes" —Jewish, Muslim, and Christian (see Acosta-Sánchez 1979; Barkai 1984; Caro Baroja 1977; Américo Castro 1973, 1983; De Bunes Ibarra 1989; Guichard 1976; Harvey 1990; Sánchez Albornoz 1960, 1983).

31. Unfortunately for me and for my readers, this old peasant never consented to taping our conversations; so, as many anthropologists do, I have reconstructed a narrative from the notes that I made after each interview with him.

32. See Mintz (1982) for a description of a similar domestic construction that also symbolizes peasants' attachment to the land, use of local resources, and poverty.

33. This narrative is very similar to one discussed by J. Moreno (1987), and it is not clear who has influenced whom. My informant played a major role in guiding the author to write his book.

The Communist local council with which he was closely associated was very active in fostering a particular social vision of the village that included a collective "imagining of the past" and of "imagining traditions." With this objective, the council organized exhibitions of local traditional labor and domestic instruments, promoted a group that revived local musical folklore, and also enlisted Moreno, a friend of the village, ex-priest and sociologist, to write a book about the village (J. Moreno 1987).

34. See Hobsbawm 1959, 1990, 18ff.; Collier 1987; Martínez Alier 1971; Mintz 1982; Sevilla Guzmán 1979.

35. See Balibar 1991; Gilroy 1987; Miles 1993.000

2. Contested Boundaries

*O*ne summer day in 1994 I was chatting with some African friends in a central spot in Alfaya, close to the bus stop and the bar Ramiro, where most hiring goes on. A couple of years before, we would have gone to the bar for coffee and to pass time while waiting for some employer in need of a couple of hands to help him with his work. But the bar, owned and managed by a former emigrant to Germany, was a place where only local men now felt at home: after a couple of incidents with Arab immigrants he decided to refuse to serve them whatsoever. Even though the owner has never refused to serve a black African, they all know they are not welcome to pass their free time there. For my part, as a woman and an anthropologist, I preferred to remain outside with the Africans.

Most of the Africans were irregular immigrants in danger of detention if caught by the Civil Guard, but at this time of the afternoon nobody except us or some bored old men would think of abandoning the cool of Andalusian houses. We were talking, as usual, about the production of tomatoes and lettuces, about new Africans coming from the Gibraltar Straits or from elsewhere in Spain, about the Civil Guard and their most recent arrests, about the so-called papers, about a casual quarrel, the near implementation of a program for immigrants in the village, or village politics, always fertile in rumors and eternal revenges. A car from Barcelona passed by, and we commented on how many villagers come back for vacations. There were cars in Alfaya from all corners of Europe and northern Spain. Assane told me that he knew many of their owners and gave me details about particular families in the village whose relatives live abroad. "They now come in very good cars, you see, they look as if they are rich now. It's the same back in Senegal, where emigrants feel superior and have to show it with good clothes, cars, and gold jewels. This is the way they forget how they suffered abroad, with money, you see? And when they are here, these emigrants don't want to look at us because it brings memories of their own pain and humiliation. They want to forget everything, so that only gold sparkles."

Notes for this chapter begin on page 71.

Assane actually introduced me to various people from the village, where many people knew him well. He had been one of the pioneer African migrants to Alfaya and cherished villagers for having supported his cause when the first arrest of a so-called illegal was made in the area. At this point in his life, he said "I am half from this village and half from my father's village." Yet even as he was telling me this, Alfaya was no longer the little village where people invited him to their homes to eat when they found he didn't have lunch. "Alfaya is now like the big places. People don't look at you, people only mind their own business. Alfaya is already like New York City, you see? Like Paris, like London. It is not Alfaya anymore. It is Alfaya City. And here, as in New York, I can be persecuted just because of my skin. There I would be a Harlem Negro; here I am a black Muslim from Senegal."

* * *

In this chapter, I describe in broad outline the relatively recent arrival of African immigrants to Alfaya, Andalusia, and in Spain in general, and some salient aspects of their structural position. Their arrival was faced with a very active construction in hegemonic discourses of a European imagery symbolically opposed to the purportedly threatening and primitive others coming from the Third World. Both the tone and the terminology resuscitated old fears of African and Islamic invasion, which have historically been used in the forging of a Spanish Catholic nation-state. The enactment of the Alien Law, or LOE 7/1985,[1] is the single most important factor in drawing the political and legal boundary between Africans as foreigners and Andalusians as European citizens. But at the time, the new borders of Europe were strongly contested. As I will show here, these borders were challenged not just by Africans who defied the law by "illegally"[2] crossing the Mediterranean—Africans who actively appropriated Andalusia's Arab past in claiming a right to belong—but also by Spaniards who did not yet give much credibility to the legitimacy of the law in a country where the law has for decades served the powerful. The ethnographically rich testimony of Assane, the first Senegalese immigrant in Alfaya, which concludes this chapter, serves to illustrate spaces of resistance to the Alien Law and to the imaginary of belonging that sets communities apart by legal and ethnic criteria. The case of Assane allows me to introduce a number of topics that will be analyzed in detail later in the book, showing how immigrants were received in the context of the inclusive criteria of belonging discussed in the previous chapter. Thus, the processes that I describe in the rest of the book can be seen as displaying the creation of ethnic boundaries—inner borders fracturing the social structure of Alfaya—through the combined action of many factors, but especially through the state administrations and legal framework.

Crossing Boundaries

Since the late 1980s, an increasing number of Africans are risking their lives in their efforts to cross the Straits of Gibraltar in small boats (one-engine barges, or *pateras*) that transport them for a high price from Morocco to Andalusia. Many suffocate in the overcrowded boats or drown when forced to jump too far from the coast. Those who reach shore risk being returned back home if caught by the Civil Guard. The Andalusian coasts and border posts are heavily guarded by police to prevent Africans from crossing the Gibraltar Straits illegally. As Andalusians did in the 1960s, Moroccans and Senegalese are today challenging the European frontiers, increasingly settling in such places as the city of Granada and its countryside.

Immigration to Spain is related to economic changes, with Spain's political and economic incorporation into the European Community as one major driving force. With an expanding economy in a competitive European environment, Spanish employers needed adaptable, industrious, cheap, and flexible workers who could be laid off when their work was not needed. Tolerance of underground economic practices made it possible for immigrants to seek jobs in Spain and for employers to hire workers without paying social security and other taxes, and without heeding workers' rights. Africa's geographical proximity made Spain an obvious entry point; over the years it became a destination for many immigrants, who, after careful planning and investment with their families, organized their quest for work around well-established migratory networks and webs of support (see chapter 6).[3]

African migration has transformed Andalusia again into a "border area,"[4] which produces effects in predominantly Muslim migrants from Maghreb and Central Africa similar to those produced in the Mixtec migrants of the U.S.-Mexico frontier studied by Kearney: "It is by passage into but never completely through this transnational zone that the alien is marked as the ambiguous, stigmatized, vulnerable person that he or she is. This border area is a liminal region into which initiates pass via what Van Gennep might punningly have called '*raites* (rites) of passage,' but from which they never emerge" (1991, 53). Entering this border area transforms the emigrant into an immigrant in the eyes of people inhabiting the Spanish pole of the transnational social space that networks of migrants have built and maintained over time. As most migrants are forced to enter Andalusia clandestinely, they become illegals, subject to deportation by the Civil Guard or police at any time. Yet even if deported, they will return. I know people who have been stopped and deported up to three times, people whose determination and persistence nonetheless thwarted Spanish efforts to curtail, or even control effectively, clandestine immigration.

Andalusia's role as a border area pervades its history—sometimes as a schism, sometimes as a bridge between both shores of the Mediterranean. Phoenicians, Greeks, and Romans all colonized Andalusia's coast. Most important, for almost eight centuries (from the eighth century to the fifteenth century) Andalusia had a prime importance in the Muslim world. Andalusia's Arab past, marked by pacific coexistence among three religions, is still profoundly present in the landscape today, and is resolutely appropriated by immigrants (see the section "Andalusia's Muslim Imagery" in this chapter), who are predominantly Muslim and devout. According to Bernabé López García, the distinguished scholar of contemporary Morocco and Moroccan emigration to Spain, the distribution of Maghrebians in Spain today maps almost perfectly onto that of Moriscos in seventeenth-century Andalusia (1993, 17). Whether or not drawing such correspondence between two disparate historical times is valid, it illuminates historical continuities that nourish the social imagery that feeds interethnic relations. The historical images of "Moors" and Africans overlap with images of people marked by class rather than ethnic content: the poor Andalusian *jornaleros* analyzed in the previous chapter.

When a small number of African immigrants arrived in Alfaya in the late 1980s they produced a disproportionate amount of public concern and attention in the village. The reason for this, as I will show, is that African immigrants have been the negative counterfoil against which Andalusian peasants are redefining their location in the Spanish social structure, their notion of belonging to a community, and their ideological principles about people's rights and status along new criteria of European citizenship and ethnicity or culture. And yet, when the first immigrants arrived, Andalusians did not perceive them as a threat to national values or local interests, as will be discussed later in this chapter. There were few immigrants, and they were easily absorbed as a complement to the local labor force, initially propelled by labor demand during harvest time in agriculture.

Case studies of individual immigrant trajectories in the labor market of the Alfaya valley reveal two main traits in their life and labor conditions: high mobility and instability. Immigrants in Alfaya respond to the temporality of jobs with several types of strategies: (1) some work mainly in agriculture, following the harvest peaks across Spanish national territory; (2) others try to stay near an area of residence, working in Alfaya's agriculture during the summer and in other economic sectors (such as construction and services) during the rest of the year; (3) still others combine work in agriculture and other sectors across several territorial areas, that is, they "take what they can get" *(ir a la que salga).*

Given immigrants' mobility and the instability of their structural situation, the different kinds of legal limitations imposed by work and residence permits on the places and the economic sectors in which they can work push them toward irregular situations in a structural way. The combination of stringent legal requirements and a pervasive underground economy, particularly in the main sectors in need of cheap labor, such as agriculture, produces an extremely high incidence of illegal immigration. Immigrants are quite heterogeneous in rural/urban background, educational level, nationalities, and ethnic groups. Yet most immigrants I have known shared being illegal, lacking the so-called papers or being in danger of losing them.

The poorest Spanish agrarian workers have also been nomadic. Similarly, most immigrants are perpetually on the move across occupations, territories, and legality/illegality. While immigrants' nomadism may arise from changed legal and socioeconomic circumstances, it also evinces the subtle boundary deeply ingrained in collective memory between "Moors"—and by extension, Islam—and Christianity, between Arabs and Andalusians, between a European destiny and an African one.

There is a deep irony in Andalusians having come to stereotype "Moors" as false, hypocritical, fickle, dishonest, underdeveloped, cruel, and lazy, for not so long ago, Andalusian workers who emigrated to Europe to work alongside Africans embraced a different image of "Moors": they saw them as fellow workers (albeit with some pejorative features)—people who lived in the same neighborhood and buildings, among whom many were, in the words of one woman, "religious and upstanding people" (M.C., summer 1994). When African immigrants began arriving in the Alfaya Valley, they were integrated into the agrarian system as cheap and temporary labor that complemented the local labor force, and Alfayans initially perceived them to be in the same class position as other Andalusian day laborers. Andalusians worked together with Africans in the same crews, and most Africans received the same salary as locals, due to the strong class consciousness of most small peasants who employed them. Remembering their own experience of emigration to Northern Europe, Andalusians identified with immigrants and with their right to "have bread." Often from a revolutionary Marxist ideology, as in the case of Alfaya's valley, they nourished a national or regional imagery of Andalusia as a forgotten land, always condemned in Spain to the lowest position. This identification with the subaltern Spain, to the south, is present everywhere in the popular culture of Granada and Andalusia (Burgos 1972; see the debate in the press about Spanish racism against Andalusians and the perpetuation of the folkloric image of Andalusian happiness, *la Andalucía de la pandereta*).[5] From Andalusia, and in the larger context of multiple "ethnogenesis" produced in democratic Spain (Greenwood 1992), most peasants in Alfaya were also skeptical of the homogeneous cultural national identity touted by Francoist nationalist imagery.[6] Finally, the fact that most immigrants were considered "illegal" under existing migration legislation (see the section "Enactment of the Alien Law" in this chapter) was not considered an impediment to hiring them, because at the beginning of the 1990s, almost half of the production and one-third of autochthonous labor contracting was not registered in official transactions. Immigrants' "illegality" was simply not as relevant as their structural situation of poverty, homelessness, and chronic nomadism, which for Andalusians conjured up memories of their own distress and deprivation as impoverished migrant workers. As a result, Andalusians initially welcomed Africans and showed solidarity toward them, as I describe later in this chapter.

But racist prejudice against Africans has acquired a quite different meaning in the context of semiperipheral late capitalism. Various social institutions actively contribute to the formation, consolidation, or transformation of stereotypes today, often in contradictory ways. Mass media and the use of sociological polls are two important producers of public opinion, and in the case of recent immigration, both have created a systematic imagery of invasion and of a national limited good (Foster 1965) supposedly threatened by foreigners (of a rather specific kind, not all of them). In effect, the state and dominant discourses were busy erecting mechanisms of exclusion around the categories of legality, nationality, and culture, as I will discuss next.

By crossing boundaries, the title of this section, I also mean to refer to the spaces of solidarity that openly defied these mechanisms of exclusion, such as the comuna described in the testimony of Assane at the end of this chapter, or the volunteer shelter and camping grounds described in the next chapter. Crossing boundaries means contesting boundaries. But first, let us see how these boundaries were created, focusing on dominant discourses and the new legislative framework.

The Making of a European Spain and Southern Immigrants

Fostered by tourism, industrialization, and a new capitalist rationality,[7] Spain's economic growth since the 1960s, linked to the establishment of a stable democratic system in the 1970s, paved the way for the country's gaining full membership in the European Economic Community (EEC, or simply EC) in 1986. Spaniards have consolidated political and socioeconomic rights for citizens in the last quarter of the century. Membership in the renamed European Union (EU), meanwhile, virtually guarantees that these changes are here to stay. Membership deeply entwined the Spanish economy with other European economies[8] and has drawn Spain into European decision making that affects political and economic areas previously reserved for the nation-state. Membership also sharpened the significance of Spain's external frontiers with Third World countries to the south precisely at the time when the flows of foreign labor into Spain from North and Central Africa swelled.

Until very recently Spain was a country of emigrants, but it has now become a locus of immigration. Both stages have responded to the needs of global capitalism for the kind of mobile labor force, needed for accumulation and profit. Yet Spain's location in the international division of the labor market has been dramatically transformed. As a consequence, new alignments of national and supranational borders have emerged in the northern margin of the Mediterranean, traversing

Andalusia and the Levant of the Iberian peninsula, marking the new limits of Spain and Europe, and, of course, of the First World. Dominant discourses legitimize the relocation of the border in terms of Europe's supposed homogeneity, both in terms of sociocultural, political, and economic processes and in terms of race and ethnicity, unifying Europe in symbolic opposition to the "other."

This homogeneity is being constructed through nationalistic discourses appealing to a purportedly national common interest in the rebordering of the Mediterranean.[9] This is clear, for instance, in the 1991 Spanish government document "Basic Lines of the Spanish Migration Policy," the first official recognition of immigration in the country: "National interest as well as the imposed obligations derived from our membership in the EEC, require us to take measures to articulate a rigorous control at the [southern] border" (Spanish government 1990, 16). The reason national interest requires control measures upon a very specific group of immigrants from the southern Mediterranean shore is articulated in this document in cultural and ethnic terms: "Spanish migration policy has to vigorously manage immigration according to the interest of the state, taking into account migrants' origins, temporality, professional profile, and capacity for integration.... [Migrants from] less developed countries often produce many integration problems, because migrants from these countries come with very different social habits" (Spanish government 1990, 18, section on "Social Integration").

Dominant discourse plays a major part in the construction of a space in which ethnic difference is seen as disruptive and threatening. Spain's inclusion in the group of developed capitalist countries is creating both symbolic and material borders with a Third World characterized in the dominant discourse as having endemic economic inequalities, high levels of poverty, and unstable politics which all allegedly promote extremist social behavior. Such characterization of southern immigrants generates an alarmist image of threat to the security of Spanish society, linking illegal immigrants to the increase of violence within the national borders. The government and other politicians in Spain use crime statistics to legitimate the state's use of force against immigrants: "given the marginality and illegality of clandestine immigration, an increase in delinquency has been proven" (Spanish government 1990, 19 section on "Strengthening Police Action").[10]

A final characteristic emphasized in the dominant discourse is demographic. The image here is of an old Europe—or better, an old white Europe—unable to fend off the flow from the uncontrolled population growth of underdeveloped countries. A high official of the Civil government of Barcelona claims that "in the next twenty years around 25 million emigrants from North Africa will unquestionably try to find jobs in Europe" (Planas Cercós 1990). Alarmism is used to stir up old fears of a silent invasion of the Iberian Peninsula.

Similarly, in our analysis of the newspaper accounts of migrants in *El País* (Suárez-Navaz and Hernández 1993), we detect a consistent propensity to represent immigrants as a problem because of their illegality, their poverty, and their purported criminality. The press invites readers to articulate their own identity in opposition to that of the immigrant, by way of symbolic inversion. Spaniards thus become those who legally live and work in Spain, have access to public benefits, have houses, and are controllable. The press takes for granted that it is normal and rational for Spanish citizens to safeguard their personal and "national" interests in opposition to those of immigrants. Immigration is thus naturalized through concepts that equate movements of population with ethnically and economically limited groups and that represent them as a threat to Spanish well-being and security. As a corollary, ethnic confrontation is perceived as an illness or cancer of society. Interestingly enough, the state, which is in part responsible for enforcing an ethnicization of Spanish society through its discourse and practices, receives additional legitimation by purporting to provide the remedy for this disease, namely, a modern and efficient legislative apparatus. Let us now turn to an analysis of Spanish migratory legislation.

Enactment of the Alien Law

The redefinition of Spain's southern border and identity accompanied a change in Spain's location in the international labor market and enactment in 1985 of the first comprehensive legislation on foreigners' status in Spain, the new Alien Law, or LOE. The government used emergency procedures to fast-track the legislation through Parliament as a "remedy [to] the legislative chaos produced by the heterogeneity and dispersion of norms" related to foreigners in Spain. A related goal was to restrict entry of Third World immigrants, especially from North Africa and Latin America, whom Spain had traditionally welcomed (Corredera and Díez 1994, 126). In effect, this Spanish legislation secured a southern frontier for Europe as a whole, a precondition for Spain's incorporation into a European space without inner frontiers. Yet entry into the EC was not discussed explicitly by Parliament in justifying the LOE.[11] Instead, debate emphasized "intolerable situations" produced by the absence of coherent legislation dealing with foreigners.[12]

The alarmism behind the parliamentary debate did not, however, accord with public opinion, or even with state practices toward the African and Latin American immigrants who were settling in Spain at that time.[13] Most of the public paid little attention to immigrants, or even welcomed them, as I will show later in discussing the experience of Assane. It was really not until the early 1990s that immigration captured the public imagination as a problem, and then only after mass media experts and politicians began to showcase immigration as an issue, especially after the Straits of Gibraltar had taken on the character of a new Río Bravo, where immigrants almost daily risked their lives to enter Europe.

Enactment and subsequent enforcement of the LOE concretized Andalusia as a border area juridically, situating it between a new Europe and the migratory flows coming from Africa. Subsequent legislation, such as Spain's decision in 1991 to revoke Moroccans' privileged status to enter Spain without a visa (motivated by the formal membership of Spain in the Schengen group), merely tightened the inscription of the southern border begun by the LOE. The result was a definitive redrawing of the frontiers between north and south, a rebordering that has had a dramatic effect on migratory flows from the south.

Spain's immigration legislation should be understood as part of the process of construction of a common European space able to compete in the new global economy. Northern Europe had welcomed, and even assisted, immigration in the 1960s, but in the 1970s it began to restrict immigration in conjunction with post-Fordist political and economic restructuring. European nation-states began to not only close their frontiers to immigrants, but also to impose administrative regulations on those already established as minorities by limiting their rights and their access to benefits and services. The European model of citizenship creates a hierarchy of legal statutes within the European frontiers, from the full citizen who holds full social and political rights, to the intermediary status of permanent legal residents (denizens), which excludes aliens from full membership, to the exclusionary category of illegals (Hammar 1985, 1994).

The LOE reproduces this model of hierarchical citizenship in an especially hermetic and exclusionary manner inherent in the use of administrative rather than judicial mechanisms to control immigration. In Spain, it is the administration and its security forces that are responsible for establishing the conditions for the entry, stay, work, and departure of foreigners. Those affected by the security measures can appeal to the courts only on an a posteriori basis, and even then can only count on partial court intervention. A lawyer working very closely with undocumented workers described the consequences of the administrative character of the law to me as follows: "Those immigrants do not have a single right in Spain. The law anticipates all their circumstances. Basically, the message is that if you are 'illegal,' the state has only one responsibility: to deport you, without any chance to appeal such action in court"[14] (E.M., lawyer for the Human Rights Association in Granada, APDH [Asociación Pro Derechos Humanos]).

The LOE sharply distinguishes legal from illegal foreigners, equating the latter with delinquents. Even though the law was drawn up "to protect the legal rights and juridical guarantees of the legal foreigner in Spain," it does not really extend legal protection to most Third World immigrants. The principal reason for this failure is the pervasive illegality of immigrants, a key feature of immigration to Spain. The reasons for this illegality are countless: the restrictive implementation of the Alien Law, the control of frontiers, the refusal to grant visas in Third World countries,[15] the link between work and residence permits for foreigners to needs of the national labor market (in a context of high unemployment in Spain), and the need to renew the permits each year, providing documentation about work status, among others (see the section "Continuing Illegality" in chapter 4 for an analysis of the reasons for continuing illegality).

As defined by law, the distinction between legal and irregular immigrants pervades daily life as well as institutional programs for immigrants' integration. The strict division along legal criteria is not as clear in practice as it is in theory, given the slowness and inefficacy of Spanish administration in solving pending cases and the contradictions among different state offices involved in the processes. An ethnographic approach to the immigrant population prevents one from falling into the false dichotomy created by the Alien Law: there are not just legal and illegal aliens, but a myriad of legal situations in the middle of these two extremes.[16] Irregular immigrants aren't the only ones who face discrimination in the informal economy. Even those who obtain work permits are often hired illegally; more important, most work permits are granted for sectors of the economy with high incidence of nonregistered participation, such as services and agriculture. Furthermore, work permits are temporary, yet most immigrants continue to work while awaiting their permit renewal, which often takes a year or more, during which time those waiting are working illegally.[17] In Granada, for instance, almost half of the Senegalese are illegal or are awaiting official response to their applications for stay and work permits (Suárez-Navaz 1995a).

A major reason for undocumented status prevailing among Third World immigrants is their precarious participation in sectors already characterized by exploitative and discriminatory underground or informal employment. In 1985, according to a study commissioned by the Spanish government, Spain's economy employed one out of four working Spaniards in informal or underground jobs, (see Benton 1990, chapter 7). Furthermore, Spain has Europe's highest rate of unemployment, with up to 34 percent of workers unemployed or underemployed in some sectors and regions such Andalusia. Immigrants merely join the most vulnerable ranks of an already substantial informal workforce. Yet the differentiation of immigrants' status as legal and illegal in relation to worker and citizenship rights draws ethnic lines that position immigrant workers below native Spaniards in underground employment. An interview I had with the manager of an established informal urban firm illustrates a common justification for discriminatory hiring policies:

> I do not hire foreigners, and it is not that I am racist, just realistic. You see, we move many millions [of pesetas] worth of goods here every month, and none of it shows up on the books. The government would be delighted to collect taxes from what we do, and a foreigner is more likely to spill the beans if taken in by the police [the manager assumes here that a colored person is more likely to be detained and then forced to give

information about his or her employer]. Besides, foreigners are too unstable … whereas our staff is more permanent (three to four months, to years). I cannot risk people leaving the job without returning the merchandise. Spanish people generally have an address where you can track them down. If you want to find immigrants working, go over to *x;* there they really exploit those people to the fullest. We do not do that.

The fact is that Third World immigrants, either legal or illegal, are automatically suspect, prone to having the police stop them for identification.[18] Nationals involved in the informal economy thus see them as a potential threat for their own security and their profit. Such ethnic discrimination is especially acute in regions and/or economic sectors with a high incidence of informal practices, as in rural Andalusia. Yet in a society highly pervaded by black money, economic vulnerability, and a high degree of informality toward the state, employers prefer highly dependent and manageable workers, especially employees who are not so interested in the social benefits guaranteed to legal workers by labor legislation. Undocumented workers accept jobs without asking for contracts, minimum salaries, or health care benefits. Thus, while employers justify discrimination on the basis of fearing the consequences of hiring illegal immigrant workers, they do in fact employ them.

The state, meanwhile, uses the presence of Third World immigrants as a pretext for intervening in highly vulnerable economic sectors as a way of indirectly interdicting endemic underground employment practices that go on whether illegal immigrants are involved or not. In Alfaya the illegality of many day laborers during harvest time, when they are most needed, is considered one of the principal problems by local authorities, who have complained about the way the LOE is sometimes applied in the village, as we will see below. Fearing state intervention, peasants and employers are prone to siding with the state against immigrants in advocating adherence to the Alien Law. Ironically, the very employers who hire illegal workers have become the state's most efficient agents of the LOE.

In fact, the effect of the law in the restructuring of collective identities and social spaces is based not only in the explicit regulatory and punitive action of the law, but also, and most important, in the disciplinary techniques and self-regulation processes that the distinction between legality and illegality is producing in civil society, as I have shown elsewhere (Suárez-Navaz 1995a) and will discuss in particular in the section "Politics of Invisibility: A Racial Geography of Labor Relations," in chapter 5. Thus, the symbolic as well as the regulative action of the LOE is creating internal borders among the people living in Spain, based on a restricted notion of citizenship that indirectly requires potential citizens to have a relatively high economic level. Most immigrants do not have the requisite level or origin. They are condemned to the ranks of the informally employed or unemployed and to permanent persecution by the police or by other social actors who see the invisibility of their own underground practices threatened by the immigrants' presence.

Andalusia's Muslim Imagery

I came to Andalusia because I thought people here spoke Arabic, you know? We had learned about Muslim Andalusia in school, yet textbooks and teachers never mentioned Andalusia again. That's why I came here when I ran away from my father in France, and I was lucky. People don't speak Arabic here anymore, but they are not like people in Europe. They do not look at you as if they are superior, you know? Like French people do. (Assane D., summer 1994)

Arab pioneer presence in the valley, in Andalusia, and elsewhere in Spain is resolutely appropriated by Arabs and other Muslims (such as the young Senegalese Assane D.) currently living in the valley. As part of my fieldwork I would ask informants to give me a tour around the valley and the village and to show me sites that were important for them. An Algerian immigrant once insisted on going to the point where the valley opens down to the road to the Mediterranean sea. From this place, one views a typical landscape of scattered small white Andalusian houses called *cortijos,* and dry land harvested with olives, almonds trees, and cereals. This immigrant knew about the past presence of Arabs in this territory, but his approach was different from that of locals who acknowledge such a past in their own minority narratives (e.g., E.A. in the previous chapter):

Arabs lived here, and this was a Muslim land. We still are very close, see? On clear days one can see Africa from here. My family is down there, my country is down there. These mountains have seen many things, many years, many people coming and leaving. Muslims crossed these mountains before toward the south when they were expelled from Spain; now we come back because we are being expelled by our countries. We taught the inhabitants of this valley and in Andalusia everything they know about agriculture, about sciences.... Spain still does not want us. And these people [in the valley] only want us as workers, as cheap labor. Maybe things will change, only the *Mizan*[19] will tell. (T.L., summer 1994)

A Moroccan immigrant similarly historicizes the valley, Andalusia, and Spain in general, calling attention to the illusory aspect of narratives of the progress and modernization that left African countries behind:

These people are campesinos; they have suffered real hunger, they have emigrated, and now they have money, they have land, they have "Moors" to work for them. They feel superior to us and to blacks because they have progress. But it is as if you throw this lighter up: it will go up, and up, yet necessarily it will stop and will go down. Well, the same will happen to this Western society: it will go down because it has *pies de barro* [feet of clay] like those of these peasants. (A.A., summer 1994)

Arab immigrants most especially, but also African Muslim immigrants as a larger group, frequently appeal to, and thus construct, a longer historical tempo, one in which the Western notion of progress is not hegemonic anymore. This tempo nourishes new imageries where Granada is represented as a highly symbolic place of the Islamic *umma* (community, see glossary), and inspires the new claims made by Muslims as belonging to this land, a phenomenon of extraordinary interest to which I will return later in chapter 7.

Andalusia, and specifically Granada, has had a long historical interaction with the peoples of Northern Africa, which reverberates in its landscape and its regional and local identities. Granada, conquered by Castilian forces in 1492, was the last bastion of Arab rule in the Iberian peninsula, which lasted from the eighth century to the fifteenth century. In Granada, the presence of *mudéjares* (Muslims living under Christian rule) and later the *moriscos* (Muslims who converted to Christianity), persisted over forced conversions, incentives for emigration, and direct repression until the expulsion of the latter in the seventeenth century.[20]

During the next three centuries there was a consistent effort on the part of the Spanish state to make the Arab presence invisible. It was not until the late nineteenth century, in the context of the romantic movement and of colonial intervention in Morocco, that the Arab heritage was reappropriated by Spanish nationalist discourse. At the turn of the twentieth century, Spain, weakened among the ascending colonial powers of France and Britain, drew on the imperial vocation of Spain to establish military power in Morocco as a means to counterfoil the growing expansion of France in Northern Africa. As an example, Prime Minister Cánovas used to say that the southern frontier of Spain was the Atlas mountains in Morocco, while Romanones, an intellectual of the time, argued that "Morocco is Spain's last chance to keep her position in the concert of Europe" (Carr 1982, 518). After many years of struggle, the Spanish protectorate in northern Morocco was finally established in 1927.[21] And it was precisely the revolt of the troops in Morocco that marked the beginning of the bloody Spanish Civil War, with Franco at the head of a small army of both Spanish and Moroccan soldiers. Today, elderly people in Alfaya and elsewhere still remember the cruelty of the so called "Moors" in the repression of the civil population. And today in the Alhambra, in a very discrete form, some of the dead "Moors" of the Civil War rest buried in the still nonrecognized traditional Muslim cemetery.

In the new multicultural Spain, Andalusia has again incorporated the legacy of al-Andalus as its distinctive historical and cultural background vis-à-vis the rest of the seventeen Autonomous Communities, such as Catalonia, the Basque Country, and so forth. During the Franco years, the national Catholic ideology co-opted part of the Andalusian folklore as the idiosyncratic Spanish cultural expression (often pejoratively referred to by critics as *españoladas*), erasing from it references to the reality of poverty and exploitation of rural Andalusia. As a reaction, the regional government, the Junta de Andalucía, has taken pains to revive this folklore as the authentic traditions of Andalusia in the context of the broader project of modernization, as Jane has masterfully grasped in her ethno-historical approach to an Andalusian village (1991, 1997). In contrast to the homogeneity conjured up by Francoist nationalism, the regional government emphasizes the heterogeneity of its cultural roots, bringing to the forefront in many cultural and tourist campaigns Al-Andalus and *Andalusí* traditions as "the living essence of one of the richest cultures of humanity," which has to be acknowledged in order to "better our historical past."[22] The Arab culture included as part of this legacy is described as "cosmopolitan, refined, and tolerant," but it is conveniently located in a past historic time, represented "through a romantic mist ... [so that] the good stereotype does not contradict the bad one," that of current Arabs living in Andalusia as immigrants.[23]

This orientalizing imagery of Andalusia is especially strong in Granada, the last bastion of the Muslim medieval al-Andalus. The revival of al-Andalus is not just official demagoguery put forward by the Junta as part of Andalusia's nation-building processes and as an economically driven strategy to attract tourists to a safe Islamic exoticism; rather, it is a battle ground. The press is an endless source of passionate debates about the meaning of the past between those who defend Catholic Granada and those who struggle to incorporate Muslim legacy as part of a tradition "which still beats deep in the consciousness of today's Granadan" (*El Ideal,* January 2, 1992, 3). As Berard Vicent said in the special issue dedicated to the anniversary of the five hundred years of the conquest of Granada: "The prominence of Granada, our Granada, is contained in the ambiguity of January 2, 1492. There is no city more Christian and more Muslim at the same time.... In its own way, this city is a beautiful symbol for a Mediterranean world in search of its own identity" (*El Ideal,* January 2, 1992, 36). The historical imagery of al-Andalus is a common legacy of Muslims and Andalusians, and each group draws on it to negotiate and imagine a new kind of *convivencia*[24] (see Martínez Montálvez, *El País,* November 5, 1992, "Temas de Nuestra Epoca" [Themes of Our Times] 4).

There are countless examples of these ongoing struggles to turn the cultural and folkloric revival of Muslim Andalusia into real social, juridical, and symbolic recognition of Muslims' rights in this land. Endless disputes arise between Muslims and Granadans each year during the main celebration of the city, the anniversary of the conquest of the city by the Spanish Catholic kings on January 2, 1492.[25] Most of the new Islamic associations in Spain are found in Andalusia, and specially Granada, and some of them, especially those founded by Spanish converts, are slowly pushing forward juridical and social claims of their rights as "historical members" of these lands. Already in 1981 in Granada one member of this now-important Muslim Spanish community said: "We Spanish Muslims did not come to reconquer Andalusia. We came because we are from here, and we will try to practice Islam in our land, a right that nobody can take from us. And we will promote Islam.... If *Al-lah* so wants it, a society based on fraternity, generosity and knowledge will flourish here in Andalusia once again" (quoted in Alonso 1990, 6). Al-Andalus is a powerful symbol in the collective Muslim imagery, not only for Spanish Muslims but throughout the Muslim world. This "return to the motherland" of the once-exiled Islam is most acutely experienced among those Arabs, and particularly Maghrebians, who make up the majority of the new immigrants in Spain, still encapsulated in this complex symbolism of the imagery of "Moors" in Andalusia. It is as if again and again Andalusia becomes for Muslims, as the Syrian poet Nizar Kabbani beautifully expressed it, "an impossible historical emotion."[26]

"Outsider" into "Foreigner": The First Case of Enforcement of the LOE and Collective Resistance

"In Alfaya there have always been outsiders [*forasteros*]," people told me, and according to them, this is the reason people in the valley have an open attitude toward people coming from abroad (see Moreno 1987). In the past, outsiders were not perceived as "invaders" who would make illicit claims on the common patrimony. Emigrants from Alfaya who returned to enjoy their vacations in the valley, workers such as people from Málaga or Gypsies who came "to work in agriculture, or to sell lemons or oranges from the coast," or "nomads who came to vend needed commodities" are remembered with sympathy by most people[27] (P.M., spring 1995). Alfayans also remember an Arab doctor who participated locally in the revolutionary transition. Former emigrants to northern Europe referred to Yugoslavs, Italians, Moroccans, and other Mediterranean people who shared jobs and housing with them as fellow workers, no matter what the cultural differences were among them. Europeans perceived them all as culturally different because "we were all foreigners from the south" (A.A., spring 1995). Another emigrant woman underscored that "Moors" "were like us; they were religious and upstanding people [*gente formal y religiosa*]" (M.C., summer 1994).

By contrast, Andalusians clearly perceived as "invaders" the large numbers of Europeans who were visiting Andalusia's Mediterranean coasts as tourists or building homes and hotels there. In 1974, a well-known jurist wrote about the "European invasion" with a nationalist rhetoric typical of the Francoist regime: "In addition to the invasions Spain has suffered historically, we are now suffering an invasion led by tourists, foreigners who are negotiating contracts for the peripheral and island areas of our territories.... It is difficult to find another country that accords [foreigners] so many advantages while imposing so few obligations on them.... The foreign 'invader' arrives in our territory as a key player and not as an 'invited artist'; he arrives to conquer, it seems, given how part of our territory has been sold off to them" (Aznar Sánchez 1974, 7–8).[28] Economists and social scientists of the time, though not using such anachronistic national rhetoric, agreed that it was astonishing for Spain to abandon autarchy by putting the country "on sale" to European tourists and to investors from Europe, the United States, and Japan.

For their part, the Spanish emigrants working for European employers during the 1960s and 1970s believed that Europeans were phenotypically and culturally "different" from Andalusian and other Mediterranean peoples: "Europeans are very different from us. They are as cold and white as ice" (S.B., spring 1995), or "I had a very bad time at the beginning because I couldn't distinguish among all of [the Europeans]; they all looked the same to me, so blond, and so white" (M.Z., summer 1994).

The category "foreigner" is never a neutral legal status constructed in a vacuum. Geopolitical concerns of a particular historical context are largely responsible for dominant definitions of who is a foreigner. Foreigners have often been linked to particular notions of "otherness," defined historically and naturalized as having religious, biological, cultural, racial, or ethnic characteristics different from those of nationals, and are thus considered incompatible with the homogeneous values emblematic of national identity.[29]

Yet, as commented earlier, Andalusians did not perceive the African immigrants who first started arriving as a threat to their national values or their culture. But even though Andalusians did not apply the exclusionary legal concept of "foreigner" to Africans, they did see Africans as different from themselves in a racial sense, especially those who came from sub-Saharan countries—immigrants such as Assane. Several women told me about their first encounters with Assane in the village: "When people saw Assane for the first time they were astonished.... An old woman told my mother 'you wouldn't imagine what I saw today, a young boy completely burned by the sun, and as he saw I was gazing at him he greeted me with his hand and it was white! Poor thing, how badly he must have been burned by the sun!" (P.P., summer 1994). P.P. recounted this anecdote to me as very funny, roaring with laughter at the ignorance showed by the old woman. Assane himself treated this and other anecdotes about his first reception as inoffensive because of the overall hospitality he received in the village: "They were good people, even if ignorant because no black person had ever lived here. As soon as they came to know me they were curious about me and my country, and young people especially were very open.... After I sold merchandise here for several days, people helped me to find work, offered me a place to stay, and told me about the political struggle going on in the valley to make the life of peasants a better one.... Everybody was very good here, very common people, most of them Communist and solidary" (Assane D., summer 1994).[30]

Assane frequently contrasted Andalusia to northern immigration sites, such as those in Catalonia or France, where he felt he was considered a foreigner, an "inferior" person: "I came to Andalusia because I thought people here spoke Arabic, you know? We had learned about Muslim Andalusia at school, and then textbooks and teachers never mention Andalusia again. That's why I came here when I ran away from my father in France, and I was lucky. People don't speak Arabic here anymore, but they are not like people in Europe. They do not look at you as if they were superior, you know? Like French people do."

Assane liked Alfaya from the very beginning. He quickly developed a group of friends with whom he shared leisure and work. He had an Alfayan girlfriend and lived "as a member of the family" with several villagers. Alfayans welcomed him into a local organization called la comuna, a collective inspired by anarchist ideals of sharing land, work, and daily life. As a member of the collective, Assane participated in assemblies and contributed his opinions and votes to decision making. Although he was not unfamiliar with collective modes of agricultural production in Senegal (in the Senegalese religious cooperatives *da'ara* described in chapter 6), he learned about the Andalusian workers' discourse of individual rights and the collective effort to break down hierarchies of power based on age, religious authority, gender, and the like. In contrast to the *da'ara*, which emphasized submission to a collective project, the comuna gave priority to equality. And whereas Assane had experienced the puritan work ethic of Mourid religious identity in Senegal, here he found that people were building ties of solidarity not just through work but also through play and through shared participation in cultural activities.

The ideology of the comuna was related to the climate of acceptance that people like Assane experienced. The comuna's leaders looked for inspiration in Third World revolutions and anticolonial struggles for independence (Cuba, Nicaragua, El Salvador, Algeria, the Sahara, and the like). They drew upon global perspectives on world inequalities to critique measures such as the LOE as illegitimate and racist. They did not link a conception of citizenship, as entitlement to rights, to nationalist notions of identity, but rather to local participation in social and labor networks. In their view, the state was obliged to acknowledge local definitions of community membership and autonomy, and the security and administrative apparatuses of the state were conceived as accountable to the inalienable rights of the persons legitimately living in the territory. In addition, the comuna embodied a rich legacy giving priority to local moral notions of justice over those of a centralized legal system of rules. "Justice stands above legality.... Personal judgment, custom, and convention are therefore the juridical reality, the 'law' governing the activities in the *pueblo*"[31] (Lisón Tolosana 1966, 225).

Such a legacy traditionally legitimized subaltern groups' "juridical noncompliance" with or resistance to the arbitrary interventions of the state that maintained unequal relations of power (see chapter 1). Resistance to the law thus invoked higher principles of justice. During the transition to democracy, Andalusians resisted the law frontally. At other times, they employed everyday forms of covert peasant resistance (Scott 1985). But at the time of initial implementation of the LOE, when Alfayans of the comuna mobilized to protest the arrest of Assane, they broadened resistance from a class-based sociopolitical struggle to a broader, multidimensional protest that questioned not only class inequalities but also national criteria of rights and belonging. They invoked the category of citizen of the world to challenge the enactment of the LOE, thus building on new, deterritorialized notions of rights inspired by growing recognition of human rights.

As Assane's testimony illustrates (in the discussion that follows below), immigrants incorporate this deterritorialized notion of a person's rights as part of their daily resistance to the law. Yet in doing so they acknowledge the limits of this kind of discourse in a Western world dominated by legal rules and procedures that exclude them as illegals. Immigrants' resistance to the law is based upon a critique of disparities in justice and of the purportedly impartiality yet patently partial enforcement of the law to the detriment of immigrants. They couch their protest in normative terms, objecting to the a priori criminalization of immigrants and advocating an alternative morally grounded notion of what makes a person "illegal." Such protest, however, is highly dependent on the support of national groups that hold the legal standing from which claims can be made against the national state. In the following I incorporate Assane's testimonies about identification, detention, and resistance to the enactment of the law.

Act 1: Hailing and Resistance

In the comuna both men and women took turns cooking for the others, and that day it was my turn … so after working along with the others I went to the supermarket to get the food. Just as I was returning, I saw a car of the Civil Guard … and he whistled. I heard him, but I ignored him, because I refused to acknowledge a whistle…. After all, I'm not a dog, he could talk to me, right? I did my shopping and again he whistled to me. I didn't stop. People took heed. They came out to look, all of them standing out there. As I continued walking, the guy followed me with the car and hailed me:

"Hey, ain't I talking to you?"

"You are not talking to me, I am not a dog or a goat; I understand everything. If you're in the car and I am walking, you should get out of the car to talk to me, because you are a civil servant. Were you a friend, you could call me from the car 'Hey you!' But the proper way for you to behave is to approach me and tell me 'Excuse me sir,' and then tell me whatever you have to say."

He then told me:

"The 'papers.'"

My heart was jumping in my chest, pum, pum, and still does so today, when I remember what happened. Trembling inside! Because I thought about many things in a flash—everything came to me suddenly! He repeated, "the 'papers,'" and I told him, "Well, man, right now I will give you the 'papers,'" and I gave him some receipts for the merchandise I had bought—that's what I gave him. "Didn't you ask for papers?" He hadn't asked me for personal documentation, and I was angry at how he had behaved, so I tricked him.

He told me, "What the hell is this? I want your passport and your identification!"

"OK, now I understand, let me go in to get my passport for you."

At that point, Liliana, I had spent three years in Spain, and my passport's visa allowed me to stay just three days in Spain…. I closed the door and locked myself in, because I knew he couldn't get in without a court order. The guy stood outside, more and more nervous…. When a fellow of the comuna came along, the guard threatened him: "Hey you, tell your friend to give me his passport or I'll kick down the door!" And my friend answered in the same tone: "You won't do that because if you do you will loose your hat" [threatening to put his job in danger by denouncing him]. I was terrified, and although my friend left to bring back the other members of the comuna, I finally gave the Civil Guard agent my passport.

He said that he would call Granada to tell [the authorities] what happened, and that I had to go with him….

"Sorry sir, I have been here for three years and my visa was only for three days, but I've never before been stopped, and you know why? Because I haven't had any problem…. I won't move from here … because I am here with my people."

He understood me well, even though my Spanish was not as good as today, and he replied:

"You are coming with your passport so that you won't run away. You are going to sleep in prison tonight, because you are illegal."

"I am LEGAL, I told him, because I never robbed anything, I never killed anybody, and I've never done anything bad. I am just working. I am not a drug trafficker, I do not launder money. I haven't done anything wrong. I am LEGAL. An illegal is a delinquent, whether he's a Spaniard or a black person."

By that time, the rest of the comuna arrived and I locked myself up again. The others wondered, What can we do? And of course, as usual, they called for an emergency meeting—how do they call this?—an extraordinary assembly!

I want to underscore three elements of this narrative. First, there is a strong connection between the so-called "papers" and fear. The legal requirements for obtaining a visa to enter Spain from a foreign country are increasingly restrictive. Foreigners circumvent this *ex-ante* system of control, described previously in the chapter, by crossing the border clandestinely or with a tourist visa. Such people get trapped in an effective *ex-post* system of control because the LOE deems not having a legal visa to be grounds for expulsion, which voids any further possibility of applying for a residence and work permit (Santos 1993, 113). Assane felt fear when asked for the papers, for the thoughts that ran through his mind at that moment all concerned the imminent failure of all his efforts to make a living in Spain, as well as the effects deportation would have on his family and on his own future in Senegal. According to one of the leaders of the comuna who became involved in the defense of immigrants' rights, this fear generates what he referred to as "the hare complex" among immigrants. This urge to hide is a major impediment to immigrants' integration into the receiving society. Yet, as I will explain in chapter 4, the well-intentioned efforts to eradicate immigrant practices of evasion, distrust, subordination, and vulnerability actually strengthen the fetishism of the papers conjured up by the law.

Second, I want to underscore the daily forms of resistance used by immigrants to delay or confuse the agents of the law. The "papers" constitute a somewhat ambiguous category. Local security forces rarely know all the provisions of the LOE, much less how international agreements affect migration, and they are thus somewhat inconsistent in enforcement of the provisions. Realizing this, immigrants come up with any kind of "papers" that they think will delay their detention. Furthermore, NGOs and labor unions supporting immigrants have used a myriad of juridical sophistries (as I will describe below) to provide immigrants with papers intended to confuse the security forces into allowing the immigrant to go free "this time" so as not to "cause problems"—even if the documents don't eliminate the threat of expulsion.

Finally, and most important, these petty strategies of resistance generally accompany direct challenging of law enforcers' actions in the name of legality itself. In the example at hand, Assane knows that the law restricts arbitrary arrest of suspects, such as arrest in their homes without a warrant,[32] and he repeatedly uses his knowledge of these restrictions to challenge the Civil Guard agent and put him in his place. Finally, as in this case, the charge of racism is commonly invoked to underscore injustices enforced by the law, thus casting the criminalization of immigrants of color as immoral.

Act 2: Resistance to Expulsion and Nationalism That "Goes without Saying"

In the extraordinary assembly that ensued, and in the many which followed, the comuna devised a collective strategy of resistance on Assane's behalf involving demonstrations, hunger strikes, and countless press releases and mass media interviews. Assane's case, which was one of the first of its kind, became widely known in Andalusia and throughout Spain, and Assane received widespread popular support. The civil governor (the central government's representative in

Granada) was bombarded by expressions of solidarity with Assane. Local politicians wanted to name Assane the adoptive son of the village. Assane received offers of marriage from women to help him avoid deportation. Local employers offered him work contracts to help him regularize his visa. Flyers distributed to the public during demonstrations demanded legal accreditation of Assane's rights "because he is just struggling, like other people, to get a job," and "because justice is a right of citizens of the world." Assane needed legal experts to defend his claims in the court, but most lawyers felt that his case was a lost cause. Finally a woman lawyer accepted his case, and Assane went off to the police station with her and with the local leader of the resistance movement, amidst public speculation as to what would happen to him. Assane told me what he was thinking at the time:

> The lawyer and E.A. went with me because I didn't want to go alone and didn't know what was the best way of dealing with the situation. I was being faced with being deported. One alternative for staying legally was to get married. Or I could pay five hundred thousand pesetas for a residence permit, or get a work contract, or try to get nationalized as a Spaniard. Another alternative was to apply for political asylum.... I was very nervous—I told myself, "Be careful because these people can convince me of anything they want, and I might end up not being able even to return to Senegal." I didn't want to apply for political asylum—that doesn't interest me. I want to be able to return to Senegal whenever I want without any problems, because I miss Senegal a lot and I love my people as much as you do here.... I didn't want get married—how could I do that just to get the "papers"? In the press, reporters asked people, "Would you mind if your daughter were to marry Assane?" But I told reporters I wouldn't marry because I am not in love with anybody, and I would have to get divorced, yet that is contrary to my religious principles. When you mention religion, everybody supports you, the priests and the rest.... I could ask for money to pay the card, because I am poor.... But I need to eat, I need a house, and how can I pay such an amount if I don't have it? How could I accept it as a present, if I don't owe anything to anybody? And, finally, how is it that I have to do the mandatory military service if I don't like it and if in my country only those who freely want do it? I owe nothing to the Spanish state, I have been here for only three years. I work all day long and I still haven't been able to save a cent.
>
> The civil governor was amazed, because he received letters supporting me from so many people and associations—even a French NGO, I don't remember the name. But he said, "This guy doesn't love Spain, he's fooling us, because he has been offered women and he rejects them.[33] As for money, he says that if he had money he would use it to eat and feed his family. He refuses to do military service, which is a duty for anyone who becomes a Spaniard!"
>
> We tried to get the papers deeming me an "adoptive son." We collected signatures, and E.A. went on a hunger strike. We got all sorts of documents to prove my attachment [*arraigo*]—a whole file of "papers."... Finally the governor agreed to stop the deportation procedure, but he insisted I go back to Senegal to get the visa, because

making an exception for me would be unfair to other immigrants. We agreed to this on the condition that they would guarantee that I would be given the visa in Senegal, and my friends threatened to take further actions if I was not back in twenty five days. The governor said "I believe people here love you, but why?" There was nothing special about me though, except that people did love me and they saw what was happening as an injustice. So finally the authorities signed the papers. And I left for Senegal to come back in a month.

Assane's testimony about this process underscores the importance of the solidarity with which his friends, and Spanish people in general, supported the rights he and other illegal immigrants claimed. Around this case, a group of people in the area of Alfaya started to work for the rights of immigrants, developing networks to provide them food, lodging, and work. In the next chapter I will analyze in detail how this group led by E.A. organized the resistance of immigrants in 1991 in the valley of Alfaya. As I will show, the 1991 movement encountered widespread opposition on the part of mainstream villagers, in spite of the massive support Assane's case gathered. The reason is that most villagers did not share the radical notion of human rights advocated by Assane's supporters. Assane was not categorized as an immigrant, with the negative connotations this label would come to have in later years, but as an "honest person" who did not bother anybody and was trying to make a better living for himself and his family. People told me they supported Assane's case in the name of "solidarity," "pity," "compassion," or even because Assane "was a nice boy."

Such personalization of Assane's cause was not representative of what most immigrants came to experience, because, as I will explain later, a more impersonal process of professionalization and routine began to characterize how groups, associations, labor unions, and NGOs assisted immigrants and defended their rights. Solidarity for specific persons was only common in the initial period of immigration to Andalusia and Spain (1985–1990). As a villager told me in 1994, "people are sensitive about a particular person; as immigration becomes a mass phenomenon and immigrants seem to be interchangeable, the tendency progressively is one of decoupling a given person's 'problem' from the political issues behind it" (J.O., summer 1994). Another villager explained it in a different way: "When people learn how immigrants lived and the multiple needs they had, people reacted positively. They brought food to the parish, and so, because when they see the human being—they forget about 'Moors' or 'blacks.'... When you touch the sentimental vein, you get positive attitudes. But if you approach immigrants from a political perspective, connected to local political conflicts, then people can have a very negative reaction against immigrants" (D.P., spring 1995).

Assane's account of his actual interaction with the civil governor reveals another attitude that came to count against immigrants: an implicitly nationalist reaction that immigrants lack loyalty to Spain. The governor's casual remarks during the course of negotiation over Assane's case reveal that he infers Assane's lack of loyalty from his refusal to marry, to do military service, to apply for asylum, to be nationalized, or even to invest his earnings in acquiring papers. Statements such as Assane's that "I don't owe anything to Spain" (even though Assane clearly wants to live in Andalusia and considers himself "half Andalusian") infuriated people who linked rights to national identity. Dominant discourse and practices assume that immigrants should be grateful for the restricted possibilities Spain offers them, given that Spain requires no corresponding obligations, especially in the case of illegal immigrants. In this view, for immigrants to deserve rights equal to those of Spaniards, some "basic obligations" ought to be expected of them.[34] Furthermore, those who "love Spain" should demonstrate their loyalty overtly in bureaucratic, economic, ideological, and even sentimental acts and deeds that also demonstrate the lesser importance of immigrants' links to their countries of origin. This commonsense logic of nationalism, which the reader will see in play often throughout this book, thus rejects transnational loyalties and rights in origin.

Notes

1. For a complete reference of the normative on the alien population in Spain, see note 2 of the introduction.
2. As explained in the introduction, I will retain the commonly used term "illegal" in this book. For the sake of clarity I will not use quotation marks with this term.
3. As discussed in more detail in chapter 6, this is in direct contradiction to the assumption made in some sociological literature about Spain as being only a "way through" for people migrating to northern European countries (e.g., Robin 1992).
4. I find it useful to follow Kearney's distinction between "boundaries" as "legal spatial delimitations of nations," and "border areas," defined as "geographic and cultural zones ... which can vary independently of formal boundaries" (1991, 53). The concept is analytically related to that of "borderland" used by recent literature to refer to areas where there are several cultures coexisting either in a context of domination and subordination or as creating new spaces of hybridization (Alzandúa 1987; Rosaldo 1989).
5. The Andalusian writer Muñoz Molina was accused of reinforcing latent Spanish racism against Andalusians (exemplified in the description of Andalusians by the well-known philosopher Ortega y Gasset), in his representation of Andalusian folklore and politics in his polemical article "Mandatory Andalusia," which criticizes the new search for the "authentic tradition of Andalusia": "In those obscure times, well before the foundation of the Junta de Andalucía, and through its official organ of *andalucización*, the so-called South Channel [of regional Television], almost no Andalusian knew what he or she was.... Most of us grew up without knowing that our land, apart from being poor and far away from everything, was an Andalusian land. The most salient image of Andalusia was that of the scenarios of those *españoladas* of the

[movies].... Even with democracy and leftist governments, Andalusia did not get rid of igno-rance, backwardness, superstitions, or folklore" (El País, March 13, 1996). See also the section "Andalusia's Muslim Imagery" in this chapter.

6. Although this phenomenon is clearly less acute in Andalusia, especially in rural Andalusia, questioning of "Spain" as a "nation" has rendered Spanish nationalism a rather "politically incorrect" position in most intellectual, political, and in generally progressive circles. Even though the discussion of the problematic status of a common Spanish national identity is beyond the scope of this work, readers should take into account the political and cultural force of various national identities within the Spanish territory, which are officially recognized by the 1978 Spanish Constitution.

7. After the interlude of autarky during the early Francoist dictatorship, Spain progressively aligned itself with Western developed countries, first through its military and economic pact with the United States (1953), and then through preferential commercial agreements with the EC (during the late 1960s), the death of the dictator (1975), and incorporation into NATO (1982) and the European Community (1986). The U.S.-Spain agreement established the basis of what has been called the "Spanish economic miracle," which produced accelerated eco-nomic development during the 1960s (see Colectivo IOE, C. 1987).

8. For example, over two-thirds of Spanish foreign trade is EU-related, and pan-European com-petition for increasingly liberalized markets of goods, services, and capital is a current reality in the Spanish economy. In addition, Spain has benefited from European "structural funds" designed to modernize the infrastructures and income levels of underdeveloped EU regions.

9. The common interest referred to in the text appears to stand above the many conflicts of inter-ests arising from the plurinational nature of the state. See note 6 for the problematic status of a "Spanish national identity." See Braudel 1972 for a historical approach to the Mediterranean.

10. One of the first official statistics on the relation between immigration and crime was used by Planas Cercós, chief administrative officer of the Civil Government of Barcelona (1990), who claimed that foreigners were responsible for as much as 20 percent of all criminal acts in 1988. As has been happening since then, these statistics include detentions of irregular immigrants, thus considerably inflating the numbers for "delinquency" among foreigners (see Hall et al. 1978 for a critical analysis of the use of crime statistics in Great Britain).

11. Beginning in 1985, European migratory policies were developed in several intergovernmental arenas: the Group of Schengen, the "Ad Hoc" group on immigration, and the group of TREVI. The European Parliament has several times criticized the agreements for their extra-communitarian character and for the secrecy of their resolutions. One of the main conse-quences of this is that security and administrative practices are not subject to supranational control, or even to national parliamentary or juridical control. The overall goal of these ad hoc groups is the elimination of border controls among participating countries. In practice, emphasis has been on establishing common European immigration and security policies, including the creation of a computerized database of police and judicial records, the Schengen Information System, which will deploy terminals in all border posts and police stations.

12. Records of parliamentary discussions, in Corredera and Díez 1994, 134.

13. For the first good overview on immigration in Spain, see Colectivo IOE 1987.

14. Several articles of the LOE were afterwards declared unconstitutional by the Constitutional Court, such as art. 34 to which this lawyer was referring, as well as arts. 7 and 8, prohibiting the unionizing of "illegal" workers and art. 26, on detention and expulsion procedures. In fact, at present the immigrant who wants to appeal an order of deportation can do so, but appeal will not stop deportation. In practice, most Third World immigrants are left at the mercy of inconsistent and often arbitrary decisions by administrative actors to write up a deportation order or accept a document as valid.

15. Art. 12 of the LOE 7/1985 states: "para la concesion de la visa se atenderá al interés del estado Español y de sus nacionales. La denegación no necesitará ser motivada" [in granting a visa, the interests of the Spanish state and its nationals should be taken into account. The refusal to grant the visa does not require justification]. Visa applicants have to prove that they can support themselves during their stay in Spain (around $500.00 are required, plus $5.00 for each day of stay) and that they have a job that requires them to return. They also have to show their return ticket to the authorities. Applicants also need documents from their home countries, and often have to put up money to pay for intermediaries, translations, and trips within the country, as well as to tap the network of well-positioned contacts such as religious leaders, civil servants, or policemen (see chapters 4 and 6). Poor people from the Third World find it difficult to justify self-support and to obtain required documents, and many times they just prefer to cross the border illegally, which appears to be a more accessible alternative. The coordinator of the NGO Almería Acoge told us that "nobody would risk his or her life crossing the Straits of Gibraltar in such horrible conditions if they could come with a temporal visa." NGOs in Andalusia blame the state for the continuous deaths in the Straits, with demonstrations in front of the civil government wielding the slogan "*No More Deaths in the Straits. For a Solidary Mediterranean.*"

16. The law establishes multiple formal requirements for staying legally in the country. The stay must be renewed every year in most cases. In practice many "legal" immigrants are in the process of renewing their residence and job permits. While awaiting response from the authorities (which often takes many months), they will continuing working, sometimes in an economic sector other than that approved by the Ministry of Labor, and they may move from the place designated in their residence permit without notifying the police. Any of these situations is defined by the law as illegal and can be punished with expulsion from the country (for a case study, see Suárez-Navaz 1995a, 1998b).

17. The renewal of the work permit is not, as I explained previously, automatic; it depends on the "interests of the state." Many immigrants who have acquired legal status become illegal again when their initial work permit expires, sometimes because they failed to pay required taxes, sometimes due to employers' unwillingness to hire people who might bring attention to their underground economic practices.

18. My fieldwork confirmed this: I was stopped much more frequently when I was with African immigrants, either in the car or just walking around in the street or in the village. Even though I am Spanish, the fact that I was born in Colombia (as indicated on my Spanish National Document of Identity, or DNI [Documento Nacional de Identidad]) proved to be an additional source of suspicion. African immigrants use to joke about this, saying that it was good to be stopped with me because the stereotype of Colombians being drug dealers attenuated the attention paid to them.

19. T.L. was referring to *Mizan* as a transcendental law of history, a kind of natural moral law.

20. Caro Baroja 1977; Guichard 1976.

21. See Valderrama 1956 for Spain's cultural action in the Moroccan protectorate.

22. Junta de Andalucía, brochure of the cultural and tourist program *El Legado Andalusí. El Arte de Vivir.*

23. Sibley 1995, 18; see also González Alcantud 1993.

24. The concept *convivencia* in this context refers to the Muslims, Christians, and Jews living side by side in medieval al-Andalus. Much has been published in the press about this historical epoch, but too often authors enter in a debate that reinscribes the ethnic and religious antagonism between Arabs and Andalusians, "Moors" and Christians (see Glick 1992 and the last section of chapter 6 for a theoretical approach; see also, for instance, the interviews with Domínguez Ortiz and Roger Garaudy in *El Ideal*, January 16, 1992 and January

17, 1992 respectively, or the articles by Blanco Zuloaga in *El Ideal,* July 26, 1992 and August 8, 1992).

25. Islamic associations that have been especially active are the Muslim Community of Al-Andalus in Granada, the Morabitúm Collective, and the "Andalusian Identity" platform, all of which favor artistic expressions of Muslim Al-Andalus and call for "reconciliation, peace, and tolerance, which characterize Andalusian spirit" (*El Ideal,* January 2, 1992). On the other side of the "battle," the association Bernal Diaz del Castillo (named after one of the Spanish conquerors in America) calls for Andalusians to "reclaim our heroic past, to challenge politicians, especially those who want to bury our nationality, in which we vibrantly live the reality of the old Spain" (*El Ideal,* January 2, 1992). The following press title gives the flavor of the polemic: "Proto-Islamic Groups Cry for Granada While "Ultras" Hail Victory over the Infidels" (*El Ideal,* January 3, 1992).

26. Quoted in Martínez Montálvez, *El País,* November 5, 1992, "Temas de Nuestra Epoca," 4.

27. See Martínez Alier 1971 for work conditions for "outsiders" in rural Andalusia in Francoist times.

28. I want to thank Fernando Alvarez Silva, curator of the library of the Spanish Migration Institute, for having recommended this book to me in one of my many visits to the overworked library which he and others have transformed into an unparalleled site of archival research.

29. After the end of Arab political presence in Spain by the end of the sixteen century, the construction of the "Spanish nation" characteristically depended on the construction of the "other" as a threat to the "universal destiny of Spanish civilization." "Purity of blood" is a clear example of biologist and racial criteria used by Spanish Catholic nation-building to expel Jews and Muslims during the fifteenth through the seventeenth centuries (Bataillon 1950; Castro 1973, 1983; Martínez Alier 1974). In colonial times, similar criteria were juxtaposed to more "open" notions of belonging, which required the assimilation (i.e., conversion) of the "ignorant" autochthonous peoples of the Americas and legitimized a necessary tutelage of those considered under the colonial logic as inferiors (see among others, Bowser 1974; Elliot 1987; Hamilton 1963; Lockhart 1968; Phelan 1978). The "foreign threat" also included European Protestants, who were considered "heretics" in the sixteenth century. Later, in the Francoist regime, Protestants were considered a contaminated source of liberal ideas that threatened the "eternal values of the Spanish spirit" (Arguedas 1968; Fraser 1973; Moreno Navarro 1986).

30. The following quotes are all from Assane D., a pioneer Senegalese in Alfaya.

31. Much has been written about the autonomy of "communitarian pueblos" (or other similar communities) in conflict management as flowing from egalitarian ideology (see Arguedas 1968; Behar 1986; Contreras 1991; Costa 1898; Freeman 1970; Greenwood 1987; Pitt Rivers 1966). While the original emphasis on egalitarianism has been questioned on the ground of class or regional differences, the collective basis of struggle for justice over legality prevails in these studies (see, among many others, Arguedas 1968; Collier 1987; Contreras 1991; Costa 1978; Gilmore 1980; Luque Baena 1974; Martínez Alier 1971).

32. A law passed three years later that greatly broadened police prerogatives, and was strongly opposed by political and civil society. This Organic Law of Citizenship Security (1/1992, February 21) is popularly known by the minister who passed it as "the Corcuera law," or more graphically as "the law of kick down the door." It was finally ruled unconstitutional by the Constitutional Court in the sentence 341/1993. Its application to immigrants was strongly denounced as racist. The law mandated that immigrants carry identification allowing them to reside and work legally in Spain (art. 11). The police were allowed to require "suspicious" people in public as well as in private spaces to identify themselves (art. 2). The law gave police the power to "retain" (instead of just detaining) and confine suspects for an indefinite amount of time (art. 19) (see Vidal Gil 1995, 120–21).

33. For many "illegal" immigrants, to "get a Spanish woman" is the only avenue available for regularizing immigration status. The acceptance of polygamy allows some immigrants to marry a second wife in Spain while maintaining other(s) in Senegal. In chapter 6, I will discuss how women are also used by the immigrant's family back in Senegal to preserve the links and obligations of the emigrants toward them. In both poles of this transnational social sphere, women are too often represented by men as icons of national loyalty, thus unveiling the profound sexism involved in the remaking of national imageries.

34. This is so despite strong movements of resistance to sanctioned obligations toward the state, such as the novel movement for *insumisión* (civil disobedience), an active and highly politicized social movement directed against military service and more generally against the role of the army in Spanish and world society.

3. PUTTING IMMIGRANTS IN THEIR PLACE

*T*he day I arrived in the Valley of Alfaya, Andalusia, in July of 1992, I was invited to a gathering organized by a local nongovernmental organization (NGO) working for immigrants called "Everybody's Land" in Arabic and Spanish (Ardo el-Jamia/Tierra de Todos). African immigrants waited outside for the party to begin. They sat on the stairs of the town hall, a white building that dominates one of the main plazas of the village, in which one also finds a kiosk where drinks are sold, a market, and a fountain called the Pilón. I was struck by the casual and carefree attitude of the large group of African immigrants, most of whom were probably living in Spain illegally. That summer there had been widespread and intense concern in Spain about the so-called new invasion of Africans, and it would have been unthinkable for immigrants to sit chatting at the entrance of the city hall in Granada or Madrid. The party soon began, and immigrants shared food, music, and conversation for some hours with NGO volunteers, most of them young women. After the party ended, some went to the local pubs for dancing and drinks. A few days later, I myself moved from Granada to Alfaya to begin my research, since such quotidian interethnic interactions provided me with a unique environment in which to learn more about African immigrants in Andalusia.

At that point in the summer there were more than one hundred immigrants scattered about the agricultural valley that spreads out around the village of Alfaya, most of whom slept in the open air under the chestnut trees or in small outlying farming huts *(cortijos)* in the countryside. I knew that during the previous summer of 1991 there had been an unofficial shelter for all immigrants furnished by some neighbors and by Africans themselves, but this year the project had been completely discarded. It was apparent, however, that some of the immigrants felt quite familiar with the place and they spoke self-assuredly about their

---

rights as workers. Soon I learned that most of them actually spent many hours in the main plaza and its surroundings, which was, in fact, the center of most political, commercial, and hiring practices in the village. Very early in the morning they gathered in the bar Ramiro, at the village's entrance, to offer themselves as day laborers for local peasants in the harvest of tomatoes, cauliflower, or peppers. Those who were not lucky enough to find a job wandered around hoping for a late work offer; they either had coffee in one of the bars or sat by the old fountain, the Pilón, together with some old village men, letting time go slowly by, watching the people and happenings in the plaza. Around lunchtime the peasants returned from the fields, immigrants and families sharing the ride back to the village. A mixed crew of Moroccan and Andalusian lettuce pickers might have an aperitif with their employer in the bar Ramiro while accounts were settled with workers. In the evening, while most villagers rested at home with their families, Africans gathered around the Pilón, talking about their day, telling newcomers about the village, calling their families from the pay phone next to the kiosk, or buying food for dinner with an established or improvised group. Especially on the weekends, some Africans who enjoyed Spanish nightlife put on their best clothes and went out, like other young people in the village, to have a drink at a pub, dance at the disco, and chat with young women or other acquaintances.

Gradually, however, during the time that I conducted fieldwork, things changed dramatically. As the years passed, it became evident that immigrants would continue to come, for there was considerable need for a cheap, flexible labor force at the peak of the agricultural season. Yet they had no established quarters in the village. Villagers perceived the presence of immigrants as a major problem, and local as well as regional governments initiated social programs for providing immigrants with housing to normalize the situation. The idea of the shelter was reimplemented, this time with official support and all of the legal and sanitary requirements. Immigrants organized themselves into two legally registered associations that were founded in the village. In spite of these visible processes of apparent normalization, it was indisputable that immigrants had been gradually displaced from the physical and symbolic center of the village to its margins and that they themselves were less optimistic about their ability to influence the handling of their situation. As early as 1994, immigrants found they were no longer welcome to gather in the plaza, to share the Pilón with locals as they had done before. Several bar owners had begun to refuse service to Africans, and some bars even banned their entrance. The owner of the kiosk complained whenever immigrants asked him for change to make a phone call. Knowing they were no longer welcome in Alfaya's central public spaces, most immigrants learned to avoid them. They stayed in what villagers considered was their place, with other Africans at the shelter. The number and quality of interethnic interactions were thus reduced dramatically.

As described in this vignette, there was a remarkable shift within a few years in the use of the space of the village, from interethnic sharing of public space to gradual segmentation. This chapter aims to explain the transformation illustrated by this vignette and to provide understanding of how Andalusians and Africans have made sense of it. Sociospatial segmentation was not new in Alfaya, but the peasants' political and cultural struggle in the transition to democracy constructed a new open and participatory public space meant to include all of those who "worked with their own hands" to make an honest living. The arrival of African immigrants with no place to stay and their occupation of this purportedly open public space generated tension and concern among villages, as well as political struggle over equality, rights, and privileges, in which the limits of belonging, nationality, and citizenship were negotiated.

In this chapter I describe the process of forming spaces and boundaries that determine who belongs where and why, who has the right to move across and to settle in a specific space, what the requirements are to dwell in a particular site, and how these requirements are maintained in practice. I will focus on the construction of the "problem" of immigration in the village of Alfaya and on how social perception of immigrants' lack of a place evoked a chaotic sense of immigrants' threats to morality, ideology, security, and hygiene. The socially constructed need to solve immigrants' lack of place involved not only official and alternative strategies to provide immigrants with housing, but also a broader intention of putting immigrants in their (social) place.

My interest is to better understand the processes underlying the reproduction of a segmented social space in the Andalusian rural landscape. Such reproduction of spatial segmentation among social groups should not be understood, though, as a mechanical functioning of capitalist social relations, where a new group of persons substitutes others in their location as a dominated class. Instead of analyzing the current location of immigrant workers within a space treated as "dead nature" where social relations take place, I incorporate the efforts of critical geography to understand spatiality as simultaneously a social product (or outcome) and a shaping force (or medium) in social life (Soja 1989, 7). For this purpose, I found it essential to engage in ethnohistorical research on the meanings associated with diverse spaces in the valley, as well as with the inhabitants who populate, cross, trespass, or avoid those spaces, and with the allegedly natural way of life associated with each form of relationship with certain spaces.

As I will show in the next section, the traditional forces of segmentation in Andalusian society have to be considered as actively informing today's creation of difference. My analysis illustrates through an empirical case how ethnic difference is constructed upon historical stereotypes of class and space allocation. By looking at the inner boundaries in a particular locality or territory and how they change through time, difference emerges as a social construction legitimating how dominant groups distance themselves from others located at the margins of purportedly normal styles of life, as in nomadism, in unconventional housing, and in habitation of areas represented as threatening, dangerous, or illegal.

Landscapes of Inequality

In this section I will show how the structural position of the new temporal workers reproduces routines of spatial and social differentiation present in the area since Francoist times. My argument is that spatial segmentation, residential differentiation, and forced nomadism have all produced, now as in the past, stereotypes and prejudices about the most underprivileged groups—those living in the margins of the territory or with a seminomadic lifestyle, whose members are pictured as being "closer to animals" than humans in a physical and behavioral sense. These stereotypes naturalize life conditions that result from socioeconomic and political inequalities, and more important, they situate people thus located in space in a lower level of morality, creating the collective need to "keep one's distance" from them and to keep them in their "proper" place.

The distribution of the valley's space is characterized, now as in the past, by a high degree of spatial segmentation. Up to the 1960s, the spatial organization mirrored the political and economic pyramid dominated by local *caciques* who effectively controlled the economic, political, and legal institutions with the help of the infamous Civil Guard. Theirs were the richest families, with the largest and most fertile lands, living in the center of the village. Further toward the periphery lived people with less or no power, either in economic or political terms. The group of small proprietors, who nevertheless depended on local salaried work to supplement their harvest, lived closest to the rich both in spatial and social senses. Next, a large group of poor landless families occupied the characteristic *chozas*, the thatched cottages or huts at the edge of town with enclosures shared with a few domestic animals. Finally, beyond the village, scattered around the valley and in the surrounding mountains, were people whose style of life was considered marginal, living in semiclandestine or semislave conditions, such as shepherds, *cortijeros*, or *maquis* (postwar republican rebels).

As I explained in chapter 1, the social structure was polarized between the *caciques* and the rest of the villagers, who directly or indirectly depended on salaried work provided by landed proprietors and on the decisions of political bosses. Among the villagers there were strong differences based on lifestyle, access to public spaces, and ability to combine economic resources to be able to stay in the village. Although all of them depended on elites to a degree, their location within the territory and their residential patterns clearly marked different ranks of social status. To be considered a full member of the community, one necessarily had to live within the urban limits of one of the valley villages. Children used to gang up by territorial area and challenge those living in other neighborhoods. As one villager told me: "there were four main groups in this village, and also there were groups in the other two villages. It was a spatial division and not a class one, but we all knew what our place was" (D.P., spring 1995). Segmentation and separation among the different groups was ritualized in almost every aspect of daily life: people knew what spaces "belonged" to them and where their presence was considered a challenge and a threat. There were bars for the rich and bars for the poor; the church spatially separated the front pews with comfortable seats reserved for the rich from the back of the nave, where poor people attended the mass standing. The same separations were evident in the village's movie theater, in parades, and in school.[1]

The poorest of the valley lived outside the villages wherever they could survive their desperate quest for daywork in the face of hunger, indebtedness, humiliations, dependence, and submission or resistance to the local elite. Marginal types abounded in the sierra,[2] always controlled and persecuted by the Civil Guard. They might survive on chickpeas harvested in hidden and rocky areas of the mountain, by gathering almonds, medical herbs, firewood, or coal, and by exchanging these products for bread, oil, eggs, or cash to feed their families. The *maquis* also lived in the mountains, hidden from the authorities and scarcely surviving in their desperate resistance to Francoist revenge and persecution. Many families were unable to feed their children and had to send them to work in the sierra as shepherds in exchange for food. Such shepherds lived on their own in small, isolated *cortijos*, taking care of others' cattle all day, eating some chickpeas for dinner, and sleeping with the animals directly on the straw, or if they were lucky, on some bags of wood (A.F., spring 1995, among other testimonies). Full families of *cortijeros* also lived this way, scattered in the valley and in the mountains. They rarely stepped foot in the village and formed, in the eyes of villagers, a "different" group of people whose lifestyle was closer to that of animals than "proper persons." Saying that a person "speaks as a *cortijero*" or that a woman "is only a *cortijera*" still conjures up notions of a kind of person who does not satisfy the minimum requirements of civilized life, who has never attended school, is ignorant, and whose morality is suspicious.

Poor people who were not able to live in the valley and feed their families were deemed even lower in the moral scale. These poor were the temporary migrant rural workers who were born in the village and considered themselves part of the community, but who were always on the move. Nomadism affected the poorest families, those living in *chozas* and *cortijos* in the margins of the community, functioning as a reserve army of labor to keep wages down.[3] As a general pattern in internal migration, whole families would go off to work in the cotton fields of Seville province or in the olive fields of Jaen. Migrant work is part of Andalusians' collective memory—even in recent experience. A woman who was only thirty-five years old in 1995 told me:

> Ever since I was a child, I can remember migrating with my family.... We only stayed in the village a couple of months, when there wasn't any work available anywhere else. If we returned, we would be off right away on another trip.... All of us would go, because that way we earned more money. We all worked, and they paid the work of two children like us more or less like my mother. We couldn't stay behind anyway, because there was nobody to care for us, and as emigrants we at least ate everyday.... In each trip we had to rent a truck to transport our furniture, for lack of a better name: a portable stove, four chairs, a table, and a mattress. We often had to go from one *cortijo* to another, because here in Andalusia landowners only provided migrants with empty and generally semidestroyed places for quarters. We had to clean it, we repaired the roof, we put something over the holes of the windows to keep the cold out.... Rarely could we save money, as patrons always paid us less than they had agreed to, either because we had to repay them for food, or because they would refuse to pay children, or whatever.... But nobody said a word, because there were a lot of people in the same situation. If you wouldn't accept the conditions, others would. This was worse than the Third World, this was a Fourth or Fifth World, but you had better hold your tongue because otherwise the police's response was no joke. (A.R., spring 1995)

Temporary migrant workers from Alfaya were the first to emigrate north to Europe, even though local *caciques* did their best to prevent this so as to preserve employment that kept workers in poverty and attached to the village, always anxious to work under any condition landowners imposed. *Caciques* realized that for the first time these families' high mobility might be an asset, once the foreign demand for Spanish guest workers grew, offering better work and living conditions than the poor Andalusian families had ever seen. "Abroad everything was better: the food, the bed, the money, the treatment.... We felt like kings in comparison to the living we had as emigrants in Andalusia" (C.G., summer 1994). Émigrés needed certain documents to qualify for the foreign guest-worker programs, including certificates of good conduct. But the local elite would refuse to provide them with good-conduct papers, arguing that they couldn't vouch for how migrant workers behaved outside the village and sometimes even questioning whether the workers were adequately "patriotic." But there was no stopping the emigration, which quickly swelled beyond the capacity of the Andalusian landed elite to control it. Landless workers were the first to break the chain of poverty by emigrating, and they were soon joined by smallholders and other villagers who had managed to avoid migrant work during the postwar years.

The itinerant dayworkers who initiated the exodus of workers and peasants had long experienced exclusion from the village and its institutions and stigmatization for their nomadic lifestyle, which villagers associated with Gypsies.

When I asked villagers about families of emigrants they always said something like "Poor people, they lived like Gypsies." Gypsies are perceived in Spain, and especially in Andalusia, as a "race" apart from Spanish people, characterized as "primitive," tribal, and always on the move, preferring liberty and autonomy over honest work.[4] While itinerant dayworkers resented such racist stereotyping of themselves, probably because they shared stereotypes about Gypsies and did not want to be compared to them, there was little they could do to avoid it. They knew that most villagers, even if poor, tended to look down on them as inferior people: "To tell you the truth, I have always felt very marginalized. I couldn't attend school, I couldn't go to mass or to the parade because I didn't have a proper outfit and I knew that villagers would laugh at me.... So those of us who were always on the move banded together when we returned to the village. We were friends because we worked together in the cotton fields of the Morche, in France, and other places.... A common style of life joined us. Of course, there have always been groups" (A.R., spring 1995). Exclusion and grouping thus combined to keep itinerant workers in their place at the margins of town.

Access to space in towns like Alfaya could not be struggled over during the time of the Francoist dictatorship. By the mid 1970s, however, in the midst of a national transition to democracy, grassroots mobilization in the valley began to challenge the monopoly of elite classes over the use of public spaces. The Communists who held office after the first democratic election in 1979 worked hard to redefine the closed and hierarchical notion of community. They denounced the terrible conditions under which peasants had labored and struggled to change them. By incorporating those at the margins, the Communists challenged the sharp segmentation of public space that local *caciques* had maintained. To do this, they revived memories of how elites had hounded nineteenth-century bandits and Civil War *maquis* into the hills in political persecution, and commemorated the *choza* as the most representative element of rural workers' lives. They also worked to reincorporate emigrants working abroad into the village by changing the date of the local parade to the middle of summer, when most émigrés returned to spend their holidays, and by persuading them of the political importance of their vote. These actions contributed to greater equality among the classes in distribution through and access to space. People rebuilt their houses, the *chozas* disappeared, and the *cortijos* were abandoned.

But when the first African immigrants arrived in the valley in the late 1980s, they once again inhabited the margins of Alfaya, scattered around the valley like the *maquis* and shepherds of thirty years ago. Some lived in abandoned *cortijos*, others in an irrigation pump house borrowed from a farmer. Some lived in caves or in abandoned cars. These areas at the margins of the valley had always been patrolled by the infamous Civil Guard, whose agents searched for political outlaws and penalized poor landless people who tried to plant chickpeas in the sierra to live on. Now African immigrants found themselves the object of Civil Guard surveillance, justified as the quest for the so-called illegals as well as for those who employed them without paying all of the taxes required by the state. As in the past, villagers themselves thus became indirect targets of law enforcement through the surveillance and control of the marginal areas where supposed outlaws or illegal people dwelled.

Africans in Alfaya: "No Place to Stay"

The increasing presence of African immigrants in the 1990s produced unprecedented concern and public attention in the village. This was so despite the relatively small number of Africans[5] and their fundamental similarity to other transient workers (including the so-called urban tribes and Gypsies)[6] in their socioeconomic situation and in strategies for coping with lack of housing and other basic needs. One of the main reasons for Alfayans' extraordinary concern was that the presence of African immigrants in Alfaya both refracted and resonated with two interrelated problems of national and supranational scope: (1) the redefinition of Spanish and European identity vis-à-vis extracommunitarian (i.e., from outside of the EC) immigration, and (2) the need to strengthen control of the boundaries between the First and Third Worlds.

Local construction of the so-called problem of immigration came at a time of "moral crisis" generated by mass media coverage of immigrants' crossing of the Mediterranean frontier and by other public discourses on the need to control southern immigration.[7] Akin to the way mass media were representing immigrants, Alfayans began to imagine them as a burgeoning multitude—threatening, chaotic, and polluting.

This negative representation of immigrants, however, was not the initial one. Rather, a complex interaction of current structural forces and institutional practices with villagers' own recent experience of emigration, segregation, and marginality initially led Alfayans to sympathize with immigrants as being similar to themselves in some respects. The very first African immigrants found an inclusive sense of community, which was much more welcoming to them than to later immigrants. As discussed in the first chapter, the village's narratives of origin depict humble migrant peasants as having worked arduously to forge the valley as a productive place open to all who work honestly to make a living, in opposition to the parasitic life of *señoritos*. In this narrative, a work ethic links both modern notions of people's sovereignty and indigenous peasant ideologies to a strong element of class solidarity. African immigrants, like Alfayans of an earlier era, were thought to have been forced by circumstances to migrate, and thus ought to have rights including the right to a place to stay while they worked in the valley. In this context, Africans' lack of place soon became the crucial issue in Alfayans' construction of immigration as a problem.

More than one hundred people lacked a roof to sleep under after their arduous travel, no place to prepare a warm meal, no shower to clean off residues of chemicals used in the intensive production of tomatoes. Villagers considered such circumstances immoral, unhygienic, an affront to their own ideology of worker rights, and a problem of security. Everyone was dismayed by having immigrants living scattered in ruined farm dwellings or even under the trees of a small forest cove near Alfaya. Lack of proper place was a powerful cultural symbol for chaos, misery, and unfairness, and it engendered an intense political struggle between the local NGO and the municipal council over allocation of space for migrants. Soon enough, both provincial and national governments entered the fray, intervening contradictorily—sometimes striving for an inclusive posture toward immigrants yet sometimes for their exclusion. The struggle redrew the boundaries constituting Alfayan peasant collective identity.

Sheltering the Homeless: Immigrants' Place as a Right and an Arena for Consciousness-Building

The pertinacious conflict about whether, where, and how to house immigrants blew up in May 1991, just before municipal elections. E.A., the villager leading a strong opposition movement in defense of immigrants, began a hunger strike on the doorsteps of the town hall, forcing villagers and the press to take notice and bringing immigrants' concerns to the center of the local moral landscape. E.A. argued for immigrant rights, not on the basis of his political party platform, but rather in terms of broader worker and human rights. The invocation of this ideological framework hailed a broad audience of left-progressive as well as Catholic villagers, many of whom had experienced emigration and poverty themselves and perceived migration as a legitimate endeavor.

E.A. addressed his claims directly to local authorities, demanding that they recognize African immigrants as the village's inhabitants and workers regardless of their legal status. Alluding to moral and ideological principle paramount in the valley's identity, E.A. advocated frontal resistance to the Alien Law as infringing peasants' autonomy to define rules of residence in the valley. Together with followers, E.A. and his village supporters constituted the local NGO, Everybody's Land, in defense of this autonomy and immigrant rights. The NGO organized a housing shelter in 1991 and a camping ground in 1992 as spaces both of resistance to European racism and of identity formation for immigrants. Both initiatives challenged the authority of either the national state, through the Alien Law, or the municipal council to arrogate from villagers the right to allocate space in the valley and to use public space in town. Officials countered with bureaucratic obstacles, physical threats, fines, and a spectacular Civil Guard raid on the camping ground at the end of the summer of 1992. Let us analyze this process now.

The shelter movement drew force from several complementary strands of Alfayans' moral discourse, historical experience, and class consciousness. The appeal to Catholic charity was self-evident and cut across class. Most Andalusians, peasants as well as workers, had themselves experienced the imperative to cross even national borders in search of work to provide food for their families. Migration was thus understandable to all of those who identified with the poor or with workers, whether they had migrated or not. Assane's plight had tapped all of these currents, especially among the village's majority left-aligned electorate, and municipal authorities did not want to risk measures against Africans that might be seen as attacks on vulnerable workers.

Yet Spain's new alignment with the European Community, enactment of the LOE, and construction of a new welfare system were all contributing to a new legal, political, and cultural spatial frame much less sympathetic to African immigrants than that held locally in Alfaya. Local authorities were trapped in the contradictory position of having to enforce legality at the local level (the LOE granted no right to a place for illegal immigrants) while at the same time honoring the ideological and moral principles of those who had elected them. The immigration "problem" brings crucial issues of citizenship and rights into local political struggle: What should be the scope of the welfare system and to whom should it extend? What are the requirements for belonging to the community in order to hold such rights? And should the meaning of leftist politics and class orientation mean revolutionary struggle framed in an international space, or reformist social democracy as framed in the arena of the European Union?[8]

Most Alfayans accepted that African immigrants were "a disadvantaged group of workers with limited claims to the resources and protections of the society which appropriates their labor" (Morris 1994, 138). What they disputed was whether immigrants should be considered "outsiders" who had no legitimate claim on the community's resources and protections, or "international workers" and "human beings" whose rights should be acknowledged by any democratic country. Immigrants, by their very presence, put the issue of membership on the table, that is, the issue of citizenship as Marshall established it in his classic work (1950). And in the process of adjusting membership to the new context and historical moment, the very concept of "community" began to be redefined. In fact, the allocation of a place for immigrants should be understood as part of the symbolic process through which a new moral landscape of the village was renegotiated and struggled over (Comaroff and Comaroff 1991, 200 passim).

Municipal authorities withheld official support for a shelter on several grounds. They argued that the shelter did not meet legal requirements for safety and hygiene. They declined to provide light and water services to the shelter because to do so for immigrants would be unjust to "their own people," that is, to other villagers living outside the urban center without utilities. These arguments drew a line between local citizens, to whom municipal authorities were accountable, and foreign workers. One municipal emphasized that legal and political constraints prevented public support for the shelter. Nevertheless, many councilors recognized the need to provide some sort of place for immigrants. So the council proposed to E.A. that the shelter be legalized as a cattle warehouse, thus avoiding protests from villagers sympathetic to the immigrants while sidestepping the issue of whether they could support a shelter for illegal immigrants. E.A. turned this tactic against the incumbent councilors in the electoral campaign. "Local Council in Alfaya Prefers to Provide Water to Animals Rather Than Immigrants" read one press headline. From this moment forward, the immigrant issue remained resolutely intertwined with local political struggles, a situation that has not always favored immigrants.

After the warehouse proposal from the municipal council, E.A. coordinated a group of immigrants and villagers determined to create a place where immigrants could live with dignity. They reconditioned an agricultural warehouse owned by a sympathizer into a shelter for eighty immigrants. Situated at the edge of town near the roadway leading to the northwest, the warehouse required three weeks of collective work to refurbish. One large room served as a dormitory, another smaller room for safekeeping of important papers and valuables, and a room in the west corner as a place to pray. A shower and washstand for clothes were outside by the clothesline. Putting the shelter to use, the collective prepared "humble menus" daily so that nobody would go hungry. The shelter had no electricity, so the collective made do with candles, car batteries, and two camping stoves (Jóvenes 1992, 22–25). The parish priest asked people to contribute mattresses, blankets, and kitchen tools to the shelter. Many villagers did so in the name of the leftist and Catholic principles of solidarity with the disadvantaged, even villagers who opposed official support for an immigrant shelter, such as some of the municipal councilors. Despite villagers' initial involvement, most remained detached from immigrants' problems and from the political and personal wrangling between the municipal council and the shelter's leader, who named the new collective Ardo el-Jamia in Arabic, or Tierra de Todos in Spanish (Everybody's Land). Another local political leader, somewhat detached from the conflict, explained to me that "People respond very well when you touch the sentimental vein, the human part of the story; however, if you steer the problem of immigrants toward the political side with all its local posturing and sectarian factionalism, that's what sets people's nerves on edge." (D.P., spring 1995).

The shelter was thought of in terms of rights, political claims, and an emergent concept of citizenship that equated belonging to residency and work. As described by the leader, the shelter is "a place for building human rights for the most weak and vulnerable, a place for helping the disadvantaged organize for personal and collective realization" (Jóvenes 1992, 24). Even though running a shelter for almost one hundred persons was difficult, most participants agreed that in doing so they created for themselves not merely a place to sleep and eat, but more important, a symbolic space of autonomy and dignity. Here immigrants could discuss their problems and "create a collective identity, a base for hope, and a motivation for struggle" (A.A., Moroccan immigrant, testimonies in *Diario 16*, July 28, 1996).

Leading immigrants, most of whom would later found their own immigrants' associations, were trained almost daily in meetings at the shelter under the direction of the local leader. The meetings organized daily life and discussed collective responses to racist attacks on the shelter or strategies for resisting new measures for enforcing the Alien Law, both along the physical frontier and inland.[9] Immigrants took part in local political struggles and learned about the efficacy of the discourse used to claim their rights as workers and human beings.

At the same time, however, immigrant leaders began to question E.A.'s political strategy of categorical opposition to the local council and use of the press to accuse municipal authorities of racism. Immigrants recognized, before the end of the shelter's first summer, that reactions of villagers and local politicians to accusations of racism could undermine their claims to space as a right. This realization shaped future strategies for claiming rights and defending immigrant interests while avoiding being stereotyped as African outsiders whose claims might appear as threatening and illicit.

Finally, some immigrant leaders began to resist what they considered a paternalistic and homogenizing representation of African immigrants as poor people from the Third World who lacked everything: "We are not just people without things or rights, we also have many rich traditions and important social resources that Western societies lack. In order to show respect toward us it is important to know and stress this also" (M.A., Moroccan immigrant, summer 1992).

Alfaya's shelter was in a way too visible, transgressing locals' sensibilities about of poor people's customary invisibility as well as the anonymity appropriate to private charity. One woman, whose poor family routinely had to beg from neighbors to survive in the 1940s and 1950s, argued that villagers have always wanted to shield their eyes from endemic poverty by keeping charity a private affair: "[Poverty is] to be kept out of sight, you know? People want to give a piece of bread not to stop hunger, but to feel better and stop seeing the starving" (A.R., spring 1995). Another woman, who was part of the municipal council, told me: "Conservatism prevails among peasants. They may talk about solidarity and charity in the name of their Catholic principles, you know? But their objective should be justice, not charity" (T.O., summer 1992). Many villagers also complained that press depictions of the village were unfair: "The notoriety [Alfaya] has gained in the press as a racist village is not only false, but also unfair," several people told me in interviews. Many recognized some discrimination and racist attitudes among a few villagers, but they wanted to keep the village problems within a restricted audience.

Along with the symbolic visibility of the shelter, the concentration of all immigrants in a single space helped to homogenize villagers' images of African immigrants as workers different from the rest of temporary immigrants coming to the village daily. The local press evoked fears of pollution through repeated criticism of the shelter as unsanitary and unhygienic. One of countless such articles claimed that "a shelter with no sanitary or hygienic condition … may bring drugs or sickness to the village" (*El Ideal,* July 11 1991). One young woman told me she overheard discussion of a case of tuberculosis in which several people commented that "you'll see these Moors are going to bring us even AIDS" (M.O., spring 1995).

The belligerent struggle for leadership among immigrants also transcended the limits of the shelter, taking the form of daily squabbles that were all too visible to average villagers. One woman told me: "It was frightening to see all of those men come down from the shelter. I didn't know where to go. It is fine for those emigrants to have a place to stay, poor people, they cannot just have the sky for a roof. But we villagers have also suffered a lot, and we do have a right to breathe at least in our own village, haven't we?" (M.Z., spring 1995). Quarrels took place in the evenings and often involved alcohol and violence, raising anxieties and fear among villagers that they interpreted in terms of the cultural difference of Africans, specifically of "Moors." Some claimed that quarreling was inherent in the character of "Moors," as a tendency to resort to violence, to betray one another, to force their opinions on others, and so forth.

Finally, the use of the shelter as a place for claims-making generated growing concern among villagers about immigrants' political ability to gain rights as members of the community. Some villagers accused African immigrants of claiming special privileges, such as free housing, for which there is no formal or constitutional guarantee. People acknowledged that foreign immigrants had a very difficult situation, yet they resented that immigrants seemed to receive more attention than "normal" citizens do. The mayor told me in 1992 that even though the village was solidary, it could not undertake to solve the problems of Africa. He warned that establishing a shelter would grant immigrants "refuge" independently of their working for local farmers: "We have to be wary of the ghetto effect and of attracting illegal immigrants who will not be able to find work here. Those of them who do not find a job must leave, because this village is not a refugee camp" (P.C., summer 1992). Moral concerns are obliterated by the threat of the shelter's becoming a "refugee camp," an image that conjures up misery, sadness, disease, and concomitant social and labor problems. Rights of foreign workers to have a proper place are not denied, yet moral responsibilities are limited to those who actually work and have been allowed to do so by the state.

Thus, the construction of an unofficial shelter had the unintended consequence of shrinking the initially open notion of migrant workers as entitled to a place in the valley. At the end of that summer, in an emergency meeting of the municipal council to address the "problem" of immigrants, the mayor declared: "This council will not support any discrimination against people who have done nothing to disturb anybody, and that goes for any person wherever he may come from. [Immigrants] are all temporary laborers who come to work here, and only a few have gotten involved in quarrels ... But to those Africans who come to break our rules of *convivencia* we tell them, just as we would tell anybody else, leave this place!" (Municipal Records, September 23, 1991). Immediately after the mayor spoke, a conservative councilor intervened, expressing what my interviews and conversations suggest was the mainstream opinion: "I am not racist, but I just want to lament the lack of security we have now. We want to be as we were before, with every place in town being quiet at night. This week there were a couple of nights with three or four different fights, and even though there is no racism in the village, we have to take measures!" (A.P., Municipal Records, September 23, 1991). A Socialist councilor warned about the potential racist consequences of overemphasizing immigrants' infighting and abuse of alcohol, reminding people that conflicts between local groups of young people were customary in the village: "Anything these people do seems to have much more echo than what any other citizen does. Quarrels have always come about, so we have to act with prudence and rigor if we want to prevent racist attitudes" (J.O., Municipal Record, September 23, 1991).

This councilor touched a crucial issue, that of racialization of the perceived causes of insecurity and lack of control, a feature that came to be ubiquitous in the politics of allocation of space to immigrants. The control of sanitary conditions, violent quarrels, and immigrants' claims became simplified and racialized under the urgency of controlling immigrants' behavior more generally. Increasingly, as local spaces came to be seen as threatened by a potentially polluting invasion of illegal African workers, security and control of local spaces became the dominant idiom for reorganizing the place of immigrants in the valley.

I will explore how these concerns took form in the valley in the public policies enacted since 1992 in chapter 5, while tracing the consequences for immigrants' location in the new segmented social space. But first I wish to analyze the culturally specific and historically situated idioms through which villagers came to understand this move to control immigrants. In the next section I will show how local understandings shifted away from the initially open perception of African immigrants as entitled to a place in the valley because they shared the structural position of so many Alfayans and Andalusians.

Putting Immigrants in Their (Social) Place

As illustrated in the vignette that opens this chapter, the issue of African immigration in the valley was already situated at the center of contention over Alfaya's symbolic, physical, and political space at the time I arrived in the summer of 1992. It is difficult to overemphasize how fiercely and with what passion both immigrants and villagers experienced this process. It seemed to me that nobody in this nook of Andalusia was indifferent to the presence of immigrants; quite the contrary, everybody had clear, even if often contradictory opinions about what the place of immigrants should be, and they expressed it with passion, and even violence. At the beginning of my stay in the valley, though, it was difficult for me to access the different sides of the controversy, because I started my ethnographic research through networks that situated me (and thus strongly limited me) on one side of the debate. Setting up the informal shelter in 1991, as I have just explained, had already polarized the politics of immigrants' location around two extreme positions—that of the local NGO and that of the municipal council—and personal attacks would often overshadow and even displace the debate of ideas. At the beginning of the summer, I did not know much about the cards on the table of the stormy polemic I was witnessing and experiencing. But I soon realized that to understand what was going on, I had to step outside of the dynamic of obstinate and inflexible oppositional contention which, I felt, was overwhelming not only me, but villagers and immigrants as well while obscuring subtle yet trenchant processes of exclusion and marginalization from our view.

The image of immigrants as a "problem" reinforced several stereotypes, which in turn had an important role both in configuring space in the valley and in heightening consciousness about the importance of maintaining distance between the groups. Seeing immigrants as a "problem" did not, as I have shown, directly mirror dominant national and supranational discourses about the need to control frontiers and about the threat of "pollution" and "chaos" coming from the south. While the alarmist tone of the mass media, and more generally, the "moral panic" over immigrants in Spain in the early 1990s had an impact on local perceptions of African immigrants, there were other local experiences and cultural processes that were shaping the allocation of space for African immigrants.

Yet the local NGO overlooked these crucial dynamics in its analysis of the situation, while reducing the problem of immigrants in an overly simplistic fashion to the purported racism of municipal authorities and local employers who were, according to this vision, incorporating the Alien Law to validate their vested interests. The gradual tendency toward residential segmentation and reduction of interethnic spaces is no doubt part of a broader process and it would not have taken place as rapidly without the Alien Law and the ongoing project of European Union, from which immigrants are excluded. But the process of spatial segmentation is an outcome of a more subtle move toward the disciplination of the immigrant population. Immigrants might have a right to a place, but only if they acknowledged the tacit village rules for everyday use and occupancy of the space.

Let me illustrate my argument by considering how use of the municipal council plaza has changed profoundly in recent years. The plaza is a central site in the village and valley known as the Pilón, in reference to an antique public fountain situated at the entrance of the village. It has always been a locus of politics, commerce, and labor contracting. The plaza was a place of interethnic interaction when I arrived in 1992. Immigrants would hang out around the kiosk where people drink while hiring workers or settle the accounts of the day. They would use the food store, the phone booth, and share the stone benches with elder villagers who would spend hours with them discussing common experiences of migration. When I returned to the village just a year later in 1993 I realized that villagers had begun to complain about immigrants being in the Pilón, though always in vague terms such as "they bother women" or "they are wasting their time." By this time I was living near the center of town and had detached myself from direct involvement with the local NGO, thus having a better vantage from which to observe daily interethnic interactions and to interview villagers about them. I tried to pin down what such criticisms of immigrants meant, interviewing those immigrants who spent time around the *Pilón*, the owner of the store across the street, the man who ran the kiosk, the doctors who worked in the town hall clinic, and many others. But I only uncovered reference to quarrels between two or three well-known Moroccan leaders. No woman had been harassed here, and no immigrant had ever turned down a job offer. Did the complaints simply manifest old stereotypes about "Moors" in the area, as the local NGO and some of the Moroccan leaders within its influence might have claimed?

Only later, when transcribing and analyzing the oral histories collected from villagers, did I recognize that villagers were upset because immigrants had been violating the tacit practices through which villagers segment use of the plaza temporally according to persons' specific social location as marked by class, age, gender, as well as ethnicity. Villagers thought of the immigrants as temporary workers *(jornaleros)*, as men, and as young people, and they expected them to behave as such. Yet customary rules for youthful and poor male dayworkers carefully limited their presence in the public space and required of them specific behaviors that African immigrants seemed to ignore.

As mentioned previously, poverty was something to be kept out of sight. Immigrants openly asked for spare money or for credit in stores, and though most of them avoided doing so in order to preserve their own notion of dignity and pride, villagers found it troublesome, just as they did in the past when, according to collective memories of local indigent villagers, "they didn't even dare to stare at you because shame prevented them from doing so" (P.M., summer 1994). A woman who belonged to a traditional *cacique's* family commented on people's begging: "I don't quite understand how people can ask for money—what a lack of shame! Mind you, I wouldn't do it myself. I would go to my house and keep my hunger to myself, or I'd just go somewhere to find any kind of work.... [The municipal council] should do something to prevent the shameful situation right there, right in public view, in front of everybody—men, women, and children, 'natives' as well as 'outsiders' [*propios como forasteros*]" (D.M., spring 1995). This woman went on to tell me how people in need had acted much more discreetly when she was young: "It is not that there was no hunger before ... life here was harsh for all of us, although some of us were more lucky and at least we ate daily.... I remember the poor people coming to my house, asking for some old bread or anything to feed the kids—God, that was painful! My parents always gave them something, you see? We gave them something to do, so that they wouldn't be embarrassed!"

Others described to me in detail customary practices of poor, jobless people:

When there was work in the valley the bar was full of people very early in the morning, same as today. Then the patrons or their administrators would come to choose those needed for the day: "You and you and you," they would say, pointing at the chosen ones. [L.S.: And what would people do if they were not chosen?] Well, that happened quite often, you know, because there was not enough work to go around. The situation was desperate, because if you didn't work your family wouldn't eat that day, so after all the patrons came, we went from *cortijo* to *cortijo* to offer to do anything ... in exchange for money, food, whatever. What else could you do? (M.G., summer 1994)[10]

Sequential temporal segmentation marked when it was proper for poor day-workers to present themselves in public hiring spaces. It was acceptable for elderly people to spend hours in the Pilón plaza, as many immigrants did, but villagers thought it definitely improper for youthful poor workers to do so. Implicitly, poor people did not have the right to rest and should offer to take up any kind of job if they wanted to gain respect and sympathy from other peasants. Immigrants were expected to accept the same humiliating practices that Andalusian dayworkers of the 1950s and 1960s had experienced, lest they be labeled as "lazy."

Tacit rules also prevented the mixing of men and women in public spaces. Yet youthful immigrant men were hanging out in the Pilón at precisely the time of day when women did errands, when only elder and nonthreatening men were allowed to stay there. My field diary notes countless problems and complaints stemming from the mixed presence of Africans and local women, something considered by autochthonous men as an intolerable danger.[11] Immigrants would wash themselves in the Pilón, the public fountain, in the view of women and children, and villagers considered this immoral and disorderly. It is telling that villagers dedicated the first public funding for immigrants to the building of public showers in an out-of-the-way location far from where women do errands.

The presence of young, unoccupied people in these public spaces was thus a cultural symbol of "disorder." African immigrants were not doing anything bad in the Pilón, as people acknowledged, but their mere presence at times when poor young men should be elsewhere raised villagers' hackles. Even though villagers embraced a modern egalitarian ethic and a notion of public space as open to everyone, they expected immigrants to acknowledge and follow local rules of comportment, rules that relegated immigrants to a subordinate status and confined them to marginal spaces.

When villagers underscored the need for a "proper" place for immigrants, they began to voice concerns deeper than those over infringement of customary use of public space. Implicit in the growing concern about immigrants' "disordered" presence in times and spaces where they were not supposed to be, was a derogatory stereotype about their lifestyle, their residential patterns, and the purported morality historically attached to these. Breaking the tacit rules structuring social space involved a drawing of boundaries between the groups: those situated at the center of the imagined community and those situated at its margins.

This separation must be understood in the context of change and mobility produced by the relocation of Andalusia and Alfayan peasants in the larger social space drawn by the rebordering of the Mediterranean. The arrival of African immigrants in the valley in the context of a bitter polemic redefining criteria of membership altered the former sociospatial segmentation between the groups. Villagers perceived immigrants as a threat to the newly established social order, but not because villagers wanted to perpetuate the closed, segmented, and hierarchical notion of social space that had once condemned most of them to marginalization, dependence, and ostracism. If anything, their mainstream ideology actively opposed the implicitly hierarchical political philosophy that underlay the corporatist authoritarianism of the earlier Francoist period.

However, the redrawing of social spaces was informed by a social mobility which had improved villagers' status and life conditions, and that was what should be preserved in their eyes. To assert social mobility and status, and to legitimize the urge to for distance themselves from immigrants, villagers imposed on immigrants images and stigmas associated with residential patterns, spaces, and lifestyles they themselves had left behind. Immigrants' presence in the center of the social space and their mutual interdependence was seen as a threat to the new order because their behavior made villagers "feel that any close contact with them would lower their own standing, that it would drag them down to a lower status level" (Elias and Scotson 1965, 149).

Images of "Moors" are redolent with autochthonous representations of people living at the margins of purportedly "normal" life, beyond the social control of peasant organized society. "Moors" are associated with *maquis,* who lived as outlaws in the sierra; with *cortijeros* and *choceños,* who lived crowded together with animals; and with migrant workers, whose lifestyle is considered "inferior" and is naturalized in racial terms as proper only for nomadic Gypsies. Dirtiness, odor, disordered sexualities, rudeness in talking and behaving, propensity to contagious sickness, and lack of respect toward neighbors and institutions were all thought to be natural for those living outside the bounds of "civilized" life. Villagers were beginning to assimilate African immigrants into this dominant imagery of the "uncivilized," naturalizing them as such.

When dirt, deviation, and defilement cannot be located outside the margins of the community, peoples everywhere undertake rituals of purification to separate themselves from this "dirt"—defined as "matter out of place," as Mary Douglas has noted (1968, 338). Distance and separation from "pollution" are central to the behavior of most social groups, and in the case of Alfayans' response to immigrants played an important role in redefining public and private spaces by purifying neighborhoods, houses, and public locales. This is why villagers began to refuse to rent their houses to Africans, to bar them from bars and pubs, and to monitor and restrict their use of Andalusian public spaces intended for casual passing of spare time.

Let us first deal with the thorny issue of housing. The problem of housing is chronic in rural areas dependent on seasonal outside labor. In the case of Alfaya, however, there were many empty houses, which, according to the municipal council, could have potentially served two purposes. Allowing immigrants to rent them would facilitate the "normal" integration of immigrants with neighbors, avoiding the consequences of the so-called ghetto effect. Furthermore, the development of a rental sector could boost real estate planning and urban development in the village. With these purposes in mind, the municipal council drew up the so-called Tutelary Housing Plan (Plan de Viviendas Tuteladas, or PVT) in the summer of 1992 to encourage villagers to rent out their houses.[12] But villagers did not respond favorably to the plan, and it was finally suspended after the harvest campaign of 1994.

"Why do people not seize the opportunity to earn money by renting out their empty houses?" asked a social worker in a meeting arranged to discuss immigrants' integration in the valley, "Perhaps one cannot ask people to behave with solidarity in mind, providing lodging for homeless people, but I just don't understand why people will not behave with business interests in mind, taking advantage of immigrants needs!"[13] According to interviews with house owners, they refused to rent their houses because "the effort is not worthwhile" (M.C., summer 1994). The effort they are referring to is not only the economic investment needed to ready a house for rental, nor the trouble of collecting rent monthly, which are intrinsic to any realty activity.[14] In addition, they refer to the efforts that would have to be made to adjust immigrants' behavior to standards of "normality," both in the neighborhood and within the purportedly private area of the house.

The villagers' implicit assertion was that immigrants' tendencies were "natural," and thus impossible to change. As a villager told me: "At first they beg you, they assure you that all three or four of them are friends, and you think you can do good by helping them out. But as soon as they rent the house, forget it. They live like pigs. You cannot imagine the odor they left when they vacated, after having prevented me from entering to see what had been going on. And then there were rowdy fights. They were always having problems with one another. They would multiply. You never knew who was living in the house. The neighbors would complain, but what could you do once they were in as renters? (A.C., summer 1994). Another woman who actually had empty houses for rent argued: "Things are too difficult to risk renting them anything, because they don't know how to behave, and they do not reciprocate by meeting their obligations. Most of them have not paid the rent, and they leave without paying the debts in the neighboring stores. People in the neighborhood hear them screaming in the evenings, so everybody complains" (M.C., summer 1994).

Sometimes villagers explicitly naturalized Africans' difference as beyond either Africans' or villagers' control, explaining why rental and other accommodation were "not worth while." As various people put it, "They live like animals … that goes in the blood, in the land of the Moors" (T.G.C.). "Even if you know them beforehand, know their style of life and how they react, it infuriates you—they are not responsible, they are not serious people" (S.P.). "They are like Gypsies—they show no respect for the house or neighbors, they only want to take advantage of a temporary situation" (C.G.). "It is normal for them not to know how to live in these houses. They are used to huts with no doors, no windows, like they have in Africa, you see? A lot of people together, mixed together, with no room to separate the couple from the rest of the family" (A.A.). The simple fact is that few, if any, owners of available housing will "take the risk" of renting to African immigrants, whatever public programs are enacted to promote such rental. Rental to Africans has come to be seen as risking "contamination" of the neighborhood's lifestyle. Property owners also fear that neighbors' complaints will jeopardize their own social status, while devaluing the rental property.

Similar justification lies behind the increasing refusal of the owners of the bars and pubs to let African immigrants drink alcohol in their locale, or to enter at all. Bars have always been crucial sites for Andalusian men's informal socialization. Traditionally, each bar had its own clientele, structured by residential location and class. Different groups might use the same bar, but at different times (e.g., rich people in the morning and subaltern groups in the afternoon). But the segmenting of African immigrants in bar use went beyond such temporal sequencing. Because all African immigrants up to 1995 were male, their exclusion from the bars literally segregated them from the most important informal networks of male socialization.

Although segmentation of groups in the village initially had the character of rites of purification, increasingly people experienced separation in terms of personal and group preferences. Villagers drew on their own experiences abroad, on the articulation of local political practice with regional or national politics, and on greater exposure to urban and middle-class habits and tastes. They sensed themselves as having undergone a kind of refinement or advance in tastes and preferences, now to be enjoyed in socialization and leisure, and even in domestic life. For such people, sharing housing and spaces of informal socialization and leisure with Africans seemed to threaten their own newly acquired cosmopolitan sensibilities.

When I arrived in Alfaya in 1992, there were no restrictions to entering a bar. Yet over time, immigrants found themselves not only restricted, but also categorically excluded from most bars. Although excluding customers was ostensibly illegal, bar owners claimed that they had the right to choose their clienteles, and that immigrants "do not know how to behave properly." Store owners, by contrast, welcomed immigrants who came to buy food. Why the difference?

One bar owner drew upon his own experience as a former emigrant in several European countries to explain that the difference related to how overuse of alcohol was related to aggressive violence.

> The reason for the difference is that store owners deal with immigrants in the daytime, while we have to cope with them in the evening, when they want to have fun. When you are abroad you may be very frustrated, you feel alone, and occasionally you feel desperate. Alcohol is a way out, an evasion. The problem with Muslims is that they do not know how to drink properly. It is not something they are supposed to do [according to their religion], and the more they drink, the more guilty they feel. Guilt fosters aggressivity, and once involved in these aggressive interactions, they need more alcohol to block out fear. It's almost impossible to break this chain; if they are not able to do so, then we have to intervene. That's why most bar owners refuse to serve alcohol to immigrants at all. But that doesn't solve the problem, because immigrants can buy liquor in the stores. That's why some bars have taken measures, which I think are extreme, of not allowing immigrants to enter the bar at all. (E.C., summer 1994)

Spain has more bars than the rest of Europe put together, and Spaniards socially tolerate overuse of alcohol. It was thus difficult for me to take at face value barmen's claim that they could not deal with drunken people. I have myself witnessed countless instances of drunken Andalusians who became aggressive and challenged both the authority of the bar owner and the peace of the clientele, producing momentary conflicts that bar owners and managers generally masterfully defuse. The reason for refusing immigrants entry to bars must lie elsewhere.

Part of the reason was hinted at by another informant who emphasized the importance of regular, loyal clients to bars as a reason for immigrants' exclusion: "The problem is not that bar owners deny immigrants entrance, because that in itself could be denounced [as illegal], and owners could be forced to let them in. The problem is broader: bar owners don't want immigrants coming in because then villagers will stop coming and the bars will lose their regular clientele" (J.O., fall 1994). For regular clients, bars are an intimate locale, a setting that villagers treat as part of their personal space where people have close links to one another, even if not always without friction, and where outsiders are not welcome.

Male interethnic conflicts about women were another crucial ingredient in the erection of boundaries in Andalusian locales where young people gather for leisure in the evening and on weekends, especially in pubs and discotheques. I will briefly touch on this topic in chapter 7, as the link between gender and cultural identity (be it national, ethnic, or racialized) is crucial in the perpetuation of forms of exclusion and domination.[15] In this regard, Andalusian stereotypes about Africans' purported sexual voracity and seductive appeal to local women roused Andalusian men to defend their women as vulnerable and in need of control and protection. Here again, African immigrants were imagined as threatening villagers' self-restraint and as challenging social control, in that immigrants were taken to be closer to nature and prone to breaking those codes of sexual morality that villagers had been trained to observe from childhood.

These highly racist stereotypes of Africans' purportedly natural negative characteristics not only mandated that villagers and immigrants be distanced from one another, but also implied a clear hierarchy in their separation linked to villagers' greater sociocultural proximity to Europe. The social world in which villagers and immigrants had come together seemed divided between the civilized village and the primitive areas appropriate to immigrants, the latter being closer to nature and, hence, suitable for animal-like behavior. Although this imagery was in some ways contested, it built on widely shared notions situating northern Europe at the extreme of civilized order and progress where people are cleaner, more punctual, and more disciplined. Africans were at the opposite extreme, and Andalusians somewhere in the middle: "Those [Africans] have a life style of their own, different from ours, even though we are in many ways still similar to them—the way we treat women, for example. We commonly say a man is 'very Moorish' if he is very macho and locks his wife up in the house, something that is still not so uncommon here" (S.P., summer 1994).

Emigration, according to villagers who had experienced it, was a good opportunity to learn more "advanced" customs and habits: "It is important for immigrants that we provide them with rules of discipline, that they get used to living like us, similarly to what we learned by living with Germans. It is good for them, because their children will thus learn to become more advanced" (S.B., summer 1994). Yet, in order to learn, immigrants needed a humble attitude, recognition of the "cultural inferiority" of their own styles of life, and an intention to learn from more "advanced" and "civilized" people. Humility, according to villagers who refused to rent housing to immigrants or who denied them entry to bars, is precisely what "Moors" lacked, as demonstrated by their idiosyncratic arrogance and aggressive attitudes.

Thus stereotyped, immigrants seemed "naturally incapable" of changing, having both a "primitive" culture (in ethnic terms), but also, paradoxically, a "lack" of culture (in terms of education and/or civilization). In one conversation among several young villagers, the daughter of an emigrant family who had returned to the village tried to relativize immigrants' purported aggressiveness and violence as deriving from a cultural background that even villagers once shared: "People are racist when they claim that it is typically 'Moorish' behavior to get caught up in violent quarrels. But my grandmother told me that we used to be that way here, for in this village, men would leap at another person's throat for any reason. Violence is caused by that, by lack of culture" (C.A., fall 1994). Another young villager responded immediately: "Well, you might be right, but the fact is that we cannot allow immigrants to impose their rules so much that people feel insecure in the streets.... It's necessary to teach them how to behave like proper persons, and if they don't learn, out of here!" (P.M., fall 1994). Immigrants should learn—they should acquire the culture necessary to comport themselves properly in social spaces because (according to this and other testimonies) they really have no choice: either they learn their proper place or they will have no place in the valley at all.

Naturalizing Difference

Villagers wanted to put immigrants "in their place." And by putting them in their alleged place, Andalusian citizens situated themselves in a safe space from which they constructed a new identity opposed to that of African immigrants. Stereotypes about Africans' animality, dirtiness, and wild behavior strengthened the importance of keeping the distance, and at the same time, situated Andalusians in the civilized area of an imaginary ethnocentric map, which not long ago excluded them on the basis of their unassimilable otherness. Group images and place images combine to create landscapes of exclusion, as Sibley has put it (1995, 15), and in Alfaya, both combined in the process of space allocation to designate for immigrants not only a proper place to stay, but proper attitudes and behaviors. This stress on control and surveillance of immigrants was to be almost literally translated to the enactment of public policies, as I analyze in later chapters. But unfortunately, any deviations immigrants might manifest were judged from a culturalist perspective: immigrants' original "culture" was deemed to prevent them from acquiring the necessary "culture" to behave properly.

Even though clandestinity and an activist political tradition initially evoked villagers' memories of resistance to dictatorship, and thus sympathies from most people in Alfaya, immigrants' occupation of marginal housing and peripheral locales summoned forth stereotypes of poor and ignorant people who inhabited such places in the past. Hegemonic narratives of what the community is tend to look down on styles of life of poor and nomadic people as marginal and different in both physical and moral senses. In the testimonies I collected, and in many other ethnographies of Andalusia in the 1960s, the poorest class was depicted as different from the rest of the people, not just in relation to their resources or their life condition, but in a very physical sense. The poorest of the poor are described as sunburnt, dark-skinned, badly dressed with secondhand clothes that may be unsuited to them and ridiculous to the eyes of others. Men are portrayed as unshaven, women as having manlike manners, and both as ignorant and naturally inclined to sexual lack of self-restraint and other inadvisable practices.[16] In the Alfaya Valley, those who lived in *chozas*, *cortijos*, caves, or even under the open sky, suffered the same process described by Young: "When the dominant culture defines some groups as different, as the Other, the members of those groups are imprisoned in their bodies. Dominant discourse defines them in terms of bodily characteristics, and constructs those bodies as ugly, dirty, defiled, impure, contaminated, or sick" (1990, 123).

Differences were not only embedded in the bodies, but also naturalized in forms of behavior, in moral principles associated with diverse styles of living and/or occupations.[17] In Andalusia, the poorest have always been judged as morally deviant, dominated by animal passions improper for civilized people. In 1972, Andalusian priests enunciated moral judgments when denouncing rural poverty and the crowding among poor people in ways that contemporary priests and many NGOs echo when they speak out against the "subhuman conditions of life" of immigrants both in Africa and in Andalusia (Burgos 1972, 119).

The same elements were used to denigrate both the poorest Andalusians of the past and immigrants of the present. Bodily references—to bad odor or to disordered and excessive sexuality—were attributed to both. Parallelisms of spaces inhabited, conditions lived, and styles of life practiced constituted both rural Andalusian *cortijeros* or *maquis*, and illegal Africans as chaotic, poverty stricken, and morally disordered, and these images of African immigrants came to pervade the dominant culture. The construction of African immigrants as different "others," and their exclusion from community's spaces, built upon deeply entrenched local meanings assigned to particular spaces, housing patterns, and a nomad style of life traditionally associated with the Andalusian poor. And negative group images in turn informed a wish to erect boundaries to protect the "normal" population from the defiled—in other words, to maintain the segmentation and residential differentiation which had traditionally served as a medium as well as an outcome of unequal social relations (Harvey 1992).

Having analyzed in this chapter some of the traditional notions of distribution of the social space that informed local processes of space allocation, I now turn to the broader framework where these processes take place. This leads me to analysis of the effects of the Alien Law and of the state politics of migration in shaping the Spanish civil sphere. The Francoist ideology of segmentation of an earlier era saw differences as "natural" features of a divinely drawn social order. By contrast, a new contemporary logic takes for granted that all human beings are fundamentally equal as subjects entitled to rights. Alfayans embraced such notions of fundamental equality when they initially sided with immigrants to resist the Alien Law. Yet soon enough, they came to naturalize immigrants as different and endeavored to put them into their (social) place. As I will further analyze in the following chapters, Andalusians did not deny immigrants a place in the valley, nor (by extension) in Spanish social structure. Yet the meaning of the place finally allocated to immigrants has changed profoundly, as has the civil sphere in which negotiations over this place have taken place. One of the most important factors in the sociospatial allocation of immigrants was the emergence of a consensus among people intervening in the process as Spaniards, differentiated and distanced from immigrants. How did this consensus emerge?

The new meaning of segmentation of space should be understood as part of a broader process: the shifting of the new European frontiers to the Andalusian interior and the crystallization of new social borders between Andalusian and Africans, citizens and foreigners. The spatial boundaries and the norms and stereotypes inscribed in space are part, now as before, of the creation of moral boundaries that separate "proper" from "deviant" and "civilized" from "primitive" behavior. This new moral landscape, however, incorporates a postcolonial, modernizing logic formerly absent in the region, one that inscribes Andalusia in an ethnocentric imaginary geography that accords local villagers the right to create a "safe space" for themselves and to "keep the distance" from immigrants. The advent of Third World workers from Africa has redrawn the local mapping of who belongs where according to new notions of legal status and cultural differences that deem deviation, illegality, and primitivism as coming from outside the Spanish nation-state, thus legitimating the new role of the state as a key actor in the partitioning of space. To this I now turn.

Notes

1. See also Fraser 1973; Gilmore 1980; Martínez Veiga 1991.
2. According to some romanticized accounts of Andalusian rural life, the sierra is imagined as a space of independence, in contrast to peasant organized society, which is subject to rigid order and social control. *Echarse al monte* (to take to the hills) appears in literature as flight to a space of liberty, where control could be eluded and where freedom prevails. Typical of this imaginary are the figures of *bandoleros* (brigands) who took the law in their hands and robbed rich people to distribute resources among poor peasants who silently supported them (see Burgos 1972, 108).
3. According to Marx, the relative surplus population of the unemployed or partially employed exists in three forms: floating, latent, and stagnant. Andalusian *jornaleros* belong to the third type, as part of active labor whose employment is "extremely irregular... characterized by working hours of extreme length for wages of extreme lowness" (*Capital*, 1930, 2: 710; quoted in Morris 1994, 14).
4. See T. San Román's works for the best-informed ethnography and analyses of Gypsies and their situation in Spain. For historical and cultural links of Gypsies with nomadism, see especially San Román 1997.
5. It is difficult, if not impossible, to calculate the number of immigrants who come to the village. My estimates are based on production, on my own censuses of Africans, and on several key informants, such as the agricultural agent. I conclude that the population more than triples during the summer harvest season. African immigrants were not more than three hundred altogether as compared to a de jure population of twenty-five hundred in the 1991 *Padrón de Habitantes* (residents census).
6. The label "urban tribes" refers to young people coming from the capital of the province to the valley to finance their studies or simply to work because they are unemployed in the city. Africans are referred to as "African tribes" in a like manner. Together with itinerant Gypsies, both of these "tribal" groups make up the majority of temporary workers who stay in the valley in search of work throughout the entire harvest campaign. Many more immigrants come from the surrounding villages, but they normally return to their houses after work.
7. See chapter 2, and Suárez and Hernández 1993; see also Hall et al. 1978 and Gilroy 1987 for the concept of "moral crisis" as constructed in Great Britain.
8. A detailed analysis of the complicated relationships among the different tendencies in the Spanish Left is crucial to understanding how the "problem" of immigration is created and what strategies are adopted to solve it. After a period of transition in which all progressive forces that had joined against dictatorship slowly identified with specific political projects, many activists began to show a progressive disenchantment with the modernizing and reformist democratic project and with the co-optation of popular movements by political parties. Many among these try to defend the viability and purity of their ideological tenets and, like E.A. and others, they maintain an ambiguous attitude toward mainstream politics. It is among these people, together with grassroots Catholic groups, that the first NGOs were founded in the civil sphere around themes such as feminism, racism, pacifism, ecologism, and other New Social Movements.
9. The LOE penalizes not only illegal foreigners and employers who hire them, but also any person who, though not directly hiring them, helps them secure employment. The leader of the shelter initiative was fined with $8,000.00 (equivalent to an average nine-month salary!). His case was published in *El País*, Spain's leading newspaper, and the media coverage could be read as both a warning and a critique of the LOE. When E.A. received notification of the penalty, immigrants discussed strategies for collecting money for him. This solidarity, according to him,

was the expression of a real connection of interests between himself and the immigrants as a consequence of the common struggle against racism and social injustice.

10. See similar descriptions in Fraser 1973 and Gilmore 1980.

11. See also Checa 1995; Moreno Torregosa and El-Gheryb 1994.

12. The PVT offered local owners reduced taxes, guarantees of rents, special subsidies and loans to recondition old houses, and insurance for fire or other damage. The guiding politics behind this plan was to promote immigrants' integration within the village social and residential fabric and to privatize the "problem" of immigrants' lack of space, thus avoiding any complaints from citizens about public services offered to immigrants. Despite all of these incentives, most people declined to rent houses to immigrants, and only a few—most of them related in one way or another to the municipal council—used these benefits to improve the condition of their houses and rent them to immigrant workers.

13. Meeting in the municipal council, June 23, 1994.

14. In this issue, the importance of the informal economy and fiscal fraud in the valley seems to be relevant once again. Renting out a house means two things, according to some owners: (1) it will raise income and property taxes, and (2) it will mean loss of unemployment subsidies. Villagers preferred to maintain their claimed status as unemployed rural workers in order to draw steady income from agricultural welfare. But this approach required hiding as many sources of income as one possibly could (see discussion of the legitimization of legality in the next chapter). For some peasants, however, the PVT led to a bureaucratic opening for their transformation into active producers in the real estate sector. The PVT, together with sustained demand for housing on the part of some immigrants, could be useful for surmounting peasants' reluctance to rent houses to foreign temporary rural workers, but only if enough institutional perseverance is maintained in the coming years.

15. See among others, Collier 1997; Chatterjee 1993; Parker et al. 1992; and Stolke 1993.

16. Testimonies of E.O., A.V., and R.F., summer and spring 1994–1995; also Gilmore 1980, 85.

17. See Morris 1994; for Gypsies, see San Román 1986.

4. The Symbolic and Political Manufacturing of the Legitimation of Legality

*T*he most important single requirement for a foreigner to live and work in Spain is possession of what are commonly referred to as "papers."[1] To be able to acquire papers is a dream and a nightmare for most immigrants living in Granada. It is a nightmare because most immigrants do not have them and have no idea how long they will be able to avoid being detained by the ubiquitous police and the Civil Guard, which leads to deportation. It is a dream because, as I will explain in this chapter, papers are presented as the only way for foreigners to acquire rights—to live openly "in the light." Papers become an obsession—as if they were the most precious "possession"—a shield needed to ward off persecution, exploitation, chronic forced nomadism, and hiding.

This situation in itself is not new. When laborers migrated to western Europe and North America in the middle of the century, the countries receiving them developed legal and administrative measures to regulate temporary immigration and direct it to the economic sectors in need of cheap labor.[2] After the recession of the mid 1970s slowed economic growth, however, the states that traditionally imported labor tried to restrict immigration and to limit it to those entering their territory legally. State regulation has shifted from controlling temporary immigration to interdicting illegal immigration.[3] Even though interdiction measures have been largely ineffective (Cornelius, Martin, and Hollifield 1994), the fact is that European states now treat migration as a threat to the legal framework defining who is a member of the national community and as requiring vigilance of borders, establishment of inland check points, and prodigious efforts to ferret out and expel illegal immigrants.

Notes for this chapter begin on page 130.

The conundrum for the post-Fordist era thus has become how to secure national sovereignty while still recognizing human rights, and how to use cheap and acquiescent foreign labor to benefit the economy while still honoring the social rights laborers should acquire through work and residence regardless of nationality. These contradictions have as yet no clear solution.

The contradictions are especially acute in countries such as Spain, which enacted national immigration policies, laws, and regulations at a time of deep concern about the unprecedented mobility of international labor coupled with the growing segmentation of the labor market. In chapter 2, I described the circumstances surrounding enactment of the Alien Law, or LOE, in Spain in 1985, including the preoccupation of Spain's would-be EU partners about the permeability of Spain's Mediterranean coasts as the new southern border of Europe. As discussed there, the LOE is one of the most restrictive laws regulating entry and residence of non-EU (noncommunitarian) foreigners.

A key feature of immigration to Spain since enactment of the LOE has been the growing illegality of Third World foreigners. Each year, the border controls and the Spanish consulates in foreign countries have tightened visa requirements for entry into Spain. As a result, many foreigners who entered Spain in earlier years no longer meet current requirements. Given the strict enforcement of the LOE within Spain, immigrants from the poorer non-EU countries have almost no way of regularizing legal status. They do not have to have entered Spain illegally to find themselves deemed illegal, for immigration controls confront them with a Catch-22 system that generates their illegality. When renewing their visas, for example, many immigrants are told that they don't have all the documents they need, and their renewals are denied, rendering them illegal. As a result, other immigrants don't dare to renew their visas and thus lapse into illegality. Thus, de facto illegality has become rampant, and legal immigrants find themselves in constant jeopardy of falling into illegality as a result of circumstances that scholars have deemed "institutional irregularity" (Cornelius 1994).[4]

To a certain extent, local attitudes provided a foil to the growing illegalization of immigrants. Many Andalusians resented state efforts to control the underground economy and took a skeptical view of the claim that the rule of law truly protects purportedly national common interests. Many Andalusians also felt solidarity toward those who are forced to leave their land to be able to make a living for themselves and their families. The corporatist legacy of the Francoist state weakened the dominant liberal hegemony, with its basis in a tacit contract between the state and each of its individual citizens under the rule of law. Notions of local and regional autonomy vis-à-vis national and supranational centralized authority further undermined the legitimacy of the state's illegalization of immigrants, as described in chapter 1.

At the same time, nonetheless, the rule of law conjures up a new ideological universe of impartiality and expertise that is slowly winning people's grudging acceptance of bureaucratic authority as appropriate to a legally rational and neutral state detached from normative reasoning (Young 1990, 77, 112). In Spain, this acceptance is being won through the use of both coercive and disciplinary methods framed by laws and procedures, oftentimes taking advantage of the "prodigious incoherence and chaotic character of state policies" (Poulantzas, quoted in Hunt 1993, 279).

It seems obvious to any outside observer that for Spaniards it is politically correct to show solidarity with immigrants as nomadic poor in search of an honest living through work. It also is apparent that Spaniards do not overtly connect "national identity" to the threat immigrants purportedly pose to the maintenance of autochthonous cultures. Yet Spaniards, by embracing legislation of the LOE, are participating in the notion of illegality as a threat to the construction of an internally open Europe. They are equating illegal immigration to other illegal threats to the rule of law, such as terrorism, extreme nationalism, drugs and arms traffic, and the like. What is at stake here is not simply the issue of whether it is legitimate to lump together such disparate categories as immigration and common delinquency. The more important consequence is that in coupling immigration to illegality, Spaniards are condemning immigrants to the lowest common denominator of deviancy in Western society—that of submission to and compliance with institutional measures designed to reincorporate the deviant into society.

My theoretical perspective is informed by recent scholarship in the anthropology of law and sociolegal studies that examine the interplay between coercive and disciplinary techniques in the production of new identities which embody culturally specific notions of personhood and of belonging to the community. This analytical perspective does not argue that law and administrative apparatuses completely determine subjective identities. Rather, it emphasizes the mutual constitution of the law and social identities in everyday life practices, the only arena in which legal categories and prescriptions are ultimately made meaningful for social agents.[5] I also draw upon new perspectives in contemporary political philosophy about the historical and cultural specificity of a central feature of modern society, namely, the legitimization of legality. The law is taken to be grounded in the fundamental rights of the person and to exercise rationality as its fundamental ethical imperative in an impersonal, impartial, and universal system. Law thus generates the space in which people can legitimately express a plurality of views and cultural values. Under the overarching framework of the law's fundamental rationality, there thus exists the de facto possibility of conflict, criticism, and revision of the content of particular normative standards.

In addition to these approaches to the centrality of legality in modern societies, my analysis incorporates political economic concerns about the new forms of domination embedded in the construction of "common sense" through a complex dynamic of coercion and consent, of punishment and control. This domination involves not only juridical and political control, but also a moral and cultural one that "concretely results from the organic relations between State or political society and 'civil society'" (Gramsci 1971, 52).[6] Foucault's notion of power and governmentality guided me across the analysis of processes of normalization, regulation, and disciplining through which general standards are internalized by the subject, shaping social agents' behavior and, most important, constituting them as social personas in their belonging to society (Foucault 1977, 1980). This "common sense" or "doxa," in terms of Bourdieu, even when contested and negotiated from particular regional, ethnic, gender, and class interests that characterize internal differentiation in hegemonic formations, effectively shapes the limits of social action and the specific forms of discursive possibility.[7]

In this chapter I will explore the effects of the new preponderance of the law and the modern bureaucratic system, together with the contested process of the legitimization of legality, in terms of how they regulate the allocation of immigrants in Spanish society. I argue that analysis of the social processes through which the law is put into practice in relation to immigrants discloses some basic assumptions of the new legal ideology which "go without saying," as Bourdieu has put it (1977). New notions of personhood, moral principles, and modalities of membership in the community are illuminated through analysis of the complex array of social, political, legal, and symbolic relationships that delineate and structure the new boundaries between those who belong and those who are excluded or marginalized through a subordinated legal status.

The meaning of legal categories is, as Malkki (1992, 9) has argued, "an ethnographic question to be explored through the many different social locations in which the category is actually used and struggled over." I use ethnography to explore the contested formation of a common sense that legitimizes legality as the necessary condition for struggling to achieve equality and plurality. I attend to incidents such as the detention and threatened expulsion of a Senegalese immigrant in 1989; the interaction of immigrants with civil functionaries, NGOs and labor unions, and legal experts; and the 1991 regularization program.

Andalusians initially used an open category of migrant worker to negotiate the inclusion of immigrants into society, but they ended up embracing a more exclusionary category of legal foreigner, which reinforces the subordinated status of immigrants sanctioned by the LOE. I will analyze how this shift came about through construction of Spain's new legal culture, illustrating how new political and cultural conceptions of space brought into play by the construction of the EU affected attitudes, uses, and understandings of law. We cannot take for granted as natural the historically constructed borders between nationals and foreigners; rather, we must resort to ethnohistorical analysis to trace the ambiguous and shifting meanings of legal and ethnic categories, categories such as legal or illegal; national or alien; European or Spanish, Andalusian, Moor, or African. We can thus see how new collective identities are actually constructed in daily social practices, within the framework of dominant discourses and of states' institutional practices and the way they affect people's experience and construction of spaces, borders, and otherness.

Salir a la Luz: The 1991 Regularization Process

Although the LOE was put on the books in 1985, it was not until several years later that immigrants began to feel its effects. Immigrants I interviewed who lived in Granada throughout the late 1980s all told me that their presence at that time was highly tolerated and that they experienced no efforts to control them. There were, to be sure, relatively few Third World immigrants in Granada at the time, and enforcement of the LOE for these few would have been costly. But those who were there were also fairly well integrated into Granada's society, where employers viewed them as industrious and flexible workers whose rights were minimal and who could, if necessary, easily be laid off. In addition, as workers, immigrants were commodities with an extraordinary economic utility (Hollifield 1992).

In practice, internal controls of immigration based on the LOE were not implemented until the very end of the 1980s,[8] even as growing numbers of immigrants from the Third World established themselves and worked in Spain in spite of their undocumented status. New migration networks were progressively built upon those of veteran immigrants, and slowly the community was growing and taking ground in Granada and Andalusia.

Even though the stated objective of the LOE is "to protect the legal rights and juridical guaranties of foreigners who are legally in Spain," the fact is that the LOE's rigid requirements are the principal reason for the undocumented status of immigrants now arriving from poor countries in search of jobs. The LOE defines illegality for immigrants as any status that is not explicitly spelled out within the law. As one lawyer put it, the LOE grants immigrants "not a single right and only one duty, that of leaving the country" (E.A., summer 1992).

In effect, the LOE entails illegal immigrants' invisibility (and that of peasants as well; see the section "Politics of Invisibility: A Racial Geography of Labor Relations" in chapter 5). Many illegal immigrants actually destroy their documentation before entering Spain to avoid repatriation if caught by the police. Without documentation they are not entitled to labor or housing contracts. They never pay direct taxes because their illegal status obviates the possibility of being taxpayers. They cannot obtain driving permits, open bank accounts, or apply for municipal permits. The postal service refuses to allow them to send or receive registered letters. Furthermore, the threat of deportation, coupled with instability in the labor market, makes for high mobility across the Spanish territory, engendering patterns of evasion in which undocumented immigrants avoid any visible attachment to a local community. Implementation of the LOE toward the end of the 1980s thus conjured up a new social formation for immigrants whose principal feature was clandestinity and the condemnation immigrants to exploitation, isolation, and detachment from the Spanish sociopolitical and economic order.

A study of the situation of foreigners in Spain, commissioned by Congress in 1990, concluded that measures were needed to cope with the increasing marginalization of growing numbers of illegal immigrants. After parliamentary debates, the government approved a generous program for an "Extraordinary Process of Regularization [legalization] of Foreign Workers" (June 7, 1991), as well as the first social programs for immigrants. Two earlier processes of regularization had failed due in part to poor planning and dissemination of information, so the government also agreed to modernize the public bureaucracies implementing the LOE.

With this new program the government expected to address various conflicting interests.

1. Spain needed to demonstrate to the EU that it could implement measures of control prescribed by the Schengen agreements[9] to eliminate the chronic illegality of worker statuses in the informal economy.
2. Employers in Spain needed adaptable, industrious, cheap, and flexible workers who could be laid off when their work was not needed.
3. The Spanish public wanted assurances that immigration would be controlled through the rule of law, thus mitigating the "moral panic" (Hall et al. 1978) being whipped up by inflated and alarmist press estimates of illegal immigration.
4. The government sought to dispel critiques that the LOE was too rigid, too complex, and too arbitrarily and inefficiently implemented.

NGOs, sociolegal scholars, and labor unions had been responsible for most of the critiques of the LOE. They pointed out that most immigrants defined by the LOE as illegal could not possibly comply with the law's strict documentary requirements. Most were thus trapped in Catch-22 situations, such as needing a labor contract in order to obtain a work/residence permit while needing the permit in order to obtain a labor contract. The government now turned to NGOs, labor unions, and immigrant associations to get them to disseminate the materials immigrants needed to legalize (regularize) their status.

To become legal, immigrants needed to show documents proving that they had lived in Spain with an undocumented status prior to July 24, 1985 (or May 15, 1991 for Moroccans).[10] Immigrants also had to demonstrate that (1) they previously had a valid work/residence permit; or (2) they could document having worked in Spain for at least nine months; or (3) they had job contracts, firm job offers, or an established business in which they were self-employed. There is an additional open-ended category titled "other documents," intended to present further documentation in order to prove the roots or attachment *(arraigo)* to a local community in Spain. Of the total of 108,321 immigrants legalized under these requirements, more than half were Africans (Moroccans, Algerians, and Senegalese were the most represented nationalities).

There are three major points I want to highlight here. First, the process of regularization entailed an implicit acceptance of a new legal culture. Initially, any measure taken by the state was received by the pertinent NGOs as highly suspicious, given the substantially coercive and punitive character of policies implemented up to that time. Lack of credibility was an important obstacle for the process of regularization, not only (and significantly) among immigrants, but also among those groups and individuals working closely with them. Most such groups were ideologically shaped by a Marxist interpretation of the state and of the law as instruments of capitalism's unequal relations of power. Furthermore, employers such as Alfayan peasants (as well as others hiring immigrants in urban areas) were very reluctant to adopt legal hiring practices since local customary hiring practices shielded them from state control. As I have shown in the first chapter, economic, cultural, and historical particularities nurture widespread suspicion of the state and its imposed legal system. Nonetheless, both immigrants and their peasant employers grudgingly acknowledged that something needed to be done to legalize immigrants' status. Yet the very involvement of each group in the process of regularization generated a change of attitude toward the papers, namely, an implicit acceptance of a new legal culture based on the implicit assumption that the state has a legitimate role in guaranteeing individual rights and obligations through impartial and universalistic adherence to the rule of law.

Second, the campaign to regularize immigrants' status entailed a new symbolic order of normalization linking images of modernity to the rule of law, while implicitly sharpening the line between Spaniard and foreigner. The campaign insistently entreated people to abandon chaos for order, to displace dirtiness and contamination with cleanliness and purity, to do away with obscurity and invisibility by embracing light and visibility, to free themselves from captivity by embracing liberty. One campaign slogan spread through the mass media and pamphlets exhorted immigrants (and their employers) to "Sal a la luz. Ponte en regla" (Come into the Light. Put Your Affairs in Order). Below the slogan, pamphlets showed a picture of a gloomy room with a door ajar through which blazing rays of light illuminate the interior. Significantly, the door of the room is being opened from the outside into a dazzling corridor symbolizing legality and order, the acquisition of rights granted to members of Spanish society. This symbolic treatment of legality versus illegality suggests, as Foucault put it, that "Definitive bounds to the sacred order are no longer set in terms of heresy but in terms of illegality, madness and other abnormalities constituted in law" (quoted in Fitzpatrick 1992, 167). The state creates illegality, just as the Inquisition created heresy in past centuries, as an abnormality, a deviation from "normal" and correct behavior. This condition of illegality and gloominess is nevertheless represented as "solvable" if the immigrants will but use documents to prove their attachment to Spain. By constructing the normal in antithesis to the supposedly abnormal, a central symbolic element of modernity is thus underscored, namely, the legal inequality distinguishing nationals from foreigners.

Third, the Spanish state's involvement of civil society in the campaign to legalize immigrant status marked, for Spain, a major turning point away from centralized power centered on control and punishment toward a decentered power focused on regulation of purportedly inclusive legal measures and integrative social policies. The state needed to make the process of legalization credible to Spaniards while building consent for the need to normalize the situation of immigrants' chronic marginalization and illegality. By asking civil society to join in these efforts while, for the first time, acknowledging moral obligations toward immigrants who lived and worked in Spain without papers, the state temporarily refrained from exercising its legitimate monopoly of violence, calling a halt to arrests of immigrants and sanctions against employers. Notwithstanding the apparently repressive, exclusionary, and hierarchical character of state power as embodied in the LOE, I argue that this phase of its implementation actually opened the way to "privatization" of the enactment of the law, which effectively involved the very citizens and groups who criticized the LOE. These critics now found themselves cast in the role of intermediaries between the state and the immigrants, compelled for their own part to embrace those regulatory and normalizing mechanisms of power whose effects "both challenged and reinforced the power relations inherent in immigration discourses" (Coutin 1993, 111).[11]

The Legitimation of Legality in the Spanish Civil Sphere

My aim in the next two subsections is to explore how disciplinary techniques and relations of power extend beyond the limits of the state, showing how the appearance of a "general juridical form that guarantees an [egalitarian] system of rights ... [is] supported by all those systems of micropower that are essentially non-egalitarian and asymmetrical" (Foucault 1977, 122). My perspective goes beyond a statist focus and a binary structure of domination, with dominators on one side and the dominated on the other. I look instead at the "multiform production of relations of domination that are [only] partially susceptible of integration into overall strategies" (Foucault 1980, 142). Here I focus on the way the involvement of employers and experts working in NGOs and labor unions reproduce unequal relations of power sanctioned by the LOE, especially those based on class, ethnicity, and nationality, thus reinforcing the dependence of immigrants on third parties.

At the same time, my approach highlights the fact that daily social processes underlie how legal boundaries come to separate citizens and foreigners. We cannot take for granted that citizens are already rooted in the democratic tradition; rather, we must explore how they come to be so rooted. When Spanish nationals embraced the process of regularization, I argue, employers and people working closely with immigrants embraced a modern notion of citizenship that redefined their own relation to the state. Their relation now entailed a tacit contract constituting themselves as legal subjects with rights, and also duties and responsibilities, which include "a civic commitment, centered on participation in public life … as well as symbolic and ethical aspects that confer a sense of identity and of belonging, a sense of community … where its boundaries lie, and thus which people constitute the 'other'" (Jelin 1996, 106, 109).

Peasants as Employers

The papers, it is worth remembering, are not merely physical pieces of documentation. They embody multiple daily social relations embedded in an unequal distribution of power. Spanish regularization went beyond the requirement of proof of an immigrant's official existence, as in the Italian case where immigrants only needed to produce a passport. The Spanish process forced immigrants to involve themselves actively in acquiring papers to authenticate their identity and to demonstrate their attachment to a local community and their intention to work legally in this area (and not another) and with a particular employer. Immigrants had to fill out countless forms in a timely manner to apply for legalization. In doing so, they needed to tap social resources both in their country of origin and in Spain. Their legalization depended almost entirely on third parties: employers who had to agree to sign documents committing to hiring them and to paying their Social Security taxes as well as the work/residence permit fees; legal experts to prepare applications in the correct manner; institutions in their country of origin to renew passports, provide them with medical and penal certificates, and the like; and Spanish institutions, such as consulates to accredit any visa emitted before May 15, 1991, municipal councils to affirm their place of residence, and so forth.

Because it was difficult for most immigrants to document earlier presence in Spain, many opted to legalize their status by obtaining an employer's firm promise of hire, commonly known as the precontract (*precontrato:* a "declaration of intent to hire"). Obtaining such a precontract was not straightforward because employers were not used to making such commitments. Their willingness to do so in Alfaya resulted from a complex process in which several kinds of people joined in pressuring employers. One key person was the leader who established the unofficial shelter discussed in the preceding chapter. Even though this leader (and the local NGO supporting the shelter) bitterly opposed Alfaya's municipal council, both cooperated in documenting people. Alfaya's mayor signed countless certificates of residence, based on declaration sworn by villagers and corroborated by municipal police. The council and the NGOs then called upon "progressist" peasants to use their networks to persuade other peasants to provide a *precontrato* to one or two illegal immigrants each. While it was not easy to convince potential employers that signing a precontract did not enforceably commit them to pay for an immigrant's permit or even to hire him, the most difficult task was to overcome peasants' reluctance to prove that they were themselves up to date in paying taxes and Social Security. Yet cooperate they did, for the social emphasis on acquisition of the papers converged, even if from radically opposite readings of the law and the liberal democratic system, in the almost unanimous acceptance of the need to support the process of regularization. Solidarity toward immigrants was claimed to be the primordial reason for making this effort to help them legalize their situation: "It's no fair that the state let them enter the country leaving them afterwards with no possibility to legalize their situation, with no rights and vulnerable to exploitation" (N.R., summer 1992).

Although Alfaya was the one place in Granada province in which the greatest number of immigrants became legalized, immigrants felt they paid a heavy cost in dependence on Alfayans' voluntaristic efforts on their behalf. When they tried to persuade their employers to give them precontracts, some immigrants found themselves treated in a clientelistic fashion that subordinated and humiliated them. Mohammed, who had put up with his employer's abusive work conditions, asked his boss for a *precontrato* only as a personal favor. Although the employer agreed, he did not really want to risk scrutiny of his hiring practices, and the precontract was never produced. Mohammed left this employer because "I preferred to work one or two days and get paid like everyone else instead of humiliating myself day after day, expecting that this son of a bitch would finally honor his commitment to do what in fact was his duty. Now I am still 'illegal,' but at least I have my pride" (M.A., summer 1992). Although legalization freed some immigrants from the so-called hare complex, many found themselves hiding once again less than a year later because most family farming enterprises did not have the capacity to keep them employed for a whole harvest cycle as legalization required.

When peasants offered immigrants precontracts, usually both parties knew that the contracts could not be honored fully. Most certainly the agencies handling legalization knew this as well. Yet all were complicit in creating the appearance of legality. This complicity tended to legitimate the process of legalization itself. The process thus had unintended consequences for peasant employers in that many of them abandoned their traditional reluctance to let themselves be "portrayed"[12] by the state. A change in local legal culture was thus set into motion and has gathered force ever since. Many peasant farmers now say they prefer to know that their own affairs are "in order" and above board, not just administratively but most especially in a moral sense: for having helped immigrants attain rights as workers, and, most important, as modern citizens who contribute to society by adopting a transparent legal persona vis-à-vis the state. The legitimization of legality stemming from the process of regularization now infuses daily life with a new common sense about what a proper person is. It seems that the law thus functions most effectively, not through repression, but as a system of representation whose standards and norms of behavior come to permeate civil society. Of course, the law also uses its coercive force, as shown in the section "Politics of Invisibility: A Racial Geography of Labor Relations" in chapter 5, but in an indirect way, recruiting peasants as reluctant enforcers of the Alien Law, in somewhat surprising ways.

There is an astonishing coexistence of an ideological ethos based on acceptance of "law" as the cornerstone of the young Spanish democratic state and a deeply embedded culture of evasion and of informal or underground economic practices that weakens the ability of the state to establish a bounded citizenship. In the official discourse, both are viewed as incompatible. Modernization implies the regularization of economic relations and the establishment of documented legal subjects. In view of the high prevalence of tax evasion among all classes, the state launched public campaigns depicting those who evade the tax system as betraying their families and friends. The "common interest" of the nation-state is thus portrayed as an extended network of friends and relatives who have common interests. Such "naturalization" or "domestication" is very common in the imagining of nations, as has been solidly demonstrated in the literature.[13] But among most of the people with whom I have been working, loyalty to the nation does not involve honesty as a citizen. Loyalty to concrete people does not have anything to do with paying taxes to the state. From the perspective of peasants who "scarcely make a living," as they say, the law and the state are usually regarded with suspicion as defending the interests of rich and urban people. But modern legal ideology operates through consensus rather than through coercive forces, and so it is the process of consensus building that is of interest here.

NGOs, Unions, and the Ideology of Expertism

The constituencies of NGOs and labor unions involved in helping immigrants regularize their status were similarly affected. NGOs and labor unions in Granada provided the bureaucratic structures for helping immigrants process their cases. An army of experts and intermediaries emerged, upon whom immigrants depended heavily.[14] Where NGOs and unions had once relied on volunteers to do their work, now their work underwent professionalization, especially when assisting immigrants involved juridical intervention (interviews, summer 1992 and spring 1995). The two groups most involved in this work were (1) the NGO Granada Acoge, most of whose members were Social Catholics from Christian-based communities (Comunidades de Base), and (2) a section of the Communist labor union Comisiones Obreras (initially called GISCO, and later CITE).[15] Both the NGO and the union offered their juridical assistance freely to immigrants and among them they handled the majority of legalization cases in Alfaya and Granada. Again, as in the case of Alfayan peasants and municipal authorities, these groups differed in the general strategies and ideological principles guiding their activities.[16] But both converged in the idea that providing papers to immigrants was an indispensable step for immigrants to be considered as legal subjects with rights. As a representative of GISCO said in a meeting in Alfaya: "If you don't have papers, you're not a person" (Alfaya, August 5, 1992).

The rich interaction of experts and volunteers working in the world of immigration falls outside of the scope of my analysis. I would like to devote more attention than I am able, and give more credit, to the energy and dedication these associations and individuals invest in helping immigrants. Because my focus here is on the interaction of these groups with immigrants, and on analysis of how the effects of the law work through this interaction to transform identities, I restrict myself to five major aspects of the implementation of the 1991 regularization process: (1) "the ideology of expertism" (Young 1990, 80); (2) strategies for competing for clienteles; (3) disciplinary methods evoking the "fetishism of papers"; (4) the normalizing effects of the expectations about what makes a "good immigrant" and what immigrants' behavior should be; and (5) the culturalism inherent in many of these interactions which reinforces ethnic boundaries between Spanish citizens and African foreigners.

Let us examine the ideology of expertism, which Young has identified as a new form of domination in corporatist welfare societies based on rationalized, legally bounded bureaucracies. Young draws on the Foucaultian notion of power when she suggests that expertism is a new form of domination: "Most people are convinced that issues of legislation, production, and planning are too complex to be understood except by fiscal, legal, and managerial experts" (1990, 80). As Young points out, lack of knowledge easily translates into lack of power. In their interactions, immigration experts clearly subordinated immigrants. Social workers and lawyers compelled immigrants to reveal countless personal details, to be sure with the good intention of helping each immigrant construct a "documented identity" that would conform to legal requirements of permitted immigration. It is not just that juridical counseling is a complicated matter (as everyone involved in the process can attest) in that, although the law conjures up a set of legal categories constructed as self-contained and mutually exclusive (ranging from the nonstatus of "illegal" to several statuses defined by the kind of work and stay temporary permits the immigrant has held),[17] in practice, these categories conceal countless individual juridical situations that cross over several categories (De Lucas 1996). Lawyers' technical training and the need of NGOs and labor unions to introduce efficiency and maximization of resources into their work force immigrants to submit to having their personal files open to scrutiny and their personal information absorbed into databases for statistical information and the like. Such surveillance (in the Foucaultian sense) tacitly transforms immigrants into more or less permanent clienteles, even as it maximizes the power derived from the energy and expertise invested in each case.

Not surprisingly, the experts serving since 1991 as intermediaries between the immigrants and the state have come to compete with one another for state resources, and for clienteles. Immigrants who initially found themselves confused about where best to obtain legal assistance soon found themselves beholden to a specific organization's experts. As one immigrant told me: "Normally the lawyer of the labor union *x* is the one who handles my papers. But the other day I spoke with the social worker of the NGO *y'* and she suggested another strategy and encouraged me to go next Monday to talk with their lawyer. I thought it might be useful to learn about other approaches [to my case]. But you know how much [these organizations] hate one another. Imagine what could happen if they both learn about this!" (S.A., fall 1994). Competition for clienteles occurred despite the alliances formed among the different groups defending immigrants' rights, for example, among the organizations within the Granadan alliance known as Iguales en Derechos (Equal in Rights).

Although most experts undertook their work on behalf of immigrants within an ideological framework that questioned state-imposed limitations on immigrants' rights, they nonetheless actually helped subject immigrants to disciplinary techniques of regulation through paperwork. The lengthy process of legalizing an immigrant usually involved setting up a personal file as the basis for one or more "documented identities." An obsession with documentation flowed partly from immigrants' having to prove nationality, prior immigration status, and so forth. More important, experts were helping immigrants provide those "other documents" demonstrating attachment *(arraigo)* to a Spanish community and to Spain. Given that the degree of necessary attachment was not defined by law, experts usually advised immigrants that "more was better" and encouraged them to accumulate every kind of paperwork that might strengthen their claim of affiliation to any Spanish institution or association, while updating their personal files. Such documentary habits were thus induced by the very administration of experts' intermediary roles. Papers acquired a symbolic transcendental value, as if their very existence would protect immigrants from the tribulations of immigrant life in

Spain. I will discuss this "fetishism of papers" in the next section but want to underscore here that experts were responsible for helping sew the seeds of this fetishism of papers among immigrants. From 1991 on, immigrants who did not have their official documents "in order" would carry several of these papers in their pockets, keeping the rest in a plastic bag full of frustrated statutes and identities.

Although experts ostensibly provided immigrants with value-free technical knowledge and advice, legal assistance inevitably imposed normative expectations and ideas about what a "good immigrant" should be. To a certain degree, the central government was itself responsible for such normalization in the use of the crude yet powerful symbolism of a polarized world of darkness and light that depicted immigrants' illegality as "abnormal" and exceptional, in opposition to the "normal" legality purportedly emblematic of Spanish society. It is clear that the volunteers and professionals helping immigrants did not buy into this dichotomous representation, knowing full well that Spaniards had long tolerated immigrants' supposed illegality, even as the state denied legal immigrants' basic human rights (not to mention citizens' rights). However, as Foucault puts it, in modern societies, "law functions increasingly as a norm, distinguished from the rule in that it identifies general standards" (1978, 89) that are to be internalized by the subject in the form of self-regulation, conjuring up a "normal" individual disciplined not by punishment but by the repetition of normative requirements. And the experts were helping effect the law.

Experts were sometimes imposing their own ideas of normality upon immigrants, particularly with regard to standards of tidiness, punctuality, respectfulness, sincerity, honesty, and courtesy—often evaluating immigrants negatively in these terms. Organizations often had to deal with crowds of immigrants demanding assistance and arguing whose case was most urgent. Organizations would set up timetables, give people individual appointments, and provide them with the forms they needed to fill out and advice about the documents they should bring to their appointments. Volunteers and sympathizers would engage immigrants in personal conversations that would help immigrants feel more comfortable interacting with Spaniards. These interactions often entailed implicit normative notions as to how immigrants should behave. For instance, one volunteer told me, "I often advise them about things they are not supposed to do, and there you are, they go ahead and do precisely what I told them not to do. I do not know whether this is because they don't understand, or if they do it simply to contradict me" (C.F., summer 1993).

More than once I witnessed social workers paternalistically advising immigrants about minimum standards of decency, such as the importance of cleaning one's hands before eating, of wearing clothes properly, or of taking care of the houses they rented. Many volunteers and professionals lamented the complications and delays stemming from what they thought was immigrants' lack of punctuality, propensity to lie or give ambiguous answers to essential questions, and rudeness and insolence, especially in the case of "Moors." One priest representing the Catholic Church in the area said, "We are working with a very difficult collective: we want to help them but they don't permit us to do so" (D.A., summer 1994). This kind of ethnocentrism is also illustrated with the rather naive testimony of a well-intentioned nun working full-time for immigrants: "If immigrants do not behave properly there are a lot of problems. Other people complain because they play music or even dance in the houses. They are not clean, nor do they respect minimum 'rules of education' among us. I am now thinking about offering a course to teach them about these things. I don't know what I should call it—'Rehabilitation Plan' or something like that" (A.A., summer 1992). A continuous chain of misunderstandings and mutual distrust impedes smooth relationships between immigrants and experts and volunteers. Personal case files often contain lawyers' and volunteers' comments and observations about a given immigrant, to be passed on to the next person that deals with the case (Pérez Losada 1993).[18]

The negative opinions that experts and volunteers sometimes have of immigrants readily reinforce culturalist explanations of immigrants' behavior as ethnically different from that of Spaniards. One juridical expert told me: "It is unbelievable really how these people are. Instead of saving for important things such as the cost of the permit, they allow themselves to buy lamb instead of the cheaper pork. Their fundamentalism is outrageous!" (C.A., summer 1993). Another expert told me: "It is difficult for a Moor to adapt to the Spanish scene. Moors are so proud of themselves, so demanding, and so individualistic! They only look out for their own interests. They betray one another. They are not able to organize collectively, even though this is the only possible way for them to defend their interests.... This goes with their culture, I suppose" (C.B., spring 1995).

Similar comments reflect a pernicious legacy of an orientalist imaginary that easily homogenizes members of a particular culture or nationality:

Black people are different form "Moors." Black people are honest, industrious, solidary, spontaneous—in a word, good people [*buena gente*]. It is a pity our materialist culture doesn't recognize their fundamental values. We have to teach them to behave properly, but usually because of a problem of ignorance.... We have to take into account that in Africa they do not have running water, they live in houses without doors or windows, they dance and sing in the streets.... Here they lose their customs, their traditional culture, which should be preserved because it is much better than ours. (A.A., summer 1992)

A kind of "imperialist nostalgia ... where people mourn the passing of what they themselves have transformed," as Rosaldo (1989, 69) has defined it, seems to prevail, especially among Catholics, an attitude that "licenses patronizing attitudes of condescension, such as reverence for a simplicity 'we' have lost" (Rosaldo 1986, 97). Although most members of NGOs openly recognize their own ignorance about how immigrants live in Africa, they do not recognize the link between such culturalist assumptions and racism. Instead, they conceive of racism as an attitude of refusal and hatred toward foreigners and people of color. Yet their own well-intended desire to help immigrants incorporates relations of domination masked behind purportedly positive and/or value-free attitudes and practices, in which they conceive of themselves as providing "remedies," assisting, and managing immigrants' "problems," treating immigrants as simply ignorant of "the" system or as having "wrong" understandings about "how things have to be done here."

Immigrants as Administered Subjects and the Fetishism of Papers

Fetishism: The Concept

The 1991 regularization of immigrants' status ostensibly opened the door for immigrants to acquire rights by legalizing their status, yet both the legality and the rights proved to be more apparent than real. Rather, I will argue, regularization generated the appearance of legality while treating immigrants as temporary workers whose legality and rights continued to depend entirely on third parties. We have already seen that regularization effected a cultural change in immigrants' understandings of the significance of papers. In light of what regularization actually (as opposed to ostensibly) accomplished, I now propose to analyze this change as the "Fetishism of Papers." My analysis is inspired by the Marxian concept of fetishism, the classical evolutionary anthropological perspective, the recent location of Law as a Myth, and the common understanding of fetish as "something, especially an inanimate object, that is believed to have magical powers" (*Collins Dictionary*).

Detailed treatment of the history of theoretical debates about fetishism in capitalist, democratic, and rational-bureaucratic societies is beyond the scope of my analysis in this section.[19] I want nonetheless to discuss how the concept of fetishism as used in the anthropological world inspired Marx's analysis of capitalist commodity fetishism. Toward the end of the last century, Lubbock defined fetishism as "the stage when man thinks he can force divinity to satisfy his desires" (1870, quoted in Harris 1981, 175). Frazer (1951) distinguished magic from religion as a primitive expression of science, a false idea about the regularity of processes of cause-effect. Marx analyzes fetishism of the commodity as the (exchange) value that commodity takes once the particularities of use-value are abstracted and reified in the capitalist market. What is most important here for my conceptualization of the "fetishism of papers" is Marx's emphasis on (1) the way social relations become relations among things; (2) how the social world appears to us as "natural" and permanent instead of what it really is, namely, a human product; and (3) the fact that this social world, as something objective, appears to be out of our control; and (4) commodity fetishism as both the material reality and the appearance of capitalist society.[20]

The "fetishism of papers" shares several characteristics with Marx's fetishism of the commodity. The papers acquire an abstract value, detached from social relations underlying the administration of the LOE. Immigrants, purportedly subjects of law, find that their legal status depends on a systematic commodity circulation that treats them as "an object and subjects them to the same prohibitions and quota allocations under the immigration laws as are other commodities imported across national boundaries" (Pashukanis 1989, 112 n. 12). The "fetishism of papers" is related to the "magic" involved in becoming a purportedly legal subject: some rituals regulated by administration and bureaucracy are supposed to conjure up an autonomy of the law (out of human's control) that is able to grant rights and constitute persons as legal subjects. Similarly, the (exchange) value that papers acquire in Spanish society is appropriated not by the immigrant, who is treated as an object and not as a subject of law, but instead by the state. Thus the state legitimizes the appearance of legality and renders as natural function its ability to demarcate and maintain classificatory boundaries shaping the construction of social difference, as well as the political struggles that weaken those boundaries (Corrigan and Sayer 1985). This fetishism, however, is neither a mere illusion nor an exclusive tool on the hands of state and capitalists' interests. The idea that power functions not only in a prescriptive, but also in a productive way, as established by Foucault, and that ideological struggle can be conceived as practical engagements with shifts and modifications in "common sense" in the Gramscian sense, should encourage scholars to explore immigrants' resistance to and appropriation of the "fetishism of papers" and the appearance of legality.

Continuing Illegality

Let us consider this phenomenon in a less abstract way. After the process of regularization, 108,321 immigrants received work/residence permits. Among these, 775 permits were granted to immigrants living in Granada, and 26 in Alfaya. Most immigrants received type-B permits for salaried workers or type-D permits for autonomous workers, valid for one year, in a specific territory and economic area, and renewable for one year if similar conditions were proved (having a contract or a firm offer of work) at the end of the first year. In Granada, the majority of non-EU immigrants regularized were Senegalese (though Moroccans predominated among those regularized elsewhere in Spain).[21] Most were regularized as autonomous workers to legitimize their occupations as street vendors.[22]

Yet despite the appearance of legality conjured up by the 1991 process of regularization, illegality continued to be the norm among immigrants. As a Senegalese immigrant who preferred to apply as a salaried agrarian worker told me:

> It's risky to get a permit for agricultural work, since such work is only seasonal. A permit for agriculture would restrict me to working in Granada. Yet an agricultural permit is much cheaper in terms of taxes, and it gives you the opportunity to get the unemployment subsidy. And according to the REA [Agrarian Special Regime] you don't need a contract to prove you can continue to work, but only the required sixty day jobs or *peonadas*, which, in the worst case, you can always "buy." As for the rest of the year, I live in Granada city doing odd jobs. I take risks by working in the informal economy, in construction, in services, but you know this is not very much controlled here anyway. (C.A., summer 1994)

Statistics that I collected in 1992 and from the Alfayan Office of Immigrants' Information (OII) in 1993 and 1994 estimate that 80 percent of Alfaya's immigrants were illegal. Only a few held labor contracts, two were applying for unemployment subsidies,[23] while fourteen needed another *precontrato* to renew their initial type-B permits. In sum, most immigrants were situated at the same point as before the regularization. Those who were able to renew their contracts, meanwhile, had to deal with bureaucracies endlessly to prove they were still in the same circumstances that justified their initial permits. Yet now they were also required to provide receipts to prove that taxes had been paid either by the employer or by themselves. Just as in 1991, those who missed out on regularization or who had fallen once into illegality were trying to document an identity that would fit the legal categories defined by the LOE.

There were two main reasons for continued illegality among incoming immigrants. First, the 1991 regularization did not in any way alter the restrictive and exclusionary character of the LOE. Any person who had entered Spain without an appropriate visa had virtually no access to legalization. Second, new immigrants continued to enter the country clandestinely, despite border controls, precisely because fewer and ever more restrictive visas were being given out by Spanish consulates abroad as Spain tried to conform to the Schengen agreements. For the 1991 regularization had convinced immigrants' friends and relatives abroad that they could count on immigrants already in Spain to help them if they immigrated clandestinely, without visas. (See chapter 6 for a discussion of Senegalese transnationalism and the networks through which immigrants provided refuge, contacts, and information to new arrivals.)

Indeed, as I illustrated before, control and detentions were more ubiquitous after 1991 than before, not just within the valley, but in public transportation directed toward it, in purportedly "humanitarian" temporary shelters, and in camping grounds (see the section "Local Implementation of Social Programs" in chapter 5). As a voluntary worker wrote in her diary: "We constantly learn about roundups, about the Civil Guard stopping buses to identify 'illegals,' about detentions in the streets, controls in the train and bus stations. It was as if after the agricultural campaign the authorities capriciously determined it was the moment to go out, as if they had been anxious to hunt any immigrant who dared to move" (A.M., summer 1992, 10).

Many immigrants who had been granted a legal work/residence permit for one year had subsequently lost their legal status, either because the renewal was not granted or because they had not gathered the papers required and so did not even try to the renew the permit. Furthermore, even among legal immigrants, the circumstances of labor situate them in strict reading of the law in extremely vulnerable juridical circumstances. Most immigrants legalized in Alfaya in 1991 returned in the summer of 1992 and worked as temporary day laborers with Alfayan peasants they knew. Although some peasants had provided immigrants with a *precontrato*, most immigrants worked without contracts and without the provision of Social Security costs. They were thus working illegally, even though they were legal. To do so was not considered an infraction serious enough to warrant deportation, but such immigrants were unable to obtain proof of payment of required taxes, which they needed to renew their permits (art. 50.6, Regulation of the LOE). Restrictions on the type-B permit, which is for work in a given geographical and economic sector, requires immigrants to notify the Ministry of Interior of any changes in residence or occupation and to initiate a new application for the work/residence permit (art. 14/LOE). Such immigrants are not allowed to work until the new permit is granted.[24] To conceal changes requiring reapplication, or to delay in applying are both defined as a grave infraction punishable by deportation (art. 26.e/LOE). Similarly, if the immigrant is unemployed at the moment of renewal, the permit will be denied and the immigrant must leave the country or face deportation (art 26.f/LOE). Job insecurity has thrust countless immigrants into such contradictory "legality/illegality."

Legal preferences for hiring Spaniards before immigrants also compound immigrants' difficulties before the law. Even if an immigrant obtains a firm work offer, the employer may be required to present proof from the INEM (Instituto Nacional de Empleo, or National Institute of Employment) confirming that the job position had been advertised in print (art. 37/R). An immigrant's permit or renewal can be invalidated if there are unemployed Spaniards in the economic area where the immigrant is applying to work (art. 18.1.a/LOE). Given the high unemployment rate throughout Andalusia and particularly in agriculture these two provisions can easily be invoked to limit the number of legal immigrants working in the area. In practice, enforcement of these provisions has been capricious.

At this point, the reader may ask how it is even possible for an immigrant to stay in Spain. The answer must take into account the contradictory interests of the state to be accountable to local employers' needs, to the public's simultaneous senses of solidarity with and fear of immigrants, to supranational pressures (especially from the EU) to control immigration, and to international advocacy of human and immigrant rights. The fact is that the state is neither able to nor interested in bringing immigration to a halt. The Alien Law thus functions arbitrarily and inconsistently, as studies and legal experts have testified.[25] From an anthropological perspective, the important question is not whether we can prove statistically that the LOE has failed to provide stable legal protection to immigrants with the required papers. The undeniable ethnographic fact is that an increasing number of immigrants are successfully settling in Spain and that most are considered illegal.

Chasing the Papers: Fetishism in Practice

Even though immigrants are situated at the margins of Spanish politics, law, citizenry, and culture, their presence is producing important changes in identities and notions of personhood, not only for immigrants themselves but for other Spaniards. Much as is happening in other Western countries, in Spain we find (1) a redefinition of a formal notion of citizenship as an attribute of a category of persons, and (2) a reconfiguration of the nature and scope of the public sphere. The presence of immigrants effects these changes because issues of their inclusion or exclusion within the rule of law and their access or lack of access to rights reshapes what inclusion and rights mean for other people.[26]

The perspective I take on such transformation is that identities are not logically constituted prior to engagement of concrete social agents with the public sphere, but rather that both are mutually constituted through political and sociocultural practices. Identities are constructed through both forced and formal participation, as well as through informal interactions in which people share experiences and sometimes contest their meanings.[27] The effect of law in transforming identities and practices should be understood as both shaping and enabling, coercive and productive. State-centered analyses generally overemphasize the coercive power of the state, ignoring "the ambiguities of normative law and legal embeddedness, especially the way in which law can be a source of popular empowerment ... and a central factor in identity formation" (Somers 1993, 596; see also Thomson 1968, 1971). Here I want to explore two issues that relate to nationality, while avoiding the ethnocentric presupposition that nationality is limited: (1) The first issue concerns how the disciplining of immigrants, together with their own corresponding efforts to validate rights of stay in a country, actually transforms immigrants into a new kind of (administered) social subject. In the process of transformation, immigrants use multiple and predominantly transnational sociocultural resources to negotiate, question, and fight for the appearance of legality, which relates to the second issue: (2) How does the appearance of modern legal subjectivity and belonging entail a logic of universalism and impartiality, constructed in antithesis to other similarly "magic," "mythic," or "imagined" systems of belonging and of subject constitution?

My analysis extends into the next chapter with detailed consideration of the transnational strategies that Senegalese migrant workers use. This analysis will allow me to question the traditional figure of resistance as a subject "outside" power, examining instead how immigrants resist the bounded and exclusionary binary logic sanctioned by states according to which one should submit to either-or categories of membership and personhood.

Let us begin this analysis by considering the discipline that immigrants experience. We must bear in mind that the practices and effects of discipline vary according to the shifts over time and space in how immigrants are imbedded in social relations. We have already seen how administrative regulations and experts instill "documentary habits" in immigrants and transmit the legal mythology sustaining the "fetishism of papers." Immigrants begin to respond to this discipline by creating a documented personal history in their country of origin (e.g., in efforts to construct a "valuable" presentation of the self). One young Senegalese came to Spain with papers certifying his experience in theater, dance, and football.[28] A Moroccan man wanted to underscore his language abilities and his training in tourism. An Algerian brought his education certificates and proof of his experience as an industrial worker. Each of these immigrants turned to other people in their country of origin to help document their abilities or create verifiable identities that would fit the requirements of a visa application. This process usually drew on favors entailing expectations of reciprocation, or on submission to clientelist relationships, as I analyze in the next chapter for the case of the Senegalese immigrants.

Once in Spain, immigrants need countless documents that are not simply physical pieces of papers, as we have seen, but that involve immigrants' daily struggle for recognition as inhabitants of the Spanish territory—as neighbors, as workers, as "trustworthy" individuals who adjust to the normative standards of people surrounding them. The process of acquiring papers reinforces a certain unrootedness and deterritorialization that derives from the dominant binary logic of being (or not being) a member of a territorial polity. In relation to the process of acquisition of papers, immigrants are foreigners in Europe and absent members with obligations in their countries of origin.

Immigrants experience the disciplinary practices to which they are subjected as foreigners in Spain and Andalusia, yet they increasingly take on a certain self-disciplinary agency. Well-intentioned Spaniards who assist immigrants normalize immigrants and constitute them as "administered subjects," yet at the same time, immigrants become purportedly legal subjects with supposed rights and obligations (especially as taxpayers) for which they themselves must assume social agency and responsibility. Immigrants have to learn the regulatory requirements of the LOE, and they have to repeat the processes of applying for legal status when their permits lapse. As a result, many immigrants become better informed about Spanish institutions and administrative procedures than most other Spanish citizens.[29] While NGOs, labor unions, or private lawyers may help fit them into immigration categories, the final responsibility for acquiring the papers is their own.

Thus, although disciplinary power homogenizes people into fixed categories, it also individualizes them, because each particular case is subjected to the control and scrutiny of administrative authorities. As I undertook my research, it gradually became evident to me that an important part of immigrants' daily practices were related to attending to administrative requirements. Every day, immigrants were using the telephones in Alfaya's main plaza to call institutions, associations, friends, and personal contacts in their country of origin and throughout Spain to inform themselves about legalization processes and to obtain valid documents. Often they had to travel to Granada to pursue their cases, which meant strategizing to share transportation and to avoid angering employers for being absent from work. To be successful, they needed to make timely plans, strategizing as to which document they needed first to validate the rest of them.

Administrative control and regulation is considered a humane form of regulation; no coercion is purportedly involved. People coming to administration windows are not physically punished for errors and misunderstandings.[30] They come because they "voluntarily" submit to regulations in exchange for recognition of rights, access to public social benefits, and the like. In actuality, however, immigrants' experience is otherwise. In my role as anthropologist I accompanied many immigrants on their "bureaucratic pilgrimages" because I had a car. These immigrants clearly felt more secure with my accompanying them, for I would be considered a "respectable" Spaniard; they felt less fearful of receiving arbitrary treatment.

Administrative windows are notorious in Spanish jokes, complaints, and sarcastic literary descriptions of everyday life and customs, the most famous being the nineteenth-century Larra short story entitled "Come Back Tomorrow!" which over the decades has become a popular saying. Most citizens still feel that administrators abuse their privileged occupations. Functionaries never give reasons for denying a request; they withhold explanations of technical requirements; they take ample time off for meals whenever they want, no matter how many people are waiting in line for their assistance. If this is how Spaniards such as myself view functionaries, imagine how immigrants feel when they approach an administrative window, sometimes with broken Spanish and their characteristic files or bags of countless old and wrinkled documents, identity cards, photos, and press clippings to prove who they are in their seminomadic life.

An immigrant who works as a journalist provides the following good-humored account of deciding, after collecting all kinds of papers in different institutions, that he felt ready to face the uncertainties of the last window, that of the police station:

The other day, more than one hundred immigrants were in line, and I took my place at the end of the line. This was my second attempt to wait in line for my turn. The first time I had to quit because I had to return to work. The line moved forward very slowly. For a long time I stood in front of a poster describing a "dangerous armed terrorist of ETA [Euzkadi Ta Askatasuna, or Basque Motherland and Liberty, the well-known Basque terrorist group]," and I took my time studying his physical appearance. I observed fellow immigrants, men and women with skin and passports of all colors, immigrants who, before arriving in this line, have waited in many other lines, moving slowly. Meanwhile we listened to the characteristic noise of all offices in Spain: that of the stamps applied by functionaries with vehemence and celerity. They used stamps in all kinds of sizes and forms. A document has no validity in Spain if it doesn't carry twenty different stamps. I observed the four functionaries and hoped I would be called by the young and beautiful one. But then I thought, "maybe I'll be missing a document of minimal importance and she, new in this work and determined to do a good job, will force me to return with it tomorrow, while the older fellows, more experienced in these bureaucratic tasks, may be willing to overlook a small shortcoming in the documentation." And then I thought it might well be all to the contrary, who knows? After an hour and a half, I realized with satisfaction that I was already at the head of the line. I had the impression that everyone was looking at me with envy, just as I had looked before at those in my current situation. When my turn came, we discovered that I was missing the most important documents of all: the receipt for having deposited the-20,000 pesetas ($200.00) permit fee! As I read the word "Hacienda" [Internal Revenue Service] on the list of requirements, I had instinctively brought my latest tax declaration instead. The kind functionary told me that if I came back before lunchtime she would attend to me promptly, so I wouldn't have to wait in the line again. I then started an obstacle-course race to the bank to get the money, and then to the Hacienda [IRS] building to deposit it, get a stamped receipt, and go back to the window. This is one of the things I like the most in Spain: it may be true that they impose more requirements than anywhere else, but you can always skip them. (*El País*, February 22, 1995)

This story has a good ending in that the immigrant, who calls the functionary his "guardian angel," was finally able to obtain his permit after inking a finger to stamp it with his fingerprint.

Accompanying immigrants to offices, I have witnessed many such experiences and can testify to the fear and frustration they provoke:

After one Senegalese immigrant had checked his papers over and over again to be sure they were in order, I accompanied him to the police station. When his turn at the window came, the woman behind it stamped all the papers without even looking at us and handed some of them back, saying: "These have nothing to do with the permit"; and

"This certificate of having no criminal record was issued in Madrid and is not valid here"; and "All these documents have to be presented in duplicate. Go to the store with the photocopy machine in *x* street"; and, finally, "You have to fill this out, and this form twice." She told us to come back later, saying, "You may have the time to fill them out now, but not before I close this window, so go away right now." We returned together later to present the papers once again. She kept a copy of everything and told us, "The other copy is for 'the group.' Wait here until they call you." My tamed friend was ready to leave the line, but I was astonished and could not help asking, "Group? What group?" And she answered, this time staring at me, "The group—the one that interviews immigrants." So I asked, "A group that interviews immigrants? All these papers are in order. Who has to do an interview? And about what? And when?" The woman began to get irritated and replied, "They are policemen; they belong to the 'Foreigner Operative Group,' and they do an interview to report to the civil governor, who is the person who grants or rejects the visa this guy is asking for. Wait right over there. Although I am not sure they will be able to attend to you today because they have a lot of work." As the saying goes, we had to "come back tomorrow." (L.S., extract from fieldwork diary, 1995)

However much immigrants may work to ensure that they have met all of the bureaucratic paper requirements, the immigration process thus situates them in a structural position of inferiority. Civil and security functionaries demand information from immigrants, require them to demonstrate allegiance, and even to invest money in the process. Yet immigrants are treated as if they do not have any rights, not even the right to request information. Many of my African friends, like the one in the last vignette, do not dare to ask for explanation of functionaries' behavior. This is part of a long held habitus brought from their countries of origin, where frequently only money will serve to change functionaries' mind. This kind of corruption is not open in Spain, (although it is possible, as happened these years), so we may find two attitudes, one of 'tamed' submission, the other of frustration and anger.

In addition to a feeling of powerlessness during the whole process, the effect of a refusal is shattering. I will always remember another immigrant whom I accompanied to pick up his permit who was told, once he arrived, that more money was needed. He burst into tears right in front of a Ministry of Finances functionary, a higher official behind a big black table. This official was as moved as I was by the immigrant's reaction. "Don't worry," he said, "your file is impeccable. I've known you for a long time. You are a serious, responsible, and truthful [*formal*] person. I know very well how harsh migrant life is. Look, take a little time to get the money, and this will be it." Although the immigrant really could not stop crying, he tried to put on a calm appearance and thanked the official profusely. Afterwards, when we went to have a coffee and discussed whether others in the Senegalese community might lend him the money, he told me: "I often think I won't be able to follow through, that I won't be able to do everything I have to do, but how can I give up after everything my family has done for me? I can't leave them, they need me!" (M.A., spring 1995).

Criticism and Appropriation of the "Fetishism of Papers"

Immigrants are one another's most reassuring and reliable sources of information and support. Immigrants talk with one another to try to make sense of such experiences and to help one another cope with countless deceptions, deceits, misunderstandings, and failures. They share clues as to how administrative processes really work and pool information gleaned from interaction with experts, employers, and other Spanish friends and contacts. They allow one another to ask questions abruptly, to interrupt a discussion to clarify the meaning of written instructions, and to tap others' insights as to what is "inappropriate behavior" toward Spaniards in different positions. Through discussion and debate with their counterparts, immigrants try to acquire and assess the knowledge of those who have built up more experience in Spain. Any one person's experience will be recounted again and again among members of a community, emphasizing the positive consequences of acquiring a stable status—being able to talk to Spaniards on more equal terms, gaining prestige in their country of origin, and acquiring some rights in Spain.

Immigrants have a difficult time establishing fluid relationships with Spaniards because of a growing sense of ethnic division. Immigrants always feel somehow on "the wrong side of the law," as Hall put it (1978), not only because of their "illegality," but also because they are "Moors" or "blacks," because they are foreigners, because they are Muslims. They always have to prove they are not what people think of them.[31]

Nonetheless, immigrant collectives are slowly settling, building up their own associations and using the learning acquired through interactions with institutions, NGOs, and labor unions to assert claims of their own. Immigrants critique the intermediaries through which they have to relate to the state:

They are appropriating the money budgeted for us. They always hire Spaniards. To be sure, they also need jobs, because there are a lot of unemployed Spaniards. But not with "our" money. They talk a lot about the need to organize to struggle against the LOE and stuff, but the lawyers don't really do anything; they don't resolve our situation.

Human rights are a good thing, yes, but in the end, these are only words. In reality, we continue without housing, without jobs, without money, without papers, while they—they continue eating off of our problems, with their bottoms well installed in the office, waiting for the "poor little ones" to arrive and ask for their help. (Immigrant workers in Alfaya, summer 1994)

Such critiques do not reflect lack of commitment on the part of experts, who in fact have helped many immigrants acquire the papers they have, and immigrants know this. But the promise of "light" and "normality" conjured up by the state and promoted by intermediaries—the "fetishism of papers"—seems to evaporate as a false illusion. Papers really have no magic power to effect rights and equality before the law in daily life. If lawyers and NGOs cannot resolve immigrants' problems—if they cannot work the magic that effortlessly extracts justice from the papers—why, then, are they still there?

Thrust to the margins of Spanish society despite all of their efforts, immigrants sometimes channel their depressed feelings of powerless and frustration into antagonism toward Spain in general. As one immigrant told his fellows: "We are all brothers here! All of us foreigners need the same papers—blacks, Arabs, Chinese, and even whites. It's the Spanish state that doesn't want any of us here. And if we persist, it is because we need papers, all of us!" (A.A., summer 1994). Impartiality of the law and of the state have not yet taken full root in a hegemonic formation, not just because immigrants' experiences of arbitrary and discriminatory subjection to administrative regulations, but because Spanish society more broadly includes underprivileged and critical groups and individuals.

However, I do not want to minimize the importance of having papers for the construction of immigrants as illegals. Even though immigrants experience social discrimination and racialization as an undifferentiated group, the law pervades everyday practices as well as institutional social programs that appear to offer immigrants integration. As an (illegal) immigrant expressed it: "My main problem is the [lack of] papers. I just need any paper that would allow me to walk freely throughout Spain. I would be happy with that. Now I am trying to get a contract through a guy. Let's see if I am lucky—that would help so much" (M.D., summer 1993). According to many immigrants, the bottom line in the acquisition of papers is money. If you have money, you can get papers. Papers end up being perceived as a precious (even if conditional and temporal) possession, rather than a legal status that recognizes and guarantees immigrants their rights as active, productive, and contributing members of Spanish society.

The promise of papers thus evokes a vision that immigrants, however much they are categorized as undifferentiated foreigners, should nonetheless enjoy the rights of Spanish society. As foreigners, they are required to prove, again and again, in a documented form, that they are still "attached to the country," that they are still "productive," and that they are still meeting their tax obligations, just as nonforeigners supposedly do. While others view them as nonmembers of the dominant community—as disobedient, lazy, lacking commitment, willing to take advantage of the welfare state, as not contributing to the "common" interest through taxes, and even as treasonous—these very vilifications connote that immigrants could be otherwise. Nor do immigrants hesitate to invert the negative discourse by decrying the hypocrisy of the Spanish state for not applying to them the same standards that are applied to Spanish citizens. The theme that immigrants are just as good as nationals is as yet still emergent in immigrant consciousness and conversations. It will take time and effort to turn such ideas into a coherent political struggle and claim-making discourse. Yet the universalism of the logic underlying their complaints is undeniable: If we are good neighbors, good workers, good citizens, and good taxpayers, why are we denied rights on the basis of our origin? That is not legal.

As pointed out at the beginning of the chapter, modern law claims to be grounded in fundamental personal rights exercised through universalistic and impartial rationality. As Young (1990, 77) has pointed out, assessment of "legal validity" in actual application of law risks being mechanical in its "rationality." Immigrants go beyond this critique, recognizing that the appearance of legality ultimately has a materialistic basis, which creates a mercantilized notion of citizenship. Some immigrants, however much disciplined and administered as subjects, recognize the embodied effects of the "fetishism of papers." They realize that the differentiation between purportedly legal and illegal foreign workers really simply reproduces inequalities among immigrants as well as between immigrants and nonforeign nationals. "We all need the same papers" underscores that immigrants are fundamentally equal and that they all experience discrimination. Some immigrants also recognize that the embodiment of purported legality/illegality also tends to individualize them, breaking down the solidarities of religion and moral obligation that immigrants share. One veteran immigrant working legally in Alfaya who had been trained as a religious authority in Senegal lamented that a fellow countryman had begun to act only in his own interest: "The difference between legal and illegal is very dangerous among us, because some people take advantage of it. If I have a house, I have an obligation to lodge people. Hospitality is a religious principle, you know? There are no superior laws for us Muslims. But some people are ignoring this. The fact that you have papers doesn't allow you to receive money for lodging somebody in a worse situation, nor to threaten such people so you can use them for your own profit" (C.A., summer 1994).

Some of my informants go even further in their critique of the embodiment of legality and illegality. They lament the binary logic of mutually exclusive categories that nation-states thus impose on them, especially because of the culturalist binary that it imposes, pitting the "Western" (normally referred to as either "European" or "white") against the "African." In this binary, "Western" legal culture is supposedly based on a formal equality among all human beings or members of a polity, while "African" legal culture privileges religious commitment to a transcendent notion of justice. In practice, both are compatible in immigrant's daily life through the embodiment of transcultural resources and notions of justice and of personhood, as will become apparent when we consider Senegalese transnational experience in chapter 6. Immigrants' everyday engagement of Spanish administrative regulations and of Spanish people in multidimensional interactions constitutes them as new subjects, yet it does not fully determine them as such. For they are, in fact, socially positioned as transnational subjects. And they are struggling as transnational subjects to create new citizenship practices that reconcile the Western mythology of legal impartiality and universality with other notions of justice. Yet doing so is difficult, given the hegemonic power of nation-states to generate personhoods deemed to be incompatible with one another, essentialized as "stable" attributes of "other" territorially and morally bounded cultures and nationalities.

Notes

1. Throughout this work I use the term "papers" as it is used popularly to refer to the documents enabling foreigners to legally live and work in Spain. For the sake of clarity, I will not use quotation marks to emphasize the metaphorical use of the term.
2. This occurred through the "guest worker" programs in western Europe and through the Bracero program in the United States. For a general account of post–World War II immigration, see Castles and Kosack 1985; Castles 1989; Cross 1989; Hollifield 1992; Sassen-Koob 1983, 1988; and Wilpert 1988.
3. Withol de Wenden (1988) clearly links economic transformations in core countries with creation of the problem of "illegality." She highlights the fact that France openly tolerated undocumented immigration for economic reasons and only in 1973 began using the notion of "illegal immigration" in contrast to an open category of noncontrolled immigration. See Layton-Henry (1990b) for a comparative perspective on the new policies and legal restrictions on immigration taken by European states since the mid 1970s, both at the border and inland (e.g., strengthening visa requirements, police control of the border, restrictions in residence and work permits, and curtailing immigrants' access to tax-supported public services).
4. For an analysis of the 7/85 Alien Law, see Santos 1993 and Vidal Gil 1995. According to Izquierdo (1993), by 1993 more than 25 percent of those who regularized under the 1991 regularization program had either been denied renewal or were not able to gather the documents required to renew their permits, thus causing them to refrain from applying for renewal altogether. This has proved to be a consistent pattern in the years following this research, as we found in recent analysis of the 2000 regularization program (Arango and Suárez-Navaz n.d.).
5. See, among others, Borneman 1993; Cohn and Dirks 1988; Comaroff and Comaroff 1991; Comaroff and Roberts 1981; Coombe 1989; Corrigan and Sayer 1985; Coutin 1993; Fitzpatrick 1992; Hunt 1993; Maurer 1997; Merry 1991; Mitchell 1988; Roseberry 1994; Starr and Collier 1989; Yngvesson 1993.
6. See Gupta 1995 for problematization of the conceptual differentiation of political and civil society. Scholarship on social movements has also addressed the relations between civil society and the state (see Maier 1987; Offe and Wiesenthal 1985).
7. See Bourdieu 1977; Gramsci 1971; Hunt 1993; Roseberry 1994; Williams 1977.

8. As an illustration of the increasing enforcement of the LOE from 1985 to 1990, see the figures provided by a 1990 report of the Human Rights Association of Spain: arrests in 1985: 13,898; 1986: 14,457; 1987: 16,393; 1988: 25,798; 1989: 32,496; 1990: 336,863 (APDHE 1991). By 1994 this last figure had already almost doubled (see Dirección General de Policía [Police Headquarters], Ministerio de Justicia e Interior [Ministry of Justice and Ministry of the Interior] 1994).

9. For similar measures in Europe, see Winthol de Wenden 1990.

10. These dates signal important legal and political measures implicitly assumed to be major reasons for increasing illegality among immigrants: the enactment of the LOE and the requirement of a visa for people from Morocco, who up to that time held the privileged status of not needing a visa to enter Spain.

11. I do not mean to imply that there may be a "purer" form of resistance. I follow Coutin's approach to analysis of the U.S.A. Sanctuary movement in suggesting that "Every form of political action engenders its own contradictions, and had the movement forsworn legal arguments, it would have abandoned a powerful source of legitimacy" (Coutin 1993, 108).

12. Being "portrayed" in the local idiom means that the state has accurate records of a person's economic situation (see note 23 in chapter 1).

13. See Anderson 1991; Barker 1981; Balibar and Wallerstein 1991; Chatterjee 1986, 1993; Herzfeld 1982; Gellner 1983; Gilroy 1987; Guillaumin 1995; Hobsbawm 1990; Parker et al. 1992; Rosaldo 1990, 1994b; Stolke 1996; Targuieff 1987.

14. In addition to the free service provided by lawyers and other "experts" working for NGOs and labor unions, there were many underemployed or unemployed lawyers who took advantage of the immigrants' need of legal assistance. According to many informants, such lawyers sometimes abused immigrants through corrupt or deceitful practices.

15. Comisiones Obreras is the Communist labor union (Workers Commission). A section dedicated to immigrants was created in 1992; GISCO stands for Grupo de Interés Social de Comisiones Obreras (Social Interest Group of the Workers Commission Union) and CITE for Comité de Intervención para Trabajadores Extranjeros (Intervention Committee for Alien Workers). CITE has focused its work almost exclusively on juridical assistance. Granada Acoge is an NGO dedicated to assist to immigrants in a more global way (Welcome to Granada).

16. The NGO Granada Acoge and its village affiliate, Ardo el-Jamia, held a broad notion of the integration of immigrants inspired by Christian principles of solidarity and a humanistic approach to assistance to immigrants. The labor union concentrated much more on juridical preconditions for dealing with labor conditions. Of the two groups, the union worked more closely with Alfaya's municipal council to prevent labor exploitation and competition between local and foreign workers.

17. The LOE did not even contemplate the possibility of acquiring a permit for permanent work/residence, the status that the migration literature has deemed as "denizen" (see Hammar 1990 and Brubaker 1989 on the notion of citizens and denizens). This changed in the new regulation passed by the Royal Decree 155/1996 (*BOE*, February 23, 1996). After seven years of uninterrupted legal status (an initial B permit must have been renewed twice for a total of four years and then converted to a three-year C permit), the immigrant may apply for a permanent permit, which has to be revalidated every five years (art. 75 of the New Regulation of the LOE).

18. I wish to stress that members of unions and NGOs working with immigrants, whose number has greatly increased since 1991, are highly motivated individuals, and immigrants often find their assistance invaluable, although immigrants may criticize them and question their work, as I show later.

19. The reader should keep in mind debates about subject/object, ideology and reproduction of inequalities, and the questioning of the dichotomy between symbolic and material domination as a broader reference framework (Weber, Lukács, Gramsci, Foucault, Bourdieu, among others).

20. See Pashukanis (1989) for an application of "commodity fetishism" to law. Fitzpatrick (1992, 6, passim) tries to resolve the apparent contradiction between law's autonomy and law's social dependence, arguing for the mythic elevation of law.

21. This reflects not only the presence of a strong and organized Senegalese community in the province, but also the especially strong ties that Senegalese immigrants maintained with the NGO Granada Acoge. Nonetheless, the current coordinator told me, "the organization has replaced personalized relations of an earlier period with progressively more professional organization, and this has led to a decline of Senegalese and the inclusion of other nationalities" (C.C., spring 1995).

22. In chapter 6, I explain how Senegalese transnational migration networks facilitate immigrants' incorporation into street commerce. They will apply to a D permit, which provides greater autonomy and mobility, but it is burdened with very high taxes (more than $200.00 per month). Semi-autonomous immigrants also have to pay for municipal permits to be able to sell in each of the villages they visit, and for costs of transportation such as using a car, gasoline, or daily bus fares.

23. The main problem in this case was to obtain the local residence certificate *(empadronamiento):* This has changed substantially since 1998, when, according to the Empadrónate (Get Yourself Registered in a Census) campaign, there has been a coordinated effort from institutions and social organizations to make immigrants aware of the necessity to register as residents independently from their juridical status. This campaign has also been directed toward functionaries of the Municipal Census office, since many of them have been reticent about registering [*empadronar*] undocumented immigrants.

24. Spanish administration is characterized by its extreme slowness; the resolution of a permit renewal commonly takes from six to twelve months. In more recent times slowness has remained a persistent problem and has even become more severe (Arango and Suárez-Navaz n.d.).

25. C.R., and E.M., both lawyers, summers of 1992, 1993, 1994.

26. See Brubaker 1992; Rosaldo 1994a, 1994b; Somers 1993.

27. This tenet has been central in the theoretical approach of the literature on "New Social Movements." For an updated review, see Gamson 1995; see also Baño 1984; Castells 1983; Jelin 1985, 1990; Melucci 1989; Suárez-Navaz 1996b; Touraine 1989.

28. Very few people acquire permits as artists, sportsman, or NGO experts, but these are areas in which young Senegalese are highly involved in Senegal. Given the "unproductivity" of these occupations in Spain, this kind of documented identity is often promptly discarded.

29. The law established that in order to renew the work/stay permit, the immigrant must fulfill a never-ending list of formal requirements that include (1) periodic visits to official institutions (the police, the local and provincial government, and three ministries—the Ministry of Labor, the Ministry of the Interior, and the Ministry of Foreign Affairs); (2) a payment that is the equivalent of twelve months of Social Security costs (although it is customary to accept a six-month payment in order to renew the permit); (3) presentation of certificates of good conduct and/or of no criminal record—these certificates involve authorities from the country of origin (and consequently, many times they involve payment of corruption fees), and also authorities of every single town and city where the immigrant has lived during the year; (4) a certificate of "appropriate housing"; (5) proof of medical checkups; (6) documents such as a valid passport; and (7) the mysterious open-ended category of "any other document that proves the immigrant's attachment [*arraigo*] to the country."

30. There are many exceptions to this, of course. Immigrants may receive a letter summoning them to the police station or to the Ministry of the Interior or the Ministry of Finances "for a

matter of their concern." NGOs and the Public Defender (an independent institution modeled after the Scandinavian Ombudsmen) has regularly denounced cases in which immigrants, once summoned, were informed that their permits had been refused and were held for deportation. A lawyer working in the labor union told me about many violations of human rights; "for instance, the police claim to have lost your papers, or the imprisonment of undocumented immigrants with *yonkis* [heroin addicts] and common delinquents all together in the same cell" (C.R., spring 1995).

31. See the sections "Work and Leisure" and "Immigrants as Collective Subjects in the Public Social Space" in chapter 7 for further ethnographic examples of immigrants' daily struggle to establish informal social relations.

Llano of Alfaya

One of the cars used by immigrants as lodging during their stay
as workers in Alfaya in 1993

Picking lettuce

In a lettuce field with some Senegalese friends

An agricultural work team, including young men from Alfaya and one Senegalese man

George and Jane Collier, my advisors from Stanford University, in a visit to Alfaya, accompanied by Puri, my host and friend during fieldwork

My friend Cheick, whom I met in Alfaya during my fieldwork, with part of his family

Drinking tea with some members of the Human Rights association working there
during the summer of 1992 and Senegalese agricultural workers

This is the poster we prepared to invite everybody in the village to the opening of the so-called immigrants' recreational hall financed by the Town Hall. (Literal translation of the poster: Neighbors are invited to join a party that starts at 22:00 on Wednesday the 10th. For a cultural enrichment. Participate! Participate! Participate!)

This image shows the opening party, where both immigrants and autochthonous Alfayans enjoyed and shared their "cultures," as they say on the wall. The poster reads: "May the borders not limit our friendship."

Another image of the same party, showing the way Moroccan immigrants sang and enjoyed the evening

5. The Imagining of Multicultural *Convivencia* in a Legally Bounded Social Space

African immigrants had been settling in Andalusia and elsewhere in Spain in significant numbers since the late 1980s, but the Spanish state and society were reluctant to accept the fact that immigration was an essential part of the rebordering of the Mediterranean and that immigrants were here to stay. Up to 1993, management of immigration centered exclusively on closing up the southern border of Europe, amidst a demagoguery of invasion and chaos. By 1994, however, civil society and state institutions came to accept immigration as an unavoidable phenomenon, concomitant with the modernization of the country.

Indeed, in 1994, the Ministry of Social Affairs made its début in migratory issues by publishing the Plan for Social Integration of Immigrants (PSII), the first official text in which the state explicitly and systematically included integration of immigrants as a cornerstone of migration policies.[1] Almost ten years after the 7/1985 Alien Law was enacted, the Plan for Integration shifted the emphasis away from "threats of invasion" toward the importance of incorporating immigrants into a modern multicultural democracy. A new atmosphere of consensus building and *convivencia*[2] between Spaniards and immigrants was promoted, and brand-new social policies and experts began to design integration programs across the country.

In this chapter I explore the rhetoric and models proposed in Spanish immigration policy since the new period opened by the Plan through an ethnographic description of its implementation in the Valley of Alfaya in 1994. I wish to underscore, however, that the ostensibly inclusive character of the new policies

Notes for this chapter begin on page 159.

for the social integration of immigrants did not negate the exclusionary results of measures previously taken to control migratory flows. What shifted was exclusive emphasis on control; integration became represented as the ultimate goal of immigration policies, and control became justified as the means to achieve this objective: "Measures intended only to regularize and control migratory flows are insufficient; immigrants residing in the country must be mainstreamed into Spanish society. And this is quite unfeasible unless migratory flows are controlled" (PSII 1995, 19).[3]

Ever since the PSII, Spanish immigration policy has been characterized by Janus-faced discourses and measures on immigration issues, as I show in this chapter. In addition, the decentralized model of government in Spain allowed for a neat institutional division of labor between central and regional administrations, the "Autonomous Communities." The two-sided character of immigration policies is instrumental, I argue, in advancing a legal ideology and the subsequent liberal notions of "normality" and "difference." This liberal imagery went hand in hand with processes described in chapter 3, where I explored how the construction of African immigrants as "different others," and their exclusion from community's spaces, built upon deeply seated local meanings assigned to particular spaces, housing patterns, and a nomadic lifestyle traditionally associated with the Andalusian poor. If dominant liberal rhetoric constructs immigrants as different "others" with a "culture" to be preserved, yet limited to a private sphere of subjective beliefs, local experiences and cultural processes built on negative group images informing a wish to erect boundaries to protect "normal" population from the defiled, morally deviant, and uncivilized poor people living at the margins of the community. Both cultural influences juxtapose to maintain the segmentation and residential differentiation that had traditionally served as a medium as well as an outcome of unequal social relations.

Analysis of integration policies in Alfaya furthermore illuminates the use of administrative regulation to foster disciplinary practices shaping immigrants' behavior, as explored in chapter 4 through the concept of the "fetishism of papers." I will first offer an analysis of a key document, the Plan for Social Integration of Immigrants, to unveil cultural assumptions about mainstream views of integration in Spain. Turning to ethnographic analysis of implementation of the plan, I will describe how local authorities created a new immigration program that ranged from extension of social services to immigrants and measures to combat racism, to the creation of new ways for immigrants to participate in civil affairs as social actors. Discipline and surveillance proved to be central concerns, informed by an a priori assumption about immigrants' inability to meet "civilized" standards of behavior, as I will show in the description of the official policies of space allocation launched in Alfaya in the summer of 1994. In addition, new social programs ostensibly sought immigrants' social participation and integration, yet institutional practices hardly facilitated their democratized participation in decision making. Instead, the coercive apparatus of legal implementation categorically barred illegals from participating in the civil sphere while construing legal immigrants as only partial legal subjects, granting them voice but not vote in the civil arena.

Last but not least in importance, I provide an analysis of the simultaneous measures—also inspired by the spirit of the Plan for Integration—to struggle against the underground economy, illegal immigration, and irregular labor relations fostering legal immigrants' exploitation. The tension produced by Civil Guard surveillance and occasional punishment of peasants who illegally hired an immigrant fueled fear and suspicion among both peasants and immigrants. Nationals saw Africans as a threat to the maintenance of their privileges, especially because the racial visibility of immigrants made peasants' informal economic practices much more susceptible to control by the state. Immigrants were further pushed toward invisibility and vulnerability, independently of their legal status, as racially marked scapegoats of peasants' reluctance to be accountable to the state.

Integration: The Imagining of Cultural Antagonism and Multicultural Consent

The first feature common to both the general Plan for Integration (from which I quote extensively here) and to local projects promoting *convivencia* in Alfaya and Granada was recognition of immigration as an unavoidable feature of modern Western societies. Spain and Alfaya thus had to face the challenges called forth by modernization. Immigration was conceptualized as both a consequence of modernization and as a challenge to it. In what sense is immigration a challenge to modernization? The plan signaled two main senses.

First, in a general sense, modernization goes hand in hand with the "emergence of a new and different kind of society" where some social groups, such as immigrants, women, and young adults, are discriminated against on the basis of inequalities of gender, ethnicity, and age. The challenge of modernity is defined in the plan as the need to avoid exclusion and marginalization by correcting structural disadvantages and by guaranteeing application of the law equally to all members of society. In this sense, immigrants are just one among other vulnerable social agents in need of social programs designed and enforced by public authorities to secure their equal access to the rights of legal subjects in a political community.

But there is a second sense in which immigration presents a challenge to modern societies: "The challenge to integrate diverse cultures and ethnic groups in order to establish harmonious relations and curb xenophobic and racist tendencies" (PSII 1995, 36). Thus, the specific challenge that immigration brought to modern Spain was the need to develop a model of *convivencia* that would respect cultural differences and thus counter "certain reactionary, non-solidary stances taken by European peoples with respect to ethnic minorities or social differences at different times in their history" (PSII 1995, 20).

To meet these challenges, both the general Plan for Integration and the local municipal council converged in (1) acknowledging legal immigrants as subjects with rights and obligations, and (2) emphasizing the role of public authorities in adopting public policies to curb current society's marginalization of particular groups. In this set of issues, institutional discourses at both levels were remarkable for their inclusive rationale and their commitment to a "regime of incorporation" of immigrants, as Soysal has called it (1994). The Plan for Integration went so far as to declare immigrants "not as workers, but as citizens, with needs and requirements in the areas of education, culture, health, regional coexistence, and participation in civil affairs" (PSII 1995, 36). The plan committed the state to guarantee immigrants access to universal services provided to all citizens.[4]

A major limitation of rights for immigrants, however, was the requirement of legal status: "In democratic societies, respect for and compliance with the law constitutes the fundamental basis for coexistence. In this regard, public opinion should not be swayed by pressure deriving from de facto situations, nor by those who act outside or against the law—for instance, by avoiding entry controls, entering illegally, or falsifying reasons for travel. Such persons must not be treated more favorably than others who abide by legally established procedures, and must not expect any other kind of support than emergency aid provided for strictly humanitarian reasons" (PSII 1995, 57).

This exclusion, as I showed in chapters 2 and 3, was most strongly contested at the local level, yet gradually, peasants and people working for NGOs came to submit to this non-negotiable, centralized, and top-down mandate, which used the prerequisite of legality as an instrument for controlling immigration, as shown in chapter 4. While the state effectively extended certain rights to immigrants, all of those rights were contingent on immigrants being legal subjects, a privilege that only the state could grant. The state, by retaining its purportedly fundamental right to deport immigrants, subordinated immigrants' rights to secondary status, subject to the will of the state. By contrast, rights of citizens were constitutional, limiting the action of the state. Indeed, in liberal ideology, rights are not something to be granted, but something to be respected by both the legal order and the state. But this is not so in the case of rights of immigrants, for whom equality before the law means being rendered unequally disadvantaged from the start.

In fact, the recognition of legal immigrants as citizens was at that point more rhetorical than real. As noted before, the Alien Law did not even consider the status of the foreign permanent resident;[5] despite this "minor" detail, the plan invoked the promise of the "fetishism of papers":

The legal framework also constitutes a fundamental guarantee for immigrants, since the principles of equal treatment and non-discrimination before the law are essential to their integration....The following lines of action must, then, be furthered: (1) migratory movements are subject to the rule of law like any other human activity; protection is owed to legal conduct, while irregular practices on the part of either foreigners or citizens must be rejected, particularly if such practices are discriminatory or based on xenophobic or racist attitudes; (2) stability[6] in a legally correct situation is a prerequisite for integration, and for this reason immigrants must have a clear understanding of the legislation in force. (PSII 1995, 58)

Note the emphasis on duties that this legal framework required of immigrants: as citizens, immigrants had to behave legally and understand the legislation in force. That would seem self-evident to any citizen; the need to make it explicit here was due to the fact that immigrants, in contrast to nationals, were systematically depicted as alien to this legal culture, and were thus deemed strongly conditioned by nondemocratic cultural values that were incompatible with the *convivencia* to be forged.

The framework for integration is thus given by the rule of law. Liberal law informed the model of modern *convivencia* by constructing it as a result of rational and democratic participation of autonomous legal subjects who defend their individual and collective interests in a public sphere where consensus about the common good should be reached. The basic elements of *convivencia* were conceived in the Plan for Integration as resulting from active participation in Spanish civil society and in immigrants' collectives established within the institutional framework provided by agencies of the state (PSII 1995, p. 37). The final objective of integration went well beyond the preservation of rights and enforcement of duties of legal members of the political community; it entailed creation of a "feeling of belonging to one and the same society" (p. 41). To achieve this feeling of belonging, a positive attitude and an active engagement on the part of all parties involved was needed. "[What is called for] on the part of Spanish society [is] the adoption of an open-minded and tolerant attitude of the differences and peculiarities that characterize the various immigrant groups, and on the part of the latter, acceptance of the rules and values on which democratic coexistence [*convivencia*] is based in our society" (p. 9, emphasis added).

In sum, the Plan for Integration of Immigrants was characterized by a clearly inclusive criterion of belonging, with the definition of the political community grounded in the concept of citizenship, which "is gradually beginning to become as important as the concept of nationality" (PSII 1995, p. 61). Immigrants, provided they accepted the rule of law and behaved accordingly, were deemed actors of their own integration. Spanish citizens, for their part, were asked to adopt a tolerant attitude toward the differences of immigrants, where tolerance meant "not ... lack of interest or indifference toward immigrants, but rather an appreciation of plural coexistence based on respect for human rights and the essential rules of democratic societies" (p. 48).

There were, however, two important ideologically interrelated assumptions that, in practice, hindered the necessary participation and change of mentality of all parties involved. The first was the depiction of Spain and Alfaya as having achieved modernity in contrast to other societies, such as the Spanish nonmodern past or other premodern contemporary societies (most relevantly, Islamic societies). The second assumption conjures up a cultural difference between Spaniards and immigrants, one based in the construction of immigrants as alien to the democratic culture of legality and thus culturally different to modernized Spaniards. As I show next, the plan presents a consistent link between modernity and democratic values and so-called "normal" standards of conduct, using a paternalizing rhetoric to associate nonstandard conduct with inferiority in a purported evolutionary order. Over the years, these assumptions have proved to be the most efficient and active neoracist arguments against multiculturalism in Spain, very much in the vein of the new logic of cultural fundamentalism analyzed by Stolke (1996).[7] As for the first assumption, evolutionary logic pervaded both the general Plan for Integration and the municipal council documents. Modernity is rhetorically equated with the prevalence of values of tolerance and respect toward other cultures, as opposed to attitudes of intolerance in other nonmodern periods of history. For example, the plan stated that "For a very long time Spain's national identity was linked to ideals based on ethnic, linguistic, cultural, and even religious uniformity," and later, "Societies are more democratic and coherent when there exists a tolerant attitude towards differences, appropriate mechanisms to channel and settle conflicts, and a general agreement about which elements are considered to be essential to coexistence" (PSII 1995, pp. 40, 48).

Similarly, in Alfaya, according to the municipal council, there should be no room for discrimination and racism because in this valley "there is a clear trajectory of democratic struggle and collective awareness, and the municipal council … is part of the human collective responsible for Alfaya's identity as a progressive, democratic, solidary, and peaceful village" (municipal council press release, September 23, 1991). This identity was equated with rational attitudes which, as Alfaya's mayor proclaimed to village citizens, maintain "*convivencia* and civism [in Alfaya] while rejecting irrational attitudes and lack of understanding toward those peoples who visit us from other villages and other countries" (municipal council press release May 18, 1992).

The assumption that Spaniards had already internalized modernization requirements and values was false, however. The construction of a democratic welfare state was rather recent and not yet fully completed, as I have shown. The attitude of Alfayan peasants was not one of total exclusion, however. Immigrants could acquire their rights—if they were perceived to deserve them at the local level. My ethnographic study of the implementation of social programs allows me to explore from yet another perspective the customary rules attached to the local notion of "deserving rights" treated in the first chapter. The plan's focus on the need to foster tolerance among Spaniards toward "difference" was misleading, for difference had long been "tolerated" in the Andalusian public sphere. The problematic issue in relation to the autochthonous population, was not difference, but equality. The Plan's assumption that immigrants, once granted a legal status, are citizens entitled to the same rights as nationals could not be taken for granted at the local level.

The second ideological element implicit in the plan was that ethnic plurality comes "from outside" and that migration changes a purportedly homogeneous culture. Discussion of integration, both in the plan and at the local level, made reference to two differentiated groups: Spanish society on the one hand,[8] and, on the other hand, an imaginary collective of immigrants. And the object of integration quite clearly was "[to] bring immigrants residing in Spain into the social mainstream" (PSII 1995, 9). Even though integration was conceived as a multilateral effort by both parts, how this effort was defined for each group reveals more than what was explicitly stated in the plan. The "elements considered to be essential to coexistence" (PSII 1995, 48) that immigrants must accept are not clearly spelled out. At only one point is the text explicit in this regard: "Essential principles [are] respect for individual freedom, equal opportunities for men and women, democracy as a form of social organization, and the restriction of religious convictions to the private sphere" (p. 48). Spaniards, for their part, should come to appreciate "plural coexistence based on respect for human rights and the essential rules of democratic society" (p. 48).

My argument, however, is that this rationale went well beyond a legal framework, and the way the plan puts matters makes this only too clear. When dealing with "regional coexistence," the plan underscored "strategic" factors related to immigrants' acceptance of standards of conduct. Regional planning was to promote family reunification; it should lead the immigrant to "gradually accept conduct in the society of destination, as regards housing, health, and hygiene so as to foster a feeling of belonging to that society" (PSII 1995, 60). And it should foster "acceptance, not merely formal but real, of values essential to democratic coexistence and of enormous importance. Western societies have had to come a long way to reach their current status, and all citizens, regardless of their nationality, are bound to respect and abide by such values" (p. 60). Ironically, legal immigrants were being asked not only to behave legally and understand the legislation in force; they must also embrace values and standards of conduct regarding housing, health, and hygiene deemed essential to democratic coexistence. In democracy one would expect the constitution to define essential values and principles, yet the very specific demands placed on immigrants' behavior in the Plan for Integration could not possibly be elevated to such dignity. Rather, we see in the plan the specification of the sorts of disciplining that immigrants were deemed to need in order to develop "a feeling of belonging to [Spanish] society."

At this point I wish to refer back to my 3 analysis of "putting immigrants in their place," as described in chapter 3. The rather startling connection of democratic rules of *convivencia* to standards of conduct regulating use of space and occupancy of housing bears comparison to how that connection was made at the local level. In addition to the self-restraint, cleanliness, and appropriate lifestyles that villagers deemed important, the plan expected immigrants to adjust to "normal" family practices and associated housing patterns—implicitly those of the nuclear family. Restructuring immigrants domestic life as a prerequisite to integration was thought necessary because immigrants who are away from their families "find living in standard housing incompatible with their desire to save money and eventually return to their homeland" (PSII 1995, p. 60).

Here we see a clear invasion of the private sphere to which any legal subject is entitled. The plan disguises its intervention in a cloak of modernity and legal universalism that clearly associates immigrants with the "underdeveloped," primitive, and quite openly, immoral cultural behavior of outsiders to the European cultural sphere. The plan clearly did not consider the housing patterns of groups of immigrant males of varying composition living together in houses or flats designed for a nuclear family to be fit or proper, yet such arrangements were instrumental for facilitating immigration networks and thus the economic survival of immigrants. Similarly, the plan's assumptions about standard conduct in democratic society regarded polygamy and other notions of extended family not only as not quite "normal" but probably also illegal conduct for immigrants seeking to integrate into Spanish society.

A crucial element in the integration process was participation by all parties in civil affairs. Immigrants were considered social agents who should speak for themselves. Constitutionally sanctioned civil rights for citizens, such as the "right to belong to a trade union, to association and gathering,"[9] were also explicitly acknowledged in the Plan for Integration as equally valid for immigrants, regardless of nationality. In the imagery of the dominant integration model, "the defense of [immigrants'] rights as workers" should ideally be channeled through "the existing administrative and union mechanisms" (PSII 1995, p. 58). Through participation, immigrants could also express their cultural particularities as a way to prove their common "humanity." In this regard, the plan expressed the idea that, even though misunderstanding prevails in interethnic relations, all cultures recognize "profound ... human values," and tolerance can be promoted by allowing cultural manifestation of this common "humanity" through artistic expression.

Programs flowing directly from these two specific kinds of participation (trade union or associational and artistic) were implemented at the local level. Yet the fact that immigrants did not yet participate at all in existing administrative and union associations both hindered their access to their fair representation in the worker class and induced locals to question their "real desire to adapt" to the Spanish civil sphere, as I will show in the next section. Social programs in Alfaya only indirectly forged new spaces that incorporated immigrants as active social agents in participatory democracy. Immigrants were welcome to participate, but not on their own terms, because they were deemed to not "yet" have "reasonable" sociopolitical proposals. Of course, the context of persecution and criminalization of immigrants pushed most immigrants into invisibility, a situation that does not, obviously, promote realistic political participation.

Meanwhile, the "essential democratic rules of *convivencia*" enunciated in the Plan for Integration and in municipal programs framed values and standards of behavior, not just in housing and family patterns, but also in styles of association and civic participation, further constraining how immigrants could struggle for fair representation. By depriving citizenship of the criterion of national belonging, the plan conjured up a non-ethnic, noncultural criterion of belonging that sought to instill feelings of belonging through multicultural participation in a modern civil sphere whose rules of *convivencia* are limited by the rule of law.

Local Implementation of Social Programs in the Summer of 1994

Dominant discourses—of politicians, of policy statements such as the Plan for Integration, and of mass media—always presented the issue of immigration in polarized terms, opposing an undifferentiated Spanish society to groups of immigrants, as though these were natural categories. I believe instead that implementation of integration programs actually created difference, naturalizing the line that came to divide both groups, especially in landscapes such as Alfaya's, where villagers once embraced immigrants as fellow poor workers. Ethnographic analysis of how integration programs were implemented in this local place thus illuminates more general transformations of Spanish society reshaping such basic issues as identity of the community, criteria of belonging, and the requirements for acquisition of rights.

In this section I analyze various institutionally promoted social programs designed for integration. I show how, for the most part, this goal dwindled to what social workers and other administrative actors often saw as a more pragmatic goal, that of avoiding conflicts. Contrary to the stated objectives of integration policies, tolerance often translated into indifference toward an undifferentiated "other"— so long as the other was not a cause of trouble (but just in case, hire a couple of watchmen on the administrative social services payroll). This failure of integration policies was blamed on immigrants' alleged refusal to participate, which in turn confirmed the image of two distinct cultures in the eyes of social workers.

I begin by describing programs in housing (a final institutionalization of space allocation for immigrants; see chapter 3), and then consider a consciousness-raising campaign ("Somos iguales, somos diferentes") and other planned activities. I discuss an Alfayan social worker's assessment of why these programs failed, and I offer my own, somewhat different appraisal.

Politics of Space Allocation

Principles of self-organization, workers' solidarity, and resistance to the LOE lay behind the shelter for immigrants as it was initially conceived in 1991. The shelter movement focused villagers' attention not just on the specifics of where to lodge African immigrants during the agricultural harvest, but on fundamental and intensely political issues associated with the need to sustain a cheap source of labor for family-based and resource-poor agribusiness. As the conflict drew increasing media attention and notoriety, villagers became increasingly uncomfortable and distrustful of immigrants and their advocates.

Alfayans became seemingly unwilling to invest themselves in improving immigrants' working conditions and began to pressure authorities to "take measures" to "solve the problem" of immigrants' lack of place in the valley. The municipal council tried to calm those who complained that no one was protecting villagers from threats immigrants purportedly posed to security and that Africans were capturing too much attention in council politics. The council faced growing tensions between having to abide by the state-enforced legal policies toward immigrants and wanting to act upon humanitarian concerns for immigrants' basic human rights. At the end of summer 1992, the Civil Guard raided ("invaded" as one volunteer organizer on the ground put it) the campsite set up for legal and illegal immigrants. Unpredictable labor inspections made it clear that the state had the capacity to and perhaps the will to enforce the legal restrictions, underscoring the vulnerability of illegals and reminding the council of its obligations as an agent and representative of the state. Capricious enforcement and raids in themselves may have fostered villagers' growing sense of a lack of security. Spaces of civil resistance to the LOE, such as the initial shelter and the later campground efforts, became mousetraps, and the institutionalization of space allocation (as opposed to the grassroots struggle on immigrants' behalf for a right to a place) appeared to be the only way forward.

Bent on avoiding the so-called ghetto effect, the council launched its star program of 1992: the PVT (Plan de Viviendas Tuteladas), or Tutelary Housing Program. In exchange for various tax incentives to rehabilitate vacant housing in the village, the town's property owners were encouraged to rent those houses to immigrants.[10] But over a three-year period, the PVT proved to be a total failure with very few houses rented, even after the council hired professionals in 1993 to promote the PVT to owners of more than forty dwellings that lay vacant. The problem of housing for immigrants remained unsolved. In chapter 3, I discussed several of the reasons for the villagers' reluctance to take part in the program, reluctance that bewildered those who promoted the PVT because it seemed to make good business sense for villagers to avail themselves of the tax benefits.

By 1993 the council cautiously began to take over some of the efforts initially undertaken by volunteers. Using regional funds budgeted for immigrants, the council set up another camp-ground, but only for legal immigrants. The council thus distanced itself from the unofficial humanitarian purpose of the 1992 campground for illegal as well as legal immigrants as a space of civil resistance to the law. As a result, more than two-thirds of the immigrants were unable to use the one public resource being offered to them—namely, a place in a tent. The remainder had to compete for places in one of five large tents, each applying for a permit from a social worker, who issued just thirty four permits altogether. Those excluded slept under the moon, in the segmented geography of the Valley of Alfaya.

Even more tellingly, in 1994, the council, backed up by the county, reappropriated the idea of a shelter, abandoning the argument that shelters would ghettoize immigrants. As in most council policies, access to this shelter (officially called the County's Temporary Lodging for Immigrant Workers) was restricted to legal immigrants, in a context of growing legitimization of the law within NGOs and unions, and among other actors. The council deemed it necessary to hire native watchmen to patrol both the campground and shelter to assure their cleanliness and security. Such surveillance epitomized a radical change of symbolic focus from self-organized resistance in the initial approaches to immigrants' lodging to the institutional takeover of housing policies. For the council had embraced official policy for "integrat[ing] immigrants in an ordered and controlled manner" (interview with the mayor, fall 1992) under proper conditions of health and hygiene; there were even explicit references to the specter of infection and contagion arising from the living conditions of immigrants in the absence of specific social programs.[11]

The shift thus underscored security and control through surveillance of the space, living conditions, and even lifestyle of immigrants. Although the watchmen's rituals of control and order were not very effective, the fact that they were deemed essential for preventing conflicts could be read as the political gesture authorities made as a sop to villagers' (in many cases openly racist) concerns. As we have seen, the national Plan for Integration of Immigrants equated "essential values of democratic coexistence" with behavior expected from "integrable immigrants." At the local level as well, discipline and normalization extended to the most trivial details of immigrants' daily lives, all in the name of integration. Immigrants had to demonstrate self-restraint in public places, be punctual, pay debts, obey tacit rules governing who could occupy public space and when, and comply with watchmen's explicit rules for taking showers and cleaning up living quarters. Similar expectations pervaded the discourse of both municipal and county-level meetings to plan programs for integration of immigrants.

These institutional emphases on immigrants' "ordered" participation in social services and on their living "normally" like their Spanish neighbors could be read as a "symbolic statement by the state to 'its own people' that 'their concerns' about 'immigrants' ha[d] been acknowledged and [would] be dealt with by ensuring that the numbers of immigrants entering the nation-state [village] [would] be reduced and by requiring those 'immigrants' allowed to remain to behave in an acceptable manner" (Miles 1993, 191).

In addition to these modern forms of domination, which disciplined immigrants to basic standards of conduct through social programs, the state also used, and even redefined, traditional forms of domination, which I described previously with my ethnohistorical analysis. These ever-present forms of domination are (1) the segmentation of different groups both spatially and residentially, and (2) the restriction of mobility and/or permanence of cheap temporary labor. I discuss the restrictions on mobility in the next subsection, noting here that they obviously related to allocation of space for immigrants. Administrative and institutional measures generally disfavored permanent settlement of immigrants in the valley and thus temporally limited immigrants' use of space and rights associated with it.

As for segmenting immigrants spatially and residentially, doing so served the short-term political advantage of ameliorating villagers' concerns about allocating a place to immigrants. Yet segmentation subverted medium- and long-term goals of avoiding the ghetto effects that municipal authorities originally railed against. The symbolic impacts of shelters established since 1994 proved to be essentially the same as those of the unofficial shelter of 1991. Hiring one watchman to instill law and order in immigrants' use of institutionally sponsored living quarters serve as an effective balm for villagers' concerns about the immigrants' claim to a place as a right, but the price paid in such measures was high. Spatial and residential segmentation destroyed many sites of interethnic social relations. The physical distancing of groups eventually fed into the configuring of territorial identities along racialized lines of legal exclusion and discrimination against immigrants, a phenomenon all too familiar in contemporary times of crisis and interethnic competition.

Thus, the net effect of local housing policies for immigrants was not "integration" at all but rather disciplining and segmentation. Discipline enforced norms of behavior in the shelter where a relatively privileged group of legal immigrants were allowed to live. But it also relegated the illegal majority of immigrants to the outskirts of the valley, severely restricting their use of public spaces lest they be subjected to law enforcement triggered by "unacceptable" behavior. While segmentation differentiated legal immigrants in the shelter from the illegals at the valley margins, it drew the sharpest line between immigrants and villagers. We see, then, the reproduction of rural Andalusia's historically segmented geography of exclusion with a permanent population of villagers occupying the center in family-based production and the impermanent and subordinate population, on whose seasonal labor production depended, relegated to the peripheries.

The politics of spatial allocation, while reproducing older geographies of subordination, did so around new cleavages of nationality and modernity. Social programs were, in fact, an integral part of the creation of "well-behaved" foreign workers, wrapped up in a purportedly "neutral" technocratic discourse. The modern politics of allocation prove to have been inseparable from wider differentiation of nationals from foreigners in terms of residential rights. They were also inseparable from a context in which the central state newly asserted its prerogative of determining membership in the political community, formerly a right that autonomous local communities in the Andalusian landscape reserved for themselves.

Residence, Rights, and National Privileges

National and local integration plans emphasized the development of a "feeling of belonging" among immigrants and of "attachment to 'the country' and to the 'host' society." According to liberal theory, attachment to territory, both national and local, is foundational in the relation of individuals to the state and its subdivisions. Liberal theory assumes that nationals hold certain rights from birth. Immigrants obtain rights, by contrast, by demonstrating loyalty to the state apparatus that represents citizens, loyalty that must be demonstrated again and again because it is always subject to questioning and doubt by locals and by authorities. The documentary habits required of immigrants clearly display the importance given to attachment and loyalty in the state practices toward immigration.

Immigrants' attachment, integration, and participation in the receiving society are clearly related to settlement. One can hardly become an active member of society if not allowed to establish permanent, long-term relationships with the agencies and agents of that society. And in a decentralized administration such as Spain's, it is not only legal status that counts, but also, for locally provided state services, documented proof of settlement in the village *(empadronamiento)*, which is granted by local authorities. This proof of residence is also required for access to other agencies and their services, such as those provided by the Autonomous Community of Andalusia. It thus configures a number of rights associated with residence, or residential rights. But where registration of residence is a simple matter of routine for nationals, for immigrants it is an elusive piece of documentation that local officials were much more likely to question or deny. A contradiction thus pits integration programs' goals of attachment, integration, and participation against the clear bias on the part of public officials at all levels of administration against granting immigrants opportunities to settle and legal recognition of residence.

I have already underscored how national policies kept immigrants in temporary statuses of legality in constant need of being renewed. Local political authorities also used measures to control immigrants' whereabouts while withholding recognition of settlement. A legal paradox lies behind the issue of whether local authorities should grant immigrants residence rights: Would doing so automatically accord them legal residency status in the country? That question was a stated concern of the Spanish Federation of Provincial and Municipal Councils (Federación Española de Municipios y Provincias, or FEMP), which finally decided that local registration of immigrants could go forward only if a law was passed to make explicit that such registration did not necessarily involve recognition of rights as legal immigrants in Spain (FEMP 1995, 117). The problem of recognizing immigrants as subjects of social policies was thus resolved legally by detaching local residence from formal legal status. This measure further underscored the temporality of the services provided to immigrants by the administration.

A significant political gesture at the local level in this regard was the setting of dates during which the official immigrant shelter would function. The council announced that the shelter would open each year at the beginning of the harvest season (when peasant producers began to need temporary workers) and that it would close down in mid October, regardless of whether workers wanted to stay on longer. Immigrants interpreted the schedule as clear evidence that local authorities did not want them settling in the village. Alfaya's mayor used to argue against the ghetto effect by saying that "Alfaya is not a refugee camp. We cannot solve all the problems of Africa." This political posture symbolically depicted immigrants and the potential for their permanent settlement as a situation of abnormality and chaos.

As if closing the shelter seasonally were not a sufficiently clear message to immigrants not to settle in the village, local authorities revived another mechanism for controlling the mobility of temporary workers. *Caciques* of an earlier era had controlled labor mobility through their power to refuse (or grant) certificates of good conduct and other documents that Andalusian workers needed to seek work abroad. Now local authorities began to withhold analogous sorts of documentation that residents of the shelter needed to register as resident villagers. There is ample empirical evidence in support of this claim, although municipal council spokesmen generally asserted that the council was open to recognizing immigrants as residents. The Report on the Social Program for Immigrants authored in 1993 by a social worker and a lawyer clearly identified such obstacles to assisting immigrants in attaining legal status (*Memoria Proyecto Oficial* 1993). When Assane, one of the veteran and most integrated immigrants in the valley, needed a certificate of residence, the mayor refused it, telling Assane that it was "because you have just arrived in the village," as Assane told me the morning he had been denied this particular paper.

The municipal council generally resisted providing certificates of residence to immigrants, although sometimes they were forced to do so for the few immigrants who settled in the valley on a more permanent basis, bringing their families.[12] But the bottom line was that local authorities seemed bent on keeping immigrant seasonally temporary. When asked by an NGO representative, "What do you think could be done to improve the relations between immigrants and Alfaya's people?" one Moroccan answered sarcastically, "The only thing which could improve relations is that as soon as the work is over we leave. This way [Alfayans] will accept us much better, but if we want to stay, then we will become enemies and invaders" (A.J., summer 1992).

Withholding needed documents was not the only way in which local authorities revived older controls over seasonal labor. By enforcing the bounded temporality of their stay, local authorities relegated immigrants to the nomadic lifestyle that local narratives of the Franco era attributed to Gypsies and condemned on the basis of naturalized differences (as discussed in chapter 3).

Yet times had also changed, as have the needs of capitalist relations of production for a cheap, easily discarded labor force. In the Franco era, authorities denied the papers for leaving the valley; now authorities refused papers needed to stay in the valley. In the past, being a member of the community did not involve granting any residential right, and it was convenient to keep temporary workers attached to the land in a situation of chronic poverty. Today, by contrast, a legally recognized resident has rights to all sorts of public services; immigrants have become a minority social collective with many needs and little money, and thus a potentially heavy burden on the local resources of an already slimmed-down welfare society.

An image of "limited good" was taking shape among villagers in their relations to immigrants, who were being considered as subjects of social programs. The temporality of immigrants' stay would preserve the privileges of nationals to benefit from such programs. In contrast to the Gypsies of the past, who villagers thought were innately disposed to migrate, African immigrants were generally assumed to want to stay put in order to take advantage of the community's common resources. As one villager put it, "Anything is better [for immigrants] than the way they live down in their countries. But we don't have a lot here, and if we give them some things, who knows what they'll want next. When the stomach is full, people want more, whether they deserve it or not" (P.M., summer 1994).

Promoting Participation and Understanding

Another set of social programs was concerned with promoting immigrants' participation in the civil society of the host society, through shared activities and consciousness-raising campaigns, which were aimed at making villagers more understanding of different cultures. The scope of these programs was comparatively limited, but they are equally illuminating in the meanings they transmitted.

The Plan for Integration proposed a decentralization of social programs based on the idea that immigrants were active social actors who could pave their way into Spanish society, and that the key for their integration lay in their active participation in civil affairs. It was at the local level that social agents and collectivities were deemed to interact socially to promote mutual respect and understanding and to negotiate shared or differential use of public space. Decentralization and participation were thus thought to be prerequisites for the goal of progressively inclusive integration.

Local authorities also adhered to this inclusive notion of social programs to promote immigrants' participation. The municipal and county councils created an official forum "open to anybody interested in participating," and they invited Granadan NGOs, volunteers working in the valley on immigration issues (such as myself), representative immigrants living in the valley, and anyone who wished to attend. However—and this is a critical point—decentralization did not necessarily mean using procedures of participatory democracy. That, in my understanding, was the reason Spaniards and immigrants participating in the process came to distrust one another, losing interest in the cause of solidary interethnic gathering. I wish to now describe some of the features hindering the transformation of social programs into real channels for immigrants' democratic participation and integration.

Although the municipal and county councils convoked this forum in the spirit of consensual decision making and inclusiveness, its monthly summer meetings were always scheduled in the mornings, when most immigrants were working. And local political authorities retained control of the forum's decisions, generally along the lines established by their political parties. When the forum called for input from the so-called experts, such as the social worker on the program payroll, these were normally Spaniards who had no knowledge either of Arabic or immigrants' context and culture of origin. Most of the experts were people trained to mediate between state bureaucracies and ordinary citizens—social workers, for example—and for the most part they participated on fixed and limited schedules. The hired social worker for the program refused to stay in the valley beyond her schedule and thus had limited interaction with immigrants, whose own meetings generally took place at night. Whatever the limitations of social workers' roles, clearly the kind of person assigned to this role should have had some knowledge of Arabic, training better suited to dealing with immigrants, residency in the valley, and a more flexible approach for opening up real, egalitarian interethnic participation.

On occasion, immigrants were hired to complement the activities of hired natives—but without pay and without contracts. In 1994, for instance, Assane was offered management of the bar to be set up in the "Sociocultural Center for Immigrants," but without a contract. Assane was expected to remunerate himself by selling immigrants food and drinks. Assane agreed to manage the bar because it afforded him work during a slack period, though he would have preferred a contract, as it would have facilitated renewal of his papers (for which either a labor contract or a promise to hire, i.e., a *precontrato,* is needed). Similarly, a Moroccan was asked to complement the work of the watchman, who did not live in the valley and came only on a fixed schedule. The Moroccan was given a "free place" in the shelter and a small cash "contribution" in lieu of employment, once again without any kind of labor contract, not even a temporary one. Such rather blatant legal, economic, and ethnic discrimination against immigrants severely discredited the purportedly inclusive rationale of these programs in the eyes of immigrants, as any reader would expect.

While local programs sought to foster immigrants' integration, they often did so in less than meaningful terms, as far as immigrants were concerned, leading immigrants to despair of their value, and villagers, for their part, to embrace an emergent public opinion that immigrants did not care about integration. Take, for example, local implementation of the pan-European campaign against racism and xenophobia, run under the slogan "Somos iguales, somos diferentes" (We are equals, we are different). This example deserves extended discussion:

In June 1994, the social worker hired by local authorities for the immigrants' social program organized activities directed primarily toward Spaniards under the aegis of this campaign. She ordered tee shirts and stickers inspired by the European slogan with a logo designed by a local secondary-school student. She invited schoolchildren to draw pictures exemplifying multiculturalism and exhibited forty two drawings at the inauguration of the "Sociocultural Center for Immigrants," a space for interethnic interaction and for immigrants' gatherings to which I will refer later. She distributed the tee shirts and stickers in schools, in the center for retired people, and among civic associations. Finally, she organized a "night of consciousness-raising against racism," featuring a meeting for everybody in the valley to screen a video about the similarities between Spaniards' and Africans' migratory experiences in Europe titled "I Am Not Your Enemy." The impact of this campaign was rather superficial, and many immigrants criticized its cost: "It is deceiving that, in the struggle against racism and against people's indifference toward us, the program only thinks about giving 'presents' to Spaniards" (M.A., summer 1994).

A meeting during this "night of consciousness-raising against racism" brought immigrants together with local associations and institutional actors. The social worker pitched the meeting as a wonderful opportunity to discuss migration reasonably and in an informal setting. At the outset, two municipal councilors (one affiliated with IU (Izquierda Unida, or United Left) and the other with the PSOE (Spanish Socialist Workers Party, or Partido Socialista Obrero Español)[13] set forth the basic political-economic factors to be considered when dealing with immigration. The Alien Law, local informal-sector practices, the extent of fraud in the Social Security system, and the actions of the Civil Guard, were all explored in depth. An interesting discussion of migrant experiences followed, comparing the experiences of former Andalusian emigrants to those of contemporary African immigrants. Andalusians and Africans both acknowledged the pressures put on them by the respective host societies to alter their lifestyle, and noted that they had experienced little recognition for their participation in production or in sociopolitical and cultural spheres. Everyone agreed that migration entails pain, suffering, discrimination, and exclusion. As a former emigrant said: "Migration means work and suffering. It has always been so, and it will keep on being the same way, always" (J.R., summer 1994).

During this interchange, immigrants began to bring up the urgent, very tangible problems they faced daily in the valley. Referring to the public experts and authorities who had organized the meeting, the immigrants appealed for human and civil rights to be accorded them as migrants. They received the usual reply, that immigrants had to take responsibility for seeking out greater participation in Spanish society: "What you [immigrants] have to do is to organize yourselves on your own!" (Vosotros lo que teneis que hacer es organizaros por vuestra cuenta!).

As a result of this interchange, some of the participants proposed forming a "Committee for Immigration" to meet on a regular base to air both immigrants' and villagers' viewpoints and sensibilities with the institutional authorities who were ostensibly promoting inclusive interethnic relationships in the valley. The intent was for the committee to involve all parties working locally on immigration issues. Yet the social worker and other professionals in charge of the program chose not to participate in any of the meetings that followed—which didn't fit with their schedules—thus seriously setting back the original objective of opening official programs to immigrants in ways that would include them in decision making

The social worker's lack of commitment, together with her unwillingness to take up residence in the valley to avoid a daily commute from Granada, was a constant topic of criticism on the part of immigrants and volunteers working at the grassroots. Political authorities and other professionals in charge of social programs were deemed hypocritical for calling for democratic participation while refusing to attend meetings or events that they had not arranged themselves.

Upon returning to Spain after an absence several-months during 1995, I found myself completely depressed by the report drawn up by Alfaya's social worker on integration activities of the summer of 1995, fully two years after they had begun. Her report on Alfaya's immigration program concludes a section devoted to integration activities with a gloomy complaint about immigrants' lack of response to the activities and meetings she had convoked. Her conclusion echoed an emergent public opinion among Andalusians that immigrants did not care about integration. She wrote that "[immigrants] do not deem it necessary to establish closer relationships with villagers. Nevertheless, no incident has been reported between immigrants and neighbors [i.e., "native" neighbors], and the relationship between both is not problematic." Though sympathizing with this social worker's evident frustration, I found myself irritated by the characterization of immigrants as simply "uninterested in becoming integrated," as she put it to me in a personal communication several months later. Her notion of *convivencia* had shriveled to the minimum: that of preventing problems and avoiding conflicts, even if the price was an absence of dialogue and communication.

In general, neither immigrants nor local neighbors paid much heed to the programs for integration in Alfaya Valley, which, if anything, ended up fostering distrust among both groups. Though a frustrating experience for the professionals involved, this tells us a lot about the kind of programs that were implemented. The few participatory initiatives with some potential for success, such as the interethnic meeting held during the "awareness-raising night against racism," were not followed through. Public authorities and "experts" representing the institutional programs often did not even show up for some of the interesting assemblies convoked by immigrants at the "Sociocultural Center." After calling for integration efforts, the authorities simply left the work to poorly coordinated Spanish and immigrant volunteers, who often worked with no official recognition.

The implementation of social programs, moreover, did not take place in a vacuum; additional factors worked against their efficacy. In society as a whole, structures of inequality were imposing new boundaries between citizens and foreigners, affecting broader European interests as well those of the national economy. At the local level, there was a silent but consistent effort to put immigrants in their place, a process described in chapter 3. Through activities of security forces and Labor Inspections (which I will discuss in the next section) the central state was underscoring this growing division.

In this context of overwhelming negation and marginalization, both by the mainstream population and by the state at various levels, immigrants themselves increasingly resorted to self-contained processes of identity construction based on autonomy from, and sometimes antagonism toward Spaniards. This phenomenon, recognized by many scholars working on immigration in Spain, took two forms. One involved the quest for autonomy from Spaniards, especially in efforts to create new, independent immigrant associations that could help immigrants take advantage of Spanish social services and capture support for cultural activities (which the government ironically intended to promote tolerance among Spaniards). I devote some of chapter 7 to analysis of such associations in Granada, where they are becoming increasingly important. The second form of identity construction involved a growing lack of interest in engaging in interethnic interactions. In the next chapter I will describe some of the factors shaping these phenomena, focusing on how immigrants structured power within their communities and analyzing in detail the case of Senegalese as a transnational community.

I want to end this section by suggesting some basic premises for forging *convivencia* in landscapes such as the Alfaya Valley. Factors pushing immigrants to invisibility, marginalization, and exclusion further facilitate the strengthening of intraethnic clientelist relations based on the extreme vulnerability of some and on the concentration of power in immigrants who hold a legal status, have a good network among Spaniards, and act as charismatic leaders among their compatriots, thereby hindering the potential processes of democratization and participation within the collectives. Therefore, two preconditions seem necessary for such movement toward *convivencia*. First, the Alien Law needs reform to recognize immigrants as legal subjects with all rights, including voting in local elections.[14] Second, immigrants need to be included at the local level, not just through participation, but through real representation of their vested interests in the social programs directed toward them, provided that immigrants are really promoting democratic mechanisms among themselves.

The Politics of Invisibility: A Racial Geography of Labor Relations

The government's 1994 Plan for Integration noted the existence of an underground economy where most immigrants were situated and called for state efforts to target that sector to eliminate all forms of exploitation in the workplace. Modernization implies the regularization of economic relations and establishment of documented legal subjects. The two municipal councilors who spoke at the event organized for the "night of consciousness-building against racism" clearly explained these goals. They emphasized the importance of respecting and complying with the law if the valley were to succeed in its path to modernity. The old customary rules regulating labor relations should now be framed within the rule of law, they said, and immigrants should denounce labor relations that did not comply with those agreed to in the *Convenio del Campo* (collective bargaining agreement on labor conditions in the countryside).

At the same time, however, even while local political authorities stressed the incompatibility between modernity and underground and/or fraudulent economic practices, they did little to change the situation. Their problem was inherent in the political clientelism pervasive in economic sectors of semiperipheral democratic and welfare societies: any locally designed action to uncover widespread fraud and underground economic practices is bound to pay a high political price, and, as a general pattern, municipal councils take the side of their clienteles.[15]

During the summer of 1994, the Civil Guard and the Ministry of Labor stepped up their surveillance and control of both peasants and immigrants in Alfaya as part of the government program to combat the underground economy, tax and unemployment fraud, and illegal immigration.[16] Yet the state did not take direct action against underground and informal practices. Rather, state surveillance and occasional punishment was used, generating a general feeling of fear and suspicion among both peasants and immigrants. My field notes for that summer record having seen the Civil Guard many times as they drove around the valley or as both immigrants and villagers commented on their nearby presence in daily informal conversations. The harvest was ready, lettuces were being sold at high prices, and labor was intensely needed. Already at the beginning of the harvest, all of us living in the village felt anxious, albeit in different ways. Older people using motorcycles, such as señor Paco, who would ride his motorcycle to his son's land, were stopped by the police and fined for not using the regulation helmet. The Civil Guard stopped me in my car several times to scrutinize my papers and question my reason for being in Alfaya, especially if Africans were with me. The Civil Guard would "visit" peasants while they were working their lands, or they would pass along rural paths as though they were casually driving around. Immigrants were regularly asked to identify themselves and to answer questions about specific employers. The Civil Guard also regularly paid night visits to those *cortijos* where immigrants sleep, rousing everybody to produce the papers (their documents). Almost daily some illegal African worker was arrested. And a few employers were fined for local underground economic practices uncovered by episodic and unpredictable Labor Inspections.

Such constant surveillance shaped behaviors and discourses that, in turn, reinforced the relations of inequality sanctioned by the Alien Law (LOE). Distrust and generalized suspicion grew among and within groups. Who was informing the Civil Guard about what was going on in the valley? In my interviews and daily conversations I heard all sorts of people blame one another. A lieutenant of the Civil Guard told me that it was the "Moors" themselves who denounced their compatriots: "They are the ones who tell us, 'this one and this one are illegals.' They notify us of the arrival of new people and advise us about their whereabouts. And then we go and many times we find them there" (summer 1994).

Immigrants also speculated about informers, both in their midst and among Spaniards. Abdula, a Moroccan who was himself suspected of once having been an informer for the Civil Guard, blamed a villager who at the time played an important role in the municipal assistance programs for immigrants: "He's in a privileged position, you see. Both municipal councilors and immigrants trust him because it seems he wants to help. But he is just a good actor. He knows how to milk money intended for us immigrants, because he gets paid by the council to do his job. But he also receives money from the Civil Guard. Do you think he could afford his style of life otherwise, as he is a drug consumer? The other day he told me: 'Look out man, watch your step, because I have balls enough to drive you out of this village if I want, through the Alien Law' " (A.A., testimony, summer 1994).[17] Various immigrants confirmed that Civil Guards were paying up to 5,000 pesetas ($35.00) for accurate leads identifying illegals and natives who disregarded the Alien Law. Moroccans blamed Algerians and vice versa. In such ways, surveillance by the state security forces engendered anxiety that sometimes flared up in violence but more usually metamorphosed into people's prejudiced control of one another.

These feelings of endemic disorientation and chaos generated an interesting reassessment by Andalusian emigrants to the North of their own experiences of migration. However much they disliked the way the state surveyed peasants' activities and spaces, they began to argue that Spain needed to embrace more "civilized," more "European" customs and attitudes with respect to the law: "Here nobody respects the law, we all know that. But we are slowly changing, and this is necessary for the country to advance. Here everybody minds his or her own business, in contrast to the North, where the law is respected. People complain, but if we got the fine we deserved, no one would be able to stay here" (R.A., spring 1995). As another former emigrant put it: "There was no illegality there [in the North]. We had a contract even before leaving to go there. They checked up on us as though we were slaves in a medieval market; only the best people passed. But what is happening here is worse, even for us. Because up there, if there was an illness, you could vaccinate; and if people did not behave properly, you knew who they were with name and last name, and people had to be responsible for their acts—not like what's happening here, because here they end up having no rights or duties" (C.G., summer 1994).

Former emigrants, as well as other villagers, while advocating the need to become law-abiding citizens in order to construct a "developed" society, emphasized their location in the Spanish social structure as poor rural people. The same emigrant who advocated vaccines and contracts for immigrants said:

I find it proper that "Moors" come, because there is plenty of work here. The problem is that many people work land *a medias* [sharecropping], and of course a *medianero* can not hire a *jornalero* and pay all the expenses of Social Security; it is too much … [Civil Guard and Labor Inspections] are restricting things too much, yet there are a lot of "fat people" who are always stealing whom they do not touch…. Meanwhile, they come here to survey us, to identify who is getting unemployment [subsidy] and who's not, who has a boy weeding the plants.... It shouldn't be this way! Tomatoes have to be picked, so what else can we do for a living? how else are we going to eat! (C.G. and his wife, summer 1994)

Surveillance by the Civil Guard and Labor Inspections were undeniably transforming everyday employment practices and uses of public spaces. Carlos went on to illustrate the effects of these policies on his family:

People are scared, of course. For example, my daughter and her husband used to receive unemployment [checks] all year, you see? Well, they had to take themselves off the unemployment rolls here and register themselves in his village so that they don't get hassled here. OK, I see this is correct, even though we all get less. Why should they go around being scared about who they're going to run into along the road? Most people won't hire a black or a "Moor"; they don't dare to, because otherwise they would hire many more. Here in Alfaya the Civil Guard pressure is too much!! I don't know why. If I need a couple of *jornales* I worry that they will catch me, like what happened to [another *medianero*] who paid dearly for it—half a million pesetas!!! [$3,500.00]. So there is a lot of fear. People are always worried. This village has never been this way before. Never! Not even in the times of Franco's dictatorship. Never before has there been so much fear. Well, even when one rides a motorcycle to the fields you may get fined 2,000 pesetas for not wearing a helmet and 10,000 for not wearing a belt. Why is that? I don't understand why the [security forces] are now more "rebellious." (C.G., summer 1994)

Carlos's words illustrate a general feeling of disempowerment and lack of autonomy. The politics of fear appeared as an enduring instrument used by the central state in the reproduction of a segmented and stratified social structure (see the section "Peasants in Francoist Times" in chapter 1). Analysis of the actual cases of arrests and fines for illegal practices shows that this fear was similar to the constructed moral panic identify by Hall et al. in their seminal research on racism in Britain (1978) in that threat of state action proves more powerful than the actual consequences. The owner of Alfaya's most important *gestoría* (a private firm managing legal and administrative procedures for clients) confirmed my impression that most fines punishing irregular labor relations among autochthonous peasants do not actually end up being imposed: "People perceive this pressure, and they complain because the state is pressing to normalize productive relations here. But, in fact, people are not affected in general because the way the state is acting is arbitrary, poorly informed, and ineffective.... In the countryside it's very difficult to control legal requirements, and peasants effectively use a thousand tricks to escape enforcement of the law. All the papers stay in the *gestoría*, so if somebody is accused of working in an illegal situation we will sign for him on the agrarian card so that he will be legal in the eyes of the Labor Inspection" (S.Z., spring 1995).[18]

The important fact that these testimonies together unveiled was that people refrained from hiring "Moors" or blacks because they were much more visible and because the control of security forces on their legal status was much stronger than that of native peasants. This was a direct threat to the interests of peasants to stay as invisible as they could to the security and labor authorities in order to make the most of available resources, mainly cheap labor and unemployment benefits. Even though the second testimony leads us to think that the possibility of actually controlling peasants' strategies of evasion was slim, those things people believe to be true are true in their consequences, as is commonly said in social sciences. Under the perceived threat of a visit by labor authorities, peasants opted for being as invisible as they could be; they did not want to take a risk hiring visible immigrants who might beg them to offer them the contract they needed for maintaining legal status, if they even had a recognized legal status. Immigrants, of course, bore the brunt of this situation: given the racism apparent in inspections that mostly monitor those who hired immigrant workers,[19] employers had become the most efficient agents of the Alien law, which was acting indirectly through peasants scared to be singled out and punished by the state.

At the same time, constant surveillance of Alfaya, and especially of African immigrants tended to render illegal aliens invisible in ways that both isolated immigrants and made them increasingly vulnerable to the most degrading working and living conditions. Given the pervasive underground economy and African immigrants' racial visibility within it, even those who had the legal right to work were at risk of detention and punishment. Forced visibility ironically engendered invisibility, as well as practices of evasion, among all of those alien workers who did not meet the strict requirements of the law. Invisibility took many forms. Some immigrants destroyed or hid documentation from their home countries that might compromise them. Others restricted their comings and goings to avoid social spaces in which they might be vulnerable. They felt they had to avoid the two bars where most hiring took place, and they often slept in the mountains to avoid surprise nighttime inspections by the Civil Guard. Legal restriction on their access to public programs forced illegals to live at the outskirts of the village. Peasants' fear of Labor Inspections thus engendered an invisible racialized geography of labor relations that restricted immigrants to work on lands situated outside of the view of casual passersby.

Over the years since its enactment, enforcement of the LOE has become widely accepted. In a 1994 interview, a Socialist councilor who had lived in France for fifteen years told me about immigration:

> At the time of the demonstration of illegals in 1992, I was in charge. I talked to the Civil Guard, to the governor in Granada [to try to avoid arrests].... I thought the council did not deserve a demonstration, because we know about emigration. We

know that the difference between legal and illegal is not a person's difference [that is, it is an artificial difference, not a real one]. But we, as political authorities in charge, should be responsible, shouldn't we? And I think now that the LOE is not a Spanish issue, it's a European one. We are bound to it because we have problems with Africa, the same way Germany has problems with Eastern Europe. We all have to cooperate. (A.P., former emigrant and councilor, summer 1994)

In recent years, people have taken greater cognizance of Spain's situation in Europe and its competition with Morocco on some important issues concerning agriculture and fishing. Resonating in an interesting way with remnant historical imageries, this rationale was one of the justifications increasingly present among villagers' testimonies about the need to "keep 'Moors' under control." Interethnic competition was inscribed in daily labor relations, especially among young men working as *jornaleros* or as members of *cuadrillas* (teams of workers) picking lettuces. An Andalusian *jornalero* who came from a neighboring province with his family told me:

I like "Moors"; I have worked with them, and I know people do not treat them as they should. But you know? They have to adapt themselves to their situation. They are *jornaleros*, just as I am. But I am Spanish, and, you know, Spain has a strong competitor in Morocco, which exports tomatoes and other things. It is fair that they work here now, as I once worked in Switzerland.... The "Moors" have a very special feeling for Andalusia, you know? Granada, or Córdoba, my own city—they dream about having it again. I think it is fair for them to work here, but if they try to use Córdoba's mosque I will oppose them, because it is ours. We fought for it, the same way we fought against dictatorship, and to change our economy. So we are now in Europe. And we didn't do all this so Moroccans can harvest the fruits of our efforts. (M.A., summer 1994)

Peasants are thus embracing (European) citizenship as an identity category, fusing together ethnic loyalties and membership rights that depict Andalusians and "Moors," or Europeans and Africans, as rivals. The labeling and criminalization of immigrants was thus part and parcel of the legitimization of social control and construction of modern legal subjectivities, which, in turn, perpetuated the stratified and segmented social structure of rural Andalusia. Now, as before, the needs of capital accumulation situate the poor, nomadic, and propertyless person somehow "on the wrong side of the law," as Hall et al. have put it (1978), condemning them to the recourse of a clientelism in which rights are interpreted as "favors" and "privileges."

Yet the surveillance and control of immigrants' activities as Third World foreigners was also being appropriated by African immigrants into their own identities and forms of resistance. The requirement imposed on them as foreigners to present their official documents (taxes, contracts, a permanent address, etc.) to the authorities each year in order to work and remain as residents in the country generated a discourse that denounces the hypocrisy of the Spanish state for not applying the same standards to Spanish citizens. A crucial requirement that further forced visibility upon immigrants was that they have to pay heavy Social Security taxes every month, which they experienced as a discriminatory requirement, for many Andalusian workers were not paying Social Security taxes: "The Spanish state doesn't allow poor immigrants to stay; if you do not have money to pay [taxes], you don't get the papers." This discourse is being appropriated by immigrants' associations in Alfaya and Granada, and poses indirect resistance to the hierarchical model of citizenship that grants citizens some rights denied to immigrants (both legal and illegal) on the exclusive basis of place of origin. As one immigrants told me: "Politics here in Andalusia are very much like politics in our country [Morocco]—lots of words and few real rights. The fact is, if you pay, you get your papers; if tomatoes need to be picked, the Civil Guard forgets about us. That's the underlying law, the reality of European society" (R.A., Moroccan immigrant, summer 1994).

Notes

1. In 1993, a symbolically important political decision was taken through the Royal Decree 1173/1993 of July, the General Directorate for Migration was transferred from the Ministry of Labor and Social Security to the Ministry of Social Affairs. The transfer was intended to help implement social programs for availing state social services to legal immigrants and was supposed to help guarantee immigrants rights to which they were entitled as legal subjects. In a meeting of the Council of Ministers on December 2, 1994, almost ten years after enactment of the Alien Law, the first Plan for Social Integration of Immigrants (PSII) was approved "as a guide for the Central State Administration, a proposal for action for the Autonomous Regions and Municipalities, and a channel for civil society to participate actively in the integration of the immigrant population" (PSII 1995, 15.)

2. See note in introduction.

3. I will quote directly the English version of the plan. *Convivencia* is translated as "coexistence," and I will respect this translation when quoting, although I will adhere to the Spanish version in my own analysis to retain the special meaning and historical connotations of the concept in Spain.

4. The specific commitment to "make existing social services available to immigrants" (PSII 1995, p. 60), even though unspecified in scope, explicitly recognized rights of legal residents. In practice, the most pertinent social services were health care and access to the extensive system of public education, be it schooling for the youngsters of immigrants in settlements where a second generation exists, or adult education and language training of the kind implemented for immigrants in Granada. Authorities at the local level sought to implement this notion of incorporation of legal immigrants through a series of measures to provide immigrants housing, offer them Spanish classes, and guarantee their access to health services.

5. "Denizen" is the term popularized by Hammar to refer to foreign permanent residents in Europe. He opened a debate about the consequences of their lack of voting rights for the democratic model. See also Brubaker 1992; Costa-Lascoux 1989; Layton-Henry 1990; Soysal 1994; Withol de Wenden 1988. For a brilliant analysis of these issues in Spain, see De Lucas 1994.

6. In only in one instance is "stability" related to the LOE requirements, whereas references to the need to comply with the rule of law are reiterated throughout the text: "The need to comply once and again with certain formalities can often be a hindrance to maintaining documented status and may indirectly contribute to marginalization. The adoption of measures intended to ensure legal residence is therefore essential to integration" (PSII 1995, p. 48). In the reform of rules implementing the LOE undertaken in 1996, permanent residency appears as a status, but the effects of this measure go beyond this ethnography.

7. See the debate about multiculturalism and racism in Spain since 2001 and the impact of the El Ejido racist attacks, which I will not discuss here; see Azurmendi 2001; Castaño 2000; Martín Díaz 2002; Martínez Veiga 2001; Sartori 2001. See De Lucas and Torres 2002 for a good update and interesting contributions.

8. I have already mentioned that the presentation of Spanish culture as a homogeneous whole does not accord with the political organization of the country, the constitutional recognition of multiple "nationalities" within Spain, and the enormous administrative development involved in the division of the country into seventeen Autonomous Communities, each with its Parliament, government, and an established administrative apparatus that inevitably promotes some form of "localism" as a sign of differentiated identity. In this remarkable process of ethnogenesis (Greenwood 1992), nation, folklore, and tradition are reinvented—seventeenfold.

9. "Right to gathering" *(derecho de reunión)* was, at this time, taken for granted as tacit common sense on the part of Spaniards as democratic subjects, but during Francoist times, any meeting of persons exceeding a very limited number (e.g., ten) required explicit administrative authorization by the dreaded "Ministry of Public Order." In the Alien Law 8/2000, this and other essential rights of foreigners were forbidden to illegal immigrants; see Arangón 2001 for a discussion about the unconstitutionality of the Alien Law 8/2000.

10. See note 12 in chapter 3 for a detailed description of related benefits.

11. *Plan de la Mancomunidad para la Inmigración,* 1993 [County program for immigration]. I know of no cases documented or reported in the press where such health concerns could be justified as playing such a salient role in the relationship with immigrants. This lack of evidence for alleged fears of contagion is remarkable given the repetitious nature of such concerns in dominant "literature" such as policy documents, media representations, and records of local meetings.

12. This is one of the most crucial factors for the settlement of seasonally temporal rural workers in a village, as bringing the family means less mobility and a need to establish more permanent roots in a particular place. This phenomenon, which has began to take place among some Moroccan immigrants, opens new possibilities for the incorporation of immigrants into the village landscape—in neighborhoods, schools, and throughout the social fabric.

13. At this point, the municipal council was dominated by the Spanish Socialist Workers Party, or Partido Socialista Obrero Español (PSOE), with the most traditional Communist leaders included as key representatives in this party's local list. Meanwhile, the United Left Party, or Izquierda Unida (IU), a political grouping to the left of the PSOE and nationally integrated by former Communists, had only one councilor in Alfaya.

14. As I mentioned previously, in 1996 the outgoing Socialist central government enacted a reform of the implementing rules of the Alien Law, which included some of the most urgent remedies to the pernicious effects produced by the law in the "integration" of immigrants. This acknowledgment of the importance of providing politic, social, and legal machinery for the integration of immigrants became real through the preparation of the reform of the LOE

(4/2000). Nevertheless, after a controversial parliamentary process, this law was reformed in a much more restrictive way, giving rise to the current law (8/2000).

15. In 2002, in spite of the unanimity among politicians about the need to reform the Agrarian Special Regime (Régimen Especial Agrario, REA) and the fraud associated with it, no political party has dared to embark on reform because of the political price of such an action.

16. In February 1994 the Ministry of the Interior, the Ministry of Labor and Social Security, and the Ministry of Social Affairs signed joint instructions to strengthen the struggle against clandestine labor practices by intensifying Labor Inspections and penalization of these practices (*BOE*, February 25, 1994).

17. As Driessen and others have shown, male interactions in Andalusia enact a ritualistic affirmation of manhood, which generally hints at potential recourse to violence and aggression under a sexual metaphor (Driessen 1991; Brandes 1980; Gilmore and Gilmore 1979; Luque Baena 1974; Moreno 1974).

18. This informant, who was a former emigrant himself, was elected as the new mayor in Alfaya when I was finishing my fieldwork. He headed the same "left collective" that has governed the village since the first municipal election in 1979. However, his election was in itself a symptom of the transformations that were occurring in Alfaya. In the times of transition to democracy, where ideologies proliferated, the former mayor was a teacher, a humanist and a Communist-trained man. Nowadays, however, the man who leads the left is the one who owns the *gestoría*, a central spot to deal with bureaucracy and the new rule of law, to evade legal obligations and, at the same time, preserve welfare state benefits. I disclose his identity because he allowed me to do so in the consent form, something that was also highly unusual in the peasant culture under consideration.

19. There are peasants known for hiring immigrants and for paying them the same salary granted to any *jornalero*. These peasants have been most negatively affected by Labor Inspections, and they complain about the open-ended regulations that restrict immigrants from attaining a fully legal status.

6. THE SENEGALESE TRANSNATIONAL SOCIAL SPACE

Survival and Identity in the Interstices of State Reproduction and Global Economy

I have argued that the normalizing policies implemented in Spain as a result of the presence of Third World immigrants are part of a broader cultural and moral project whereby a modern citizenry (and alienness) is created. The legitimization of the rule of law, as the major ideological transformation underpinning the shaping of Spanish civil society, constructs a public space where legal subjects are guaranteed by the state the fundamental rights of the person through a bureaucracy that claims to be founded in an impersonal, impartial, and universalistic rationale. Although I have characterized this normalization process as a contested one, the ethnographic scrutiny of the daily social processes through which immigrants were "put in their place" has disclosed the disciplinary efficacy of social and bureaucratic forms of domination in reinforcing legal and ethnic boundaries between citizens and foreigners, Europeans and Africans.

The ubiquitous illegality of immigrants is conceived by dominant hegemony as an abnormality that threatens the modernizing path of Spanish society. To resolve this problem, the state has implemented a double strategy. On the one hand, the central apparatuses of the state used their coercive power to control immigrants' presence in the Spanish territory while dictating the timing and limits of processes to legalize immigrants and ostensibly to incorporate them into Spanish civil society as legal subjects with rights. On the other hand, local and regional state administrations implemented social policies directed toward immigrants' integration into the local social sphere through consensus building in civil society (immigrants' associations, NGOs, and labor unions). As I have

Notes for this chapter begin on page 186.

shown, the daily social practices through which institutional measures came to life evinced a pervasive, though heterogeneous, evolutionary and neocolonial rationale, mapping the world into antagonistic categories dear to modernization ideology: developed versus underdeveloped societies, secular versus religious public spheres, civilized versus primitive and national versus tribal identities. Migrant workers exposed to this double strategy experienced the de facto denial of their status as legal subjects in the Spanish civil sphere, together with the imposition of normalizing public programs that inscribed their cultural difference as an impediment to modernization.

This imagined landscape of bounded cultural differences, hierarchically classified according to civilizational level, was, in fact, the main ideological tenet of European colonial enterprise. As the literature on law and colonialism in Africa has shown,[1] the colonial administrations employed both direct and indirect rule in a complementary way to conjure up a scenario where citizenship was constructed as a privilege of the civilized and the maintenance of custom as the priority of the uncivilized. As Mamdani (1996) has demonstrated, a racialized civil society governed by the rule of law excluded free native peasants, who were instead subjected to a variety of state-enforced, semiautonomous customary powers. Colonial rulers legitimated spatial and institutional autonomy of native peasant communities in terms of moral and cultural segregation rather than on the basis of race: "What is aimed at is a segregation of social standards, and not a segregation of races. The Indian or the African gentleman who adopts the higher standard of civilization … should be as free and welcome to live in the civilized reservation as the European, provided of course, that he does not bring with him a concourse of followers."[2] It may seem odd to compare Spain's contemporary situation with colonial legal apartheid, which segregated the "civilized" civil sphere from a "primitive" sphere of multiple locally enforced ethnic and religious customs. But the fact is that for newcomers, part of the effects of the normalizing politics of space allocation and proper behavior was to perpetuate a legal apartheid in which state-enforced cultural "others" were constructed more as subjects of tutelage than as legal subjects entitled to rights.

My objective in this and the next chapter is to illuminate the link between the politics producing a culturally differentiated immigrant worker in Spain, and those producing a culturally abiding emigrant worker in Senegal. Linked together, such politics serve as a major mechanism through which nation-states perpetuate their clienteles in late capitalism. In this chapter I focus on the contested social space where Senegalese migrant workers negotiate, resist, or adopt this transnational postcolonial framework. In earlier chapters I analyzed how Andalusians bring cultural and historical particularities of their background into their experience of the new legal and ethnic inner boundaries shaping social space. Here I provide an analogous case study of Senegalese diaspora and how it

builds on the legacy of the racialized colonial civil sphere and the state's reproduction of relatively autonomous, culturally encapsulated, indigenous authorities. I will show how idiosyncratic Senegalese modes of social organization
successfully extend into a migratory transnational space to incorporate youth
from the lowest ranks of the global labor market and at the margins of a trans-
statal[3] civil sphere where legal subjects are acknowledged. I explore how these
new transnational practices reinvent a relatively autonomous space from which to
challenge global inequalities, and I examine the extent to which Senegalese organization in diaspora facilitates or hinders the questioning of the national status
quo. Once the particularities of the Senegalese transnational social space are
spelled out, I will return to Alfaya and Granada in the next chapter to examine
how different understandings of integration, or *convivencia,* work out in daily
social processes. There we will see how dominant and alternative notions of culture and legality intertwine, overlap, and contradict each other in the making of
global social spaces where power and morality are struggled over.

The Forging of a Modern National Tradition in Senegal:
Black Islam, Peripheral State, and Global Capitalism

For centuries, the West African territory that later became unified politically as
Senegal occupied a strategic location in global capitalism and in the encounter
between black African indigenous population, Islam, and colonial Europe. As my
informants repeatedly told me, Senegal is the door to Africa, and relations with
the *toubab* (white people) and other cultures are old. The Wolof who inhabited
the heartland of the country had a highly hierarchical social structure based in
part on the slave trade, as did the Toucoulers of the northern Futa Toro region
under the Moorish protectorate (Ingham 1990, 115–16). French and Islamic
expansion into Senegal took place slowly in the eighteenth century on the basis
of slave and mercantile trade, which contributed to the power of local military
and commercial elites. Both Islamic and European traders "dovetailed with preexisting African circuits of exchange, not altering their basic structure but merely
adding to the flow of goods through them."[4] The nineteenth-century abolition
of the slave trade redirected French and Islamic leaders to other forms of economic and political hegemony over the many indigenous kin-organized lineages
in autonomous social and economic territories governed by "divine kings." Islam
began to plant more profound roots with the expansion of the Arab brotherhood
Tijaniyya, led locally first by Al Haj Umar Tall, and later by Ahmadou Bamba,
who founded the Senegalese Muridiyya brotherhood. Meanwhile, the French
had strengthened their economic hegemony in the region. Failing to restrain the
accelerated spread of these Mouride and Tidjane brotherhoods, which actively

opposed them as an imposed alien culture, the French sought their leaders' cooperation to ensure political stability.

The successful cooperation between the central French colonial state and the Islamic brotherhoods marked "the beginning of an important partnership which was later to contribute significantly to Leopold Senghor's successful takeover of the whole country when Senegal became independent" (Ingham 1990, 117). French authorities established political and economic indirect rule based on the production and export of groundnuts, organized in tandem with local authorities along the lines of the earlier slave trade. Local authorities, especially the *Marabouts*, Islamic religious authorities, were accorded autonomy over labor-intensive productive relations provided that they encouraged their followers to grow groundnuts. Over the years this partnership strengthened, with the *Marabouts* guaranteeing the French loyal support from their followers in cooperatives they had organized (the *da'aras*),[5] and the French offering the *Marabouts* a variety of concessions and financial help for building mosques and expanding their clienteles. In addition, Wolof-speaking authorities received training in the French administrative system and were sent out to govern areas where indirect rule was incomplete. Extensive "wolofization" thus accompanied the expansion of Islam and of French colonization.

Senegal has a reputation as an exceptionally stable and nonviolent political unit in comparison to other African countries. The key to this stability is the role played by *Marabouts* and Wolof elite as intermediaries between the free peasantry and the central government, creating a national political culture that successfully transcends ethnic, class-based, religious, and regional differences. This national political culture, however, involves a precarious balance of forces that has to be continuously renegotiated and protected rather than an established civil culture that links citizens with the state. The two principal components of the shared nationalist ideology are, on the one hand, Islam, and on the other the doctrine of *négritude*, which Senegal's first independent president, Leopold Senghor, promulgated as one of its main intellectuals. Since independence, political leaders have taken pains to maintain the allegiance of the rural social base controlled by relatively autochthonous leaders. One mechanism for doing so has been to stress the strong religious bonds of peasants to intermediaries in Sufi brotherhoods, and to link the brotherhoods to the country's modernization. Black Islam is thus taken as the moral and cultural heart of the modernizing project of a socialist secular state. As Leopold Senghor (himself a Roman Catholic) put it in 1979: "It is a duty for the public powers to provide the best conditions for citizens to face their religious obligations; the religious authorities have an eminent role to play in moral and civic education to consolidate the state and the unity of the nation" (quoted in Copans 1988, 251).

Thus, paradoxically, the political stability of the state since independence has strongly depended on spaces of semiautonomous religious and local loyalties conjured up by the colonial system. The new state faced an extended economic crisis when the price of groundnuts fell in the global market and as the terrible drought of the 1970s brought famine. In exchange for much-needed support, the World Bank (WB) and the International Monetary Fund (IMF) pressured Senegal to implement liberalization policies and to attract foreign investment through multinationals and development agencies. Liberalization implied reducing the traditional autonomy granted to local and religious authorities as part of the state's modernizing project of incorporating society into the space of direct state control. Yet the social base needed to legitimize new socioeconomic arrangements remained attached to clientelist and patrimonial networks controlled by the Sufi brotherhoods (Coulon and Cruise O'Brien 1989, 151). Local and religious authorities engaged in the modernizing project of the state by extending their socioeconomic activities and clientelist networks into the urban areas where proletarianized peasants—the principal victims of the crisis— rehearsed new strategies of survival as city-dwellers. Meanwhile, peasants, students, and new political groupings based on leftist, "fundamentalist," and regional movements resisted the liberalization efforts. These proved not very effective, in the end, rendering uncertain the contingent balance of forces on which democratization in Senegal depends.

In the face of the negative consequences of the liberalization imposed by international agencies, traditional intermediaries struggled to maintain both the political and economic privileges granted them by the central state in return for their support and the allegiance of devout followers. To legitimize continued collaboration with the state, traditional authorities needed to offer clienteles and followers new avenues of incorporation into the socioeconomic sphere. The traditional authorities took control of the burgeoning commercial sector and developed new structures of mutual aid, protection, and collective identity in the urban areas, the *da'iras*.[6] This positioned religious authorities in an ambiguous and shifting relation to the state and to global political economy. On the one hand, they tried to preserve their role as spiritual leaders of an anti-Western black Islamic ideology of resistance. On the other hand, they sought out alternative spaces to ensure their role as powerful socioeconomic agents by playing key roles—especially in the organization and control of overseas Senegalese commerce—shaping the flows of Senegalese into the flexible and controllable transnational labor force needed in late capitalist relations of production. In doing so, Islamic brotherhoods such as the Mourides (who gained influence in the country at the expense of the traditionally more numerous Tidjanes) transcended their former role as intermediaries between the dispossessed and the state by expanding the sphere of influence of their mystic cosmology and economic practices into the arena of diasporic, deterritorialized Senegalese emigrant workers.

Tradition and Cosmopolitanism in Emigration:
Reproduction and Change in Senegalese Society

The peculiar eclecticism of Senegalese nationalism challenges a priori categories for thinking about the new social agents upon whose shoulders families impose the task of achieving autonomy and improving social conditions: the emigrants. Who were the young people who left the country in a steady stream beginning in the 1980s to establish new Senegalese communities all around the world? How were they perceived by their families, by the Sufi brotherhoods, and by the state? What were their own objectives, expectations, and dreams, and how did they pursue them? Did they reproduce the familial, political, and religious organization within which they were raised? Or did emigration transform the delicate balance of forces upon which the Senegalese status quo had depended? The answer to these questions requires close, comparative ethnographic attention to new transnational Senegalese communities in the multiple sites where emigrants maintain, negotiate, and challenge the eclectic bonds Senegalese have to national ideology.

I intend to explore these issues through an ethnographic approach to transnational practices of Senegalese in Granada.[7] In this section I analyze social agents shaping emigration in the Senegalese territory: the family, the *Marabouts*, and the state. I will describe some of the ethnic, class, gender, age, and religious axes through which power forged representations of the "good emigrant." I will also explore how the positioning of young emigrants in national and international spheres generated alternative understandings of the transnational social space.

The emigrants with whom I have worked in Granada can be characterized as young male Wolof black Muslims.[8] They are part of the kin-based lineages of Wolof families that had engaged in groundnut production as free peasantry in Senegalese territory under colonial policies of administrative indirect rule. The Wolof inhabited the heartland of the country in the Djambout and Baol regions from which most Senegalese immigrants in Granada hail.[9] Despite the traditional agricultural occupation of their parents, the younger generation experienced rural exodus and the hardships of postcolonial structural adjustment that condemned them to either unemployment or informal sector work, mostly as street sellers.[10] The young males who made up the majority of immigrants in Granada had experienced extreme dependency on their extended families before migrating, due to the scarcity and instability of jobs available to them and their very low earnings.

Given the historic role of the Wolof as administrators and intermediaries in the Senegalese political economy, most Wolof families had direct or indirect experience with migration prior to the emigration of young men abroad, as I found in Senegal when I visited the families of Wolof who had settled in Granada. That role characteristically stretched Wolof families beyond the limits of residentially based units of production and reproduction in networks spanning Wolof territory in the places where family members served local colonial councils. The resulting form was extended, polygamous, and patrilineal, but with more of an imaginary of belonging than of clearly limited, territorially concentrated membership (see Blash et al. 1994). As had been true of their parents in Senegal, many recent emigrants grew up away from biological parents while living with others of their extended families who were geographically or economically better situated. It might be that a young man's parents could not afford to raise him, or that they wanted him to attend a particular Koranic school—the reasons for placing youth elsewhere in the family network were manifold. Young men sometimes remembered displacement painful, for it forced them to depend on others, but it also afforded them opportunities for learning and for building family networks that proved useful when they migrated abroad.

The fact is that almost any young male was perceived by family members as a candidate for emigration to earn resources for the family residential unit where they lived, the *keur,* roughly defined as those who eat from the same bowl. Interests of individuals within the unit were structured by power relations based on age, gender, and social status. Elders held authority over juniors, men over women, those of higher caste over those of lower caste, and those men educated in religion over the laymen. Generally the eldest man (or, in his absence, either the eldest woman or the wife or widow of the eldest man) heads and directs the family, weighing whether or not to invest in the emigration project of a young family member. The efforts and resources needed to send a family member in migration are usually familial, and many young men had emigration imposed on them as a compulsory duty to the family. B.D., for example, thought he had been living in the golden age of his life when his elders told him to emigrate. He lived in his sister's family, a *keur* of more than thirty members in which he was second in terms of prestige and authority. He was also respected among his cohort. He didn't want to emigrate, but his sister, his parents (living in another *keur*), and other elders in the family told him, "You are a young man and your family needs you to go" (B.D., winter 1995).

Young men also thought of emigration as a way of earning enough money to gain independence by forming a family of their own. "We are many young people in the same situation, as there are no jobs for us. It is very difficult to save up the money needed to form your own family, thus getting some independence. Many families are not even able to feed their children, so the young male has to look out for them and for himself" (M.G., winter 1995). Emigration abroad was one of the few ways of helping one's extended family while saving up to form one's own family as an independent, adult man.

When one member of a family unit migrated, others held expectations or imposed obligations on them. Parents generally expected sons to help them raise their brothers and sisters, but the extended family with whom the emigrant had lived also expected help. Once established abroad, an emigrant was expected to help another young family member emigrate, providing money for travel and information to make the voyage a success. Women to whom emigrants were married or engaged also expected remittances, phone calls, and visits, even though their own location in Wolof families required them to submit to the family's decision to send their men abroad, staying behind to take care of children, and accepting the hardships of their men's emigration without complaint.

The family thus held out a specific model of what an emigrant should be: a man who sacrifices himself for his people and struggles against adversity in *Toubab* land (the land of white people). Whatever legal and social difficulties he might encounter along the way did not matter. The family looked at such obstacles with skepticism, while expecting the migrant to send gifts, shipments, and letters, and make telephone calls and frequents visits. An emigrant who could fulfill these expectations would acquire social prestige and authority while strengthening his identity as an adult man. The image of the good emigrant as fulfilling family obligations was deeply instilled in the Senegalese emigrant, working powerfully to maintain and reproduce a transnational social space.

Religion also strongly structured both Wolof peasant society and emigrants' understanding of their travel as strategies of black Muslims to resist dispossession and marginalization. Islamic brotherhoods are a key element in children's socialization and ideological formation. Children receive Koranic education based on obedience, self-control, and anti-individualism. Senegalese Islam reinforces the idea of migration *(hijra)* as part of a process of learning and self-abnegation that should serve the well-being of the community of origin. Likewise, it advocates solidarity and hospitality with fellow disciples in the diaspora. Families consulted *Marabouts* in preparing a member for the voyage, often asking their assistance with bureaucratic matters such as obtaining a visa.[11] Sometimes it was a *Marabout* who recruited a *taalibe* (religious follower) to serve as émigré, arranging his departure and financing the voyage. Senegalese believe misfortune will result if a *Marabout* does not bless the voyage and provide a *gri-gri* (protective charm) to protect the traveler from *Jinn* (supranatural forces or spirits).[12] Senegalese recount stories of young men who drowned while crossing the Gibraltar Strait or faced arrest and deportation because they ignored the advice of the religious leaders. The bond with the *Marabout* is personal and must be renewed periodically, even in migration. In Mouride ideology, every *taalibe* must emulate the life of the founding Cheick Ahmadu Bamba in exile, sanctifying himself through hard physical labor and asceticism, sacrifices that must be part of a virtuous life.

The dominant religious ideology in Senegal is deeply intertwined with politics and with nationalist discourses. The *Marabouts* generate a postcolonial nationalist discourse (which is also Africanist and Muslim) that emphasizes the bravery of the Senegalese people. In the context of the extended economic and social crises hindering the emergence of a modern Senegalese state and socioeconomic structure, religious brotherhoods assumed unprecedented roles in urban areas by taking control of commercial trade in Dakar (Ebrin 1990) and by taking advantage of associations such as the *da'ira* (see note 6) as sources of labor for setting up commercial branches in strategic locations abroad. Many young immigrants in Granada arrived there through the mediation of brotherhoods that financed their travel and incorporated them into one or another of these commercial branches as street sellers. The brotherhoods' bonds and mutual obligations intertwined and overlapped with those of the *keur* and the extended family in their extension into the transnational social space. They functioned as sources of help, support, and collective identity, but also as mechanisms of social control to maintain the status quo by regulating emigrants' projects and behaviors.

Recent shifts within the Senegalese state to countervail the authority of religious brotherhoods has nonetheless afforded the most recent generation of young Senegalese emigrants a somewhat different location vis-à-vis the state and the international arena. In the national sphere, Senegalese are no longer defined as subjects of customary authorities as in the colonial regime. Even though religious and local authorities function as intermediaries between the state and its citizens, young Senegalese are, in theory, entitled to rights as Senegalese citizens. Furthermore, the Senegalese state has its own interests in offsetting the power of Islamic brotherhoods so as to incorporate citizens under its direct control. As Coulon and Cruise O'Brien have argued, "[w]ithout overtly seeking to eliminate intermediaries, this new state seeks to develop its own instruments of domination and to create a more homogeneous and malleable political and economic space, which is to be more closely controlled" (1989, 151). A peripheral state may not be able to implement modernization policies similar to those I have analyzed for the Spanish case, yet Senegal did enact some comparable juridical reforms, such as the Family Code (1972), the law on the national domain (1964), and unified legislation for all groups—ethnic, caste-based, regional, or religious. Such policies enabled the Senegalese state to intervene in sensitive spheres formerly controlled by customary age-based or religious authorities, such as in allocation of land and in family relations. In addition, the state has established a system of compulsory education that has changed the socialization of the youngest generation of Senegalese emigrating to Spain and elsewhere. More than half of the Senegalese immigrants in my Granadan sample had received secular schooling in French along with Koranic education. The state has also ventured jointly with multinationals and development agencies into major economic projects that have profoundly transformed some key Senegalese rural and urban areas. Many of these ventures have failed, yet groups responding to the failures have been incorporated into the public sphere as civil associations—youth or women's groups, or economic interest groups such as the GIE (Groupe d'Intérêt Economique)—that form independent but legalized platforms from which to develop survival strategies and to claim rights to which members are entitled as citizens.

Other challenges to the status quo in Senegal's systems of stratification flowed from Senegal's dependent position in the context of global capitalism and the growing cultural influence of North America and Europe on Senegalese youth, especially men. This cultural influence forged new cosmopolitan cultural practices in youth that are perceived by those in positions of authority as potential sources of "contamination" of purportedly authentic African traditions. Traditional Wolof structures of age, gender, and religious authority required young males to work in family agrarian production in exchange for the dowry needed to marry and form families of their own. Elders could thus appropriate the work of their junior kin while legitimating their own authority. The socioeconomic crisis following the collapse of prices for groundnuts in global markets left Wolof families with scant economic resources for reproducing kin-based lineages and the systems of authority in this way. While investing in young men's emigration enabled elders and religious authorities to reclaim some of the authority over juniors lost in the breakdown of more traditional productive relations, emigration itself gave youth access to cash and exposure to Western liberal ideology in new discourses and practices that seemed to undermine the idiosyncratic Senegalese system of stratification.[13]

Cosmopolitanism began to shape the popular culture, strategies, hopes, and expectations of Senegalese youth. As one Senegalese immigrant in Granada told me, there was a widespread belief among young males that, "in order to move your country, your family, and your own life project forward, you must travel abroad, struggle in life, suffer if necessary, and learn from those who have more" (A.D., summer 1994). Thousands of young men in Senegal embraced this challenge. Amadou, twenty-four years old, was a typical case. IMF impositions had forced Senegal to restrict the quota of those who could enter university study, thwarting Amadou's aspiration for higher education. "Now that they have denied me entrance to the university, I have no other option than the streets. And you know? The streets are cruel. My family has nothing to offer me. I won't find work because there are thousands like me. Anyway, the salaries here barely pay anything. I can't marry [pay a dowry], nor form a family. I don't want to leave [Senegal] never to return, but rather to better the situation here. We can barely do anything from here" (A.N., winter 1995). Preparing to emigrate, Amadou engaged in daily practices of youth culture that constructed him as one of Senegal's burgeoning pre-emigrants[14] whose sights have turned abroad. Like Amadou, young males try to save up whatever earnings they can from odd jobs in the informal economy, while investing time and energy in obtaining information and developing networks to facilitate hoped-for travel. Amadou worked hard to transform himself into a cosmopolitan person able to understand and control Western cultural patterns. He studied languages such as English, Italian, and Spanish by speaking to emigrants who returned to Senegal or to visitors like myself. He asked about all kinds of specific aspects of everyday life in foreign lands, such as the cost of rent, utilities, cars, and food. In his speech, he mixed languages, for example, by combining French and English in the word *cool-ment*; he dressed in American fashions; and he soaked up reggae and Youssou N'Dour, appropriating the cosmopolitanism that he felt on the verge of gaining.

Senegalese youth preparing to leave the country did not merely reproduce cosmopolitan cultural patterns and identities unchanged, as some of their elders alleged. They were not simply passive recipients of postcolonial ideology and structures of power. Rather, young Senegalese, "as active participants at several social and cultural borders … talk about, interact with, negotiate, and enact change.… They generate their own visions from a repertoire of contemporary identity politics, through processes of selection, modification, and enactment. They formulate their responses and reactions in terms of calls for change at the intersections of the local, national, and transnational environs they occupy" (L. Soysal, n.d., 1). As I will show, fluid transmission of information across transnational social space created by migrant workers opened up new challenges both to traditional autochthonous authorities in Senegal and to the state's demagoguery of modernization and democratization.

Let us now consider how Senegalese have emerged as a visible collective in a new transnational and geographically disconnected public space while retaining facets of their country's idiosyncratic autochthonous social structures. I will show how Granada has become a Senegalese place through material and symbolic practices of community building, and how transnationalism has conjured up a new contested public space where migrant workers both incorporate and challenge structures of global and national inequality.

Community in the Diaspora: The Construction of Granada as a Senegalese Place (1980–1995)

Senegalese peasants have a long tradition of migration, produced more often than not by the intervention of colonial powers. Scholars have studied the migratory patterns of specific ethnic groups within the frontiers of Senegal, across African states, and, finally, across continents, in Europe and the United States.[15] The three migratory patterns are linked with one another, not only through the complex networks that connect personal and collective trajectories, but more generally, as part of strategies of reproduction of capital and labor.[16] Global and local conjunctures intertwine in the shaping of the migratory social space. As for the Senegalese emigration to Spain and Italy, its very recent incorporation in the migratory landscapes is closely related to France' shifting migratory politics toward its former colonies in West Africa, and the restriction of privileges historically granted to Senegalese.[17]

Senegalese entered the Iberian Peninsula in three successive waves, each time facing greater restrictions on access and greater risk in conjunction with changes in foreign and immigration policy, both in the Western world and in Africa.[18]

1. From 1980 to 1985 there were four principal avenues of entry: (a) via France, which still does not require visas of Senegalese but offers them little possibility of regularizing a stay in France; (b) via Morocco, where they could easily "negotiate" a Moroccan certificate of residence to obtain a tourist visa in the Spanish consulates; (c) via Gibraltar, where they were allowed to enter despite the fact that the authorities retained their passports, which they afterwards requested from Spain; and (d) directly from Dakar, via the Canary Islands.

2. From 1985 to 1989, France and Gibraltar began to interdict immigration, leaving the Canary Islands and Morocco as principal venues for immigrating Senegalese.

3. From 1990 to 1995, Spain enforced visa restrictions in Morocco and the Canary Islands, forcing growing numbers of Senegalese to join other Africans crossing the Straits of Gibraltar clandestinely. In this later phase, immigrants crossed in small boats, or *pateras,* organized by new transnational mafias that maximized profits by overcrowding barges with people willing to risk anything to cross over to Europe's nearest foothold, Andalusia.

The first Senegalese to arrive in Granada in the mid 1980s were part of a broader emigration of Wolof, originally from the regions of Djambour and Baol, who found themselves trapped in the accelerated urbanization brought on by the decline of the *da'aras*.[19] Most came through France, taking advantage of familial or religious networks with the community already settled there.[20] Many went first to Catalonia, in northeastern Spain, primarily to Barcelona, attracted by rumors of an imminent regularization which in 1986 would enable them to obtain documents permitting entry elsewhere in Europe. But the regularization of 1986 was very restrictive; most of those who applied did not receive papers. Instead they stayed in Spain, taking advantage of initial tolerance toward foreigners and their petty commerce. Once in Spain they began traveling, seeking out new commercial enclaves where they could free themselves from the hegemony already established in Barcelona.

Omar was among the first to arrive to Granada. Like other pioneers, Omar tried to break his dependence on Africans already established in Catalonia who controlled the commerce of new arrivals. He traveled to Granada to look for a place where African commerce was absent, affording him an opportunity.

In Barcelona, Senegalese were living in several hostels, but once you got there, you had to submit to the rules imposed by the elders, and I was already an independent man because I had worked in the army in Dakar.... So I moved down south and I went to Granada, where I found only three other Senegalese. People in Granada were very friendly and open. There were many opportunities for selling because of all the tourism. There were all kinds of people in the streets—Gypsies, "Moors," tourists— and the police tolerated street vending and didn't enforce the Alien Law. So we felt good, and we started to organize ourselves in a hostel. We sought out alternative providers of merchandise in the coast of Málaga, and we distributed ourselves around for selling (O.N., spring 1995).[21]

Progressively more Senegalese came to Granada through the Canary Islands, Morocco, or Gibraltar. By 1989, before the government almost completely restricted the granting of visas in Morocco, Granada already had a visible (though largely illegal) community of Senegalese.[22] Most had been recruited through migratory networks based on familial, village, or religious relations to help take advantage of the opportunity that Granada afforded. As they arrived in a growing diaspora, they began to deploy idiosyncratic Senegalese structures of authority and mutual aid in new ways—for example, in housing. The first hostel (to which Omar referred above) rapidly overflowed into another one. All Senegalese in the hostels engaged in daily meetings to distribute domestic tasks, contributing to a common pool of money, and exchanging information on immigrants' experiences. Functioning as collectives, they extended solidarity to newcomers, allowing them a free month's stay while they established themselves. They thus extended Senegalese familial and religious practices into new forms for organizing domestic units in Granada, transforming this reterritorialized space into a socioeconomic resource, a kind of social capital that migrants use to make their project possible.

Yet while building new structures of solidarity, Senegalese were also beginning to struggle over leadership of their community in ways that both drew upon and resisted older Senegalese structures of authority. The Senegalese in Granada were a heterogeneous group in terms of origins and situation in the Senegalese national social structure, and they used capital acquired in the Senegalese pole strategically to preserve and improve their positions of power in the new transnational social space. Some brought the organization and authority of the *Marabouts* with them, and worked to extend this basis of tradition and religion into the new arena. Others came as dependents of the *Marabouts*, submitting to their authority while accepting the benefits of *Marabout* support, thus reinforcing the classic clientelist system described in the literature.[23] But other immigrants wanted to take advantage of their new social space to free themselves from structures of authority that they felt were oppressive. Omar, for example, complained that "they wanted you to be like them, to obey the *Marabouts* blindly, to contribute money for religious celebrations, to live in a Senegalese island in Spain. I didn't want to do all this, even though I am a believer, and I became more and more isolated from the resources they control" (O.D., spring 1995).

By 1989, Senegalese from the Granadan hostel collectives had begun to develop alliances with Spanish volunteer organizations, notably Granada Acoge (Welcome to Granada), an NGO whose members began to help Senegalese expand out of the hostels into apartments by intermediating for the Senegalese with apartment owners. The volunteers of Granada Acoge were, for the most part, mature Spanish women who acted more on the basis of their Catholic liberation ideology than by any knowledge of Senegalese culture and structures of power. The volunteers felt they saw similarity between the solidarity and habitus of paternalism in Catholic base communities and Senegalese Islamic brotherhoods.[24] As they built personal relations and alliances with Senegalese leaders, they began to feel that the Senegalese were harder working and more organized than other immigrants. As one volunteer put it: "They are very organized people: Each house has a coordinator who takes care of the domestic organization and tells us about their needs. They are industrious workers and they help each other a lot, not like "Moors," who don't seem to trust each other. We have very good relations with the coordinators, and this form of organizing makes our task much more effective" (A.A., volunteer at Granada Acoge, summer 1992). But the volunteers tended to misperceive the nature of Senegalese leadership and organization. What Spaniards saw as the democratic selection of a "coordinator" to manage domestic resources and tasks in an organized way was instead usually an extension of idiosyncratic Senegalese modes of hierarchical authority, which were proving their efficacy for incorporating newcomers into the highly surveyed European social space.

As literature on Senegalese immigration in Europe and the United States reveals,[25] there are four elements that permeate the ongoing expansion of Senegalese communities across a transnational social space:

1. At the base, Senegalese use a hierarchical division of labor to organize the domestic sphere and productive relations. An extreme form is that of Mouride residential units.
2. Senegalese develop semiautonomous networks of transnational trade able to absorb newly arriving Senegalese into street commerce.[26]
3. Senegalese deploy a complex and continuous flow of persons, commodities, and information across residential units in places such as Granada as well as across the geographically scattered sites of the Senegalese global diaspora. They use networks of religious, familial, territorial, and commercial ties to create and maintain their migratory circuits, which are daily strengthened by informal visits, phone calls, and letters, remittances, commercial and financial exchanges, and religious rituals.

4. Senegalese underscore the primacy of common religious and cultural values over ethnic, political, or religious differences among Senegalese people. The most important among these common values are those of solidarity and hospitality, of a strong work ethic, of emigration as a process of learning and struggle for their own community, and of collective life as part of the self-denial inherent in purity and religious virtue.

Senegalese used all of these elements in establishing themselves in Granada, which has become an important site of the Senegalese transnational imaginary, with more than seven hundred members in 1995 distributed in domestic units ranging from four to ten individuals.[27] According to the 1994 survey cited above, more than 80 percent of them came directly to Granada, 75 percent arriving since 1990, when the Spanish government announced the regularization of 1991. These figures reflect the efficacy of highly organized networks for facilitating migration through careful planning, from departure to destination.[28] Emigrants plan their travel months or years in advance, with the help of their family and of *Marabouts* in Senegal and abroad. They seek out information on the cost of different ways of entering the peninsula (including bribes and transport on mafia-run *pateras*) and scrape together money by selling part of their personal or familial patrimony. They memorize the addresses of contacts in Spain so as to carry no paperwork that could facilitate deportation if caught by the Civil Guard. They seek out information about countries at war, such as Liberia or Rwanda, in case they wish to claim political asylum as refugees.[29] They acquire a powerful *gri-gri* (amulet; see note 12), "which allows us to be unnoticed when crossing the frontiers" (A.D., winter 1995). Once in Spain, they contact a member of their extended family or *keur*, their brotherhood, or their native village to guide them to their final destination. Arriving in a Senegalese house, the emigrant will be lodged for free for at least one month. He will help in the domestic tasks while being instructed by his compatriots about Spanish legislation and police control, the distribution of commercial enclaves, and access to civil associations dedicated to helping immigrants.

These informal economic, social, and cultural mechanisms prove very effective for helping Senegalese confront the economic and juridical uncertainties and sociocultural exclusion of being African immigrants in Spain. Although building from autochthonous, home-state organizations such as the *da'ira* or the *keur*, it is not surprising that they acquire a life of their own. Migratory processes involve a series of "rites of passage" that have the capacity to change traditional structures, remodeling them to help craft a deterritorialized space in which the projects of emigration are viable and within which Senegalese can find a strong sense of belonging, even in the face of exclusion and marginalization.

The linkages of domestic and labor structures to commerce are a crucial material foundation for Senegalese diaspora. These linkages are especially strong among the Mouride, where the "head" of the residential unit is usually a *grotisse,* or trader, who mediates transnational commercial exchanges controlled by Mouride *Marabouts,* both in Senegal and abroad. Such organization is not exclusive to the Mouride, however. Most Senegalese began their lives in Granada by entering one of the similarly organized residential units, taking credit arranged through one of the Senegalese warehouses or through family or religious mentors, and selling merchandise with their housemates.

Most Senegalese had to transform their ideas about migration upon arrival in Granada. As African emigrants they arrive with the intention of being responsible family members and good Muslims but without a realistic sense of what they will find. Yet Spaniards perceive them differently, ignorant of their efforts and their plight. As immigrants in Spain, Senegalese encounter difficulties and suspicion that belie the widespread imaginary of a European "paradise." "When you return to Senegal, many approach you for help to leave. You tell them how difficult things are here. You tell them about the need to get the papers, about the lack of houses, about the difficulty even Spaniards have in finding a job, and about racism, but they don't believe you. They won't listen to you. They think you say so out of self-interest, because you don't want them to leave. It is impossible to stop people. Only when they are here already do they begin to understand what we meant" (A.N., winter 1995).

The solidarity and hospitality afforded by Senegalese residential organization proves crucial for immigrants coping with disillusion and with the socioeconomic marginality and instability of their juridical status. The residential units serve as informal structures of support and as spaces for reaffirming black Muslim sociocultural identity in Europe. Senegalese mark their doorbells in the buildings they inhabit to facilitate one another's visits and thus combat isolation and spatial dispersion. "There are so many of us that people often rang at the wrong house, provoking the complaints of neighbors and problems. So we mark our doorbell with nail polish, and this helps to avoid confusions. You know you are knocking at a Senegalese house" (A.D., summer 1994). Even in situations of overcrowding and extreme poverty, Senegalese can count on one another for a place to sleep and warm food to eat. If a person falls sick, has severe problems, or dies (as has actually happened), the Senegalese community will quickly collect whatever money is needed for the emergency, no matter the quantity.

Senegalese in Granada also sustain, renew, and reconstitute linkages to the different places within the Senegalese diaspora, or "deterritorialized nation-state," as Blash et al. (1994) have termed this new hegemonic configuration.[30] The figure of the courier (messenger or transporter) as a professional, though informal, occupation, reflects the solidity of these transnational networks. Similar to the transnational migrant circuits studied by Rouse in his analysis of the social networks between Aguililla in Mexico and Redwood City in California,

Senegalese networks involve a representation of community that transcends national territorial limits. As much so for Senegalese as for Aguilillans, "Through the continuous circulation of people, money, goods, and information, the various settlements have become so closely woven together that, in an important sense they have come to constitute a single community spread across a variety of sites" (Rouse 1992, 15).

Kinship and religion are two principal forces shaping Senegalese transnational migration circuits in their deterritorialized community. Traditional systems of authority, though contested, have succeeded in making their interests prevail and impose specific notion of community and of what being a good emigrant-immigrant means. Yet this is also the result of ongoing negotiation between social agents differently situated in the transnational social space. As Kearney suggests with his description of a border area, Senegalese have to deal daily with the perception and expectations that Spaniards have of them. The interaction with the Spanish state and civil society (members of NGOs, friends and fiancées, employers, and civil servants) instills in Senegalese a new preoccupation with individual projects and legal recognition, as I have shown in chapter 4. While family or brotherhood members back in Senegal may see such concerns as threats to their own structures of kinship and religion, both emigrants and non-emigrants continue to deploy familial and religious power strategically to strengthen the links between people in the diaspora and at home.

The construction of Granada as a Senegalese place involves a reappropriation and redefinition of the space of migration, even though the structure of this space is shaped by objective forces independent of the actual interaction of social agents, such as global political-economic inequalities, class relations, gender, and age systems of authority. People situated at the Senegalese extreme of this transnational social field use their particular social, economic, and symbolic capital strategically to perpetuate the image of emigrants as indispensable members of the community, even if not present in the territory. This notion of community emphasizes mutual obligations among Senegalese members of the same extended family, *keur*, or brotherhood—(even across national borders)—obligations that reproduce structures of authority along the lines of age, gender, social status, and also, more plainly, wealth. The fact that Spaniards consider immigrants as dispensable foreigners despite their presence in the territory further strengthens Senegalese representation of community in familial, lineage-based, and religious imageries of belonging linked to autochthonous social structures. For their part, transmigrant Senegalese who take an active part in redefining this space also periodically renew their links with the extended family, the *keur*, and the religious community (Tidjane and Mouride brotherhoods). In doing so, they use their image as indispensable emigrants as capital to negotiate what Senegalese back home can reasonably expect of them as good Muslims and responsible family members.

In strategies developed back home, for example, families may offer an emigrant a woman to marry, preferably one close to the family.[31] Such offers extend a family claim on the emigrant's remittances while underscoring his ongoing obligation to participate in life-circle celebrations that are the basis of a complex, reticular economic system of wealth distribution.[32] Similarly, religious social structures such as the *da'ira* underscore mutual religious obligation binding each *Marabout* to his *taalibes* (followers), even when they extend abroad. A *da'ira* in Granada collects *taalibes'* contributions and sends them to *Marabouts* back in Senegal. *Marabouts* from the highest strata of the Mouride hierarchy in Senegal periodically visit the different *da'iras* of the diaspora where they have *taalibes*. Celebrations welcoming them include mystical songs, prayer, and displays of submission. All emigrant members of the brotherhood gather the contributions to turn over to the *Marabout*, in part for his own well-being and in part to improve living conditions of people back home (schools, hospitals, mosques). Such practices strengthen the image of Granada as part of a community of faith and are particularly strong among Mourides.

Senegalese networks linking home to Granada and into the diaspora also serve as effective forms of social control. Word of imputed "deviations" travels fast through Granada's residential units, back to Senegal, and through the diaspora. Definitions of the "good immigrant" vary from inflexible and puritanical expectations of those most deeply involved in religious organizations to milder expectations on the part of young Senegalese who have opened up to interethnic relations and to Spanish styles of leisure and organization. Yet across this spectrum, Senegalese share an understanding of migration as a process of learning that entails suffering and self-restraint. Senegalese will strongly reprove compatriots who fall into delinquency (especially if related to drugs), who forget the family and the country they left behind, and who behave as Europeans or Americans (as they refer to them). Such people will be censured as improper Africans.

Yet there is reaction among Senegalese against religious conservatism. Some of the more devout religious units condemn Senegalese relations with white women as sinful and potentially corrupting, and they compel people to stay at home after work to participate fully in religious collective life. Other Senegalese criticize such requirements as extreme and as enabling religious leaders to profit from Spaniards' exclusionary practices by driving immigrants back into a hermetic space dominated by the authority of elders, mentors, and religious bosses. As a Senegalese immigrant told me:

> The *Marabouts,* who have all the privileges back at home, come here and stay the same. They take advantage of all these illiterate boys who come here and believe anything the *Marabout* tells them, just because they live in constant fear of the police and of magic forces. It is not true that in order to be a good Muslim one has to avoid any

contact with people in Spain, or that you have to come home directly after work. Everybody begins this way, with the rosary in their hands and seeing only other Senegalese. But here the situation is different. We learn more about our rights as persons, and we realize that nobody is necessary to intercede for you in front of God. (A.N., spring 1995)

Such criticisms, however, do not flow from national struggles in Senegal among brotherhoods (Mourides versus Tidjanes, for instance), between Islamic brotherhoods and the state, or between dominant structures and alternative, albeit relatively powerless, ideologies of radical Islamic politics favoring an Islamic state (Villalón 1995, 70–71). In other words, resistance and redefinition of what is a "good migrant" and of what are the rules of the community are not organized along purely national imageries. Other processes are at work. I argue in the concluding section of this chapter that both collective identity construction and contestation flow from the clash of Senegalese and Spanish cultural hegemonies in the global political-economic context in which they are differentially situated. Through the case study of Senegalese community representations in Granada, I will show how transnational processes involve both a reproduction of national structures of power through the struggle to reproduce the dominant representation of the nation, and at the same time, a transcendence of nationalism.

Strategies of Belonging and Structures of Power: The Challenge of a Transnational Social Space

Granada and other places of Senegalese diaspora are being constructed as such at the interstices of the global economic forces tending toward decentralization, mobility, and deterritorialization, but also as a result of the interplay of national institutions and power groups seeking capital accumulation in Spain and Senegal. Hundreds of Senegalese migrants in Granada facilitate the expansion of transnational trade networks controlled by religious organizations, thus serving the interests of Mouride and Islamic religious elite in Senegal and their balance of power vis-à-vis the Senegalese state.[33] This same army of street sellers is also available as temporary, cheap, and flexibly deployable laborers when work is needed in economic sectors such as agriculture or construction in Andalusia. The surplus value that young Senegalese workers generate in transnational social space is appropriated by groups of people only tangentially situated in the transnational social matrix. To secure their interests and privileges in the context of an increasingly global economy, Senegalese religious and lineage authorities, similarly to Spanish employers, strategically use their relative power positions at the national level to achieve control of transmigrants as an obedient and cheap labor force.

Senegalese national elites maintain their role as mediators between the Senegalese state and its citizens, to a great extent as a consequence of their control of commerce across the strategic sites in the diaspora where they have established "delegations." Conversely, their control of the diaspora is possible because they preserve their role as national socioeconomic actors able to generate resources for disempowered Wolof families. In the representation of the community and the nation they emphasize a symbolic imagery that goes well beyond the territorial limits of the state but doesn't challenge the secular channels of participation marked by the Senegalese state.

In Senegal, these elite facilitate capitalist projects of modernization while, at the same time keeping a prudent distance from the state as spiritual leaders of anti-Western resistance based on the so-called authentic traditions of black Islam. Their community of belonging is, as Blash et al. (1994) suggest, nationalist, building on the anticolonial role of the brotherhoods and delineated in terms of "race" (the ideology of *négritude*) and religion (whether the *umma*, or international Islamic community, *dar el-Islam*, or the particular symbolic territory of the brotherhood). Yet in contrast to the case studies explored by Blash et al., their nationalist discourse does not necessarily reinforce the state but rather their own role of linking the state to its people. Their appeal to moral and religious bases of power thus reinforces local (rather than national) systems of authority and dependence while producing "culturally abiding" clients, disciples, and family members.

On the Spanish side of the transnational social space, intermediaries and some Senegalese also seek to maximize the symbolic power of discourse representing Senegalese immigrants as "cultural others," or as ethnically differentiated groups. In Granada, for instance, NGOs, unions, and (more recently) municipal and regional institutions have consistently supported Senegalese associationism as part of purportedly progressive efforts to mitigate postcolonial domination, capitalist exploitation of Third World countries, and European racism. Senegalese in Granada, whether they support or criticize more traditional structures, strategically deploy the economic and political resource of associationism in alliances with those Spanish organizations and institutions controlling social funds directed toward cooperation and integration. Seeking control of the funds for integration and cooperation programs, Senegalese migrants, like the Mexican indigenous Mixtec transnational migrants analyzed by Kearney, project their political strategies toward powerful allies in global contexts who can help them "realign their relationships with their own states to their advantage" (Kearney n.d., 1). Such interethnic alliances help immigrants improve their situation both in Senegal and in Spain, and may potentially open up new spaces for challenging the dominance of traditional systems of authority and social control within the deterritorialized community.

Interethnic alliances in these transnational spaces entail some structures of inequality that are open to criticism. An important cleavage entails cultural constructions of gender, given that most Spanish volunteers working in cooperation and integration issues are women and most Senegalese immigrants are men. Some young Senegalese have begun to problematize the African and Islamic model of polygamy (see note 32 of this chapter), but most Senegalese men want to retain the privileges granted to them by this particular cultural model, evoking misgivings and denunciation on the part of Spanish women, most of whom are progressive, and even feminist. In the daily interactions of Senegalese men with Spanish women, however, there is an ongoing exchange that clearly opens up new fissures in the model perpetuated by traditional authorities. Although Senegalese women's emigration is still unusual, such women's interaction with Spanish women may also open new lines of contestation within the deterritorialized community.

Other frictions arise in the alliances linking Spanish volunteers to Muslim men, yet both also cooperate in grassroots efforts to ameliorate the normalizing power wielded both by states and by institutional mediators (Islamic brotherhoods as well as powerful NGOs) in the definition of cooperation and of integration. These grassroots efforts are, in fact, opening some lines of multiethnic dialog at the local level across geographically discontinuous sites in the transnational space.[34] Yet the possibility for informal alliances between groups and individuals are constrained by the scarcity of resources for subaltern projects.

Most cooperation efforts have in fact been channeled through the state's social programs of integration, through powerful Western NGOs, and through immigrants' autochthonous social organizations, such as the brotherhoods, effectively directing economic resources through their strong preexisting networks of mutual aid and collective well-being. Many of these programs draw upon essentialist notions of cultural differences and of development stages that may, as Blash et al. have suggested, "contribute to the belief that each of these states has a discrete and viable national economy ... [and yet they] are pulled into developmental schemes that actually make the home country even more subordinate to global capital" (1994, 277). Thus, in contrast to the case of the Mexican indigenous transnational migrants explored by Kearney, Senegalese transnational alliances based on ethnic identities and cooperation do not necessarily produce a relaxation of the power of the closed corporate community, and may even serve to reaffirm local autochthonous powers. The Senegalese case seems to illustrate the possible conservative consequences of the revalorization of a transnational ethnicity in Western countries of destination.

In contrast to alliances between Spanish associations and Senegalese groups that emphasize migrants' cultural distinctiveness, there are interventions that involve much more radical criticisms of Western models for incorporation of "cultural others." The criticisms flow from a confluence of post-Marxist internationalism and militant Islamic analysis, which denounces both internal colonialism and the cooperation between Islamic brotherhoods and the state. Here we find "Westernized" intellectuals and "arabisants" as allies in challenging the legacy of colonial domination that is evident in the partnership between state and Islamic brotherhoods for the reproduction of the Senegalese national project. Such critiques may become the basis of profound challenges to the mutual feeding of the global and national status quo.

The militant Islamic and post-Marxist internationalist critics coincide in denouncing the internal colonialism perpetuated by secular states and institutional mediators in places like Senegal. Both call into question the role of a powerful Senegalese bourgeois commercial elite, empowered by a legal system that grants them juridical privileges denied to most Senegalese, and thus enable them to use clientelism to take advantage of immigrants' vulnerable situation while strengthening their own positions of authority. These critics see the symbolic violence exerted on immigrants by Mouride authorities as either exploitative, or non-Islamic, or both. Such criticism nonetheless joins leftist intellectuals and militant Islamics in an egalitarian logic that proves to be embedded in evolutionary and neo-colonialist frameworks that map the world into a hierarchical array of less or more civilized cultures. *Marabouts* resort to "magic" in establishing networks of dependence among disciples (e.g., *gri-gris*-making practices; see note 12). *Marabouts* also exact extreme forms of allegiance from their *taalibe* followers, such as the act of submission, or *njebbel*.[35] The Mouride brotherhood appropriates the symbolic power of the anticolonial struggle of black Africans by appealing to the anticolonial, but specifically Senegalese, struggle of the saint-founder of the brotherhood, Cheick Amadou Bamba, a black Wolof Muslim who is claimed to represent the interests of the nation of Senegal. Radical criticisms interpret all of these phenomena as "primitive" practices based on animistic beliefs. Such modernist rationales clearly incorporate racist prejudices of both Arabs and Europeans toward black Africans who engage in such practices as "authentic" African traditions.

Senegalese include themselves in the larger Islamic community as it has spread in Europe and Spain. Like other Muslims, Senegalese struggle to counter the pervasive Western conception of Islam as a threat to modernity's purported rationalism, egalitarianism, and democracy. As I will illustrate in the next chapter, for some Muslim groups in Granada, Islam emerges as an alternative political and moral rationale, one that questions the legitimacy of secularism imposed by the materialist and "sinful" hegemony of the United States. The power of this antagonist imagery, however, is rather limited in Spain and Andalusia, and in the case of the Senegalese, is further undermined by the racist prejudices of many Muslims toward black Islam, as well as by the efficacy of *Marabouts* in reproducing "culturally abiding" subjects.

It is appealing to think that transnational formations might be able to challenge state-bounded categories of participation, yet in practice, the challenge is still minimal. Migration processes seem primarily to strengthen the hand of those mediators who can tap public resources directed toward marginalized people, typically those who are still segregated from full participation in the civil sphere and who have little or no access to democratic decision making. The fundamental issue is not just legal entitlement, but real empowerment. Migrants who are citizens in Senegal and, with luck, semi permanent legal residents, may be legal subjects entitled to rights and subjected to duties within both Senegal and Spain. But they are constructed as subjects of tutelage, as political clients, as assisted by and dependent upon those who hold control of decision making at the local level—be these traditional or customary authorities, NGOs, or municipal and regional administrations. Unless participation in the name of difference is backed up by democratization at the local level, it may remain as a new form of colonial indirect rule, unintentionally perpetuating pernicious legacies of racism, ethnic conflict, and particularism (or so-called tribalism).

As recent sociolegal scholarship has demonstrated, colonial administrations conjured up ethnic, national, and racial categories in politically enforced indirect rule. Senegal's characteristic socioreligious Islamic brotherhoods both struggled against and complied with colonial modalities of governance. The Mouride and Tidjane leaders are well known for their anticolonial struggle in the colony and for joining secular politicians in struggles for independence and for racial desegregation of the civil sphere. Yet their complicity in the colonial order as traditional authorities also set the foundations for strong socioreligious social structures that now facilitate the weak Senegalese state's indirect rule over citizens. These socioreligious structures help incorporate despairing young people into productive enterprises. They create empowering imageries of belonging and identity. Yet they are also powerful instruments of social control over "culturally abiding" subjects who perpetuate traditional systems of authority and the national status quo in the name of their religious allegiance. The context of migratory processes and transnational formations may forge new collective identities that are able to transcend both state and institutional mediators, but the process will be slow.

The snail-paced change is due in part to the mode of rule that constructs immigrants as different "others" with only partial (if any) rights to full participation in the Spanish civil sphere. I have shown throughout this book how a particular notion of immigrants' difference is created, enforced, resisted, and negotiated at the local level. Dominant ideology and political discourses defend a liberal perspective that categorizes difference as cultural in the form of a right to private and subjective belief. Local implementation of social programs prioritize issues of control and security, developing disciplinary techniques intended to normalize immigrants' behavior, or in other words, to erase those cultural impediments to "normal" integration into the Spanish civil sphere. Immigrants' interactions with institutional mediators, such as unions, NGOs, or civil servants, further discipline standards of appropriate behavior and habits required to fit state-sanctioned migratory categories. In these daily interactions, I have shown, Spanish intermediaries unintentionally reproduce the "fetishism of papers" and the evolutionary rationale intrinsic to modernization policies that construct immigrants as subjects of disciplinary programs, of tutelage, or, more plainly, as clients.

As Mamdani masterfully argued regarding African postcolonial politics in *Citizen and Subject*, "The antidote to a mode of rule that accentuates difference, ethnic in this case, cannot be to deny difference, but to historicize it. Faced with a power that fragments an oppressed majority into so many self-enclosed culturally defined minorities, the burden of resistance must be both to recognize and to transcend the points of difference" (1996, 296). This is surely the challenge of *convivencia*—both to recognize the importance of difference and yet transcend it in order to be able to really live together.

In the next chapter, I will explore *convivencia* through analysis of relevant ethnographic material. *Convivencia* requires a theoretical approach to ethnic relations that looks beyond conflict to processes of exchange, mutual respect, and understanding. My notion of *convivencia* draws on Jewish and Spanish historians' recognition of the centrality of this facet of ethnic relations in medieval Spain, for which the term was originally couched. I follow Glick's (1992) notion of *convivencia*, where cultural exchange is not deprived of "the complexities of the social dynamics of cultural interaction." I will argue that in order to transcend categories and structures of difference, the analyst should take full account of these complexities as they shape day-to-day interactions, where rivalry and suspicion go hand in hand with mutual interpenetration and creative influence. To appreciate the complexities of the social dynamics of cultural interaction, the analyst has to attempt to transcend difference by relativizing it, in addition to historicizing it.

In other words, the forging of moments and spaces for *convivencia* does require that the groups and individuals involved recognize the multidimensional character of their social interactions. As Glick put it in his article on medieval Spanish cultural interchange, "*Convivencia* ... must encompass the ability of persons of different ethnic groups to step out of their ethnically bound roles in order to interact on a par with members of competing [*sic*] groups" (1992, 4). I will thus explore examples of social interactions in which immigrants manage to both use and yet transcend roles structured by ethnicity, religion, social class, and legal status. Such moments and spaces of *convivencia* configure them as social agents who, in their daily lives, actively step out of the ethnic and legal categories imposed on them, winning acknowledgment of their roles in broader society as neighbors, friends, members of a religious community, and potential sociopolitical collaborators. As I will show, difference does not disappear from these interactions, yet they allow for cultural exchange.

Notes

1. For a recent review, see Merry 1991; see also Chatterjee 1993; Cohn 1989; J. Collier 1992; Comaroff 1989; Comaroff and Comaroff 1987, 1991; Cooper and Stoler 1989; Fitzpatrick 1992; Messick 1992; Mitchell 1988; Moore 1969; 1986; Snyder 1981; Vicent 1990. For an overview of similar issues in Latin America see Stavenhagen and Iturralde 1990 and Chenaut and Sierra 1995.

2. Lugard 1965, 149–50, quoted in Mamdani 1996, 16.

3. Kearney (1995, 548) distinguishes global processes as "largely decentered from specific national territories" from transnational processes as "anchored in and transcending one or more states." To emphasize the conflict between these transnational processes with limited civil spheres sanctioned by particular states as their legitimate jurisdiction, he proposes the term "trans-statal." See also Appadurai 1991 for anthropological views on transnational issues.

4. Wolf 1982, 206; see 204–20 for the use of preexisting slavery mechanisms in West Africa by European traders.

5. *Da'aras* were organized most especially by the *Marabouts,* or religious leaders, who brought their followers (*taalibes*) with them to work in the groundnut fields. Some of these *da'aras* were monastic sites where hard work was emphasized as a purifying and sanctifying activity. Other *da'aras* formed around traditional *chefs du villages* (villages authorities) who coordinated the work of the free peasants of the village who had to give part of their production to the local chief and to the French authorities. Common to all of this was the hierarchical organization of labor, in which bosses were exempt from manual labor but responsible for administrative functions for the local state and for prayer (Copans 1988.)

6. The *da'iras* began as independent cohort associations in the urban areas and later spread as the most successful form of association in the rural environment and in the diaspora. They commonly relate to a given *Marabout,* but they are independently run by an elected board organized for bureaucratic functions (Copans 1988; see Carter 1997 and Ebrin 1990 for an ethnographic account of *da'iras* in Milan and New York, respectively; see Evers Rosander 1997 for a focus on gender issues).

7. In addition to conducting fieldwork in Alfaya and Granada from 1992 to 1995, I went to Senegal in the winter of 1995. I undertook fieldwork in Dakar and in the regions of Thiès (Mbour, Sébikotane) and Djourbel (Louga). In Sébikotane I designed a questionnaire together with two Senegalese, one of whom was an immigrant in Granada (Ahmat Tidjane Niang) and the other a university student in Dakar who was interested in emigration in his region (Ousseynou Ndiaye). We administered the questionnaire to a pool of thirty emigrants who normally lived in Spain and Italy. I thank my Senegalese aides for help in this study.

8. According to a survey designed by Professor Javier García Castaño, University of Granada, in cooperation with the NGO Granada Acoge, for one hundred male Senegalese immigrants in Granada in 1994 (at this point there were no Senegalese women living in Granada; they began to arrive in 1995), 76 percent of the sample were younger than thirty-five, more than half were bachelors, 67 percent had no children. Eighty-eight percent declared Wolof as their first language, and 95 percent were Muslims. Although the questionnaire unfortunately did not inquire about brotherhood affiliations, my own ethnographic work suggests that Mourids prevailed over Tidjanes.

9. It should be noted that the volunteers who administered the survey did not have any information about Senegal, not even a map to locate the village, town or region to which immigrants referred when asked about their places of origin. I therefore found it difficult to interpret some of these responses, but the result clearly indicates that most immigrants came from

Djambour, and specially Louga (more than 23 percent), and Baol (around 30 percent from Touba, Diourbel, Mbacke, Ndagal, Ndame, Ndiane, and Darou Mousty). Other significant places of origin are Dakar (13 percent) and Kaolack (14 percent).

10. Almost 35 percent of immigrants in the poll declared commerce as their former occupation in Senegal, followed by 20 percent engaged in a variety of jobs in the service sector, and 17 percent were unemployed.

11. See Ebrin 1990 for a description of the links between the Mouride brotherhood and Senegalese emigration in New York. In my interviews in Senegal it was widely recognized that *Marabouts* are the only ones who have access to visas to come to Spain or elsewhere. The consul in the Spanish Embassy confirmed to me that generally the *Marabouts* are granted visas because "they travel a lot, they go back and forth to visit their *taalibes* abroad…. But they live here very well, and they do not have any reason to stay in Spain, which is what we are supposed to prevent. We know that sometimes they travel with *taalibes* who will stay … there are thousands of tricks they use to fool us, but we cannot control them all" (Dakar, winter 1995).

12. Many of the references to the *Marabouts* are associated with their roles as intermediaries between the lawmen and the supranatural beings from whom one needs protection. As Carter has explained, "The gri-gri of Islam have been appropriated and combined with notions of spirit and divinities from pre-Islamic ideology … [It] is a little bit of baraka [divine grace] which transforms the body of the follower into a channel of this transformative power and subordinates other 'forces' to its logic…. The gri-gri cannot be worn by another, and gri-gri are often sent to migrants from Senegal; when a powerful gri-gri maker is found people will travel great distances and have another belt made to protect their children abroad. Many Senegalese have gri-gri made for them specifically for going to Europe that they might not be harmed by police or other 'forces.' The gri-gri in fact encircles the wearer in a world of the community of faith and protects and promotes free movement in dangerous or potentially dangerous situations" (Carter 1997, 13–15).

13. See Collier 1994 for an analysis of similar transformations in the traditional system of stratification in the Chiapas highlands, Mexico.

14. I thank Angela García Moreno for suggesting this concept to me while doing fieldwork in Senegal.

15. See Barou 1987; Bredeloup 1992; Carter 1997; Cruise O'Brien 1971; Cohen 1971; Diop 1965; 1988; Ebrin 1990, 1992: Ebrin and Lake 1992; Meillasoux 1981; Schmidt di Friedberg 1993.

16. Barou's analysis of the Soniké, a transnational ethnic group originally from the Senegal River Valley located between the boundaries of Senegal, Mali, and Mauritania is one such case in point. According to his research on Senegalese immigration in France, the Soniké made up the most numerous African group living in France in the mid 1980s (60 percent of the black African population), and 14 percent of the Sonikés were scattered across Senegal, Mali, Mauritania, and other African countries. Soniké authorities acted from the eleventh century onward as middlemen in the trans-Saharan trade of slaves and gold, forging a royal dynasty that was able to exact taxes and preserve its independence. During the nineteenth century they lost power and began to migrate to the Congo and Zaire to engage in new trade, and to central Senegal as seasonal laborers in the peanut fields, as salaried workers in the coal and fish industry in the Senegal River, and also to France, where they enlisted in the colonial troops. After World War II, many stayed on in France and tried to enlarge their communities through migratory networks that made strategic use of both France's changing migratory policies and the Soniké elite's resources at home (Barou 1987, 80–81)

17. See Barou 1987 and Schmidt di Friedberg 1993. France had recruited labor from its colonies before World War II, but until the late 1950s there was no real competition for labor among the industrial European countries, and so no serious migratory policy was implemented. The early settlement of Africans employed by the French army and navy facilitated the development of

migratory networks that were further promoted by agreements between France and Senegal, Mali and Mauritania in 1962 to recruit workers. Apart from following France's National Immigration Office (ONI) and its documented recruitment processes, many entered the country using informal networks. France eventually acknowledged these populations by legalizing their status as guest workers (Barou 1987, 79 and 81). In contrast to the later predominance of Wolof migratory networks directed to Spain, Italy, and United States, this first Senegalese immigration in France was predominantly comprised Soniké.

18. Here I limit myself to migration to Europe, and I focus on strategies for emigrating to Spain, although most cases included earlier migration patterns, both within Senegal (as part of the rural exodus), and across several African countries, such as Mauritania, Mali, the Ivory Coast, Guinea Bissau, Gambia, as well as some labor-importing Arab countries, such as Saudi Arabia (see Robin 1992 for a statistical analysis of West African emigration).

19. Diop 1988 and Cruise O'Brien 1971.

20. Some family members of immigrants living in Granada are French citizens or have a residence or work permit in France; immigrants brought them to France as family members, and they later traveled to Spain to take advantage of the promised legalization of 1991. The example of Assane, described in chapter 2, is one such case in point. Here again we see how papers have become a precious possession, treated in the Senegalese cultural context as a collective resource. The papers of any given member of the family or brotherhood is imagined as, and at times converted into, common patrimony that can be tapped by any "pre-emigrant" trying to maximize the success of his particular emigration project.

21. In Granada's local newspaper *El Ideal* September 1 1991, the spokesman for the Senegalese Immigrants' Association (Cheick Amadou Bamba) claimed that "Andalusia is the most hospitable community in Spain," and that "many Africans come to Granada because is a wonderful city and also because we can take advantage of tourism."

22. According to the testimonies collected, there were about 100 to 150 Senegalese living in Granada in the late 1980s. Only three or four of them have managed to meet the requirements of the LOE to receive a work/stay permit.

23. These mutual obligations are based in Senegal on cultural sanctioning of dependence inscribed in the clientelist relationships that permeate civil society. As Villalón has argued: "dependence involves not only degrees of authority but also obligations on the part of the holder of the superior position.... Rather than being perceived as inequitable and therefore unjust, concentrations of wealth are actually desirable for everyone concerned—as long as the holder of wealth recognizes and acts on his (rarely her) obligations to those in dependent positions. The surest guarantee against hunger for many people is that their patron be well supplied" (1995, 59).

24. This initial relationship among the founders of Granada Acoge, Senegalese leaders, and average immigrants did not distribute power along clearly cut lines. Senegalese men establish personal and affective relations using symbolic capital attached to gender relations in Senegal. Though a very interesting ethnographic site for exploring the intertwining and clashing of gender and race structures of power, I deal only marginally with these aspects in this book.

25. See among others, Barou 1987 for France, Schmidt di Friedberg 1993 and Carter 1997 for Italy, and Ebrin 1990, 1992 and Ebrin and Lake 1992 for New York. Unfortunately, most recent work on the Senegalese diaspora in the United States and Italy, which shares with Spain the preponderance of Wolof peoples, focuses on the Mouride brotherhood. Even though my own research acknowledges the importance of the Mouride brotherhood in the creation of the Senegalese community in Granada, my ethnographic approach did not take this brotherhood as a unit of analysis, but rather the Senegalese community as a whole. The emphasis on the Mouride brotherhood is also patent in the literature dealing with Senegalese social structure. Villalón's ethnographic study in Senegal (1995) clearly proves that the disproportionate attention paid in

the literature to the Mouride brotherhood misrepresents the multistranded organization of Senegalese civil society, in which not only other brotherhoods should be taken into account, but also alternative Muslim activist formations, political parties, ethnic cleavages, NGOs, and other forms of civil association that are deeply intertwined with one another.

26. Senegalese participate in the burgeoning street commerce of Granada, sharing this space with other foreign immigrants such as Moroccans or Peruvians, Gypsies, and other traders who earn their living from the city's tourism.

27. This figure is based on estimates of the Senegalese association M'bolo moy Doole and the NGO Granada Acoge.

28. These results challenge the assumption made in some sociological literature about Spain as being only a "way through" for emigration to other northern European countries (see for instance Robin 1992).

29. The fact that this was a strategy used by several immigrants in Spain should be put in contrast to the practices of Moroccans, for instance, who relegate this strategy to the last choice for fear of possible negative consequences for their families under repressive regimes such as the Alauitan monarchy. Ignorance of Africa's history and the difficulty of dealing with asylum applications in the early phases of immigration in Spain made it a good strategy, by contrast, for some Senegalese who were not actually living in a regime of daily politically based human rights violations.

30. In contrast to the notion of diaspora, where belonging to a common "nation" or "people" is not necessarily linked to a particular state or territory, Blash et al. suggest that a characteristic of these deterritorialized people is that they may be "anywhere in the world and still not live outside the nation-state" (1994, 269).

31. It seems important to point to the gender and age systems of authority as shaping these interactions, though I won't expand on the ethnographic accounting of these relations here. Undoubtedly, women seem to suffer the most disadvantaged position, especially young girls, for whom marriage is still an unavoidable requirement and emigration is not encouraged. They are the ones who are supposed to stay behind, taking care of the children, awaiting the irregular remittances and visits of their absent husbands. Some emigrants are challenging this dominant tendency, bringing their nuclear family with them to Spain. As the first Senegalese in Granada to bring his wife and daughter once told me: "I want her to live here with me, so that she will understand more how life is here and can share everything with me. If I change, then she will change accordingly. The same is true for the baby. I want her to have an opportunity to go to a good school here, and also to maintain contact with her family there. One has to take the best of both worlds" (C.N., summer 1994).

32. Villalón refers to the way the Senegalese state has tried "to legislate limits to the 'wasteful' excesses [of such ceremonies] ... always unsuccessfully"(1995, 59). I rely on his work for analysis of the role of ethnic, caste, and religious cleavages in Senegalese civil society and its relationships with the state.

33. For an ethnographic approach to state-society relationships in Senegal, see Villalón 1995. Unfortunately, Villalón does not explore the role of emigration in the maintenance or transformation of the delicate balance of power in Senegalese society between religious and political authorities. (Villalón only briefly mentions contact with the Mouride community in Granada in note 73 of chapter 2, p. 283.)

34. I know of several grassroots projects that generate criticism of the reproduction of power structures in the world of international cooperation. I myself have participated in one of these projects, as part of an extended network of people living in a particular area in Senegal, Senegalese emigrants originally from this area who are now living in different places in Spain, and Spanish people living in Andalusia and Madrid.

35. The link between the *Marabout* and the *taalibe* (follower) is an individual one based on sub-mission of the follower to the authority of the *Marabout*, which among Mourides takes an extreme form ritualized in the act of submission, *njebbel*, through which the *taalibe* promises blind obedience to the *Marabout:* "I place my soul and my life in your hands. Whatever you order I will do; Whatever you forbid, I will refrain from" (quoted in Villalón 1995, 119). Among Mourides, and in contrast to orthodox Islam, the *Marabout* is thought as a necessary intermediary between God and any believer. The personal relationship goes far beyond the spiritual and religious dimension, however; it involves material benefits for the followers, inscribed in the widespread clientelistic functions of Islamic brotherhoods in Senegal. As Villalón explains, to have a "good *Marabout*" is thought of as part of overall strategies for advancement and survival. A good *Marabout* will use his social and political power (resolving disputes, facilitating access to goods, services, and jobs, or protecting a *taalibe* in legal trouble) to mediate between the state and the follower (Villalón 1995, 121).

7. A NEW *CONVIVENCIA?*

Belonging and Entitlement from the Margins

*T*he integration of immigrants in the Spanish public sphere is blended into the larger strategy of the Spanish state to accommodate cultural difference while preserving an integrative framework of a common political community. This expansion of the model of citizenship to foreign non-national residents and the emphasis on a nonhomogeneous cultural belonging is linked to other key transformations of the model of national citizenship within the Spanish state. In Spain cultural diversity is constitutionally sanctioned, in contrast to other countries such as France, with its restrictive emphasis on equality and republican nationalism. Cultural difference is treated in its own political terms through the institutional system of the "Autonomous Communities." In this model, citizenship is considered as resting upon a legal (versus. cultural) bond among individual legal subjects and culturally diverse collectives, serving as "a device to cultivate a sense of community and a common sense of purpose."[1]

This notwithstanding, I have shown that in the particular case of African Muslim immigrants, their cultural difference is constructed as a threat to the fundamental principles of modern liberal democracies. This emphasis on immigrants' need to comply with the law, as shown in analysis of the Plan for Integration in chapter 5, was related to the systematic depiction of immigrants as alien to modern legal culture, most notoriously when referring to African Muslims. The enclosing of immigrants in self-contained cultural units conceived as incompatible with and a hindrance to the acquisition of democratic and modern values helps legitimize their treatment in many integration programs more as subjects of tutelage than as legal subjects with rights.

At the same time, in spite of the dominant construction of African Muslim immigrants as alien to modern legal culture, here we pay attention to a vernacular understanding of *convivencia,* which incorporates powerful cultural connotations in Spain's historical imagery as a multicultural land, both for Spaniards (most of them Catholic, although this is slowly changing), and Muslims (mostly foreigners, but also Spanish). *Convivencia* is also the term used in the local context to refer to personal and social relations among people at various levels: the family, the neighborhood, the village or city, or the country at large. In this sense, *Convivencia* is an exercise of negotiation that assumes difference as a basic fact of life, and the need to make room for dialog among all members of society, respect for one another, and sharing the public social sphere.

In this chapter I am concerned with the way immigrants engage in the active construction of *convivencia,* as the forging of common rules of social behavior (ultimately, a shared notion of justice), and of common belonging to a shared civil sphere that makes room for a non-homogeneous and transnational cultural identification and belonging (ultimately, a shared multicultural citizenship). I will first describe some theoretical points informing my analysis of multicultural *convivencia.* In the next two sections, I draw on several ethnographic examples to explore moments and instances of *convivencia* where immigrants struggle to achieve respect as concrete personas, resolutely drawing on local customary notions of rights to be granted to those who honestly work with their own hands to maintain the pride and dignity every person is entitled to defend. In the last section, I will look at collective processes of *convivencia,* drawing mainly on the case study of Muslims in Granada, and contrasting their strategies of entitlement and belonging with the formal recognition of rights as different "others." From the perspective of most immigrants, *convivencia* implies a daily negotiation of and resistance to racism—namely, prejudices, attitudes, and discrimination practices toward different "others" shaping their marginal location in the civil sphere. I will show how, nonetheless, the revaluation of cultural identity and of human rights as privileged channels of participation in the civil sphere opens up spaces of struggle for civil participation and representation in the Spanish social sphere.

I will argue that the localized process through which *convivencia* is forged in the public sphere shows a lived coexistence of liberal universalism and religious particularism embedded in social agents' practices as noncontradictory cultural repertoires. My interest here is to emphasize that rather than culturally or legally determined, these practices are the "outcome of political, legal and symbolic practices enacted through relational matrices of universal membership rules and legal institutions that are activated in combination with the particularistic political cultures of different types of societies [and collectives]" (Somers 1993, 589). The hegemonic processes within which *convivencia* is forged at the local level contain as effective cultural repertoires not only the dominant model of liberal democratic *convivencia* (based on universalistic rational and secular principles), but also other residual or emergent cultural repertoires, such as religious and ethnic particularism

(Williams 1977). Whether or not these residual or emergent cultural repertoires become alternative or antagonist social movements challenging the limits of citizenship is not a question of intrinsic incompatibilities between competing cultural repertoires, but of concrete historical conjunctures where local forms of resistance to unconditional incorporation are successfully articulated.

Convivencia and Citizenship from an Anthropological Perspective

From the standpoint of an anthropologist like me, who became involved in social processes surrounding implementation of social programs for integration and the enforcement of the Alien Law, the notion of *convivencia* is not merely a theoretical issue but a practical challenge embedded in daily social relations. The essential rules of daily *convivencia* are not set in stone; they are continuously negotiated, struggled over, imposed by force, and resisted by both immigrants and villagers. The privileged position of participant observer has allowed me to experience *convivencia* in multiple social spaces and temporal conjunctures. These instances and moments of *convivencia* range from tension, crisis, and conflict, to happiness, interethnic mating, and mutual understanding. Both sides of *convivencia*—on the one hand, conflict, punishment, and control, and on the other, negotiation and the coexistence of people on a daily basis—were present in my own perception of the situation at the end of my fieldwork in Alfaya. The chiaroscuros of *convivencia* at the daily and local level are marked in my field notes by a disordered mix of optimism and pessimism. Sometimes after a good meeting or an informal interethnic gathering, my expectations about the possibilities of bridging the ever-growing boundaries between immigrants and nationals rose. At other times, misunderstandings, suspicions, and mutual demonization seemed to make the struggle to establish interethnic personal relations on the basic of mutual respect an impossible one.

What remains clear after my experience as an active participant observer in the daily processes shaping interethnic relations in Granada, and as a social scientist interested in sociopolitical, cultural, and legal construction of identity and difference, is the fact that one cannot take for granted what *convivencia* (and integration or citizenship) means for any given group. Instead, the challenge is, as Rosaldo has argued, to keep as a methodological priority "cultural analysis, the recognition of divergent subject positions, and studies of contestation ... to discern historical processes of conflict and change rather than to discover timeless essences of universal human nature" (1994b, 11–12).

As I have shown throughout the book, a particular model of *convivencia*, that of democratic citizenship, has succeeded in becoming hegemonic in Spain. I have argued that this was not a process only requiring legal and political transformations, but also moral and cultural ones. In a modern state, where governamentality as defined by Foucault is a major concern, the need for a homogeneous and predictable polity is secured through processes of normalization, regulation, and discipline to instill general standards in social agents, shaping not only their behavior, but indeed seeking to constitute them as social personas in their belonging to a political community. Immigrants or minority groups cannot escape "the cultural inscription of state power and other forms of regulation that define the different modalities of belonging" (Ong 1996, 738). Their processes of enfranchisement and community building take place in the context of a dominant imagery of a multicultural society that does not erase difference, but implicitly and explicitly constructs it.

The dominant model of *convivencia* constructs difference implicitly, because liberal law constructs people as "having identities of various sorts that they should be equally free to express without hurt or hindrance."[2] And it constructs difference explicitly, through what appears as a "natural" function of the state, the application of legal and administrative categorical identities and public programs. This dominant construction of difference does have a transformative effect on the way people behave and identify themselves, and it shapes the sociopolitical struggles of enfranchisement of immigrants in particular countries and locales. Although I am more concerned here with exploring processes of claiming space, rights, and cultural practices that go beyond the intentions of the state, these vernacular notions of membership and belonging cannot be thought of as "pure" spaces of resistance. As I have argued in this book, a more complex approach to power and resistance should transcend the ingrained temptation of presenting this social structure as one that is polarized between dominators and dominated peoples.

Hegemonic processes are always contingent because they are a lived "complex of experiences, relationships, and activities, with specific and changing pressures and limits ... [that have to] continually be renewed, recreated, defended, and modified. It is also continually resisted, limited, altered, challenged by pressures not all its own" (Williams 1977, 112). Citizenship, as the model for democratic *convivencia* in Spain, provides cultural repertoires for legitimizing inequality but also for claiming social justice in one or more political communities.

I look at *convivencia* as the daily social processes through which people negotiate minimum norms of behavior and a common sense of belonging to one (or more) political community. My perspective includes the challenge that globalization and transnational formations pose to social science (Kearney 1995). In this sense, I do not assume that the public sphere in which social agents engage in daily *convivencia* is nationally bounded, that the notion of belonging to the political community necessarily means a cultural identification, nor that the notion of effective politics is limited to the channels established in a state-framed civil sphere.

To explore the essential sociocultural and moral rules disputed in daily relations of *convivencia*, one has to avoid assuming a priori any unitary subject positions by using social categories as analytical tools, for two main reasons. First, identities are not formed prior to participation in the public sphere; instead, it is through social agents' participation in daily social interactions that identities are shaped and constructed. And second, social agents engage in daily practice from an "intersection of multiple subject positions" shaped by a multidimensional structure of power conditioning their structural positions (class, gender, ethnicity, or "race") as well as their mental dispositions and schemes of perception and thought embedded in the agents' very bodies.

This theoretical approach to *convivencia* requires a methodological emphasis on the localized character of citizenship practices, as a result of concrete political, legal, and symbolic practices of social actors with multiple and overlapping identities, as family members, group members, consumers, producers, citizens, foreigners, and so forth. Furthermore, by emphasizing social agents' practices in particular institutional settings, *convivencia* is necessarily seen as a process rather than a particular model of social interaction. And finally, *convivencia* incorporates the necessity of dealing with major moral cleavages in the public sphere, be they religious or secular ethics. These cleavages inform diverse modes of social contestation in the moral and cultural project of consensus building upon which hegemonic projects are based.

Convivencia at Home: The Case of Zoheir and the Blanco Family

Localized processes of successful interethnic *convivencia* are based on the negotiation of what constitute the duties and rights for being considered a person. These processes take time, because notions about duties and rights are not given a priori, detached from local social interactions; on the contrary, according to this logic, nobody deserves anything if he or she does not behave as a person. Customary ideologies of personhood are not abstract constructs based on an individualist rationale, but a practical cultural mastery of collective social norms regulating behavior and justice (see the sections "Rights and the Experience of Emigration" and "Alfaya in the Narratives of the Past" in chapter 1). An immigrant, as any other villager, is required to behave as a "person" to deserve respect, autonomy, and consideration of his or her rights. Indigenous egalitarianism imposes a moral system of mutual obligations with which everybody is obliged to comply. One has to "prove" (and most especially in the case of African immigrants) that he or she deserves these rights by adhering to certain moral values such as being a "good worker," "noble," "grateful," "respectful of commitments," and not provoking or betraying others. Even if, as I have demonstrated in this book, this localized notion of what a good *convivencia* is tends to reproduce global and national inequalities that put immigrants in their (social) place, it also opens a space for negotiation and struggle to achieve respect as persons and rights as workers, and as residents engaged in multidimensional social relations (however informal and flexible they ended up being).

In the case of immigrants, as in the case of former indigenous poor nomads, *cortijeros,* or *choceños,* personhood was put at risk by their belonging to social, ethnic, or racially defined groups that purportedly have by "nature" some primitive, asocial, and deviant tendencies. The circumstances have changed much in the last thirty years, however. Today there are several imageries of fluidity among social groups that occasionally foster contestation of social boundaries. In this section I will look at the negotiation processes in the case of *convivencia* between a Muslim Algerian who worked in Alfaya and a local family who, as they said, "adopted" him as part of their family. What were the spaces of agreement and consent building and what were the boundaries that separated them?

The example of the *convivencia* between the Blanco family and Zoheir was one of a sincere and consensual effort to live together as members of a family. Zoheir was an Algerian immigrant who arrived into Spain from Germany, where he had a temporary residence visa. As soon as he arrived in the valley of Alfaya in search of work, he was informed of the existence of a "Sociocultural Center for Immigrants," or rather, as a villager told him, the "bar of the Moors." Coming from Germany, Zoheir knew about social programs and public resources open to immigrants in Europe, but a bar for Muslim people was a rather new and bizarre concept. In the bar, located in the Sociocultural Center for Immigrants, the Senegalese in charge directed him to the municipal council where he could borrow a camping tent. Zoheir was one of the Algerians who passed through the valley that summer, some of whom were escaping from the latent civil war going on in Algeria. In contrast to the Moroccans, most of whom were of rural background, Algerians' behavior was much more individualistic and urban. Zoheir asked for classes on Spanish language and was interested in learning as much as possible about this part of the world, Andalusia, so close geographically and culturally to his own memories of the Algerian village in the Mediterranean coast where he was raised. Zoheir spoke fluent Arabic, French, English, and German, and soon started to learn Spanish following an orderly grammatical pattern. He slept in the borrowed tent, and spent his leisure hours in the center, like most immigrants, where he participated daily in the informal conversations going on among immigrants and with Spaniards who visited the place, employers, old people, the social worker, the "watchman" of the shelter, volunteers of varied background, and people like me.

After a few weeks in the valley, working *peonás* (day jobs) every other day for different employers, he was hired by the head of the Blanco family, who needed a worker for a longer period of time. Juan Blanco provided Zoheir with a small *cortijo* where he could stay for free as long as he worked for the familial peasant agricultural enterprise. Juan was one of the most prominent leaders of the progressive grassroots collective involved in the struggle for democratic rights (see the section "Politics of Change" in chapter 1). He was very sensitive to the new inequalities being brought into the valley as a consequence of peasants' involvement in capitalist agriculture. He systematically compared the economic function of today's immigrants to that of autochthonous *jornaleros* in Francoist times. He was well aware of the global relations of inequality between the First and Third World, on which the valley's prosperity depended. At the same time, he was concerned about the political situation in neighboring countries such as Algeria. In the past he had hired a Russian peasant; now he hired Algerians. His interaction with Zoheir was based not only on labor relations, but on Zoheir's being a "good and honest worker," conduct that Juan appreciated highly, as would any peasant in the valley.

Zoheir understood perfectly well local common sense about what it took to be considered a "good guy," deserving consideration and respect as a person. He tried hard to be "a good worker": one who was industrious, responsible, and willing to learn. He was sincerely grateful about the living quarters provided by Juan. And he kept up the expected distance and respect toward women of the family during labor in the field. In addition, according to Ms. Blanco, Zoheir kept the place clean and orderly, in contrast to the fellow Algerian living with him, a musician with no interest in agricultural work. Zoheir called Juan "boss" and behaved respectfully toward him during labor hours, even as he gradually developed more familiar relations with him outside of work.

At the end of the agricultural season, like other immigrants, Zoheir left the valley to look for a new place to earn money in Spain. Zoheir had a friend in Barcelona who told him about a good qualified job, so he moved there, happy to be able to take advantage of his training as a textile engineer. In Barcelona, his Algerian friend cheated him. Broke, he returned to the village and asked Juan for work. When I returned to Alfaya in March of 1995, after my fieldwork in Senegal, I was happy to learn from a villager that "the Moor who worked for Juan last summer was now living in his house, with the rest of the family."

Living with the Blanco family, Zoheir came to know many people in the valley. He played with children; he visited all the bars with Juan and met other villagers in the daily informal meetings where males discuss current social, economic, and political issues. The Blanco family shared food with him, offering him alternative dishes if he could not eat a particular food, such as pork. The mother of the family cleaned and ironed all his clothes as though he were another one of her children, and Zoheir entrusted Juan, the head of the family, with all his earnings except for what he wanted for personal expenses. Zoheir tried to obtain the residence and work permit with the help of Juan Blanco, who presented all the documents needed to legalize him. Unfortunately he was not successful, as we expected; the high unemployment rate in the agricultural Andalusian sector, meant the denial of work permits for foreigners.

I shared in many of the interactions of the extended Blanco family, often as they drank coffee after the daily 3 P.M. meal. An open topic of discussion was Islamic fundamentalism, religious differences, and coincidences between "Moors" and Catholics, and equality, justice, and fate. Of course, many conversations were pedestrian and prosaic; there were discussions about work, the family, the village and the valley, the news on Television. What linked Zoheir to the rest of the family was that they all enjoyed conversation and all wanted to know more about one another. Juan was the family member who spent the most time with Zoheir. In spring of 1995, Juan told me of the interethnic *convivencia* being experienced by all members of the family with Zoheir:

> He is an intolerant man in his principles, but knows how to negotiate daily about where the limits of *convivencia* are. In addition, he is authentic, sincere, "noble," industrious, and an affectionate person. We made a commitment to him and he made a commitment to us. It is an extraordinary experience, mind you. It is a situation of interculturality, of trying an exchange. Problems arise not because he is of another race, but because he is of a different culture. People simply are ignorant of normal things in their culture, and misunderstandings occur, producing conflicts. To know more about each other is very important, and this can only be achieved in a personal interaction, where negotiation occurs in an improvised way. We have a good *convivencia*, both at home and at work. (J.O., spring 1995)

This *convivencia* was evident despite the fact that Zoheir was a firm Muslim believer and had no qualms about saying what he thought about "major errors" of Catholic religious dogmas, such as the adoration of Christ and the Virgin Mary as if they were God's son and mother. In the Blanco family there were firm Catholic believers (generally the women) as well as active atheists and agnostics, such as Juan Blanco and some of his brothers. Everybody, however, started from the open recognition of one another's right to think and to express thoughts freely. Despite firm beliefs, in practice, no one was dogmatic about the limits of their own involvement with others' practices and beliefs. Zoheir, for instance, attended the village festivals with the rest of the family despite the highly religious symbolism of particular celebrations. He even went to Granada to see the renowned *pasos,* or platforms bearing sculptured scenes from the Passion of Christ carried through the streets in overcrowded processions during Holy Week. Juan's wife treated Islam and Zoheir's beliefs with respect and always emphasized the common unique God that unites Muslims and Catholics. Juan and the rest of the family, for their part, considered Islam as a private religious belief deserving respect as any other belief.

Juan, in particular, went beyond tolerance by asking Zoheir to explain Islamic beliefs that Juan was curious about.

An important element in Zoheir and the Blanco's mutual understanding was acknowledgment of a shared popular cultural heritage, despite major religious differences. Zoheir used to refer to this Andalusian legacy, evident in the coastal area of Algeria where he was raised, especially in music and in popular sayings common to both Spanish and Arabic. Zoheir normally listened to flamenco songs, as well as the classical *andalusí* style, which Algerian music had absorbed and transformed over the years with "local colorings and variations" (Broughton et al. 1994, 126).[3] Similarly, Juan and many people in the valley who interacted with Zoheir and other "Moors" emphasized traits shared by Andalusian and Maghrebian cultural expressions. I will return to this issue later in the last section of this chapter.

In spite of mutual respect for one another's religious beliefs and common cultural heritage, religion informed mutual ethnic stereotypes and some major moral disagreements between Zoheir and the Blanco family. Perhaps the most important illustration of this is the divergence between Juan and Zoheir in basic assumptions about nature and social life. Juan was optimistic about humans' ability to improve their environment, to use nature to benefit people's living conditions, and to struggle socially for equality among human beings. Juan's ideological take reflected a humanistic and leftist secular tradition in Europe, which takes for granted that social progress and modernity go together, an assumption questioned by the "losers" along the path to modernization, especially in postcolonial and impoverished societies such as the one in which Zoheir was raised. Juan's views thus epitomized progressive Andalusian peasants' cultural logic of anthropocentrism. Zoheir's views, by contrast, evinced the Algerian peasants' religious vision of the world (a vision that is not, after all, so foreign to Spanish cultural legacy, incidentally). Zoheir's narratives always appealed in one way or another to a transcendental law of nature, a kind of ingrained divinity that transcends everything men can imagine through social means. Zoheir was rather pessimistic about social efforts to gain social equality, and he readily dismissed politics as a corrupted affair. His attitude was one not easily accepted by Juan, who engaged in an active proselytizing discourse about the good of collective action, emphasizing the duty of a man like Zoheir to struggle for the rights of people whom Juan conceptualized as his peers: the immigrants.

Zoheir resented and actively resisted the link that Juan posited between him and the rest of "his fellows immigrants." Zoheir in no way denied his condition of being Arab and Muslim; much to the contrary, he was happy to talk extensively about his customs and beliefs and to defend them vigorously in countless social interchanges. Yet he was critical of the organizational process lead by a group of Moroccans and of some of the attitudes and practices of fellow North Africans. Zoheir participated actively in meetings, and he participated in the sociopolitical processes around immigration in the valley, yet he wanted to retain his critical approach to a project monopolized by a group that, according to him, was authoritarian and did not incorporate a democratic plurality of perspectives. That was the reason he argued with Juan when Juan pressed him to organize with others as immigrants.

Another issue that caused resentment for Zoheir was being subjected to the highly racist stereotyping of "Moors" as "fundamentalists" in daily relations with mainstream villagers. Zoheir claimed the right to be treated like any other person, without being repeatedly shoved into prejudicial images:

> It is important they acknowledge the fact that although I am quite a pacifist, I am not one of those who turns the other cheek. Now things are different, you know? It is not that people care about you, but it is another matter completely to have a family behind you—they support me, and their trust in me is an attitude that they transmit to the village, to all people. I have met everyone here, everywhere the door is open for me.... But yesterday we were in the new bar after work and a young child said to me: "Don't you know this place isn't for Moors?" He was joking, of course, and we played together afterwards. But a child only repeats what he hears, and when he meets me this is all he will see: a Moor.... The worst thing is prejudice—what people think of you before-hand, before they greet you, before even talking to you.... Well, one has to negotiate. I am a pacifist.... There are many levels: first I am an immigrant, then I am a Muslim, and in addition, we are neighbors. There are many levels, but we have to negotiate, don't we? And one cannot do it with everyone; one cannot go on proving to everyone that one is not what they think.... I say, leave people alone, minding their own business! [yo lo que digo, ¡que dejen a la gente en paz!] (T.L., spring 1995)

Lack of respect and homogenization of all immigrants under the same category, such as "fundamentalists," "Moors," and even "immigrants," is a major concern for all Africans trying to integrate into the Spanish public sphere. Let me clarify further the way this explicit, and occasionally violent, culturalism pervades many interethnic relations. The case of Zoheir illustrates how an Algerian who in his country and among his family would be perceived as rather "Westernized" was routinely accused by villagers of being an Islamic "fundamentalist" when he expressed his opinions about marriage, religion, and politics. Meanwhile, some Moroccans living in Alfaya viewed Zoheir with suspicion and distrust because of his ability to incorporate into Alfayan social structure. The border marking membership in the community was continuously being problematized, both by North Africans and by villagers.

Like some villagers, even a few members of the Blanco family viewed Zoheir with suspicion, as was evident in a conversation I overheard reflecting the ambiguities of local attitudes about "Moors." One afternoon, Margarita, Juan Blanco's sister, joked with Zoheir about how to get a local girlfriend and told him: "Register yourself as a resident here and as a voter, and you will see how quickly you get in-laws!" Juan's brother Antonio answered back: "No way! Then this guy wouldn't allow his wife to vote; he is a fundamentalist!" and displayed an open smile to imply he was joking and could thus avoid challenging Zoheir's sense of honor. Zoheir laughed with the rest of the family and comically gave Antonio a few taps on the arm as if to admonish him for his loose tongue. This was only one of several occasions in which Antonio and other members of the family, less sensitive than Juan to racist prejudice, explicitly questioned Zoheir's ability to become one of them because of his religious beliefs.

This incident perfectly illustrates how difference and equality may or may not play antagonistic roles in shaping the local public sphere and the possibilities of harmonious and fair *convivencia*. The case of Zoheir and the Blanco family was one of friendly coexistence of diversity within the family, one in which social agents' everyday practices actively negotiated inclusion in and exclusion from the community. Spaces and moments of *convivencia* where Zoheir's cultural difference was not at all seen as a threat were plentiful. This did not mean that difference (as shaped by hegemonic processes) dissolved into an idealist consensus where relations of power seem to fade into the background. Much to the contrary, as these testimonies attest, the hegemonic perception of difference as a threat plays an important role in shaping inclusion and exclusion of Muslim immigrants as equal members of the community entitled to full citizenship rights. This accounts for the reaction of Juan's brother to the potential inclusion of Zoheir as a local resident in the valley.

Convivencia is possible not as an idealistic harmonious interaction, but as the product of daily negotiation and struggle over contested sociocultural and moral imageries.

Work and Leisure: Rights as Workers, Respect as People

The case of Zoheir and the Blanco family illustrates an exceptional instance of intimate interethnic *convivencia,* based on both work and personal relations. The members of the Blanco family shared their work and leisure with Zoheir and in numerous ways made him feel like another member of the family and, by extension, of the local community. But for most immigrants, work and leisure are clearly differentiated. Immigrants share work with Alfayan peasant families and with Andalusian *jornaleros* who are part of the same work team *(cuadrilla).* Many spaces of interaction and harmonious *convivencia* take place at work. But after work, the lives of immigrants and the Andalusians with whom they work generally split, and increasingly so, as a consequence of the processes shaping segmentation and stratification among social groups.

The split between work and leisure is, in my opinion, a major force in shaping immigrants as "foreign workers" and "cultural others," reproducing the difficulties in rendering compatible a model of *convivencia* that includes difference as an effective right to achieve social justice. Immigrants who have successfully made themselves valuable in the eyes of villagers as "good workers" and "good neighbors" find it difficult to erase the pernicious racist and culturalist prejudices against their difference. Especially relevant here are views of immigrants as being "dangerous men" in their leisure time, based on the mutual construction of racist and gender naturalization and the split between public and private spheres.

As I have mentioned throughout this book, most African immigrants in Alfaya were male, although this will change as immigrants begin to bring their wives and families with them. With their arrival in the valley, immigrants established good relationships with many young women, gathering with them in public spaces such as pubs, streets, and plazas. Heterosexual relationships opened up an important site for immigrants' integration into the community and for the creation of everyday interethnic *convivencia*. Gradually, however, the racist stereotypes of Africans' purported sexual voracity and seductive appeal to local women roused Andalusian men to defend their women as vulnerable and in need of control and protection. That racism and sexism are found together in the most extreme forms of violence showed by villagers in the valley is not a coincidence, but "a historical system of complementary exclusions and dominations which are mutually interconnected" (Balibar 1991, 49). The overarching function of racism against immigrants is connected to practices of normalization that build upon the trope of nation-as-women.[4] The increasing segregation of immigrants from Spanish youth in leisure time, most especially women, closed spaces of *convivencia* and limited immigrants' ability to claim rights in the workplace as persons. As good workers, immigrants challenged this split between work and leisure by claiming the right to be respected as individual persons who engage in multidimensional social interactions. Such respect, I will conclude, is imperiled when Spaniards consider immigrants as temporary legal subjects, as disposable workers, or as incompatible cultural others, free to maintain some rather "inadequate" cultural "peculiarities" in a private sphere segregated from women.

Work is indeed a space that should be privileged when dealing with modes of integration, as I have argued in describing the relationships between Zoheir and the Blanco family. Everyone respects the local work ethic(which was explained in detail in chapter 1), as a criterion for due respect and entitlement to rights. Correspondingly, it is in work that immigrants most energetically deploy strategies of integration, given that jobs are the chief concern of an economic immigration like that of Alfaya's Africans. As I have explained, local requirements for being considered a "good worker" have to do with the basic sense of honor held by any person who struggles for his *autonomía* (autonomy). One is a good worker when work is well done, when the employee shows interest in learning about specific tasks, and when he takes responsibility for finishing tasks as a personal duty *(cumplir)*. In labor relations, the employee is not supposed to take advantage of the trust showed by the employer; but rather, he should prove he deserves it.

To be a good worker is ingrained in Andalusia's rural notions of personhood, and specifically in those of manhood. A *jornalero* from the Andalusian province of Córdoba who came to work in the valley told me: "In the *cuadrillas* there has always been a sort of rivalry between us about who is the best worker. People make efforts to go far ahead in their work, to rest only the minimum amount, and to prove that one is a strong man.... It is a vicious circle, and always has been so in Andalusia, even though it ultimately benefits the employer, that [to be a good worker] is embedded in Andalusia as the way you really make yourself valuable [acaba haciéndose la forma en que tú realmente te haces valer]" (M.C., summer 1994).

And, in fact, those immigrants who have "made themselves valuable" in the eyes of the employer are the ones who have slowly settled into better conditions in the valley. Of course, the circumstances in which immigrants have made themselves valuable differ. Some have developed stable labor relations in the village with one or several employers and through one or more agricultural seasons. Stability facilitates solving housing problems as well. Occasionally, some employers will provide housing (most often, an abandoned *cortijo* or *motor* [where tools and the irrigation motor are kept]). But even if they do not, the very fact that an immigrant is known to work for somebody on a regular basis, or that an immigrant is a good worker facilitates the task of renting an apartment in the valley.

The way this integration of the immigrant worker takes place, however, differs a great deal from what is imagined by official discourse. In practice, social networking based on labor relations means (in rural Andalusia, but more generally in most economic sectors where immigrants work) a compliant attitude on the part of immigrants toward villagers' informal economy and the widespread fraudulent use of unemployment checks. Integration does not take place within the boundaries of the dominant imagery of legality, but rather in a context where customary hiring practices and local resistance to central state control are rampant. This means that what papers say about immigrants' labor situation does not reflect the local complexity of social, economic, and labor relations into which the immigrant integrates. As immigrants develop their social networks in the valley through labor relations, they usually get information about who can offer a promise of hiring (the *precontrato*, which is required to get a job permit in agriculture the first time), about who is able to "sell" the signing of work days (the *peonás* which are required to get an unemployment subsidy) in exchange for money, and, of course, who can actually offer them jobs. As happens for Andalusians as well, the employer who offers a *precontrato* or to sign the *peonás* may not be the same employer who actually hires the immigrant. The papers needed can be asked as a favor from somebody with whom the immigrant has established a clientelist or a friendly relationship.

Immigrants may use customary rules and habits strategically to their own advantage, but by doing so they subject themselves to the pernicious effects of a personalized consideration of rights. The assessment of mutual obligations between a good worker and an employer is thus conditioned by concrete circumstances and particular interests beyond the control of the immigrant. Even though this is also the case for most poor workers, widespread prejudices against different "others" and institutional discrimination against foreign workers situates immigrants in a much more vulnerable position. Yet immigrants still appeal to customary as well as universal and fundamental rights of the person to claim the right to be recognized as persons entitled to human dignity.

Let us examine, for example, the case of a Senegalese worker, Ahmat, whose ability to deal efficiently with work provided him with well-deserved prestige and improvements in his social position. Ahmat resented the fact that his being "black" continuously put the respect he had won as a good worker and peaceful neighbor at risk. The following anecdote clearly illustrates this point:

> The other day I saw a family of Gypsies taking our tomatoes, and since I am the one in charge, I went after them in my car. When I caught them in front of the bar by the road, the men got out of their pickup and threatened me with their knives. But nobody in the bar tried to stop them. I was very frustrated and upset. Afterwards I returned to the bar, told people what happened, and asked them why nobody did anything. And the response was pretty clear: they told me they hadn't intervened because they thought it was our business, as if we were having trouble over drugs or God knows what, and they excused themselves by saying that these things happened with Gypsies and blacks, they knew! You know, they all know I have been working for P.L. for some years, and I deserve better than that. I am not just a good worker, I am also a good and honest person and I have done nothing to make people doubt it. (A.N., summer 1994)

As a different "other" in leisure time, Ahmat experienced prejudice and racism that he felt especially painful in light of his diligent efforts to establish personal relationships beyond the workplace, especially with women. In 1993, for instance, he was seeing a young local woman, but as he told me: "She was neurotic all the time about villagers seeing us, so more and more the relationship was becoming something to hide. When I wanted to see her, I had to talk to Carlos [a young villager who was a close friend], and he would pass a message to [Ahmat's girlfriend's] sister as to a time and place to meet so that nobody would see us. But I did not like this situation, why should she be ashamed of talking to me?" (A.N., summer 1994). Relationships with local women were increasingly made invisible so as to avoid gossip and pressures on women from their families. Such invisibility, of course, only served to further criminalize immigrants' activities outside the workplace. People who established relationships with immigrants were also tainted by the pernicious racist stereotyping of immigrants as "dangerous others." Women who associated with immigrants were subjected to rumors that categorized them as virtual prostitutes, and men were suspected of being involved in dishonest business activities. Carlos, Ahmat's friend told me, "I am trying to rent an apartment because I want to be independent from my parents, now that I have enough money, but here everybody knows me, and they tell me: if I rent you the place, you are going to bring your friends, the immigrants, with you!" (J.P., summer 1994).

At the same time, an immigrant's recognition as a good worker may situate him in a position of power in relation to Andalusians, tending to erase difference and to promote equalization. Ahmat was hired as a *jornalero* by a local villager in 1992 and continued working for him during 1993 as the person responsible for coordinating work *(encargado)*. In 1994 he turned down this position because:

> People did not like my being in a position of authority. They don't like to follow orders from a black man. I was designated *encargado* because I am responsible, but people do not accept this easily. They don't like my telling them what is to be done. They did not finish their work, and as soon as the employer was absent they refused to maintain a proper rhythm of work. They'd say to me, "What's up with you, guy? You are a *pringao'* [easy to cheat] just like us. Sit down and let's wait for the employer to come and tell us what is next." When I had to make myself heard, the relationships with them were much worse than normal, so I prefer to keep up good working relations and let someone else assume the responsibilities of the employer. (A.N., summer 1994)

Many immigrants greatly appreciate informal egalitarian relations with fellow workers and other Spaniards. When labor competition is involved, these informal relations are at risk. The response of immigrants to the problems that arise as a consequence of labor competition are varied. Some of them privilege having good working and neighborly interethnic relations, as Ahmat did. Others struggle instead to make their difference valuable in labor relations, claiming that employers prefer them to other Spaniards because the latter are no longer as good workers as Andalusians used to be. This was the position taken by an especially well-integrated group of veteran Moroccan immigrants who specialized as work teams for lettuce picking (*cuadrillas de lechugueros*). Up until 1994, *cuadrillas* of Moroccans predominated among the teams who offered to pick lettuce and load the trucks, and they became renowned for their efficiency. A leader of one of these *cuadrillas* proudly told me: "Truckers always prefer to hire us, because they know they can ask us to work at any hour, and we are ready. They know that we don't rest until the truck is going to leave, even if it is raining cats and dogs, because people from here have become very 'delicate' [que los de aquí se han vuelto muy señoritos]" (A.A., summer 1993).

After 1994, young people from Alfaya began to form their own *cuadrillas de lechugueros*, to take advantage of the easy cash made in this occupation. Directly competing with renowned Moroccan *lechugueros*, they claimed privileges as village "natives" vis-à-vis the "newcomers." Moroccans, in turn, made use of every resource to compete with locals. Some Moroccan *cuadrilla* leaders, for example, would underpay fellow illegal immigrants, taking advantage of their vulnerability. Moroccans also underscored their rights as good workers. As one of the lettuce *cuadrilla* members told me: "These people [the Andalusian lettuce pickers] are very racist. They don't want us to work. They tell truckers and dealers that they should respect their rights as Spaniards to have work, which is understandable, but they also tell them not to hire us just because we are Moroccans and our country is competing with their products ... I have been working in this valley for five years now. Everybody knows me here—this is a small place—and I want to continue here. I have all my papers and my house, but I need the work and it's not fair what these people are doing to us now" (A.A., [different person from above], spring 1995).

The ability of immigrants to claim rights on the basis of their being good workers is also weakened by their unstable legal status. In order to renew papers, immigrants need documentation of their work situation, and they depend on employers' compliance with the law. Even for those immigrants and employers who have presented all the required documents to legalize a work relationship, granting the permit is conditioned by the situation of the Spanish labor market. This was the case for Zoheir, who was denied a permit because of unemployment among nationals in agriculture. The lack of official recognition of a de facto work relationship rendered Zoheir an illegal immigrant, with no rights in the civil sphere. In the summer of 1995, when the papers Zoheir presented to the ministry to legalize his situation were being processed, Zoheir had a problem with a villager who threatened him aggressively. Zoheir wanted to denounce this villager to the Civil Guard, despite the fact that his own papers were in the process of renewal. I remember several people telling him he was "crazy" to press charges because of the close relationship between the Civil Guard agents and the person who had threatened him. He considered, however, that it was an issue of human dignity and of preserving his prestige as a "peaceful" person who did not want to engage in conflicts with villagers. He felt this irregular situation would not endanger his staying in the valley, since everybody knew him and his status.

The claim of immigrants like Zoheir, Ahmat, and several Moroccans is that everyone has the right to be recognized as a "person" if he has "proven" compliance to customary rules, as a neighbor and resident, as worker, as friend, as member of a family. Such recognition at the local level is different from official recognition of their rights, a claim imperiled by restrictions imposed by the Alien Law and well beyond their control. What they deeply resent is local discrimination against them as concrete persons on the basis of racist prejudices and practices. They feel trapped by stereotypes steeped in centuries of prejudice, despite the fact that their cultural difference, in the sense of particular religious or cultural habits, is not an issue in daily interethnic relations in the workplace and beyond. As a general rule, immigrants do not ask for special favors on the grounds of their cultural particularities. For example, they work through the five daily prayers expected of Muslims. "The Koran provides specific norms of behavior for the Muslim who is in a non-Muslim place. You are not obliged to stop working in order to pray, for instance, and you don't need a special place like a mosque to pray to God…. This way our religion facilitates adaptation to the circumstances we have here" (T.L., summer 1994).[5] An employer may sometimes grant particular cultural rights, as Juan Blanco did to Zoheir, allowing him to follow his religious practices, including prayers or the fast of Ramadan, without any conflict whatsoever with the rest of the family. The Blancos could accept such practice as normal in the long run because villagers easily tolerate religious or cultural practices, provided that different "others" acknowledge the local rules of social control and behave accordingly.

The main obstacle to proper *convivencia* from the point of view of immigrants was thus not lack of tolerance toward their cultural habits and religious beliefs, but rather their stigmatization in a collective way as disposable people, as persons who could be easily interchanged with others fulfilling similar functions. Such treatment denied basic human dignity, based on a notion of equal respect, which immigrants thought fundamental to *convivencia*, much more than mere tolerance of difference. The central importance of respect was evident in a young Senegalese man's account of how his employer once snubbed him by passing through without greeting him. We were together in a group, having coffee in a bar, and Musa's attitude suddenly changed. He was rather upset and responded to our concern by saying, "I am pretty sure he [the employer] saw me, he looked at me and I was starting to say hello when he left without greeting me, as it is due to any person whom one knows and respects" (M.A., summer 1994). In countless instances, immigrants who have made themselves valuable as workers complain about the fact that outside work they are invisible to their employers; they feel as if they are nobodies. Respect means both more and less than tolerance. It means less, because it does not require from people an appreciation of another person's culture, but rather of basic personhood. And it means more, on the part of Spaniards, because it includes considering any immigrant as a person, as a member of a face-to-face community. It is not a question of appreciation of plurality in the abstract, but rather an appreciation, so to speak, of people as instances of diversity.

Immigrants as Collective Subjects in the Public Social Space: A New *Convivencia* in Granada?

Up to this point I have focused on ethnographic examples of interpersonal *convivencia* to explore, first, some areas of consent, the ever-contingent system of mutual rights and duties and rich cultural exchange, and second, the most common fractures, mechanisms of exclusion, and areas of cultural impermeability and segregation. Now I wish to advance my exploration of *convivencia* and cultural citizenship by considering the collective processes of *convivencia*. How do people negotiate their social relations as self-differentiated groups in public spaces and institutional settings? What kinds of collective strategies are developed by "different others" to enfranchise themselves as social actors in the Spanish civil sphere?

In the context of modern democratic Spain and of the dismantling of central nationalism in the Spanish state, Andalusia's regional government engaged in a new process of nation-building that sought to underscore the regional cultural particularities of Andalusia vis-à-vis the rest of the "Spanish nations." The imagining of the Andalusian "nation" or people is, of course, a cultural product that involves a particular representation of the past promoted by the regional state and elites.[6] In the case of Andalusia and Granada, this nationalist imagined community reinscribes the imagery of medieval *convivencia* in al-Andalus as a central feature shaping Andalusia's cultural uniqueness. In contrast to other "Autonomous Communities," such as Catalonia or the Basque Country, the dominant representation of Andalusia as a territorial and cultural unit does not challenge in any way its accommodation to a larger legally defined political community (the Spanish state and the European Union). The location of Andalusia as a borderland embodies a tension between its belonging to Spain and Europe and its strong identity as a poor southern area, trapped in a folkloric and exotic imagery. The future links Andalusia to a modernizing European landscape where its past, as it is constructed by local authorities, connects it to the unique blend of Islamic, Jewish, and Christian cultures of the medieval al-Andalus.

I am especially interested in the peculiarities of Granada as a highly symbolic place for Muslims and in the effects of the revival of medieval *convivencia* in al-Andalus on citizenship practices, both at the level of identity (in the construction of imageries of belonging), and at the level of claims-making (in the development of strategies of enfranchisement). The key aspect I want to underscore is that, as in any nation-building process, the imagining of the Andalusian community involves some naturalization processes that, once created, may be used to legitimate diverse claims-making and imageries of belonging, as well as to create new criteria of inclusion and exclusion. In this sense, Granada is a perfect example of how the production of symbolic places nourishes dominant as well as subaltern imageries of belonging and of how spatial and territorial areas are naturalized in cultural terms.

The superposition of medieval religious *convivencia* and contemporary multicultural *convivencia* makes room for strategies of enfranchisement of Muslims as the contemporary representatives of an "indigenous" form of belonging. However, are all Muslims equally included in this appropriation of the dominant imagined community? Do religion and the broader antagonism between the West and Islam appear as a crucial battleground shaping ethnic identities and claims-making? To what extent does the legal framework of common citizenship as a vital integrative function counteract claims for a primordial allegiance of "different others" to alternative systems of justice based on religious or lineage authorities?

In exploring these fundamental issues, my objective is rather modest. I wish to show how Muslim immigrants engage in collective practices to assert their belonging and entitlement to Granada in a way that incorporates both liberal universalism and religious particularism—while making these compatible with one another—as part of their struggle to subvert national and transnational forms of domination. I will explore these issues by drawing on my ethnographic work among Senegalese in Granada and Senegal, situating them as collective actors in the larger context of a contested public space where legitimacy and allegiance are central axes of identity building, power, and domination in Granada and beyond. I will first describe the dominant imagery of multicultural *convivencia* and the way Spanish Muslims and North Africans redefine and appropriate it to claim (competing and highly naturalized) forms of alternative belonging and entitlement, and I will point out the national cleavages shaping this imagery. Then I will look at the Senegalese, a Muslim collective that is excluded from this imagery in racial terms, as non-indigenous representatives of the Islamic Andalusian *umma*. I will show how their participation as cultural others in the framework of contemporary multicultural *convivencia* is part of an effort of enfranchisement as residents entitled to rights in the Spanish civil sphere, emphasizing the way this participation is linked to a struggle for power in the Senegalese transnational community.

Granada as a Multicultural City: The Imagining of the Past and the Challenges of the Present

Granada was the last bastion of al-Andalus, the most important medieval Muslim power in Europe, whose reign lasted seven centuries (from the seventh century to the fourteenth century). It is recurrently remembered as the jewel of Muslim civilization, characterized by the harmonious *convivencia* of Muslims, Jews, and Christians, and by a flourishing cultural atmosphere. Christian troops, directed by the Catholic kings, conquered the city on January 2 1492; this date was marked with major festivity in the city, and Granada became a highly symbolic focal point in the imagery of the new Spanish Catholic nation-state. Although initially some arrangements were made in the Capitulation of Santa Fé to preserve the rights of the Jewish and Muslim communities, the criteria for belonging to the Spanish nation-state was subsequently based on a racist criterion called "Purity of Blood." Non-Catholic people were subjected to forced conversion, persecution, and finally expulsion—not just Jews and Muslims living in Christian territory *(Mudéjares)*, but also Muslims who had been forced to convert to Catholicism *(Moriscos)*. Despite the consistent efforts made in past centuries to render Islamic influence invisible, it still reverberates in the landscape and in cultural expressions, and it has been an important part of Granada's appeal to tourists and travelers.

That Granada still partially lives and defines its identity based on Muslim legacy is sarcastically pointed out by some immigrants, especially Moroccans: "Spain does not allow us to stay here, but this city was constructed by us, and people here still eat from what we were forced to leave behind" (R.R., summer 1995). The dependence of Granada's economy on tourism makes this assertion partially true, an argument used by North Africans to challenge the dominant European mapping of civilizational rank between "modern" European Andalusia and "backward" North Africa in countless social interactions. While Granada suffers one of the highest rates of unemployment in Spain, the city is also the one place in Spain most visited by tourists from every corner of the world, generating one of the most important sources of income for its residents. Tourists come to admire the Muslim palace of La Alhambra; the old Jewish commercial district, where traditional Spanish merchant families now share part of this privileged space with new Moroccan traders; and El Albaicín, Granada's older and Arabized district, traditionally inhabited by Granada's working class and Gypsies, and now slowly being reappropriated by an important Muslim community to the extent that some of its streets are almost completely filled with Muslim businesses and people—tea houses, restaurants, jewelry shops, perfumeries, pastry shops, and stores selling traditional *andalusí* ceramic work.

The image of Granada as a multicultural city, reinscribing the medieval *convivencia* onto the contemporary sociolegal landscape, is a polysemic one. In 1994–1995 the city was papered with a poster of the cultural project "Legacy of al-Andalus," carrying the statement: "You Are Part of the Legacy: Live It!" Accordingly, the city included testimonies of multiculturalism in its celebrations, inviting important Arab writers and artists to inaugurate the city's festivities and to participate actively in them. The press heralded an image of Granada as a city of encounters between Mediterranean cultures. A North-African Arab musician who was invited to the festivities said, "In Granada we feel at home … because here the bonds between Andalusia and Muslim peoples are still present" (*El Ideal*, June 28, 1994). Similarly, the well-known writer Amin Maalouf said that Granada "was the most global experience, the most meaningful one … a place of encounter [of Muslims] with Christianity and an important Jewish community … an experience that produced in this place a kind of magical alchemy ... [that] should be a model not just for the past, but for the future" (*El Ideal* June 10, 1995).

But for immigrants who now live in Granada, excluded and/or marginalized from public spaces and institutional settings of decision making, and condemned to an almost never-ending legal vulnerability, the imagery of multicultural Granada evokes sarcasm. The irony of the city's invitation to "Live the Legacy" was wonderfully captured in an alternative poster produced by the NGO *SOS Racismo*: situated at the center of the image, under the logo "You Are Part of the Legacy," the image shows a Moroccan immigrant as he is being arrested by two policemen. This poster was received among immigrants as a wonderfully apt response to official multicultural demagoguery, which most immigrants take as a hypocritical characteristic of Western political regimes.

The revival of an Islamic presence in Granada is the outcome of a complex social process involving not just the cultural policies of municipal and regional governments, which imagine Islam in somewhat folkloric terms, but also the establishment of diverse Muslim groups in the city. Granada is represented, imagined, and materially constructed as a symbolic place by different institutions and social agents with very different objectives and interests. Especially relevant for making Granada a symbolic place for Islamic *umma* are the several groups of Spaniards who converted to Islam in the late 1970s and 1980s, establishing the city's first Spanish Islamic community in five hundred years. Linked to other groups in equally symbolic places such as Córdoba, the Spanish converts claim to inherit the legacy of the Spanish Muslims of al-Andalus, the *Moriscos* who were forced to convert by Catholic authorities.

The small but very active Muslim Spanish community in Granada settled right at the center of the city, in El Albaicín, and initiated a struggle "to conquer its own vital space" (*La Gaceta de Granada* 1994). The expression of cultural difference and the realization of a real multicultural city was much more than a folkloric issue for this group; it involved the use and control of key public spaces, and the autonomous management of justice. For this and other groups of converts, the Islamic *umma* emerges as an alternative political and moral imagery of belonging and entitlement, one that questions the legitimacy of secular states as co-opted by the materialist and sinful hegemony of global and national capitalist systems. After years of struggle against the opposition of political leaders as well as segments of the local population, Spanish Muslims have successfully gained the right to construct a sizeable mosque right in the middle of El Albaicín, considered a "sacred site" for all Muslims in Andalusia.[7] Despite a chronic pattern of divisions and competition between different tendencies among them,[8] Spanish Muslims appeal to common objectives: the expansion of Islam in Andalusia and, particularly for those in Granada, the recognition of the rights granted (and violated) by the Catholic kings to Muslims in the Capitulation of Santa Fé in 1492.

The Spanish Muslim communities in Granada claim their right to use and manage their "sacred spaces" as Spanish citizens and as leading members of the Islamic *umma* in al-Andalus. As Spaniards, their belonging to the national community is a legal fact, although as one member told me, "There is still much to be changed for people to accept that one can be Spanish and not be Catholic" (A.A., summer 1995). Spanish Muslims in Andalusia have focused up until to now on what Kymlicka has called "polyethnic rights," that is, public support and legal recognition of their cultural practices, such as bilingual education and exemption from laws that would disadvantage them, due to their religious practices (Kymlicka 1996, 156). Citizenship grants them legal legitimacy to struggle for their right to be different and to achieve collective rights for self-determination, similar to other peoples and nationalities within the Spanish state who appeal to their "differential fact" *(hecho diferencial)* in order to claim self-government (such as Catalonia or the Basque Country): "We Muslims have a different law. We accept that we are subjected to the law of the country in which we live, but it is a completely different thing to renounce the struggle for more autonomy"[9] (*El País*, December 7, 1997). Some Spanish Muslim leaders dream of a new hegemony of Islam in al-Andalus, and similar to other nationalist struggles within the Spanish state, their final objective includes the constitution of their own political community in the Andalusian territory, as the president of the Islamic Foundation in al-Andalus, Hamza Aby Yaser, clearly expressed it: "the objective and duty is to work for the return of Islam to Andalusia ... to recuperate its sovereignty as a people and a national identity [lost] after a terrible repression ... [that forced] Andalusian communities to disperse around the world, so that they can return and find their identity as Andalusian Muslims in the framework of the Islamic *Umma*" (Alonso 1990, 6). Crucial in understanding the claims made by these groups is the fact that they appeal to the spiritual legacy of *Moriscos* in highly biological terms, in an effort to distinguish the purportedly "authentic" *Andalusí* Islam from that of Muslims coming to Granada and Andalusia from Third World countries.[10]

The relations between these associations and the new Muslim immigrants is highly ambiguous, crisscrossed not just by different religious interpretations of the sacred book, the Koran, but by cleavages of class, race, and nationality. In contrast with immigrants, Spanish Muslims are nationals, entitled to full rights as members of the political community. They are not racially marked, and their middle-class status makes it easier for them to establish and build a community with their own resources. Whereas religious identity is the central source of community building, claims-making, and access to resources for Spanish Muslims, both from the Spanish state and from Islamic states, immigrants situate themselves in a different institutional setting, which defines them mainly as foreigners and immigrants.

In contrast to Spanish Muslims, immigrants' location in the Spanish public sphere is still strongly shaped by dependence on the support of local associations and experts who function as intermediaries between them and the Spanish state and society (see chapter 4). Legal instability and labor vulnerability, together with racist discrimination, systematically hinder immigrants' efforts to settle in Granada. Most experts and volunteers working in NGOs and labor unions are Catholic and Marxist militants at the same time, and they perceive immigrants as the new underclass in Andalusia. Despite the quest for autonomy as social agents, Muslim immigrants do not yet claim collective religious rights in an organized way, probably because there is too much to struggle for before religion becomes a priority, and because the international context makes it difficult to develop a noncriminalized Muslim identity.

In addition, there are some crucial cleavages between the different Muslim immigrants along ethnic and national origins. The imagery of medieval *convivencia* is one that North Africans living in Granada, and especially Moroccans, can easily appropriate. Many dispute the "authenticity" of Spanish converts as leaders of the Islamic community in Granada. It is not uncommon to hear Moroccans emphasizing the cultural and historic links between Granada and their own Moroccan cities, where many of the *Mudéjares* (Muslims living under Christian rule) sought refuge after being expelled from Andalusia during the sixteenth and seventeenth centuries.

The links between Moroccans and Granada are not confined to a distant past. Several generations of middle-class Moroccan men from Tangier and Tetuán have customarily come to Granada to study at its prestigious university. The most recent and important group of these students resent and complain about the obstacles to such study caused by the rebordering of the Mediterranean. The Alien Law (art. 18.3.f) excludes Moroccans from the preferential treatment accorded to other people who are considered culturally and historically linked to Spain, such as Shephardis, Latin Americans, and others. There is heterogeneity and antagonism between those who support the Moroccan Hassan II regime and those who oppose it, as there is between "Westernized" and more religiously oriented Moroccan groups. Yet a common feature emerged in my interviews with leaders of several Moroccan associations[11] in Granada: the claim that they are members of the Granadan landscape in their own right, as inheritors of the Muslims expelled from the peninsula, or as neglected neighbors of Andalusia. This imagery of belonging will continue to be an important source of enfranchisement and legitimization of Moroccan rights to live in Andalusia and Spain.

Moreover, among Moroccans and other North Africans in Granada, Islamic identity is no doubt acquiring a newly politicized character previously absent, for the most part, in their personal trajectories. Such politicization takes shape in the local context of the claims advanced by Spanish Muslims, as well as in the broader national and supranational antagonisms between Islamic and Western countries.[12] This is especially true after September 11, although Muslim leaders strongly refuse and struggle against the link between Islam and criminal organizations. Among immigrant rank and file, however, and especially in the rural areas where exclusion and marginalization are pervasive, there seems to be a higher tendency to associate with religious movements. This is also linked with the failure of NGOs and unions to counter open forms of racism against "Moors" and the policing and restrictive bent of the new government in power. In the new international and national context, stereotypes about "Moors" have deepened, acquiring new meanings linked with terrorism and fanaticism, which can only serve to exacerbate the already notorious ethnic prejudices and animosity present at the local level.

Black Islam in Granada

The case of Senegalese in Granada contrasts with the highly territorialized and naturalized imageries of belonging appropriated by Spanish Muslims and North Africans in Granada. Even scholars interested in Islam in Spain treat the Senegalese as a "special case," evincing an unconscious prejudice against non-Arab Islam, which scholars share with Spanish Muslims and North African immigrants. Both groups largely ignore the way black Muslims relate to and resist the highly racist stereotypes of their cultural habits and religious beliefs. Like North Africans living in Granada, Senegalese find their location in the Spanish public sphere to be shaped by their condition as foreigners from Third World countries. A common religious identity as black Muslims imbues their social gatherings, their deterritorialized imagery of belonging, their resources, and their practices of community building. In contrast to North Africans, Senegalese held no links to Andalusia before immigrating there, so Senegalese strategies of enfranchisement in Granada have been created from scratch. Senegalese have suffered repeated racist attacks, such as the burning of one of their houses in El Albaicín, systematic burning of their cars, refusal to rent them houses, and violent attacks on street sellers. Reacting to this, and in contrast to the heterogeneous Hispanic-Arabic communities that have settled in central locations in Granada, Senegalese have settled in workers' districts at the city outskirts, such as La Cartuja, Pajaritos, or El Zaidín, sharing space with the local working class and with Gypsies. Yet, as I described in the previous chapter, Senegalese have settled in Granada in a steadily increasing pace, gaining the acceptance of many locals and associations (which contrasts sharply with the experience of the despised "Moors"), becoming one of the most important Senegalese communities in Spain.

Senegalese have systematically claimed to belong to the Islamic *umma* in Granada, and they occasionally participate in public interethnic religious celebrations, yet they tend to find themselves discriminated against and despised as black Muslims. Many testimonies of North Africans confirmed this view during fieldwork; to them, black Muslims do not practice "authentic" Islam.

In fact, racism is also pervasive among Muslims in Granada. North Africans as well as Spanish Muslims draw on an evolutionary rationale that imposes a neo-colonial map on Islam, dividing the Islamic world between "civilized" and "primitive" cultures, seeing the Senegalese as among the latter. In reaction to this, Senegalese brotherhoods claim to lead an "authentic" black-African Islam. In a powerful nationalist version of this stance, the Mouride brotherhood claims to be the one legitimate representative of the interests of the Wolof people, and by extension, of the Senegalese nation. In contrast to the territorialized imagining of belonging to an Islamic *umma* forged by Spanish Muslims, Senegalese displace the center of the religious imaginary of belonging to a deterritorialized Senegalese diaspora. Both subaltern imageries draw heavily on naturalized notions of the community, based on ethnic and racial lineages and an almost biological inheritance of cultural "authenticity." As I have argued in the last chapter, traditional religious and lineage authorities profit from the forces of exclusion that Senegalese immigrants find in Spain and Andalusia, which strengthens these authorities' power as intermediaries between them and the Spanish and Senegalese states.

Following the political tradition of coexistence between a secular state and powerful socioreligious structures, the Islamic brotherhoods, and the amazingly hybrid forms of organization such as the *da'iras* (see chapter 6, note 6), Senegalese immigrants have opted to organize as a cultural collective, secular in form and also in many of its objectives. As a collective, Senegalese immigrants have developed a mutually informing double-sided strategy, one directed toward Senegalese enfranchisement as social actors in the Spanish civil sphere, and the other focused on how the transnational deterritorialized community is shaped. On the one hand, Senegalese have established formal and informal alliances with Spanish associations to gain access to social resources and powerful allies in advancing claims as foreigners suffering discrimination before the law, public institutions, and civil society. They have also organized as a cultural association vis-à-vis the local and central Spanish state and actively use this channel to make their presence visible in Granada. On the other hand, some Senegalese have developed several strategies to strengthen their transnational networks and the deterritorialized imageries of belonging that frame their location as vulnerable social actors in a global scenery, while, at the same time, challenging the powerful role of intermediaries between them and the Senegalese state.

Senegalese consider the room made for cultural difference as a privileged channel for collective participation in the Spanish civil sphere an important resource for their enfranchisement as foreign immigrants. They also recognize that difference shapes a site for struggle between different ways of understanding the migratory project. Initially, Senegalese organized with other black Africans, but soon they formed their own Senegalese association in an effort to establish autonomy from other black communities, some of whom enjoy a privileged status in Spain (such as the people of Equatorial Guinea, a former Spanish colony). The first Senegalese organization was a Mouride association, named after the saint and founder of the brotherhood Cheick Amadou Bamba. The association caused distress in the community because it was seen as discriminating against non-Mouride people. Misuse of public resources by leaders prompted critics to form the current Senegalese association, Mbolo Moy Doole (the Union Makes Strength). The objectives of this association, according to its leaders, are to struggle for Senegalese integration in Granada, to denounce racist acts, to participate in public institutions and sociopolitical platforms, and to disseminate Senegalese "culture" in Andalusia.

To help them write up projects and obtain funding for the association, the Senegalese turned to local NGOs, which knew how to obtain money from public institutions and were themselves interested in fostering immigrants' free cultural expression in Granada. Although Senegalese religious authorities wanted to use the funding for their own celebrations, the Senegalese community repeatedly rejected this on the grounds of an overarching nationalism that crosses religious and ethnic cleavages. This strategy reproduced the tactic that Senegalese political authorities used during the early period of independence, embodied in a law forbidding political parties based on religious, ethnic, or regional identities. Even if reproducing Senegalese nationalism, the strategy has served in Granada to reduce the economic and political power of brotherhoods in representing Senegalese immigrants vis-à-vis the Spanish state. Despite Spanish pressures to devote public resources to the cultural expression of Senegalese particularities, the focus of the association has been the struggle for the rights of Senegalese immigrants as residents and workers who are paying their taxes to the Spanish state every month to comply with the requirements of the law.

The informal alliances between the Senegalese community and local NGOs have helped Senegalese gain access to space for meetings and associations, and for protesting the racism of both the Spanish state and civil society. Senegalese related to NGOs in the same open way they welcomed solidary relations with associations of various ideologies and religions. Thus, they obtained support from the Human Rights Association, which loaned them their locale for the meetings of their association Mbolo Moy Doole, and they have always been very close to the most active NGO working for immigrants, Granada Acoge. Similarly, the Neighborhood Association of El Zaidín shares the public locale allocated to them with the Senegalese living in this neighborhood as with any other resident group, and it is in El Zadaín that most meetings of the Mouride *daï'ra* take place on a weekly basis. Even the radical association "Alternative Left" has

loaned a meeting place to the Senegalese to celebrate the important Islamic festivities of the Sacrifice of the Lamb (Aid al-Adha). Senegalese thus use manifold
strategies for entry into the Spanish social sphere, as persons entitled to human
rights, as residents in good relations with neighbors, or as part of Granadan alternative social movements.

All Senegalese welcome the participation of their association in public cultural
events that make their presence visible in civil society through music, cultural
workshops, or exhibits of the folklore of countries of origin. Yet there is dissent
as to whether Senegalese should embrace some of the requirements for participation in the Spanish civil sphere, as I explained in the previous chapter. Religious leaders, for instance, do complain about adoption of non-Muslim forms of
participation, such as the very popular *chiringuitos* (street stands to sell refreshments) that many local associations (and now Senegalese immigrants) organize to
raise funds during Granadan parades, for it is problematic for Muslims to sell
alcohol. Other more traditional Senegalese also question the importance that
some of their compatriots attach to creating interethnic and multireligious spaces
of *convivencia*, such as the celebration of the Sacrifice of the Lamb referred to
above, given that the purpose of the celebration is more social than religious.

At the center of the polemic is the issue of the legitimacy of the inclusive
model of Spanish *convivencia* based on the rule of law, especially as this issue
intersects with Senegalese religious authorities' own claims to hold legitimate
authority over the Senegalese community. Islamic brotherhoods in the diaspora
claim their right to establish the criteria of proper social behavior, based on moral
and socioreligious authority. Similarly to Spanish Muslims, Senegalese brotherhoods are highly critical of Western civilization's "lack of values" and consumerism, and they charge Senegalese who challenge their authority with having
fallen victim to Westernization. Yet the brotherhoods do not question either the
split between public and private spheres or the liberal understanding of religion
as a subjective belief, both of which have traditionally served to maintain their
power as intermediaries between the Senegalese state and its people. Their strategy is to struggle for the representation of Senegalese as cultural others in the
Spanish civil sphere, and of Senegalese citizens as culturally abiding subjects both
in Senegal and in the diaspora.

In contrast to this position, other Senegalese criticize a folkloric notion of
multiculturalism, emphasizing how cultural difference hides inequalities both in
relation to Spanish citizens and to traditional forms of domination. These Senegalese point to racism, exploitation, and legal discrimination in Spain, but they
actively appropriate the legal system to struggle for rights acknowledged them in
order to circumvent their dependence on traditional hierarchical structures of
power. Some of them, for example, are challenging the linkage between gender
and nationalist structures of power that leaves women back in Senegal as needed

to preserve purity of lineage and tradition. Some immigrants are bringing their wives to Spain under the provisions for family reunification acknowledged by the law, despite the concerns of Senegalese authorities about the dangers involved. In doing so, they challenge the traditional system of age and religious authority for determining their way of life. They thus seek new ways to create a collective (versus individualist) spiritual experience compatible with the enjoyment of interethnic spaces. Other immigrants, more politically motivated, emphasize the need to keep strategic alliances with local associations to gain power and influence in the issues that dramatically weaken Senegalese possibilities for participating as full legal subjects in the Spanish social sphere.

What is at stake in the Senegalese case is the issue of the power of ethnic groups to control their own members, or what Kymlicka has termed "internal restrictions" of collective rights. Whether the spaces opened by an imagery of a multicultural *convivencia* can be transformed into an instrument of power by those representing minority communities is a question of their degree of internal participatory democracy. And successful internal democracy depends on the immigrants' ability to challenge the structures of power from outside hegemonic national formations. Undoubtedly, the revaluation of cultural difference and of human rights in the context of liberal multicultural citizenship opens up spaces for the struggle for equality and participation in Spanish civil society, as I have shown. But at the same time, immigrants' socioeconomic marginalization, legal exclusion, and lack of effective channels of political participation, as well as the cultural consequences of the "fetishism of papers," only fuel the new international imagery of ethnic confrontation in terms of religious principles. We can only help counter this sad panorama by contributing to immigrants' efforts to achieve harmonious *convivencia* at the local level, respecting and acknowledging them as persons, as neighbors, as workers—as concrete human beings.

Notes

1. Heater 1990, 295, quoted in Kymlicka 1996, 162.
2. Collier et al. 1995, 2.
3. The links between Andalusian and North African musical expressions are well known and are not merely reminiscences, but actually very much alive in the repertoires of both Andalusian and North African current artists. Although the roots of Andalusian flamenco are "a subject of great debate and obscurity," it is clearly a Gypsy expression, which in the sixteenth century "was fused with elements of Arabic and Jewish music in the Andalusian mountains, where Jews, Muslims, and 'pagan' gypsies had taken refuge from the forced conversions and clearances effected by the Catholic kings and Church" (Broughton et al. 1994, 135). Even the word

flamenco is thought to be an Andalusian mispronunciation of the Arabic words *felag* (fugitive) and *mengu* (peasant), according to the same source. Similarly, the classical Andalousí orchestras who were forced into exile greatly influenced musical expressions in the north of the Maghreb. Known as *al-âla* in the Maghreb, the classical suite called *nuba* in its current forms is very much alive, popular, and greatly loved. The contemporary Algerian *Rai*, is influenced by flamenco among other traditions, like the protest songs of refugees from Franco's dictatorship who visit Algeria or settled there. In short, "both Moroccan [and, in general, Magrebian] music and flamenco have strong links with Mauritanian music and the three together emphasized a Moorish, as distinct from Arab, cultural sphere all too often forgotten" (109).

4. Parker 1992; Yuval-Davis 1990.

5. See Maribel Fierro (n.d.) for an analysis of the doctrine of the *hiyra* (emigration) and the rules of conduct for Muslims in non-Muslim lands (*dar al-kufr*, or land of infidels).

6. Anderson 1991; Gellner 1983; Hobsbawm and Ranger 1983.

7. The mosque also includes a cultural center, a library, and an Islamic school. As a member of the Spanish Muslim community puts it: "[the mosque] is a place where our heart, our aspirations, our intelligence grow. For the mosque is 'the' place … that reconstitutes the Muslim in the world. An existential place. A constitutive place. Thus, after five hundred years, Spanish Muslims reinvent a relation with the world…. Thus, we are no longer dispersed men, nomads without a place, without constitutive land … and despite this, the only thing that a Muslim needs … is a piece of clean land" (*La Gaceta de Granada* 1994). They also claim the right of Muslims living in Granada to use the Islamic cemetery situated in the highly symbolic *Alhambra*, and their religious celebrations are increasingly held in public spaces where they invite members of other Muslim and non-Muslim associations, significantly those NGOs working closely with immigrants.

8. According to the research of Alonso, half of the first Muslim associations legally recognized in Spain from July 1989 to October 1990 (a total of thirty one) were located in Andalusia, and half of these were in Granada. Together with a preoccupation about the unity *(tawhid)* of the Islamic *umma* and its ability to incorporate difference (captured in the dictum of the *sharia* "ikhtilaf al-umma rahma" [difference within the Islamic tradition is a blessing]; Asad 1995, 9), there has been a tendency within Islam toward conflict, division, and antagonism among its leaders since the times of the succession of the prophet Muhammad *(fitna)*. The Spanish Muslim community has not escaped this tendency, lamented by its members in the local press: "Why so many Islamic associations … [if we continue this way] there are going to be as many associations as Muslims in Granada…. Haven't we learnt from history? When Muslims divided in Granada … the conquest by the peoples coming from the north was facilitated…. I am ashamed of these struggles and factionalism among us … we are Muslims and that is that!" (Abraham López *El Ideal,* June 17, 1994).

9. In Islamic political language, what these communities are aiming for is the special status of the *dimma*, an Islamic sociolegal arrangement by which the Muslim central power guarantees "protected groups," such as Jews and Christians, internal autonomy, freedom to practice their religion and apply their law, and the inviolability of their spaces, in exchange for the payment of some special taxes (Fierro n.d., 1). In this system, the juridical individual and the notion of equality was simply not relevant: everyone was within a group that had its juridical place within the larger sociopolitical arrangement (see Aaron Rodrigue 1995).

10. The names of some of these associations are highly significant: Andalusian Front of National Liberation, Islamic Yamaa of Al-Andalus," and the Morisca League, founded by the controversial Abderrahman Medina in Córdoba.

11. Moroccans are organized around three main groups. First, there are the students who have developed their own associations in Granada, such as UNEM (Unión Nacional de Estudiantes

Marroquíes, or Moroccan National Students' Union). Second, there are the immigrants who are more focused on labor issues and linked with Spanish labor unions, such as ATIME (Asociación Trabajadores Inmigrantes Marroquíes en España, or Association of Moroccan Immigrant Workers in Spain). Third, there is a growing group of Moroccan Muslim believers and activists who establish connection and alliances with Spanish Muslim communities while at the same time seeming to maintain some distance and autonomy.

12. See Aguer 1991; Carmona 1993.

CONCLUSION

One of the main puzzles facing the analyst of the contemporary world is to explain why it might be, as Harvey puts it, "that the elaboration of place-bound identities has become more rather than less important in a world of diminishing spatial barriers to exchange, movement, and communication" (Harvey 1993, 4). The unification of Europe, which has almost completed its project of becoming a unique market with internal free circulation of goods, services, capital, and people, stands as an important example of the paradox to which Harvey is pointing. Contrary to the expectations of both modernist and Marxist theorists, new nationalisms and regionalisms are arising in European countries, and ethnic conflicts are becoming a central feature of advanced industrialized countries.

Literature on European immigration has identified two major forces contributing to the growing importance of cultural difference and ethnic identity in contemporary industrial societies and to the mushrooming of racist and xenophobic attacks on Third World workers. On the one hand, global socioeconomic forces, the constitution of transnational socioeconomic and political institutions such as the EU, and the international division of labor of late capitalism, draw people from the impoverished south to the industrialized north and produce the current racialization of class relations in Europe. On the other hand, scholars emphasize the role of nation-states, whose reliance on the principle of nationality shapes categories of belonging and of national identity, and whose classificatory functions and technologies of power strongly influence the constitution of bounded identities along ethnic and legal lines.

This book provides an empirically based analysis of the reinscription of cultural difference and ethnic identity as a major force shaping social boundaries in a borderland area situated at the periphery of the newly constituted Europe. While this project is framed by a consideration of the global political economy underlining the rebordering of the Mediterranean, my main concerns are the cultural and moral repertoires informing the translation of these boundaries to the innerland. The anthropological perspective, informed by an ethnohistorical and multisited methodology, proves to be instrumental in questioning some implicit assumptions held in migration and ethnic studies.

First, I argued that the racialization of class relations in Europe should not be based on a priori notions of "race" or ethnic difference. Rather than assuming the internally stable properties presumed by social categories (such as peasants, immigrants, Europeans, or "southerners"), we should show how identities are constructed dialectically, in the particular relationships in which actors are embedded. The experiences of Andalusians illuminated the extent to which ethnic, political, and class identities depended on particular sociospatial locations. They experienced a profound shift in the way their ethnic and class identities have been categorized by both social research and political authorities in Spain and abroad. I also showed how the racialization of African immigrants in Andalusia drew on local historical stereotypes of disadvantaged social groups situated at the margins of the imagined community. The emphasis on the mutual feeding of class and ethnic naturalization of differences helped me avoid the tacit primordialist notion of contemporary ethnic and racial structures of exclusion. Social categories do have a transformative effect in agents' identities, however. When certain social groups are categorized as different, and their difference becomes naturalized, these social categories will have an impact on social relations. But the way this takes place becomes an empirical question, because identities shift over time and space, and those identities, rather than constituting stable social categories, become the source of sociopolitical action.

Second, by looking at the case of Andalusia in the new multicultural Spain, I have demonstrated that the imagining of an homogeneous national community cannot be assumed as a given, and that sociospatial inequalities within the national social formation have to be taken into account in a serious way. In Granada, immigrants were not perceived as a threat to a national style of life or cultural identity, as scholars of the new racism argued for Britain, France, and Germany. Moreover, the fact that such a small number of immigrants could evoke such a disproportionate reaction to put them in their place, belies those scholars who posit the so-called threshold of tolerance to explain racist and xenophobic behavior.

Last but not least, the ethnographic analysis of the boundaries drawn between Andalusians and Africans is that the "cultural stuff" of immigrants—their cultural difference in the sense of ethnic customs and habits—was not at all a source of conflict. The problem at the local level was not the fact that the new others belonged to a different culture, ethnicity, religion, or "race." The problem was rather that they had "no place" in the sociospatial and moral landscape and were subjected to effort to "put them in their place." Instead of constructing the conflict as primordially ethnic, it should rather be analyzed as a conflict of social inequality framed in the anxiety produced by the ambiguous boundaries of a redefined national membership, where social entitlements of residents are purportedly detached from cultural belonging and nationality. Local people and the state resisted most fiercely the acquisition of equal rights by newcomers, not the presence of yet another difference in the national territory. In the context of a multicultural Spain, the national discourse is redefined through the re-creation of a kind of inclusive yet primordially unequal caste system, a multiple and hierarchical system of legal statutes that perpetuates global inequalities and reinscribes class and ethnic racism in the form of legal exclusion and marginalization.

The ethnohistorical, non-nationally bounded anthropological perspective on the redrawing of social boundaries in the Andalusian landscape brings to the forefront a disturbing reproduction of a stratified and segmented social space. I use the concept reproduction reticently, for even while acknowledging the endurancing hegemonic formations and dominant ideologies in the naturalization of class, ethnic, and gender inequalities, I also perceive them as fragile, plural, and contested in multiple social sites. Let us consider the transformation of Andalusian peasants during the past three decades. Rural sociospatial structure since the end of the Civil War was shaped by the control of elites of the economic, legal, and political apparatuses. Those who could not "live on their own" struggled to gain the autonomy and respect they deserved as persons, as people who honestly worked with their own hands, to make a living. They did so through emigration, dismantling the agrarian system that was based on peasants' attachment to the land and their inability to sell their labor force, and thus overcame dependence on and submission to clientelist and paternalist relationships. They also did so by engaging in intensive agricultural production and by struggling through political mobilization against a national-Catholic ideology that conjured up a controlled, segmented, and hermetic social sphere. The utopia of universal sovereignty, of democratic participation, and of economic autonomy seemed to be achieved in the early 1980s. As people said to me, despite the persistence of inequalities in wealth, villagers had "leveled off," and the egalitarian landscape imagined in the social vision of rural Andalusia seemed to have become much closer to realization.

Nonetheless, there was a widespread feeling of disenchantment with the consequences of modernization. The presence of immigrants in the valley served to confirm the suspicion of local leaders that the peasants who had struggled for universal principles of sovereignty and autonomy had become something else in the process. Villagers seemed to have given up local peasant class identity, and with it the popular culture of participatory democracy through which they might create a new destiny for themselves. Many informants described villagers as obsessed with production, money, and markets, closed up in their new houses full of modern commodities, and indifferent to the sociopolitical issues that extended beyond their own interests. New forms of dependency, on loans and markets as well as on welfare subsidies, undermined the will and ability of peasants to organize politically.

Meanwhile, poverty, humiliation, and exclusion reappeared in the bodies of African immigrants. Their presence was constructed at the local and national level as a problem, and a regime of regulation was deployed to solve the problem. Local and national cultural and moral repertoires were used in a conflictual way in daily social practices to put immigrants "in their place"—a temporal, segmented, and conditional place marked by class, age, ethnicity, and gender, as well as by legality. Again, through the complex dynamic of coercion and consent that characterizes hegemonic formations, a fractured landscape was conjured up. The new "open wounds" (Anzaldúa 1987, 3) of this borderland are not quite the same as those of Andalusia's past, yet in the context of the expectation of progress and equality created by the process of modernization, they stand as a fatalist rationale naturalizing inequality as unavoidable ("there will always be poor people … that's the way life is") and as proof of the limits of the utopia of democratic and legally bounded polities where equality is not just a formal right, but a social entitlement ("we suffered it before; now, unfortunately, it is their turn").

In the global symbolic framework where we navigate today, the role of the states is still crucial. The nationalist ideology, however much delinked from a culturally homogeneous imagined community, conjures up the globalizing landscape as a reason for nation-states' inability to control immigration, and masterfully uses this danger to legitimize further investment in the control of frontiers and of those inner enemies that pose a threat to national security and well-being. Among these threats, "illegal" immigration from the Third to the First World is frequently depicted in the mass media as the so-called challenge of the new millennium. Erased from this picture are the empirical data suggesting that most of the great population journeys take place within that undifferentiated Third World where most human beings live. Immigration is a crucial element in the symbolic strategies deployed by welfare states to redefine their own role in the context of the aggressive transnational power of financial capital and of the powerful neoliberal ideologies.

To justify the alleged need of the state to control immigration, dominant discourses resort once again to the image of the phantom of the south, with the south depicted as a hostile landscape inhabited by ignorant and primitive people who are inclined to engage in not quite rational behavior, such as continuing to give birth to children who have little or no future, or risking their lives to cross frontiers. Such images hardly impact people anymore—we have become so accustomed to watching others' distress on television. Rather, they draw power from how representation of an irrational and threatening south draws on the legacy of the European colonial imagery that served to uphold Western civilizational superiority.

They play an important role in the criminalization of immigration. But in addition to these symbolic resources, and perhaps because it is not quite true that people buy into them so readily, the state intervenes in many other ways to materialize the criminalization and externalization of immigration. And this is where Law comes into play, with its powerful symbolic resources to mark out the new deviancy: "illegal" immigration.

What is at stake here, as I said before, is not simply the issue of whether it is legitimate to lump together such disparate categories as immigration and common delinquency, as the Alien Law does. The most important consequence for the translation of boundaries to the innerland is that the construction of immigration from the south as a problem sets the basis for the deployment of a mode of regulation of that problem. A mode of regulation, following scholars such as Corrigan and Sayer (1985), and especially Hunt (1993, chapter 13), includes explicit laws and administrative regulations, but also the institutional setting and the norms and social practices by which regulation comes into being as a normalizing force.

Regulation contains both exclusive and inclusive mechanisms. There is first, at least from the experience of immigration in Spain, a basic overwhelming exclusion: illegality. As Foucault put it, "Definitive bounds to the sacred order are no longer set in terms of heresy but in terms of illegality, madness and other abnormalities constituted in law" (quoted in Fitzpatrick, 1992, 167). The state creates illegality (recall the Catch-22 system generated by the Alien Law) just as the Inquisition created heresy in past centuries—as an abnormality, a deviation from normal and correct behavior. By constructing the normal in antithesis to the supposedly abnormal, a central symbolic element of modernity is thus underscored, namely, the legal inequality distinguishing nationals from foreigners.

This condition of illegality and gloom was nevertheless represented as solvable if only the immigrants would submit to and comply with institutional measures designed to reincorporate the deviant into society. On the one hand, administrative regulations required immigrants to obtain and renew a limited legal status as foreigners with rights. On the other hand, integration policies were put forward to incorporate immigrants into larger society. Such was the Janus-faced mode of regulation that the state deployed to purportedly "solve the problem" of immigration, but which also ultimately had a profound impact on civil society, both on the formation of identities and subjectivities and on the repositioning of social agents vis-à-vis the state.

First, this mode of regulation strengthened the tacit contract between the state and its nationals (e.g., employers), creating a multiple and hierarchical system of legal statutes that secured the interests of the state's political clientele. Yet at the same time, by constructing nationals as citizens with privileges, the state enforced their duties as taxpayers, contrary to their entrenched economic survival strategies in the informal economy. This was a painful learning of citizenship, one that was not without consequences for immigrants, as I have shown. Second, regulation promoted the creation of national intermediaries who were in charge of implementing social programs to assist and incorporate immigrants into the mainstream, thus transforming them into agents of regulation (Coutin 1993). The state thereby acquired credibility with those groups, such as NGOs and trade unions, that hold the state accountable based on an open notion of citizenship rooted in human rights. Yet at the same time, this mode of regulation transformed those sectors of civil society into efficient agents of the flourishing social field of humanitarian work, who found themselves competing for public resources. Humanitarian work became privatized, and in some instances depoliticized, in ways that served and efficient and decentralized use of state resources for social services. Yet as a result, immigrants' access to services came to be seen as gifts rather than as entitlements.

This mode of regulation also transformed immigrants by constituting them as administered subjects. Administrative regulations became embedded in immigrants' daily practices, and through their repeated bureaucratic pilgrimages, immigrants became experts in creating a coherent documented identity. As Foucault has noted (1978), the power of administrative regulations is in creating self-responsible individuals, operating not so much by way of negative prohibition as by positive, productive application. Of course, immigrants were not free to choose whether or not to subject themselves to regulations, but they did expect something in return: the acquisition of rights and their own constitution as legal subjects. The most important transformative effect of administrative regulations was thus two-sided: immigrants became individualized in their relations vis-à-vis the state, and they became "proprietors" of rights as something they could buy. This "mercantilized" vision of rights did not go unnoticed by immigrants. Immigrants recognized that those among them who could pay the onerous taxes required of them had little difficulty in obtaining papers, and therefore, acquiring rights. As I have shown, the idea of rights as "bought" was itself not alien to Andalusian peasants, who were also suspicious of abstract rights and prioritized proper behavior in terms of persons being members of a collective. The perception of rights as a commodity available to those who have money evoked moral criticism of the purported universality and legitimacy of the law. But it also transformed both peasants' and immigrants' customary rules. Especially for immigrants, most of whom were excluded from acquiring stable legal status, the resulting construction of multiple legal statutes actively restructured relations of power within their communities, not just because individual projects came to be frequently prioritized over moral obligations toward other immigrants, but also because legal status served to strengthen clientelist relationships, as an additional resource that secured transnational and traditional forms of authority.

The state's general strategy of integrating immigrants in to the mainstream entailed a very inclusive notion of membership involving, in addition to legality, immigrants' participation. Participation was two-sided, emphasizing equality as well as difference or cultural plurality. First, immigrants needed to incorporate in to those sociopolitical organizations, institutions, and social services available to any other citizen. Yet the implementation of social programs for the incorporation of immigrants began to have an opposite effect. Discourses about equal rights in the public sphere tend systematically to make differences invisible, often obstructing social programs that address immigrants' specific needs on the grounds of unequal treatment with respect to nationals. The emphasis on equality thus paradoxically conjures up "a sphere prior to the public sphere where inequalities flourish" (Collier et al. 1995, 2). In the context that considered immigrants' presence problematic, threatening, or polluting in some crucial public sites, to make difference invisible is to obviate the forces that excluded immigrants from public spaces in which to negotiate their membership in the community and to make claims on society.

At the same time, discourses about culture highlight difference. Official strategies for promoting immigrants' participation tended to conceive of immigrants as purportedly natural carriers of cultural difference and identity, clearly distinguished in ethnic terms from a category of Spaniards construed as homogeneous. National, regional, and local administrations emphasized cultural identity as a privileged channel for social mobilization, but not just for immigrants, as I have explained. Identity and cultural difference were reinscribed in this political landscape as a "meaningful discourse of participation, and it [identity] is enacted as a symbolic tool for creating new group solidarities within and beyond national boundaries … it becomes a universal category (that everyone should have an identity, the core definer of their selfhood) and affords the means for participation in the public sphere and mobilizing resources in the national and world polities" (Soysal n.d., 2). Immigrants became "proprietors" of culture, and they used it to draw resources from the state and to make room for participation in the civil sphere. In the context of widespread local reticence toward embracing immigrants on equal terms in existing channels of participation and decision making, immigrants resolutely made use of resources available to them as cultural others. The revaluation of cultural identity in the context of multicultural Spain did carry with it the danger of "otherizing" the participation of immigrants, but it also opened up social spaces from which immigrants could engage in a struggle for equality on their own terms.

Although authorities seemingly welcomed immigrants' expression of cultural identity, a subtle though systematic distinction differentiated the cultural identities of peoples within the national formation from those of African immigrants. The cultural difference of immigrants came to be represented as primordially incompatible with culture internal to Spain, a potential threat to the integrative function of the constitutional rule of law based on secular, rational, and universal respect of the rights of the individual. Multicultural discourse emerges as a privileged channel for promoting cultural difference and tolerance, yet at the same time, it constructs difference as belonging to the private sphere, as bounded, and essential. Immigrants' cultural peculiarity could better be described as an "excess" of culture, a kind of primordial attachment and loyalty to bounded and unified cultures that could and would be "corrected" though their resolute compliance to the rule of law.

If immigrants seemed to have an "excess" of primordial cultural attachment, this was because Spaniards implicitly viewed them from the vantage point of the fundamental tenet of the European colonialist enterprise that deems full citizenship a privilege of the civilized and the maintenance of custom as the priority of the uncivilized. My case study of Senegalese migration underscores this imagined landscape of bounded and hierarchically differentiated cultural differences privileging the kinds of cultural identity associated with modern Western civilization. It may seem odd to compare Spain's contemporary situation with the colonial legal apartheid that segregated the so-called civilized civil sphere from a primitive sphere of multiple locally -enforced ethnic and religious customs. But the fact is that the Janus-faced mode of regulation of immigration reproduced just such an effective form of power in the contemporary migratory panorama. As the state "normalized" the allocation of space and the behaviors appropriate for immigrant newcomers, an unintended consequence was to perpetuate a new kind of legal apartheid based on a kind of "caste system," in which state-enforced cultural others were construed more as subjects of tutelage than as full legal subjects entitled to rights.

Could immigrants circumvent the pernicious effects of such regulation? I concluded my analysis by exploring the multidimensional ways in which immigrants, through practices of *convivencia*, try to negotiate common rules of social behavior and access to social entitlements as members of a nonhomogeneous and non-nationally bounded civil sphere. Localized citizenship practices and *convivencia* emerge as a way of understanding ethnic relations not as inherently conflictual, but rather as facilitating mutual exchange, respect, and understanding. Difference need not disappear from such negotiations for respect and social entitlements. My ethnographic exploration of interethnic relations showed that rather than disappearing, historically constituted notions of cultural difference were systematically reinscribed, both in terms of a so-called traditional biological hierarchy of cultures and races and in the purportedly new imagining of the insurmountability of equally valuable cultural differences (Balibar 1991). Nevertheless, immigrants deployed a myriad of strategies of entitlement and belonging to resist having their participation as members of several communities reduced to their cultural difference. They actively engaged in local informal negotiation of rights as neighbors, workers, or family members by claiming the respect due to any person who conforms to the customary rules of behavior regulating *convivencia* (especially at the local level) and by appealing to their compliance with legal requirements vis-à-vis the state as a basis for equal treatment.

The mode of regulation deployed at the local level to "normalize" and "solve" the "problem" of immigrants brought unintended consequences for both immigrants and citizens, but also for the state, because in interaction with state practices of regulation, new spaces of resistance are opened. Hegemonic formations effectively shape the limits of social action and the specific forms of discursive possibility. People act within a multidimensional structure of power conditioning their structural positions (class, gender, ethnicity, or "race") as well as their mental dispositions and schemes of perception and thought, constituting them as agents. Yet there are no a priori, unified social categories from which social agents engage in practice. Rather, it is through participation in daily social interactions that identities are shaped and constructed. The imagery of a multicultural *convivencia* conjured up by the state, where all parties involved reach consensus about the essential rules and values to which everybody should submit and comply, is no doubt a contested one. There is no unique challenge to the model. Rather, there is a complex and dynamic array of regional, transnational, class, ethnic, religious, gender, and legal locations from which the moral and cultural hegemonic formations can be challenged and their normalizing techniques resisted.

My ethnographic account of the localized practices of citizenship unveils a contested public sphere, a dynamic and changing process where consensus is never complete and where the hegemonic cultural and moral repertoires legitimating the use of coercion are seen with suspicion from a complex array of situated identities and particular social interests. Both among Andalusians and immigrants there is widespread disenchantment with democracy and the rule of Law, a symptom of the contradictory way in which the utopia of equality coexists with the material consequences of global capitalist relations. I do not want to imply that civic commitment to equality and representation disappears, for it is well alive. Nor do I want to suggest that people wish to live in a kind of moral vacuum produced by the modern rational and impersonal authority of legal imagery, as Weber seemed to suggest. What I find undeniable, and worth considering in cultural analysis of change and transformation in modern societies, is that this disenchantment responds to a fragility of hegemonic processes. Indeed, points to the limits of the ideological representation of a global neoliberal political economy as situated beyond humans' control. Disenchantment is a good disease, so to speak, a symptom of unrest, which may be manifest itself in either political, cultural, or moral terms. As Roseberry (1994, 357) argues, paraphrasing Scott, "the dominated know they are dominated, they know by whom and how; far from consenting to that domination, they initiate all sorts of subtle ways of living with, talking about, resisting, undermining, and confronting the unequal and power-laden worlds in which they live"—and by which they are indeed constituted as social personas.

The fractured landscape I have considered here reveals a disturbing ability of reproduction, but it is also fragile. Yet conspiratorial perspectives that conjure up a singular and unified subject of this power (the state, capitalism, Western racism or atheism, among so many others) only undermine our ability to struggle against hegemonic formations and dominant ideologies. Social sciences and history have largely demonstrated the dispersion of the sites of domination, the multidimensional character of inequality, and the mechanisms of mimesis and metamorphosis as basic factors in the re-creation of forms of domination and for its legitimization. The emphasis of Foucault and Bourdieu on the embodiment of power is a disturbing one, but once again, history has proved that reproduction does not ever take place without resistance, that empires fall, and that people defy order by moving and acting out. As Bourdieu reminds us: "Science has a time which is not that of practice. For the analyst, time no longer counts: not only because—as has often been repeated since Max Weber—arriving *post festum* he [*sic*] cannot be in any uncertainty as to what may happen, but also because he has the time to totalize, i.e. to overcome the effects of time" (1977, 9). I fear that social scientists are forced to refrain from temptations to impose utopia on the analysis of social processes, not because detached objectivity is ever possible, but rather because their own utopias are not likely to coincide with those of people engaged in practice.

GLOSSARY

Aid al-Adha: Islamic festival of the Sacrifice of the Lamb.

andalusí: Refers to Al-Andalus, or "the Muslim Spain."

Aparceros: *See* **arrendatarios**

Ardo el Jamía/Tierra de Todos: Everybody's land.

arraigo: Attachment; to be deeply rooted or settle down in a place.

arrendatarios, medianería, medianeros, aparceros, or comuneros: *Arrendatarios* are land renters; *aparceros* and *medianeros* are sharecroppers to whom the landowner supplies land, seed, capital, investment, and other kinds of clientelistic favors, while the worker contributes the animal team and labor. Finally, *comuneros* are more strongly linked to a particular land plot, paying a minimum rent and acquiring some rights to the land over the years, and even across generations linking owner and worker families.

bandoleros: Brigands.

Boletín Oficial del Estado (BOE): Official State Bulletin.

buena gente: Good people.

cabeza de comarca: Head of county.

caciques: Originally meant "the principal person in a village," but in the nineteenth century it acquired negative connotations referring to anybody who is considered to hold power in an illegitimate, arbitrary, and corrupt way. Uses of the term are related to the ascendance of a local bourgeoisie in the creation of a capitalist agrarian society (Contreras 1991, 503; Joaquín Costa 1978).

campesino: Peasant.

chiringuitos: Street stands to sell refreshments.

chozas, choceños: In the village, poor people used to live in *chozas,* a term that was actually the first name of the village. In his wonderful piece of ethnohistorical research, Mintz describes *chozas* as thatched cottages or huts. (See Mintz 1982 for a description of a similar domestic construction that also symbolizes peasants' attachment to the land, use of local resources, and poverty.) *Chozas* are usually located at the edge of town, and have enclosures shared with domestic animals.

chozas, choceño *(cont.)*
Choceños are the people who lived in the *chozas*.

CITE: Comité de Intervención para Trabajadores Extranjeros; Intervention Commitee for Alien Workers.

comarca: County

comuna: A close-knit community of people who share local interests. Any community organized for the protection and promotion of local interests and those of its members, who are called comuneros, but in a different sense from those who rent and cultivate somebody's else land. In this context, *comuna* refers to a specific local organization: a collective inspired by anarchist ideals of sharing land, work, and daily life.

comuneros: *See* **arrendatarios**

Comunidades de Base: Christian-based communities.

construyendo pueblo: Building *pueblo*.

convenio del campo: Collective bargaining agreement on labor relations on labor conditions in the countryside.

convivencia: Translated literally as "living together," *convivencia* was the concept coined by historians to refer to the coexistence and cultural intermixing of Muslims, Jews, and Christians in medieval times, just before the Spanish nation-state was founded as a territorial unit in the Iberian peninsula. Today it is a somewhat loose term that applies to a formal/informal meeting with a spiritual, congregational, or ecumenical approach (the sense in which it is used above); daily interaction among people; or a particular model governing collective rules of a political community, as in the expression democratic *convivencia*.

corredores: *Corredores* (literally runners) are those who link individual producers with customers, obtaining a good commission for each business deal. In the eyes of peasants, this way of earning money is considered immoral, because no (physical) work is involved, no risk is assumed, and because *corredores* enrich themselves at the expense of both producers and consumers.

cortijos, cortijeros: In contrast to the typical Andalusian elite rural houses with the same name, the *cortijos* to which we refer in the Valley of Alfaya are small houses scattered in the valley, and are used today to keep the tools for working the land. Sometimes they are used by the family to eat and rest in the countryside, most times while working. Some farmers arranged for immigrants to live in *cortijos*. In the past, as today, *cortijeros* refer to those persons who live permanently in the *cortijos*, and the term has a derogatory sense.

courier: Messenger or transporter.

cuadrillas: Teams of workers. A special type of agrarian team work is the *cuadrilla de lechugueros*, which is devoted to gathering and loading lettuces. *Cuadrillas* are generally hired as a group for this purpose and they get paid by the job.

cumplidor: Person who keeps ("respects" in the text) commitments.

cumplir: To take responsibility for finishing tasks, as a personal duty.

da'aras: Rural cooperatives organized primarily by the *Marabouts*, who brought their followers with them to work in the groundnut fields.

da'iras: Urban cohort association generally linked to a *Marabout*.

denizen: Word used by Hammar and others to describe the predominant status of foreign immigrants in Europe.

Dirección General de Migraciones (DGM): General Migration Headquaters.

Dirección General de Policía: Police Headquarters.

Documento Nacional de Identidad (DNI): Spanish National Document of Identity.

El País: An important Spanish newspaper.

embrujo: Bewitchment.

empadronamiento, padrón: The *empadronamiento* is the act of getting registered in the Residents' Census, which is managed by the municipal authorities. *Padrón* is short for Padrón de Habitantes.

en buena ley: In honest law.

encargado: The person responsible for coordinating work under the direction of the employer.

españoladas: Exaggerated portrait of Spain. Any action, performance, or literary work that exaggerates the Spanish character. Pejorative term often used by critics to refer to Andalusian folklore as an idiosyncratic Spanish cultural expression during the Franco years.

fandango: (1) A lively Spanish or Spanish-American dance in triple time, performed by a man or a woman playing castanets. (2) A piece of music for such a dance or one having its rhythm.

Federación Española de Municipios y Provincias (FEMP): Spanish Federation of Provincial and Municipal Councils.

feria: Fair.

feria del campo, de ganado: Agricultural, livestock fair.

forasteros: Outsiders.

gente de paso: Passersby.

gente formal y religiosa: Religious and outstanding people.

gestoría: A private firm managing legal and administrative procedures for clients.

GISCO (Grupo de Interés Social de Comisiones Obreras): Social Interest Group of the Labor Union.

Granada Acoge: Welcome to Granada; the main volunteer organization dedicated to helping immigrants in the Andalusian province of Granada.

gri-gri: Protective charm.

grotisse: Trader who mediates transnational commercial exchanges controlled by *Murid Marabouts*.

hecho diferencial: Differential fact.

hijra: Idea of migration.

Iguales en Derechos: Equals in Rights.

Instituto Nacional Empleo (INEM): National Institute of Employment.

ir a lo que salga: To take what you can get.

Izquierda Alternativa: Alternative Left. A nonparliamentary group, which can be traced to one of the minor Communist parties.

Izquierda Unida: United Left. The Spanish parliamentary group made up of former Communists and other left-wing groups.

Jinn: Supranatural forces or spirits.

jornaleros: Day laborers, often without land of their own.

jornales: The daily pay a *jornalero* receives for his or her work.

Junta de Andalucía: The Regional Government of Andalusia.

keur: Literally "those who eat from the same bowl," *keur* refers to the group of people living in a domestic unit,

keur *(cont.)*
whose members generally belong to
the same extended family (it also frequently includes friends and adopted
children).

la tierra para quien la trabaja: Land for
those who work it.

latifundistas: Quasi-feudal landowners.

Legión, la: The Legión was a pseudo-
paramilitary force in Franco times
linked to the Moroccan protectorate
and to hyper nationalist symbols, such
as the flag, destiny of the Spanish
nation, and the national-catholic
regime. The Legión has recently been
given a new role as part of the Peace
Corps of the NATO (North Atlantic
Treaty Organization) or the UN
(United Nations).

Ley Orgánica de Extranjería: Popularly
known as the *Ley de Extranjería* but
officially as the Organic Law 7/1985,
July 1, on Rights and Liberties of Foreigners in Spain. The law is further
elaborated in the associated Regulations (*Reglamento*), Royal Decree
1119/ 1986, May 26. Additional legislation includes European Council and
other international agreements.

malagueños: From the province of
Málaga, adjacent to Granada. Situated
within the southwest border of the
province of Granada with Málaga,
Alfaya has always maintained a
stronger connection with the neighboring villages of the province of
Málaga.

maquis: People who fought with the
Republican band in the Civil War,
and lived hidden in the mountains
afterwards.

Marabouts: Islamic religious authorities.

Mbolo Moy Doole: The Union Makes
Strength.

a medias: Sharecropping.

Medianería, medianeros: *See* **arrendatarios, a medias**

Memoria del Plan de Inmigrantes:
Memorandum of the Immigrants
Plan.

Ministerio de Interior: Ministry of the
Interior.

Ministerio de Justicia: Ministry of Justice.

Ministerio de Trabajo: Ministry of Labor.

moriscos: Muslims who converted to
Christianity.

motor: Narrow booths where tools and
the irrigation equipment are kept, and
where many immigrants live.

mudéjares: Muslims living under Christian rule.

Muridiyya: Senegalese brotherhood
founded by Cheick Amadou Bamba.

négritude: Postcolonial philosophy and
ideology in defense of Back African
culture and rights, which was instrumental in the independence of African
countries since the 1950s.

njebbel: Ritualized act of submission of
the follower to the authority of the
Marabout, through which the *taalibe*
promises blind obedience to the
Marabout.

no meterse con nadie: To refrain from
provoking or betraying others.

no pagábamos derechos: "We never paid
any rights."

nos hemos igualao: "We have leveled off."

nuestra forma de ser: "Our way of being."

¡olé!: Typical Spanish interjection used to
encourage or applaud someone; it
could be translated as "bravo!" or
"well done!"

Padrón de Habitantes: Residents' Census.

pagar derechos: To pay someone's rights.

paro, el: *Subsidio de Desempleo Agrario*
(SDA); Agrarian Unemployment Subsidy.

Partido Socialista Obrero Español (PSOE): Spanish Socialist Worker's Party.

Pasos (de Semana Santa): Platforms bearing sculptured scenes from the Passion of Christ, carried through the streets during Holy Week.

pateras: One-engine barges that transport emigrants for a high price to the northern shore of the Mediterranean; generally, they are very small and overcrowded.

payo: A person who is not a Gypsy.

peonadas: Each working day carried out by a *peón* or *jornalero*.

Peonadas or peonás: Day jobs.

Pilón, el: Old public fountain situated at the entrance of Alfaya.

Plan de Empleo Rural (PER): Rural Employment Plan.

Plan de Viviendas Tuteladas (PVT): Tutelary Housing Plan (1992).

Plan for Social Integration for Immigrants (PSII): First National Plan in Spain to address the problems of integration of immigrants, passed by the Ministry of Social Affairs in 1994.

política de cupos: Annual quota system (set up by the government in 1993).

precontrato: Precontract; a declaration of intent to hire.

pringao: Pejorative adjective used to designate someone who is not very important and who is easy to cheat.

propios como forasteros: Natives as well as outsiders.

pueblo: Village; also people.

pueblo, ha nacido la esperanza: *pueblo*, the hope is born.

Régimen Especial Agrario (REA): Agrarian Special Regime. The current rural fiscal and labor model, which is designed to address the problems specific to agrarian production, such as chronic unemployment.

Representantes: In agrobusiness, *representantes* (agents) of a particular firm establish a direct contact between the customer and the agroproducer, generally imposing a price.

retratados: In this context it means "being portrayed by the state"; it is a common idiom to refer to the state's acquisition of accurate records of a person's real economic and labor situation, thus preventing tax and unemployment fraud.

Río Bravo: River, United States and Mexico, rising in the San Juan Mountains of Colorado and flowing first east and then south into New Mexico, through that state in a general southerly direction, and southeastward along the border between Texas and the Mexican states of Chihuahua, Coahuila, Nuevo León, and Tamaulipas. Although the lower part of the river is navigable, it has been closed to navigation by international agreement. In this context, Río Bravo is a metaphor used to evoke the danger of the Straits of Gibraltar, where almost daily immigrants risk their lives to enter Europe.

salir a la luz: To come into the light.

secano: *Cultivo de secano*: dry farming; *campo de secano*: land used for dry farming.

señorito: "well-to-do landowner who does not work but lives from the rental of his property or by the effort of his foremen and workers" (Mintz 1982, 323).

ser agradecido: To be grateful.

Sindicato Obrero del Campo (SOC): Rural Workers' Union.

somos iguales, somos diferentes: We are equals, we are different.

Subsidio Desempleo Agrario (SDA): Agrarian Unemployment Subsidy.

taalibe: Religious follower.

¿tan raros somos que quieres estudiarnos? Are we so strange that you want to study us?

terrateniente: *See* **latifundistas.**

Tijaniyya: Arab brotherhood first led locally by Al Haj Umar.

Toubab: Blanco; *toubaland*, the land of white people.

umma: Literally "community," refers to the international Islamic community *dar el-Islam*, or more restrictively, the particular symbolic territory of the brotherhood.

vivir de lo suyo: Literally, "to live on someone's own"; took on meaning in the agrarian class system of Andalusia in relation to landed property. Without property, or with insufficient property, a man would have to work for others, hence losing the personal autonomy of the self-sufficient property owner, who in turn could hire others and thus control others.

yonkis: Heroin addicts.

REFERENCES

Aceves, Joseph. 1971. *Social Change in a Spanish Village.* London: Schenkman Press.

Aceves, Joseph, and William Douglas. 1976. *The Changing Faces of Rural Spain.* Cambridge MA: Schenkman Press.

Acosta-Sánchez, José. 1979. *Historia y Cultura del Pueblo Andaluz.* Barcelona: Anagrama.

Aguer, Beatriz. 1991. "Résurgence de L'Islam en Espagne." *Revue Européenne des Migrations Internationales* 7.

Alonso, E. 1990. "De las Taifas a la Federación. La larga marcha hacia la unidad de las Asociaciones Islámicas Españolas." *Encuentro Islamo-Cristiano, 222* (October).

Anzandúa, Gloria. 1987. *Borderlands/La Frontera. The New Meztiza.* San Francisco: Spinsters/aunt lute.

Anderson, Benedict. 1991. *Imagined Communities. Reflections on the Origins and Spread of Nationalism.* London: Verso.

Appadurai, Arjun. 1991. "Global Ethnoscapes: Notes and Queries for a Transnational Anthropology." In Richard G. Fox (Ed.), *Recapturing Anthropology,* Santa Fe: School of American Research Press.

Aragón, M. 2001. "¿Es constitucional la nueva ley de extranjería?" *Claves de Razón Prácticas* 112.

Arango, Joaquín, and Liliana Suárez-Navaz. N.d. *Regularización 2000 y el Mercado de Trabajo.* Madrid: Ministerio de Trabajo y Asuntos Sociales (Ministry of Labor and Social Affairs). Instituto Migraciones y Servicios Sociales (IMSERSO); Institute of Migration and Social Services.

Arguedas, José María. 1968. *Las Comunidades de España y Perú.* Lima: Universidad Nacional de San Marcos.

Asad, T. 1995. "Modern Power and the Reconfiguration of Religious Traditions: Interview by Saba Mahmood." *Stanford Humanities Review,* 5(1), 1–16.

Asociación Pro-Derechos Humanos en España (APDHE); Human Rights Association. 1991. *Informe Anual Derechos Humanos en España 1990.*

Aznar Sánchez, Juan. 1974. *La Extranjería.* Madrid: Montecorvo.

Azurmendi, Mikel. 2001. *Estampas del Ejido.* Madrid: Taurus.

Balibar, Etienne. 1991. "Racism and Nationalism." In Etienne, Balibar and Immanuel Wallerstein (Ed.), *Race, Nation, Class. Ambiguous Identities* (pp. 37–67). London and New York: Verso.

Balibar, Etienne, and Immanuel Wallerstein. 1991. *Race, Nation Class: Ambiguous Identities.* London and New York: Verso.

Baño, Rodrigo. 1984. *Lo social y lo político: consideraciones acerca del movimiento popular urbano.* Santiago: Flacso.

Barkai, Ron. 1984. *Cristianos y Musulmanes en la España Medieval (El enemigo en el espejo).* Madrid: Rialp.

Barker, Martin. 1981. *The New Racism. Conservatives and the Ideology of the Tribe.* London: Junction Books.

Barou, J. 1987. "In the Aftermath of Colonization: Black African Immigrants in France." In H.C. Buechler and J.-M. Buechler (Eds.), *Migrants in Europe:The Role of Family, Labor, and Politics.*

Barth, Frederik. 1969. *Ethnic Groups and Boundaries.* Oslo: Scandinavian University Books.

Bataillon, Marcel. 1950. *Erasmo y España.* Mexico: FCE.

Behar, Ruth. 1986. *The Presence of the Past in a Spanish Village.* Princenton: Princenton University Press.

Benton, Lauren. 1990. *Invisible Factories. The Informal Economy and Industrial Development in Spain.* Albany: State University of New York Press.

Berger, John, and Jean Mohr. 1975. *A Seventh Man. The Story of Migrant Workers in Europe.* Baltimore: Penguin.

Blash, Linda, Nina Glick Schiller, and Cristina Szanton Blanc. 1994. *Nations Unbound. Transnational Projects, Postcolonial Predicaments, and Deterritorialized Nation-States.* Langhorne, PA: Gordon and Breach Science Publishers.

Borneman, John. 1993. "Uniting the German Nation: Law, Narrative and Historicity." *American Ethnologist,20,* 288–311.

Bourdieu, Pierre. 1977. *Outline of Theory of Practice* (Richard Nice, trans.). Cambridge: Cambridge University Press.

———. 1987. "The Force of Law." *Hastings Law Journal. 38*(5), 805–853.

Bowser, Frederick. 1974. *The African Slave in Colonial Peru, 1524–1650.* Stanford: Stanford University Press.

Brandes, Stanley. 1975. *Migration, Kinship and Community: Tradition and Change in a Spanish Village.* New York: Academic Press.

———. 1980. *Metaphors of Masculinity: Sex and Status in Andalusian Folklore.* Philadelphia: University of Pensylvania Press.

Braudel, Fernand. 1972. *The Mediterranean.* New York: Harper and Row.

Bredeloup, Silvie. 1992. "Itinéraires Africains de migrants Sénégalais." *Hommes et Migrations* (1160), 16–22.

Brenan, Gerald. [1957] 1991. *Al Sur de Granada.* (13th ed.). Madrid: Siglo XXI.

———. 1980. *The Spanish Labyrinth.* Cambridge: Cambridge University Press.

Broughton, Simon, Mark Ellingham, David Muddyman, and Richard Trillo (Eds.). 1994. *World Music. The Rough Guide.* London: The Rough Guides.

Brubaker, Rogers. 1992. *Citizenship and Nationhood in France and Germany*. Cambridge: Harvard University Press.

———. (Ed.). 1989. *Immigration and Politics of Citizenship in Europe and North America*. Lanham, MD: University Press of America.

Buecher, H.C. (Ed.). 1991. *El secreto de los Reyes Magos: flexibilidad del empleo de los emigrantes gallegos en Suiza*. Madrid: Taurus.

Burgos, Antonio. 1972. *Andalucia, Tercer mundo?* Barcelona: Círculo de Lectores.

Candel, Francisco. 1967. *Los otros Catalanes*. 3rd ed. Barcelona: Ediciones Península.

Carandell, Lluis. 1970. *Celtiberia Show*. Madrid: Maeva Ediciones.

Carmona González, A. 1993. "Los nuevos mudéjares. La Shari'a y los musulmanes en sociedades no-islámicas." Paper presented at the Comunidades Islámicas en España y en la Comunidad Europea (Islamic Communities in Spain and in the European Community), El Escorial, Madrid.

Caro Baroja, J. [1957] 1977. *Los Moriscos del Reino de Granada*. 2nd ed. Madrid: Istmo.

Carr, Raymond. 1982. *Spain, 1808–1975*. 2nd ed. Oxford: Oxford University Press.

Carr, Raymond, and Juan Pablo Fussi. 1979. *Spain. Dictatorship to Democracy*. 2nd ed. London: Unwin Hyman.

Carter, Donald. 1997. *States of Grace: Senegalese in Italy and the European Immigration*. Minneapolis: University of Minnesota Press.

Castaño, Angeles. 2000. *Informe 2000 sobre la inmigración en Almería*. Seville: Observatorio Permanente Andaluz de las Migraciones (Permanent Andalusian Migration Observatory).

Castells, Manuel. 1983. *The City and the Grassroots*. Berkeley: University of California Press.

Castles, Stephen. 1989. *Migrant Workers and the Transformation of Western Societies*. Ithaca: Cornell University, Center for International Studies.

Castles, Stephen, and Godula Kosack. 1985. *Immigrant Workers and Class Structure in Western Europe*. 2nd ed. London: Oxford University Press.

Castro, Américo. 1973. *The Spaniards. An Introduction to Their History*. Berkeley: University of California Press.

———. 1983. *España en su Historia. Cristianos, moros, y judíos*. Madrid: Grijalbo mondadori.

Cazorla Pérez, José. 1965. *Factores de la estructura socio-económica de Andalucía Oriental*. Granada: Caja de Ahorros.

———. 1989. *Retorno al Sur*. Cadiz: OCAER and Siglo XXI.

———. 1994. "El clientelismo de partido en la España de hoy: una disfunción de la democracia." Paper presented at the I Congress of the Spanish Political Science and Administration Association, Bilbao.

Chatterjee, Partha. 1986. *Nationalist Thought and the Colonial World: A Derivative Discourse?* London: Zed Books.

———. 1993. *The Nation and Its Fragments. Colonial and Postcolonial Histories*. Princeton: Princeton University Press.

Checa, Francisco. 1995. *Invernaderos e Immigrantes* (program 313-H. number 94.172.003494). Madrid: Dirección General de Migraciones (General Migration Headquaters).

Chenaut, Victoria, and María Teresa Sierra. 1995. "La antropología jurídica en México: temas y perspectivas de investigación." In Victoria Chenaut and María Teresa Sierra. (Eds.), *Pueblos indígenas ante el derecho* (pp. 13–44). Mexico: CIESAS/CEMCA.

Cohen, A. 1971. "Cultural Strategies in the Organization of Trading Diasporas." In C. Meillassoux (Ed.), *The Development of Indigenous Trade and Markets in West Africa.* Oxford: Oxford University Press.

Cohn, Bernard. 1989. "Law and the Colonial State in India." In June Starr and Jane Collier (Eds.), *History and Power in the Study of Law. New Directions in Legal Anthropology.* Ithaca and London: Cornell University Press.

Cohn, Bernard S., and Nicholas B. Dirks, 1988. "Beyond the Fringe: The Nation-State, Colonialism and Technologies of Power." *Journal Historical Sociology, 1*(2), 224–229.

Collier, George A. 1987. *Socialists of Rural Andalusia: Unacknowledged Revolutionaries of the Second Republic.* Stanford: University of Stanford Press.

———. 1994. "Seeking Food and Seeking Money: Changing Production Relations in Zinacantán, Chiapas." In C. Hewitt de Alcántara (Ed.), *Economic Restructuring and Rural Subsistence in Mexico* (pp. 81–98). La Jolla: Center for U.S.-Mexican Studies, University of California, San Diego.

Collier, Jane. 1986. "From Mary to Modern Woman: The Material Basis of Marianismo and Its Transformation in a Spanish Village." *American Ethnologist, 13*(1), 100–107.

———. 1991. "Bullfights and Sevillanas: Gendered 'Tradition,' Engendering Nationalism." Paper presented at the meetings of the American Ethnological Society, Session on Nationalism and Gender, Charleston, SC.

———. 1992. "The Anthropology of Law. A Review" (manuscript).

———. 1997. *From Duty to Desire.* Princeton: Princeton University Press.

Collier, Jane. F., Bill Maurer, and Liliana Suárez-Navaz. 1995. "Sanctioned Identities: Legal Constructions of Modern Personhood." *Identities. Global Issues in Culture and Power. Issue on Law and Identity, 2*(1–2).

Comaroff, John. 1987. "Of Totemism and Ethnicity: Conciousness, Practice and Signs of Inequality." *Ethnos, 52*(3–4).

———. 1989. "Images of Empire, Contests of Conscience: Models of Colonial Domination in South Africa." *American Ethnologist, 16*(4), 661–685.

Comaroff, John, and Jane Comaroff. 1987. "The Madman and the Migrant: Work and Labor in the Historical Conciousness of a South African People." *American Ethnologist, 14*(2).

———. 1991. *Of Revelation and Revolution: Christianity, Colonialism, and Conciousness in South Africa,* Chicago: University of Chicago Press.

Comaroff, John, and Simon Roberts. 1981. *Rules and Processes: The Cultural Logic of Dispute in an African Context.* Chicago: University of Chicago Press.

Contreras, José. 1991. "Estratificación Social y Relaciones de Poder." In Joan Prat, Ubaldo Martinez, Jesús Contreras, and Isidoro Moreno (Eds.), *Antropología de los pueblos de Espana* (pp. 499–519). Madrid: Taurus Universitaria.

Coombe, Rosemary J. (1989). Room for Manoeuver: Toward a Theory of Practice in Critical Legal Studies. *Law and Social Inquiry, 14*(1).

Cooper, Frederick and Ann L. Stoler. 1989. "Introduction. Tensions of Empire: Colonial Control and Visions of Rule." *American Ethnologist, 16*(4), 609–621.

Copans, J. 1988. *Les Marabouts de L'Arachide.* Paris: L'Harmattan.

Corbin, J. 1979. "Social Class and Patron. Clientelage in Andalusia: Some Problems of Comparing Ethnographies." *Anthropological Quarterly, 52*(2), 99–114.

Cornelius, Wayne A. 1994." Spain: The Uneasy Transition from Labor Exporter to Labor Importer." In Wayne A. Cornelius, P.L. Martin, and James F. Hollifield (Eds.), *Controlling Immigration. A Global Perspective.* Stanford: Stanford University Press.

Cornelius, Wayne. A., P.L. Martin, and James Hollifield. 1994. "Introduction: The Ambivalent Quest for Immigration Control." In Wayne A. Cornelius, P.L. Martin, and James Hollifield. (Eds.), *Controlling Immigration. A Global Perspective.* Stanford: Stanford University Press.

Corredera García, M.P., and L.S. Díez Cano. 1994. "La política de 'extranjería' en España." In Jesús Contreras (Ed.), *Los Retos de la Inmigración. Racismo y Pluriculturalidad.* Madrid: Talasa Ediciones.

Corrigan, P., and D. Sayer. 1985. *The Great Arch: English State Formation as Cultural Revolution.* Oxford: Basil Blackwell.

Costa, Joaquín. 1898. *Colectivismo agrario en España.* Madrid.

———. 1978. *Oligarquía y Caciquismo.* Madrid: Ediciones de la Revista del Trabajo.

———. 1982. *Derecho Consuetudinario y economía popular de España.* Zaragoza: Guara ed.

Costa-Lascoux, J. 1989. *De L'immigré au Citoyen.* Paris: Notes et Etudes.

Coulon, Christian., and Donald Cruise O'Brien. 1989. "Senegal." In Donald Cruise O'Brien, John Dunn, and Richard Rathbone (Ed.), *Contemporary West African States* (pp. 145–164). Cambridge: Cambridge University Press.

Coutin, Susan B. 1993. *The Culture of Protest. Religious Activism and the U.S. Sanctuary Movement.* Bolder: Westview Press.

Cross, Malcolm. 1989. "Migrants and New Minorities in Europe." *International Review of Comparative Public Policy,* 1 (Immigration in Western Democracies: The U.S and Western Europe).

Cruise O'Brien, Donald. 1971. *The Mourides of Senegal: The Political and Economic Organization of an Islamic Brotherhood.* Oxford: Clarendon Press.

De Bunes Ibarra, Miguel Angel. 1989. *La Imagen de los musulmanes y del norte de Africa de los siglos XVI y XVII. Los caracteres de una hostilidad.* Madrid: CSIC, Instituto de Filosofía.

De Lucas, Javier. 1994. *El Desafío de las Fronteras. Derechos Humanos y Xenofobia frente a una Sociedad Plural.* Madrid: Temas de Hoy.

———. 1996. "Un Pais en Tránsito: España ante las exigencias de la UE y la transformación de la immigración: incoherencias e incapacidad de respuesta." Paper presented at the seminar "Migration Political Challeges," Instituto Ortega y Gasset, Madrid.

De Lucas, Javier, and Francisco Torres (Eds.). 2002. *Immigrantes: ¿Cómo los tenemos? Algunos desafíos y (malas) respuestas.* Madrid: Talasa.

Díaz del Moral, J. 1984. *Historia de las Agitaciones Campesinas.* Madrid: Alianza Editorial.

Diop, A. B. 1965. *Societé toucouleur et migrations, Initiations et études* (Vol. XVIII). Dakar: IFAN.

———. 1988. *La société Wolof: Traditions et Changement, les sistèmes d'inegalité et de domination.* Paris: Khartala.

Douglas, Mary. 1968. "Pollution." In D. Sills (Ed.), *International Encyclopedia of the Social Sciences.* Vol. 12, pp. 336–342. San Francisco: Macmillan and Free Press.

Douglass, William A. 1975. *Echalar and Murelaga. Opportunity and Rural Exodus in Two Spanish Villages.* New York: St. Martin Press.

Driessen, H. 1991." Sociabilidad masculina y rituales de masculinidad en la Andalucía rural." In Joan Prat, Ubaaldo Martínez, Jesús Contreras, and Isidoro Moreno (Eds.), *Antropología de los pueblos de España* (pp. 710–718). Madrid: Taurus.

Ebin, Victoria. 1990. "Commerçants et missionnaires: une confrérie musulmane à New York." *Hommes et migrations, 1132* (May), 25–30.

———. 1992. "A la reserche de nouveaux 'poissons'. Strategies commerciales mourides par temps de crise." *Politique Africaine, 45* (March), 86–99.

Ebrin, Victoria and R. Lake. 1992. "Camelots Sénégalais à New York." *Hommes et Migrations* (1160), 32–37.

Elias, Norton, and J.L. Scotson. 1965. *The Established and the Outsiders.* London: Frank Cass.

Elliot, J. H. 1987. *The Spanish Conquest: Spain and America before 1700.* Cambridge: Cambridge University Press.

Evers Rosander, E. (Ed.). 1997. *Transforming Female Identities. Women's Organizational Forms in West Africa.* Uppsala: Nordiska Afrikainstitutet.

Federación Española de Municipios y Provincias, (FEMP; Spanish Federation of Provincial and Municipal Councils) 1995. *Los Municipios y la Integracion Social de los Inmigrantes. Analisis y propuestas de Actuacion.* Madrid: Federacion Española de Municipios y Provincias.

Fernández-Kelly, Maria Patricia. 1983. *For We Are Sold: Women and Industry in Mexico's Frontier.* Albany: State Universitty of New York Press.

Ferrer, A. 1982. *Paisaje y Propiedad en la tierra de Alhama (Granada, siglos XVIII-XX).* Granada: Universidad de Granada.

Fierro, Maribel. N.d. "La Emigración en el Islam: Conceptos antiguos, nuevos problemas" (manuscript).

Fitzpatrick, Peter. 1980. *Law and State in Papua New Guinea.* New York: Academic Press State.

———. 1992. *The Mythology of Modern Law.* London and New York: Routledge.

Foster, George. 1965. "Peasant Society and the Image of Limited Good." *American Anthropologist, 67,* 293–315.

Foucault, Michel. 1977. *Discipline and Punish: The Birth of the Prision.* New York: Pantheon Books.

———. 1978. *The History of Sexuality.* Vol. I. New York: Vintage Books.

———. (Ed.). 1980. *Power/Knowledge: Selected Interviews and Other Writings, 1972–1977.* Brighton: Harvester Press.

Fraser, Ronald. 1973. *Tajos: The Story of a Village on the Costa del Sol.* New York: Pantheon Books.

———. 1979. *Blood of Spain. The Experience of Civil War, 1936–1939.* New York: Pantheon Books.

Frazer, J.C. 1951. *La Rama Dorada.* Mexico: Fondo Cultura Económica.

Freeman, Susan T. (1970). *Neighbors. The Social Contract in a Castillian Hamlet.* Chicago: University of Chicago Press.

Frigolé Reixach, Joan. 1981. "Caciquismo." In R. Valdés (Ed.), *Las Razas Humanas.* Barcelona: CIESA.

———. 1991. "'Ser Cacique' y 'Ser Hombre' o la negación de las relaciones de patronazgo en un pueblo de la Vega Alta del Segura." In Joan Prat, Ubaldo Martinez, Jesús Contreras, and Isidoro Moreno (Eds.), *Antropología de los pueblos de España* (pp. 556–573). Madrid: Taurus.

Gamson, J. 1995. "New Social Movements and Identity Politics." *Contemporary Sociology,* 294–298.

Garamendía, J.A. (Ed.). 1981. *La emigración española en la encrucijada.* Madrid: CIS.

García Muñoz, Adelina. 1995. *Los que no pueden vivir de lo suyo. Trabajo y cultura en el Campo de Calatrava.* Madrid: Ministerio de Agricultura (Ministry of Agriculture).

Gavira, L. 1991. "La estructura segmentada de trabajo rural en Andalucía." *Revista de Estudios Regionales* (September–December), 87–104.

Gellner, Ernest. 1983. *Nations and Nationalism.* Ithaca and London: Cornell University Press.

Gellner, Ernest and John Waterbury (Eds.). 1977. *Patrons and Clients in Mediterranean Societies.* London: Duckworth.

Gilmore, David D. 1980. *The People of the Plain. Class and Community in Lower Andalusia.* New York: Columbia University Press.

Gilmore, David, and M. Gilmore. 1979. " 'Machismo': A Psycodinamic Approach (Spain)." *Journal of Psychological-Anthropology, 2,* 325–349.

Gilroy, Paul. 1987. *There Ain't No Black in the Union Jack.* Chicago: University of Chicago Press.

Giner, Salvador and Juan Salcedo. 1978. "Migrant Workers in European Social Structures." In Salvador Giner and M.S. Archer (Eds.), *Contemporary Europe* (pp. 94–123). London: Routledge and Kegan Paul.

Glick, Thomas F. 1992. "Convivencia: An Introductory Note." In Vivian B. Mann, Thomas F. Glick, and Jerrilynn D. Dodds (Eds.), *Convivencia. Jews, Muslims, and Christians in Medieval Spain* (pp. 1–7). New York: George Braziller and The Jewish Museum.

González Alcantud, José Antonio 1993. *La Extraña Seducción. Variaciones sobre el imaginario exótico de Occidente.* Granada: Universidad de Granada.

Gramsci, Antonio. 1971. *Selections from the Prison Notebooks* (Quintin Hoare and Geoffrey Nowell-Smith, trans.). New York: International Publishers.

Greenwood, Davydd. 1976. *Unrewarding Wealth: The Commercialization and Collapse of Agriculture in a Spanish Basque Town.* Cambridge: Cambridge University Press.

———. 1977. *Continuity and Change: Spanish Basque Ethnicity.* Ithaca: Cornell University Press.

————. 1987. "Egalitarianism or Solidarity in Basque Industrial Cooperatives: The Fagor Group of Mondragón." In J.G. Flannagan and S. Rayner (Eds.), *Rules, Decisions, and Inequality in Egalitarian Social Groups*. Farnborough: Grover Press.

————. 1992. "Las Antropologías de España: una propuesta de colaboración." *Antropología. Revista de pensamiento antropológico y estudios etnográficos, 3* (October), 5–33.

Gregory, David. 1978. *La Odisea Andaluza: Una Emigración hacia Europa*. Madrid: Editorial Tecnos.

Guichard, Pierre. 1976. *Al-Andalus. Estructura antropológica de una sociedad islámica en Occidente*. Barcelona: Barral Editores.

Guillaumin, Colette. 1995. *Racism, Sexism, Power, and Ideology*. London and New York: Routledge.

Gupta, Akil. 1995. Blurred Boundaries: The Discourse of Corruption, The Culture of Politics, and the Imagined State. *American Ethnologist, 22*(2), 375–402.

Gupta, Akil, and James Ferguson. 1992. "Beyond 'Culture': Space, Identity, and the Politics of Difference." *Cultural Anthropology, 7*(1), 6–23.

Hall, Stuart, C. Critchen, T. Jefferson, J.Clarke, and B.Roberts, 1978. *Policing the Crisis. Mugging, the State, and Law and Order*. London: Macmillan Press.

Hamilton, Bernice. 1963. *Political Thought in Sixteenth-Century Spain. A Study of the Political Ideas of Victoria, De Soto, Suárez, and Molina*. Oxford: Clarendon Press.

Hammar, Thomas. 1985. *European Migration Policy*. Cambridge: Cambridge University Press.

————. 1990. "Denizen's Political Interest and Participation. Voting Rights in the Nordic Countries."(in French) In Ida Simon-Barouh and Jean-Pierre Simon (Ed.), *Les Etrangers dans la ville.Le Regard des Sciences Sociales*. Paris: Editions L'Harmattan.

Harding, Susan F. 1984. *Remaking Ibieca. Rural Life in Aragón under Franco*. Chapell Hill: University of North Carolina Press.

Harris, Marvin. 1981. *El desarrollo de la teoría antropológica. Una historia de las teorías de la cultura*. Madrid: Siglo XXI.

Harvey, David. 1989. *The Condition of Postmodernity*. Cambridge, MA: Blackwell.

————. 1992. "Class Structure and Residential Differentiation," In *The Urban Experience* (pp. 109–124). Oxford: Basil Blackwell.

————. 1993. "From Space to Place and Back Again: Reflections on The Condition of Postmodernity." In Jon Bird, Barry Curtis, Tim Putnam, and George Robertson, (Eds.), *Mapping the Futures. Local Cultures, Global Change* (pp. 3–29). London and New York: Routledge.

Harvey, L. P. 1990. *Islamic Spain. 1250–1500*. Chicago: The University of Chicago Press.

Herzfeld, Michael 1982. *Ours Once More. Folklore, Ideology and the Making of Modern Greece*. Austin: University of Texas Press.

Hobsbawm, Eric. 1959. *Primitive Rebels: Studies in Archaic Forms of Social Movement in the Nineteen and Twenty Centuries*. Manchester: Manchester University Press.

————. 1990. *Nations and Nationalism since 1780*. Cambridge: Cambridge University Press.

Hobsbawm, Eric, and Thomas Ranger. 1983. *The Invention of Tradition.* Cambridge: Cambridge University Press.

Hollifield, James F. 1992. *Immigrants, Markets, and States. The Political Economy of Postwar Europe.* London: Harvard University Press.

Hunt, Alan. 1993. *Explorations in Law and Society. Toward a Constitutive Theory of Law.* London: Routledge.

Ingham, Kenneth. 1990. "Senegal: Unity in Diversity." In *Politics in Modern Africa. The Uneven Tribal Dimension* (pp. 115–134). London: Routledge.

IOE, Colectivo. 1987. *Los Inmigrantes en España.* Documentación Social. Caritas Española.

Iszaevich, A. 1991. "Emigrantes, solteronas, y curas: la dinámica de la demografía en las sociedades campesinas españolas." In Joan Prat, Ubaldo Martinez, Jesús Contreras, and Isidoro Moreno (Eds.), *Antropología de los pueblos de España* (pp. 280–293). Madrid: Taurus.

Izquierdo Escribano, Antonio. 1993. "Semejanzas y diferencias en el perfil demográfico y laboral de los marroquíes que solicitaron la regularización en 1985 y en 1991" (manuscript).

Jelin, Elisabeth. (Ed.). 1996. "Citizenship revisited: Solidarity, Responsibility, and Rights." In Elisabeth Jelin and Eric Hershberg (Eds.), *Constructing Democracy. Human Rights, Citizenship, and Society in Latin America* (pp. 101–119). Boulder: Westview Press.

———. (Ed.) 1990. *Women and Social Change in Latin America.* London and New York: Zed Books.

———. 1985. *Los Nuevos Movimientos Sociales.* Buenos Aires: CEAL.

Interview to E.A. 1992. "Tierra de Todos," *Jóvenes,*(22–25).

Kearney, Michael. 1991. "Borders and Boundaries of State and Self at the End of the Empire." *Journal of Historical Sociology,* 4(1), 52–74.

———. 1995. "The Local and the Global: The Anthropology of Globalization and Transnationalism." *Annual Review of Anthropology, 24,* 547–565.

———. 1996. *Reconceptualizing the Peasantry. Anthropology in Global Perspective.* Boulder: Westview Press.

———. N.d. "Desde el indigenismo a los derechos humanos: etnicidad y politica más allá de la mixteca" (manuscript).

Kymlicka, W. 1996. "Three Forms of Group-Differentiated Citizenship in Canada." In S. Benhabib (Ed.), *Democracy and Difference. Contesting the Boundaries of the Political* (pp. 153–170). Princeton: Princeton University Press.

Layton-Henry, Zig (Ed.). 1990. *The Political Rights of Migrant Workers in Western Europe.* Vol. 25. London: Sage.

Lisón Tolosana, Carmelo. 1966. *Belmonte de los Caballeros.* Princeton: Princeton University Press.

Littlewood, P. 1979. "Campesinos, producción y patronazgo." *Agricultura y Sociedad, 13* (October–December).

Lockhart, James. 1968. *Spanish Peru, 1532–1560.* Madison: University of Wisconsin Press.

López García, Bernabé (Ed.). 1993. *Inmigración Magrebí en España. El retorno de los Moriscos.* Madrid: Mafre.

Luque Baena, Enrique 1974. *Estudio antropológico social de un pueblo del sur.* Madrid: Tecnos.

Maier, Charles S. (Ed.). 1987. *Changing Boundaries of the Political.* Cambridge: Cambridge University Press.

Malefakis, Edward E. 1970. *Agrarian Reform and Peasant Revolution in Spain. Origins of the Civil War.* New Haven: Yale University Press.

Malkki, Liisa H. 1992. "National Geographic: The Rooting of Peoples and the Territorialization of National Identity among Scholars and Refugees." *Cultural Anthropology*, *7*, 24–44.

Mamdani, M. 1996. *Citizen and Subject. Contemporary Africa and the Legacy of Late Colonialism.* Princeton: Princeton University Press.

Marshall, T.H. 1950. *Citizenship and Social Class.* Cambridge: Cambridge University Press.

Martin Díaz, Emma. 1991. "La inmigración andaluza en Cataluña: causas, sistemas de organización y trasplante de la cultura andaluza." In Joan Prat, Ubaldo Martinez, Jesús Contreras, and Isidoro Moreno (Eds.), *Antropología de los pueblos de España* (pp. 299–307). Madrid: Taurus.

———. 2002. " El Ejido, dos años después. Realidad, silencios y enseñanzas" In Javier De Lucas and Francisco Torres (Eds.) *Immigrantes: ¿Cómo los tenemos? Algunos desafíos y (malas) respuestas.* Madrid: Talasa.

Martínez Alier, Juan. 1971. *Labourers and Landowers in Southern Spain.* London: George, Allen and Unwin.

Martinez Alier, Verena 1974. *Marriage, Class, and Coulour in Nineteenth-Century Cuba: A Study of Racial Attitudes and Sexual Values in a Slave Society.* New York: Cambridge University Press.

Martínez Veiga, Ubaldo 1991. "Organización y percepción del espacio." In Joan Prat, Ubaldo Martinez, Jesús Contreras, and Isidoro Moreno (Eds.), *Antropología de los pueblos de España* (pp. 195–255). Madrid: Taurus Universitaria.

———. 2001. *El Ejido. Discriminación, exclusión social y racismo.* Madrid: La Catarata.

Maurer, Bill. 1997. *Recharting the Caribbean: Land, Law, and Citizenship in the British Virgin Islands.* Ann Arbor: University of Michigan Press.

Meillasoux, Claude. 1981. *Maidens, Meal and Money.* London: Cambridge University Press.

Melucci, Alberto. 1989. *Nomads of the Present: Social Movements and Individual Needs in Contemporary Society.* Philadelphia: Temple University Press.

Merry, Sally E. 1991. "Law and Colonialism." *Law and Society*, *25*(4).

Messick, B. 1992. *The Calligraphic State: Textual Domination and History in a Muslim Society.* Berkeley: University of California Press.

Miles, Robert. 1993. *Racism after "Race Relations."* London: Routledge.

Mintz, Jerome. 1982. *The Anarchists of Casas Viejas.* Chicago: University of Chicago Press.

Mitchell, T. 1988. *Colonizing Egypt.* Cambridge: Cambridge University Press.

Moore, Sally F. 1969. "Law and Anthropology." *Biennial Review of Anthropology.*

———. 1986. *Social Facts and Fabrications: Customary Law on Kilimanjaro, 1880–1980.* Cambridge: Cambridge University Press.

Moreno, José Antonio. 1987. *Alfaya* [pseudonym]. *El polje y su cultura.* Alfaya: Iltrmo. Ayuntamiento.

Moreno Navarro, Isidoro. 1974. *Las hermandades andaluzas: una aproximación desde la antropología.* Seville: Publicaciones de la Universidad de Sevilla.

———. 1986. "Fieldwork in Southern Europe and Scientific Colonization: The Andalusian Case." Paper presented at the Thirteen European Congress of Rural Sociology, Braga.

———. 1991a. "Desarrollo del Capitalismo Agrario y Mercado de trabajo en Andalucía." *Revista de Estudios Regionales, 31*(September-December), 19–29.

———. 1991b. "Identidades y Rituales." In Joan Prat, Ubaldo Martinez, Jesús Contreras, and Isidoro Moreno (Eds.), *Antropología de los pueblos de España* (pp. 601–636). Madrid: Taurus.

Moreno Torregosa, P and Mohammed El-Gheryb. 1994. *Dormir al Raso.* Madrid: Eds.Vosa.

Morris, Linda. 1994. *Dangerous Classes. The Underclass and Social Citizenship.* London and New York: Routledge.

Offe, Claus, and Hans Wiesenthal. (1985). Two Logics of Collective Action. In Claus Offe and John Keane (Ed.), *Disorganized Capitalism.* Cambridge, MA: MIT Press

Ong, Aiwa. 1996. "Cultural Citizenship as Subject Making. Immigrants Negotiate Racial and Cultural Boundaries in the U.S." *Current Anthropology, 37*(5), 737–761.

Palenzuela, Pablo. 1991. "El Estado no es inocente: naturaleza perversa y eficiencia de la política asistencial en el medio rural." *Revista de Estudios Regionales, 31* (September–December), 213–228.

———. 1992. "Antropología Económica del campesinado andaluz." In Eduardo Sevilla Guzmán and Manuel González de Molina (Eds.), *Ecología, Campesinado, e Historia* (pp. 357–374). Madrid: La Piqueta.

Parker, Andrew, Mary Russo, Doris Sommer, and Patricia Yaeger. (Eds.). 1992. *Nationalisms and Sexualities.* New York: Routledge.

Pashukanis, Evgeny. 1989. *Law and Marxism. A General Theory.* Worcester: Pluto Press.

Pérez Losada, D. 1993. "Análisis de los expedientes de extranjeros atendidos en la Delegación Diocesana de Immigrantes (1986–1991)." In C. Giménez Romero (Ed.), *Inmigrantes Extranjeros en Madrid* (Vol. 1, pp. 461–497). Madrid: Comunidad de Madrid (Autonomous Community of Madrid)

Phelan, John Leddy. 1978. *The People and the King. The Comunero Revolution in Colombia, 1781.* Madison: University of Wisconsin Press.

Piore, M. (1979). *Birds of Passage. Migrant Labor and Industrial Societies.* Cambridge: Cambridge University Press.

Pitt-Rivers, Julian A. 1954. *The People of the Sierra.* Chicago: University of Chicago Press.

Portes, Alejandro, Manuel Castells, and Lauren Benton (Eds.). 1989. *The Informal Economy. Studies in Advanced and Less Developed Countries.* Baltimore and London: Johns Hopkins University Press.

Plan for the Social Integration of Immigrants (PSII). 1995. Madrid: Ministerio de Asuntos Sociales, Dirección General de Migraciones (Ministry of Social Affairs, General Migration Headquarters).

Rhoades, R.E. 1978. "Intra-European Return Migration and Rural Development: Lessons from the Spanish Case." *Human Organization, 37,* 136–147.

Robin, N. 1992. "L'espace migratoire de l'Afrique de l'Ouest." *Hommes et Migrations* (1160), 6–15.

Rodrígue, Aaron. (1995). "Difference and Tolerance in the Ottoman Empire." Interview by Nancy Reynolds. *Stanford Humanities Review,* 5(1), 81–92.

Rosaldo, Renato. 1986. "From the Door of His Tent: The Fieldworker and the Inquisitor." In James Clifford and George E. Marcus (Eds.), *Writing Culture: The Poetics and Politics of Ethnography* (pp. 77–97). Berkeley: Cambridge University Press.

———. 1989. *Culture and Truth: The Remaking of Social Analysis.* Boston: Beacon Press.

———. 1994a. "Cultural Citizenship and Educational Democracy." *Cultural Anthropology, 9* (3), 402–411.

———. 1994b. "Social Justice and the Crisis of National Communities." In F. Barker, P. Hulme, and M. Iversen (Ed.), *Colonial Discourse/Postcolonial Theory.* Manchester and New York: Manchester University Press.

Roseberry, William. 1994. "Hegemony and the Language of Contention." In G.M. Joseph and D. Nugent (Eds.), *Everyday Forms of State Formation. Revolution and the Negotiation of Rule in Modern Mexico* (pp. 355–366). Durham and London: Duke University Press.

Rouse, Roger. 1992. "Making Sense of Settlement: Class Transformation, Cultural Struggle, and Transnationalism among Mexican Migrants in the United States." In Nina Glick Schiller, Linda Basch, and Cristina Blanc-Szanton (Eds.), *Towards a Transnational Perspective on Migration. Race, Class, Ethnicity and Nationalism Reconsidered.* Vol. 645, New York: New York Academy of Sciences.

Said, E. W. 1978. *Orientalism.* New York: Pantheon Books.

———. 1981. *Covering Islam. How the media and the experts determine how we see the world.* New York: Pantheon Books.

San Roman, T. (Ed.). 1986. *Entre la marginación y el racismo. Reflexiones sobre la vida de los gitanos.* Madrid: Alianza Ed.

———. 1997. *La Diferencia Inquietante. Viejas y nuevas estrategias culturales de los gitanos.* Madrid: Siglo XXI.

Sánchez Albornoz, Claudio. 1960. "España y el Islam." In A. del Río and M. J. Bernadete (Eds.), *El concepto contemporáneo de España.* Buenos Aires: Losada.

Santos, Lidia. 1993. "Elementos jurídicos de la integración de los extranjeros." In G. Tajiros (Ed.), *Inmigración e integración en Europa.* Madrid: Itinera Libros.

Sartori, Giovanni. 2001. *La Sociedad Multiétnica.* Madrid: Taurus.

Sassen-Koob, Saskia. 1983. "Labor Migration and the New Industrial Division of Labor." In June Nash and Patricia Fernández-Kelly (Eds.), *Women, Men, and the International Division of Labor* (pp. 175–204). Albany: State University of New York Press.

————. 1988. *The Mobility of Labor and Capital.* Cambridge: Cambridge University Press.

Schmidt di Friedberg, Olivia. 1993. "L'Immigration africaine en Italie: le cas sénégalais." *Révue Etudes Internationales, 24* (March 1), 125–140.

Scott, James C. 1985. *Weapons of the Weak. Everyday Forms of Resistance.* New Haven and London: Yale University Press.

Sevilla Guzmán, Eduardo. 1979. *La evolución del campesinado en España.* Barcelona: Ediciones península.

Sevilla Guzmán, Eduardo, and Manuel González de Molina (Eds.). 1992. *Ecología, Campesinado, e Historia.* Madrid: La Piqueta.

Sibley, David. 1995. *Geographies of Exclusion. Society and Difference in the West.* London and New York: Routledge.

Snyder, Francis G. 1981. *Capitalism and Legal Change. An African Transformation.* New York: Academic Press.

Soja, E.W. 1989. *Postmodern Geographies. The Reassertion of Space in Critical Social Theory.* London: Verso.

Solé, Carlota. 1982. *Los inmigrantes en la sociedad y en la cultura catalanas.* Barcelona: Ediciones Península.

Somers, M.R. 1993. "Citizenship and the Place of the Public Sphere: Law, Community and Political Culture in the Transition to Democracy." *American Sociological Review, 58* (October), 587–629.

Sopeña Monsalve, A. 1994. *El Florido Pensil. Memoria de la escuela nacionalcatólica.* Barcelona: Critica.

Soysal, Yasemin. 1994. *Limits of Citizenship. Migrants and Postnational Membership in Europe.* Chicago: University of Chicago Press.

————. N.d. "Boundaries and Identity: Immigrants in Europe" (manuscript).

Spanish Government. 1990. "Situación de los extranjeros en España. Lineas Básicas de la política española de inmigración"

Starr, June, and Jane F. Collier. 1989. Introduction: Dialogues in Legal Anthropology. In J. Starr and J. Collier (Ed.), *History and Power in the Study of Law. New Directions in Legal Anthropology* (pp. 1–28). Ithaca and London: Cornell University Press.

Stavenhagen, Rodolfo, and D. Iturralde, D. (Eds.). 1990. *Entre la ley y la costumbre.* Mexico: Instituto Indigenista Interamericano/Instituto Interamericano de Derechos Humanos (Interamerican Indigenous Institute/Interamerican Human Rights Institute).

Stolke, Verena. 1993. "Is Sex to Gender as Race is to Ethnicity?" In Teresa del Valle (Ed.), *Gendered Anthropology* (pp. 17–37). London: Routledge.

————. 1996. "Talking Culture: New Boundaries, New Retorics of Exclusion in Europe." *Current Anthropology, 36*(1), 1–24.

Suárez-Navaz, Liliana 1995a. "Law and Surveillance in Non-Core Europe: A Case Study in the Andalusian Countryside." *Political and Legal Anthropology Review (PoLAR), 18* (2).

————. 1995b. "La Construction d'une communauté transnationale: les Sénégalais en Andalusia, Espagne." *Mondes en Développement, 23*(91).

————. 1996b. "Women's Popular Collective Mobilization in Santiago de Chile." Paper presented at the Second Spanish Anthropological Congress, Latin American Social Anthropology, Zaragoza.

————. 1997a. "Political Economy of Mediterranean Rebordering. New Ethnicities, New Citizenships." *Stanford Humanities Review*, 5 (2), 174–200.

————. 1998a. "Los procesos migratorios como procesos globales: El caso del transnacionalismo senegalés." *Ofrim*, diciembre.

————. 1998b. "Las politicas de la invisibilidad: una geografía racial de relaciones laborales en el campo andaluz." *Migraciones*, Vol 4, diciembre 1998.

Suárez-Navaz, Liliana, and Aída Hernandez Castillo, 1993. "La inmigración norteafricana en España: Un análisis de su representación en El País" (manuscript).

Targuieff, Pierre-André. 1987. *La Force Du Préjugé. Essai sur le Racisme et ses Doubles*. Paris: Ed. La Decouverte.

Thomson, E.P. 1968. *The Making of English Working Class*. New York: Vintage.

————. 1971. "The Moral Economy of the English Crowd." *Past and Present, 50*, 77–136.

Touraine, Antoine. 1989. *América Latina: Política y Sociedad*. Madrid: Espasa-Calpe.

Valderrama Martinez, F. 1956. *Historia de la Acción Cultural de España en Marruecos (1912–1956)*. Tetuán: Editora Marroquí.

Velasco, Honorio. 1991. "Signos y sentidos de la identidad de los pueblos castellanos. El concepto de pueblo y la identidad." In Joan Prat, Ubaldo Martinez, Jesús Contreras, and Isidoro Moreno (Eds.), *Antropologia de los pueblos de España* (pp. 719–728). Madrid: Taurus Universitaria.

Vicent, Joan. 1990. *Anthropology and Politics: Visions, Traditions, and Trends*. Tucson: University of Arizona Press.

Vidal Gil, Ernesto, 1995. "Los derechos de los extranjeros. Un análisis crítico de la legislación y la jurisprudencia." *Revista de Serveis Socials* (1), 117–135.

Villalón, L.A. 1995. *Islamic Society and State Power in Senegal*. Cambridge: Cambridge University Press.

Wallerstein, Immanuel. 1974. *The Modern World System*. New York: Academic Press.

Waterbury, John. 1977. *North for the Trade. The Life and Times of a Berber Merchant*. Berkeley: University of California Press.

Withol de Wenden, Catherine (Ed.). 1988. *La Citoyenneté*. Ediling: Foundation Diderot.

————. 1990. "The Absence of Rights: The Position of Illegal Immigrants." In Zig Layton-Henry (Ed.), *Political Rights of Migrant Workers in Western Europe*. Vol. 25, pp. 27–46. London: Sage.

Williams, Brackette F. 1989. "A Class Act: Anthropology and the Race to Nation Across Ethnic Terrain." *Annual Review of Anthropology, 18*, 401–444.

Williams, Raymond. 1977. *Marxism and Literature*. Oxford: Oxford University Press.

Wilpert, Czarina. (Ed.) 1988. *Entering the Working Force: Following the Descendants of Europe Immigrant Labour Force*. Aldershot: Gower.

Wolf, Eric. 1982. *Europe and the People without History*. Berkeley: University of California Press.

Yngvesson, Barbara. 1993. *Virtuous Citizens, Disruptive Subjects.* New York and London: Routledge.

Young, Iris. 1990. *Justice and the Politics of Difference.* Princeton: Princeton University Press.

Yuval-Davis, N. 1990. "Women, the State, and Ethnic Processes." Paper presented at the Conference Migration and Racism in Europe, Institut für Migrations- und Rassismusforschung, Hamburg.

INDEX